The Garden in Victorian Literature

The Garden in Victorian Literature

MICHAEL WATERS

Scolar Press

First published 1988 by
SCOLAR PRESS
GOWER PUBLISHING COMPANY LIMITED
Gower House, Croft Road, Aldershot, GU11 3HR

British Library Cataloguing in Publication Data

Waters, Michael
The garden in Victorian literature.
1. English literature, 1837–1900. Critical studies
I. Title
820.9′008

ISBN 0-85967-736-2

Printed in Great Britain at the
University Press, Cambridge

Contents

Note on Textual References

In view of the great number of works I have cited, I felt it incumbent upon me to avoid wherever possible the duplication of textual references. To this end, the majority of imaginative works are cited in the text with their dates of publication, and full bibliographical details are given only in the Bibliography. Page numbers in parenthesis refer to the editions cited in the Bibliography. This strategy has made it possible to reserve the sections on Notes and References largely for references to works other than poems and works of prose fiction.

Abbreviations

AP	*Poems of Matthew Arnold*
BP	*Browning: Poetical Works 1833–1864*
DP	*Complete Poetical Works of Austin Dobson*
MP	*Poetical Works of George Meredith*
MW	*Collected Works of William Morris*
MSW	*William Morris: Selected Writings*
RW	*Works of John Ruskin*
TP	*Poems of Tennyson*

Preface

This study has a two-part structure. In Part One the emphasis is upon the garden itself. I consider what Victorian poets and novelists had to say about gardens, the styles and theories of gardens privileged in their writings, and the relations between the garden elements of imaginative texts and the theories and practices of contemporary horticulturalists. In Part Two the emphasis is upon the functions and significations of the garden in Victorian imaginative literature. I consider the multifarious uses to which gardens are put, and the effects and significances of these uses. I focus upon both the intra-textual relations of garden elements, that is, upon their relations with other elements of the texts in which they occur, and their extra-textual relations, that is, upon their relations with other elements within the Victorian cultural milieu.

Although the two parts of this study differ in emphasis and content, they overlap and interconnect at many points. This is nowhere more evident than in the chapter on floral codes (Chapter 6). I have placed it at the head of Part Two, but clearly it straddles the boundary between the two parts.

In spite of the organizational framework I have imposed upon it, I have tried to allow the subject to speak through me. To this end, I have resisted the temptation formally to define the concept of 'garden', with the effect that my use of the term is consonant with its multiplicity of applications in Victorian imaginative literature.

Since this study is proffered as a contribution to scholarship rather than to literary theory, I have refrained in the main from commenting explicitly upon the critical theories which have informed it. Perhaps it is worth pointing out, however, that my policy has been to make use of whatever critical ideas and practices have seemed to me appropriate to a subject both diverse and culture-specific. This has led me to make assumptions to which some modern critics may possibly take exception. For instance, it will be evident that I have granted literary texts a high degree of referential stability, and that I have refused to reduce the author to a decentred function of the text. I imagine that most readers will not find these procedural practices disagreeable.

I am grateful to Dr Malcolm Andrews for his enthusiastic support of this study, and to Dr Graham Clarke for having read and commented upon parts of it. I should like to thank Marika Rush for having produced the typescript with considerable patience and alacrity. My greatest debt of gratitude is to Lynne, Anna and Louise for having allowed me to devote their time as well as my own to the production of this book.

M.W.

Publisher's note

This book was prepared for publication before the publication of *Victorian Gardens* by Brent Elliott (Batsford, 1986).

PART ONE

Introduction

I wish to address myself to a subject largely neglected by literary scholars and garden historians[1] alike: the relations between Victorian imaginative literature and contemporary garden theory. I am concerned with what poets and novelists have to say about gardens, with their ideas of what gardens are or ought to be, and with the styles and features favoured or disfavoured in their writings. In the main, their contributions are bitty, brief and widely scattered, and in no sense add up to a fully coherent informal version of garden theory which we can place securely beside the formal version as expounded in the substantial body of technical garden literature. Rather, they can be regarded as an eclectic but highly interesting and possibly influential collection of comments, opinions and descriptions which seem sometimes to articulate and support, sometimes to challenge and interrogate, the ideas and practices expressed in Victorian horticultural texts—both written and topographical.

The Victorian period was one of eclectic garden styles. No one style dominated the age; preferences and possibilities varied socially and at different times. At the broadest level, Victorian imaginative literature mimes this stylistic diversity in that poets and novelists presented their readers with a wide range of garden types, some suggesting actual or typical 'real' world equivalents. Even so, the relations between the practical gardening of the period and imaginative 'garden' literature are far from simple.

For one thing, certain kinds of Victorian gardens, particularly those of more exotic or experimental design (Chinese and Egyptian gardens, for example) and the more specialized types (such as rock and Alpine gardens) rarely if ever figure in poetry and fiction. Conversely, some fictional gardens have no exact extra-textual correspondences. For instance, the gardens in Disraeli's novels tend to be exaggerated and romanticized versions of the display gardens upon which they are loosely based. Moreover, many of the gardens described in fiction owe more to the predilections, values and desires of their authors than they do to the faithful documentation of social reality. This is egregiously the case with cottage gardens, copiously and affectionately described in the literature of the age, and frequently in terms more closely resembling, if not a literary stereotype, actual cottage gardens of an earlier period, or the gardens of the genteel cottager of modest means, than the genuine cottage gardens of the contemporary rural labourer.

If Victorian garden styles were diverse, so also were the terms by which they were linguistically mapped. Different theorists proposed different systems of classification, and often applied the same label to gardens with dissimilar formal features. As Brent Elliott notes, 'no system of nomenclature was universally accepted, not even Loudon's, although his probably had the greatest authority.'[2] This uncertainty over labels complicates the task of determining the precise structure of relations between fictional and historically specific gardens. The absence of a common and consistent vocabulary means that we cannot always be certain that garden writers and imaginative writers shared common frames of reference. Even when they used the same appellation, such as 'picturesque', 'geometric' or 'Italian', it is not always safe to assume shared definitions and applications.

These problems are compounded by the general absence in imaginative literature of explicit references to contemporary garden theorists, and to the traditions of garden design in which they felt themselves to be working. Consider the case of John Claudius Loudon. Though the most prolific and influential garden writer of his time (he died in 1843, but his influence was enduring) Loudon, as garden theorist, is cited by none of the novelists I have consulted.[3] More significantly, no novelist appears ever to have employed his most famous coinage—'gardenesque'. In one respect, this can be counted a blessing, for there was (and still is) confusion over its exact denotation, though it is generally taken to refer to a style in which plants are separated and cultivated as individual specimens so as to make each worthy of careful inspection. On the other hand, since a number of fictional gardens are clearly constructed in the gardenesque mode, at least some Victorian novelists must have been familiar with the notion of a style 'calculated for displaying the art of the gardener',[4] even if they did not or could not put a name to it. Consider the following description of a villa garden from Bulwer Lytton's *Ernest Maltravers* (1837):

> Through an Ionic arch you entered a domain of some eighty or a hundred acres in extent, but so well planted and so artfully disposed, that you could not have supposed the

> unseen boundaries inclosed no ampler a space. The road wound through the greenest sward, in which trees of venerable growth were relieved by a profusion of shrubs and flowers gathered into baskets intertwined with creepers, or blooming from classic vases, placed with a tasteful care in such spots as required the *filling up*, and harmonised well with the object chosen. Not an old ivy-grown pollard, not a modest and bending willow, but was brought out, as it were, into a peculiar feature by the art of the owner. Without being overloaded, or too minutely elaborate (the common fault of the rich man's villa), the whole place seemed one diversified and cultivated garden. (p. 70)

Clearly, this garden is intended to display the 'peculiar feature' of each plant and, by implication, the wealth, skills and tastes of its owner, the rich, fashionable and highly cultivated Mr Cleveland. It might best be described as a gardenesque garden in the Italian mode exemplifying, perhaps, what Richard Gorer has identified as the tendency to historical pastiche in the gardens of the 1830s and 1840s.[5]

Another kind of gardenesque planting is described in Disraeli's *Lothair* (1870). The subject is Chart, a park planted in the early years of the century

> entirely with spruce firs, but with so much care and skill, giving each plant and tree ample distance, that they have risen to the noblest proportions, and with all their green branches far-spreading on the ground like huge fans. . . . It was a forest of firs, but quite unlike such as might be met with in the north of Europe or of America. Every tree was perfect, huge and complete, and full of massy grace . . . (p. 61)

Here the separatist use of trees contrasts with the Brownian mode of planting in belts and clumps, and might almost have been written to bear out Loudon's declaration that the gardenesque 'may now be seen in its most decided character, as far as respects trees and shrubs, wherever Arboretum have been properly planted.'[6]

Gardenesque-like plantings appear elsewhere in *Lothair* in, for example, the description of Belmont with its 'exquisite turf studded with rare shrubs and occasionally rarer trees' (p. 126). However, it is impossible to be certain that Disraeli was fully conscious of writing in terms specifically supplied by exponents of the gardenesque. It is not improbable that he described trees as individual specimens because that is how he, with his fondness for trees, preferred to see them, for in all such descriptions particular species and specimens are distinguished even when they do not constitute recognizably gardenesque plantings. (There are excellent examples of tree descriptions, and of Disraeli's separatist mode of vision, in *Coningsby* and *Endymion*.)

There are, then, difficulties in establishing direct connections between what imaginative writers had to say about gardens and what garden writers had to say about them. These difficulties should not prove unduly bothersome, for although I shall make cross-references when it seems legitimate to do so, I intend to treat imaginative 'garden' literature and technical garden literature as separate but historically parallel kinds of writing. My main concern is to discuss imaginative literature *within the context* of Victorian garden theory and practice, not to assimilate it to them.

If it were possible to reconstruct the textual encounters of a Victorian garden enthusiast, probably conversant with contemporary garden theory, and widely read in Victorian poetry and fiction, what should we discover? Almost certainly, that he would not have found one kind or style of garden consistently and unanimously extolled to the neglect and deprecation of others. Given that Victorian authors differed in their tastes in, attitudes towards, and uses of the garden, and given also the generally mimetic orientation of nineteenth-century fiction, this is just what we should expect to find.

That nineteenth-century garden designs were diverse was attributable in part to uncertainty over and toleration towards choice of styles. Many Victorians congratulated themselves on a want of bigotry in this respect. With reference to gardens, an anonymous contributor to the *Quarterly Review* of 1855 wrote: 'If we can flatter ourselves that the taste of the present age is better than that of the past, it is because it is more tolerant.'[7]

The sympathies of many imaginative writers were certainly not unduly narrow. Indeed, the sharp-eyed garden-conscious reader may have noticed that Trollope found no difficulty squaring his admiration for trimness and order with, in *Orley Farm* (1862), his obvious affection for the 'commodious, irregular, picturesque and straggling' Orley Farm with its equally 'large, straggling trees' (I, 7); or how Bulwer Lytton could in one novel, *Kenelm Chillingly*

(1873), denounce the 'pretentious' modern garden in favour of the old-fashioned farmhouse garden with 'its straggling old English flowers' (p. 91) and, in another, *Eugene Aram* (1832), defend 'those magnificent gardens, modelled on Versailles' against the opinion that 'beauty is always best seen in *deshabille*' (p. 93), or how Disraeli in *Lothair* could lavish description upon grandiose versions of the High Victorian Display Garden, and yet devote the concluding section of the same novel to a compelling repudiation of its motivating aesthetic.

None of these writers could match Tennyson for sheer catholicity. His garden-conscious readers (and there were many of them) were presented with descriptions of and allusions to a considerable range of garden types. The rectory gardens of his Somersby home are suggested in *Song*, 'A spirit haunts the year's last hours', and figure in sections of *Ode to Memory* and *In Memoriam* (notably CI and XCV). There are rose gardens in *Maud* and *The Gardener's Daughter*, and terraced gardens in *The Roses on the Terrace*. There are aristocratic parks and garden estates in *The English Idylls*; those in *Audley Court* were 'partially suggested by Abbey Park at Torquay in the old times' (*TP*, p. 704). According to Tennyson, Sir Walter Vivian's 'broad lawns' were based upon the Lushingtons' grounds at Park House, near Maidstone (*TP*, p. 73). Also in the outer frame of *The Princess* are Gothic ruins, and in the poem's inner frame, the gardens of the Women's College have some of the distinguishing characteristics of mid-century Italianate gardens: fountains, peacocks, statues, stonework, a balustraded terrace of high elevation and exotic vegetation. Enclosed medieval gardens and bowers provide settings for consequential exchanges in the *Idylls of the King*, and there are references to the *hortus conclusus* in *The Princess* and *Maud*. Cottage gardens appear in a number of poems, including *Aylmer's Field* and *Enoch Arden*. In addition, there are sensuous eastern gardens in *Recollections of Arabian Nights*, and sacred bowers in *The Poet's Mind* and *The Hesperides*. As Robert G. Stange observes: 'Imaginary places analogous to the Eden garden are abundant in Tennyson's poems.'[8]

In itself, a catalogue of this sort does not mean very much; but it does at least suggest that, like that of many of his contemporaries, Tennyson's concept of the garden was plastic, and that he recognized the aesthetic appeal and semiotic possibilities of different kinds of gardens.

Though the reader interested in gardens would not have found in Victorian imaginative literature a single, consensually acclaimed garden ideal, he would have perceived a privileging of certain styles, features and qualities. That is, he would have noted that delightful, lauded gardens were likely to be certain things and unlikely to be certain other things. This observation provides the structural framework for Part One.

Among the qualities commonly privileged in literary texts are fragrance, old age or the appearance of old age, visual appeal, picturesqueness and the potential for pictorial representation, and a moderate but not excessive degree of artifice. I begin with the latter quality, exhibited in what for convenience can be called the trim garden.

CHAPTER ONE

The Trim Garden

If any one principle dominated the aesthetics of Victorian garden theory, then it was expressed in the view that the garden ought to be considered a work of art rather than an attempt to copy the 'natural' landscape. Sir Walter Scott gave it its simplest formulation when he declared that 'Nothing is more completely the child of art than the garden.'[1] Loudon contended that a garden ought to be natural in content but artificial in form. Likewise, Shirley Hibberd exhorted 'every cultivator of taste in gardening' to bear in mind 'that a garden is an artificial contrivance . . . not a piece scooped out of a wood', and that art rather than nature should be 'the basis of every arrangement'.[2]

From what did this emphasis on artificiality stem? Chiefly, from a general disapproval of the eighteenth-century landscape garden: for its lack of imaginative variety; for its aesthetically displeasing and socially inconveniencing disconnection of house and garden; and for its deception of the spectator, who was misled into believing that what he saw before him was a 'realistic' if improved version of the natural scene. Most Victorian garden theorists held that in perpetrating this fiction, the landscape school had displayed a want of aesthetic integrity. Since nature was an abstract concept, no garden could provide a mimetic representation of it. All gardens codified nature; all were subject to the rules and conventions of art. Moreover, as Loudon argued, if a garden excited the spectator's 'emotions of taste', it was not by virtue of its inherent properties but, as Archibald Alison had contended, 'by the associations which may have connected these with the ordinary affections or emotions of our nature'.[3] Hence, it was the gardener's job to provide designs which could not be mistaken for works of nature, and which were sufficiently imaginative to connect with the associations of the viewer.

This insistence upon artifice and variety was motivated by other considerations. Loudon and his followers believed that 'the hand of man should be visible in gardens' because they are 'intended to show that they are works of art, and to display the taste and wealth of the owner'.[4] Loudon wanted the credit for a good garden to go to the gardener or garden owner rather than to nature. Similarly, many theorists reasoned that since the garden is 'one of the last refinements of civilized life', to attempt 'to disguise wholly its artificial character is as great a folly as if men were to make their houses resemble as much as possible the rudeness of a natural cavern'.[5]

The emphasis upon artifice was ensured by at least two other developments. First, it was ensured by the influx of new plant materials, including those which became the staple of the bedding-out system, which many Victorians of means were eager to exhibit. Second, garden writers turned their attentions to the suburban gardens of the middle classes, and to the gardens of country 'residences' as opposed to country 'seats' (the distinction is Loudon's). Thus they were concerned with garden designs appropriate to grounds of comparatively modest size. To lay them out to effect demanded skills quite different from and, as Loudon insisted, often more exacting than those required for the construction of landscape parks.

Many mid-century novelists seem to have been aware of the views and developments I have outlined, and frequently imply a qualified approval of the kind of garden that wears its artifice upon its floral sleeve; 'qualified' because they were aware also of the excesses and extravagances to which the stress upon artificiality could in practice lead. More of this later. Here I wish to quote a passage from Trollope's *Can You Forgive Her?* (1864–5). It is a description of John Grey's house and gardens at Nethercoats:

> But though Nethercoats possessed no beauty of scenery, though the country around it was in truth as uninteresting as any country could be, it had many delights of its own. The house itself was as excellent a residence for a country gentleman of small means as taste and skill together could construct. I doubt whether prettier rooms were ever seen than the drawing-room, the library, and the dining-room at Nethercoats. They were all on the ground floor, and all opened out on to the garden and lawn. . . . But perhaps the gardens of Nethercoats constituted its greatest glory. They were spacious and excellently kept up, and had been originally laid out with that knowledge of gardening without which no garden, merely as a garden, can be effective. And such, of necessity, was the garden of Nethercoats. Fine single trees there were none there, nor was it possible that there should have been any such. Nor could there be a clear rippling stream with steep green banks, and broken rocks lying about

> its bed. Such beauties are beauties of landscape, and do not of their nature belong to a garden. But the shrubs of Nethercoats were of the rarest kind, and had been long enough in their present places to have reached the period of their beauty. Nothing had been spared that a garden could want. The fruit trees were perfect in their kind, and the glass-houses were so good and so extensive that John Grey in his prudence was sometimes tempted to think that he had too much of them. (I, 124–5)

There is nothing in this passage which could not have pleased almost every contemporary garden theorist. The details and emphases are exactly right: the happy interconnection of house and garden; the exclusion of nature in its wildest forms; the felicitous combination of means, taste and horticultural expertise conspiring to produce rare and perfect botanical specimens.

Trollope's novels are punctuated by similar descriptions of (often) exemplary gardens. Though few include such explicit remarks on garden theory as the one quoted above, most suggest that he was in touch with and sympathetic to prevailing attitudes towards garden design. To draw attention to some commonalities of more general significance, I should like to focus upon some interesting points of contact between Trollope's descriptions and the ideas of the garden theorists with which they tend to concur.

Trollope is at his most Reptonian in his descriptions of substantial country houses squatting in unrelieved acres of turf. As Repton saw it, 'placing a large house, not only on a naked lawn, but in the centre of it . . . so that the park might surround it in all directions . . . [was] one of the greatest errors in modern gardening.' The result, he says, is that the gardens, the pheasantry, and other features, 'become so many detached establishments'[6] banished to an inconvenient distance. Repton and his Victorian successors considered this a violation of the unity of the house-garden-park composition. Repton's response was to advocate the reintroduction of flower-beds and specialized flower-gardens near the house. This, he believed, would restore not only the art of gardening but also the social functions of the garden. That this was Repton's major contribution to the history of garden design is occasionally acknowledged in Victorian fiction. In *Kenelm Chillingly* he is credited with having originally planned the flower-garden and pleasure-ground of Leopold Travers's country estate. Trollope doesn't mention Repton by name, but Reptonian attitudes consistently inform his garden descriptions.

The gardens of the huge and 'uselessly extensive' Desmond Court in *Castle Richmond* (1860) are half a mile off from the house. 'There is no garden close up to the house, no flower-beds, in nooks and corners, no sweet shrubs peeping at the square windows', and 'the great hall door opens out upon a flat, bleak park, with hardly a scrap around it which courtesy can call a lawn' (pp. 5–6). In *An Eye For An Eye* (1879), the Elizabethan Scroope Manor is set in an extensive but unattractive park where 'there was none of that finished landscape beauty of which the owners of "places" in England are so justly proud. . . . To a stranger, and perhaps to the inmates, the idea of gloom about the place was greatly increased by the absence of any garden or lawn near to the house' (p. 3). Similarly, Bragton Park in *The American Senator* (1877) 'is somewhat sombre, as there is no garden close to the house' (p. 14), and because the flower-gardens of Clavering Park in *The Claverings* (1867) are some 300 yards removed from the house, 'the cold desolate park came up close around the windows' (p. 370).

Trollope's judgemental descriptions are by no means peculiar. In Mrs Oliphant's *A Country Gentleman and his Family* (1886), the substantial country seat of Markland suffers more even than most of Trollope's gloomy houses from the lack of modern horticultural improvements. For commercial reasons, the plantations of Markland 'had been wantonly and wastefully cut' so that the house 'stood almost unsheltered upon its little eminence'. Because it lacked ornamental gardens, and could boast but a scattering of immature beeches, it stood 'in a nakedness which made the spectator shiver' (I, 59).

If a flower-garden close to the house is Trollope's first requirement of a first-rate garden, scarcely less essential are well-tended lawns and gravel paths. His agenda is strikingly compatible with those of mid-century garden writers. An anonymous contributor to the *Quarterly Review* of 1842 wrote: 'The smoothness and verdure of our lawns is the first thing in our gardens that catches the eye of the foreigner; the next is the fineness and firmness of our gravel-walks.'[7]

Consentience is suggested also by a common vocabulary—by the word 'trim' in particular. It is Trollope's favourite 'garden' adjective, and a term much favoured by garden writers. Though 'trim' has a cluster of significations, Trollope consistently applies it to tidy, tasteful, well-tended arrangements. In the technical literature, it is sometimes used with specific reference to the contents as opposed to the overall design of gardens: to plants trimmed to perfect shape characteristic of the gardenesque style. In Trollope, this sense seems cognate with but subordinate to its larger, more general application. 'Trim' is used also for the strictly regular and symmetrical garden, but not by Trollope, who denotes severe symmetry and connotes stuffy propriety with the epithet 'prim'. Thus, with a glance at Pope, he describes Mrs Winterfield's gloomy plot at Perivale in *The Belton Estate* (1865) as 'a square, prim garden, arranged in parallelograms, tree answering tree at every corner' (p. 87).

The referential variations of 'trim' are interesting but less significant than its affective stability. In common with most mid-century garden and imaginative writers, Trollope uses 'trim' to express approval, and almost all the gardens he presents positively have the quality of trimness. In *The Small House at Allington* (1864) we learn that about the Great House at Allington 'there were trim gardens, not very large, but worthy of much note in that they were so trim,—gardens with broad gravel paths, with one walk running in front of the house so broad as to be fitly called a terrace' (p. 5). Lily Dale, we are told, took pride in her lawns at the Small House, and considered them finer than those of her uncle. In *Framley Parsonage* (1861) we learn that the gardens of Framley Court 'were trim and neat beyond all others in the country' (p. 9), and those of the house at Noningsby in *Orley Farm* 'were trim, and the new grounds around them trim, and square, and orderly' (p. 215).

Trollope's notion of trimness was evidently broad enough to license the incorporation of a certain amount of stonework close to the house; in this respect, also, his views are consistent with those of contemporary garden theorists. In *Barchester Towers* (1857) he describes the Thornes' old-fashioned garden at Ullathorne. The windows of the withdrawing-room 'opened on to the full extent of the lovely trim gardens; immediately beyond the windows were plots of flowers in stiff, stately, stubborn little beds, each bed surrounded by a stone copping of its own; beyond, there was a low parapet wall, on which stood urns and images, fawns, nymphs, satyrs, and a whole tribe of Pan's followers; and then, again, beyond that a beautiful lawn sloped away to a sunk fence which divided the garden from the park' (p. 187).

But in Trollope's estimation, even the finest of terrace gardens is aesthetically inferior to a well-kept lawn. Of Greshamsbury

House, 'said to be the finest specimen of Tudor architecture of which the country can boast', we are told: 'It stands in a multitude of trim gardens and stone-built terraces, divided one from another: these to our eyes are not so attractive as that broad expanse of lawn by which our country houses are generally surrounded; but the gardens of Greshamsbury have been celebrated for two centuries, and any Gresham who would have altered them would have been considered to have destroyed one of the well-known landmarks of the family' (*Dr Thorne* (1858), p. 10).

One wonders on behalf of which particular community Trollope considered himself to be speaking here. Not, one assumes, on behalf of those tradition-conscious members of the gardening fraternity who had for more than half a century been lamenting the destruction of architectural features like those of Greshamsbury. That Trollope's remarks were proffered at a time when many Victorians were reviving Tudor and Italian garden designs in the search for historical authenticity, makes them even more difficult to square with contemporary attitudes—notwithstanding Trollope's acknowledgement of historical appeal. What his use of the democratic 'we' does suggest is that his views about the indispensability of a 'broad expanse of lawn' were widely shared—at least among the country house community.

In general, Trollope's predilections are far from idiosyncratic or narrowly sectional, and he is by no means the only novelist to write approvingly of garden features considered by theorists appropriate to show a desirable degree of artifice. In *Wives and Daughters* (1864–6) Mrs Gaskell more than once refers with approval to the 'trim lawn' of Hamley Hall, and she also uses 'trim' with reference to the vicarage garden at Helstone in *North and South* (1854–5), and to the gardens of Cranford (*Cranford* (1853)). In Mrs Oliphant's *Salem Chapel* (1863) the reader is told, again by way of commendation, that in Lady Western's autumnal garden 'everything is in the most perfect order in the trim shrubberies' (p. 56). The perceived attractiveness of modest artifice is registered in poems as well. In Austin Dobson's *A New Song of The Spring Gardens*, the speaker hails Londoners to 'the trim gravelled walks' of Vauxhall Gardens (*DP*, p. 298).

Many novelists evidently shared with garden writers the suspicion that what attracted foreigners to English gardens was the trimness of their features.[8] Disraeli's Colonel Campion is pleasantly struck by the 'art-fulness' of English gardens. He says to Lothair: 'What I admire most in your country, my lord, are your gravel walks' (*Lothair*, p. 101). A real American abroad, Henry James, expressed similar sentiments in his travel essays and novels, as here in a description from *The Ambassadors* (1903) detailing Strether's experience in the garden of his hotel at Chester: 'The ordered English garden, in the freshness of the day, was delightful to Strether, who liked the sound, under his feet, of the tight fine gravel, packed with chronic damp, and who had the idlest eye for the deep smoothness of turf and the clean curves of path' (pp. 54–5).

On numerous occasions, James writes admiringly of English lawns, as when he sets the scene at Gardencourt in the opening chapter of *The Portrait of a Lady* (1881), or describes a 'charming old rectory' in Warwickshire, set down 'upon its cushiony lawn and among its ordered gardens',[9] which also brings to his mind George Eliot's Gwendolen Harleth and Mallinger Grandcourt. He was thinking, presumably, of the 'carefully-kept enclosure' of the archery ground at Brackenshaw Park, with its 'gravel walks and the bit of newly-mown turf where the targets are placed . . .' (*Daniel Deronda* (1876), p. 72).

In the last thirty years of the century, the term 'trim' acquired new applications and connotations. Some garden writers gave it a derogatory twist. Chief among them was William Robinson, who, in 1870, formally launched, in *The Wild Garden*, his quest for a system of gardening that 'will enable us to grow hundreds of plants that never yet obtained a place in our "trim gardens", nor ever will be admitted therein.' Robinson associated trimness with the architectural features of mid-century Italianate gardens, with a restricted and unimaginative use of plant materials, and with the bedding system, which he denounced as 'base and frightfully opposed to every law of nature's own arrangement of things'.[10] He argued instead for what he rather misleadingly called the 'wild garden'.

I shall show later that some contemporary poets and novelists shared Robinson's preference for comparatively simple and 'natural' garden styles. Here I wish to mention only one novelist: George Gissing. Like Robinson, Gissing had a passion for the English countryside and for what he took to be nature undeformed. His use of the term 'trim garden' is distinctly Robinsonian in its pejorative connotations. With regard to the thwarted ambitions of Clara Hewett, the narrator of *The Nether World* (1889) says: 'Never yet did the rebel, who had burst the barriers of social limitations, find aught but ennui in the trim gardens beyond'

(p. 277). Here, I think, 'trim gardens' has a more than figurative force—it is very much a metonym of the tediously conventional social world of the privileged classes. But it is in *The Private Papers of Henry Ryecroft* (1903) that Gissing's Robinsonian proclivities are most in evidence. Henry Ryecroft, in some respects like Gissing himself, is released from the servitude of his life as a struggling city writer by an unexpected legacy. His final years are spent in a privileged pastoral retreat, where he supervises the construction and stocking of his garden—about which he has some definite 'peculiarities'. Ryecroft informs the reader that his gardener is puzzled because he 'will not let him lay out the flower-beds in the usual way, and make the bit of ground in front of the house really neat and ornamental'. Ryecroft explains:

> The only garden flowers I care for are the quite old-fashioned roses, sunflowers, hollyhocks, lilies and so on, and these I like to see growing as much as possible as if they were wild. Trim and symmetrical beds are my abhorrence, and most of the flowers which are put into them—hybrids with some grotesque name—Jonesia, Snooksia,—hurt my eyes. On the other hand, a garden is a garden, and I would not try to introduce into it the flowers which are my solace in lanes and fields. Foxgloves, for instance—it would pain me to see them thus transplanted. (p. 100)

On this last point, Ryecroft seems to differ from Robinson, who proposed the naturalization in gardens of hardy plants, including non-native species. Otherwise, their likes and dislikes are very similar.

Robinson had opponents. Of these, the most extreme was Reginald Blomfield, the most level-headed, J. D. Sedding.[11] Like Robinson, they abominated the Italianate taste for carpet-bedding and elaborate parterres of vivid bedded-out flowers. But in contrast to Robinson, who wished to make trim gardens things of the past, his opponents wished to make trim gardens because they *were* things of the past. That is, they located the trimness they desired not in the immodest formality of Italianate compositions, nor in the look-alike plots of suburban London with, in Ruskin's words, their 'exactly similar double parallelograms of garden, laid out in new gravel and scanty turf, on the model of the Crystal Palace' (*RW*, XXVII, 529), but in the small, modestly formal gardens of the Renaissance, and of the late seventeenth and early eighteenth centuries: enclosed, rectangular, axial, pleached and pergolaed, with cubicle flower-beds edged in clipped box.

William Morris was one writer favourably disposed to such gardens. He was especially charmed by the simplicity and orderliness of the medieval pleasure-garden with its enclosed plot and trellises, its fruit trees and flower closes.[12] He believed that all (pre-Utopian) gardens should be enclosed—with almost 'anything but iron' —[13] and that inside the walls there should be a tidy arrangement of small, square, boxed-in beds. He constructed his own gardens on medieval lines.

Morris's writings bristle with references to and descriptions of medieval gardens and gardens of medievalist inspiration. Almost all of them are distinguished by their trimness, which for Morris meant more than simple tidiness—important though this was to him.[14] Morris's notion of trimness is recoverable from his imaginative writings, where the term is usually clarified in relation to its opposite. Thus, in many contexts, 'trim' contrasts with 'tumbledown'. In *A Dream of John Ball* (1888) the Victorian dreamer, accustomed to the 'tumbledown, bankrupt-looking surroundings of our modern agriculture', awakes to find himself in an unfamiliar (medieval) landscape. He is struck by 'a certain unwonted trimness and hardiness about the enclosures of the gardens and orchards', 'surprised' by 'the garden-like neatness and trimness of everything' (*MSW*, p. 200). In *News from Nowhere* (1890) the contrast is provided by the 'tumbledown picturesque'. 'Such things', Old Hammond tells Guest, 'do not please us even when they indicate no misery. Like the medievals, we like everything trim and clean and orderly and bright' (*MSW*, p. 68).

Morris's use of 'trim' is implicitly opposed to the Robinsonian applications of the term to a nature made ugly by coercion and architectural subjugation. It suggests, on the contrary, a nature both subdued *and* superabundant. In *The Story of the Unknown Church* (1856) the gardens of the medieval abbey and church appear, as Morris in a paper entitled 'Making the Best of it' (1882) said every garden should appear, 'both orderly and rich' (*MW*, XXII, 90). Their beauty is enhanced by the welcomed intrusion of wild-flowers. Near the Piccadilly of post-Revolutionary England, the visitor to Nowhere finds himself 'in a region of elegantly built much ornamented houses' with trim gardens, each one 'carefully cultivated *and* running over with flowers' (*MSW*, p. 39; my emphasis).

It is significant that Morris applies 'trim' to homes and interiors (in *News from Nowhere*, to dwellings, sheds, and workshops) as well as to gardens and exteriors. It suggests that Morris, like other Victorian proponents of the formal garden, believed in the harmonious integration of house and garden. Indeed, he held that a garden 'should by no means imitate either the wilfulness or the wildness of nature, but should look like a thing never to be seen except near a house. It should look, in fact, like part of the house . . .' (*MW*, XXII, 90).

For Morris, this happy union of house and (formal) garden came to serve as a paradigm of the relations between people and nature under ideal conditions—the conditions which obtain in the socialist Utopia presented in *News from Nowhere*. Here, men are masters, and 'won't stand any nonsense from Nature in their dealings with her' (*MSW*, p. 68). 'Trim' is the footloose adjective which sums up this ideal state of affairs.

So far, I have focused upon the protean term 'trim', and plotted some changes in its application and associations. This has served to reveal some significant areas of agreement between Victorian garden theorists and contemporary imaginative writers. In particular, it has revealed that many fiction writers subscribed, in broad terms at least, to the idea that a garden should be 'robed, dressed and beautified' (Hibberd's words) rather than a deliberate replication of the 'natural' scene.

Writers who upheld the idea of the garden as a composed landscape tended also to privilege gardens whose potential for pictorial representation has been 'realized' through articulation, so that the reader is asked to collude with the fiction that the garden described has already been painted on canvas. Of course, Victorian novelists often described objects in such a way as to imply an anterior representational status; by this means, they sought to achieve an illusion of reality. (Consider Barthes' assertion that realism consists 'not in copying the real but in copying a "painted" copy of the real'.[15]) But the effect of treating a garden as a kind of visual quotation is not simply to verify its authenticity and likeness to the real; it is also to acknowledge its visual merits, and to affirm its status as a work of art.

When garden theorists argued that a garden should be a work of art they usually meant that it should be a landscape designed with regard to the general principles of artistic composition, not one designed consciously to look like or imitate a picture. Indeed, they took their eighteenth-century predecessors to task for not having 'questioned whether a picture should be the ultimate test of laying out gardens and grounds'.[16]

Between them, Repton and Loudon largely redefined the relations between painting and gardening. Repton distinguished between the two arts, while Loudon drew attention to the underlying principles common to both. In the very first volume of the *Gardener's Magazine* (1826), Loudon declared that 'the principles of composition are the same in all the arts of taste'; hence, all should be 'guided by unity of expression as the whole or general effect, and by the connection and cooperation of the component parts....'[17] Subsequently, he reiterated and expanded upon these principles. Since they appear to be evinced in many fictional gardens privileged by a pictorial frame of reference, it will be useful to look at them in some detail.

Loudon's repeated insistence upon 'unity of expression' stems from his conviction that the mind can attend to only one thing at a time. Hence, 'when a multiplicity of objects are placed before it, they must be so disposed as to form one object or picture, so as to be seen at one glance, otherwise the mind would be distracted, and deprived of that repose which is essential to comprehension and enjoyment.' Loudon acknowledges that 'the want of unity of expression is a prevailing error in most public gardens; and, indeed, in most private ones. Not only are there too many objects crowded into one scene, so that the spectator does not know to which to direct his attention first, but even so many walks offer themselves to his choice, that he is at a loss to know which to take.'[18]

Loudon's second principle is 'variety'. He writes: 'to excite attention and to keep alive interest, one kind of scene must succeed another.'[19] Finally, he emphasizes the importance of 'Relation or Order'. 'Scenes in a garden should not succeed one another at random, but according to some principle of succession, founded on the nature of the scenes to be exhibited; and this order of succession should be recognizable from the first by the spectator.... The spectator ought never to be taken violently by surprise, or startled; for that is the character of the lowest degree of art.'[20]

Let me quote the description of a garden which seems to meet Loudon's requirements. It is from G. J. Whyte-Melville's *Tilbury Nogo* (1854). The titular hero arrives at the door of Mr Cotherstone's villa

> through a sort of half-shrubbery and half-garden, studded with evergreens and fragrant with roses. Nothing could be prettier than the house and grounds—the former a long, low building, standing so white and level on its smoothly-shaven lawn, with French windows opening in all directions on the well-kept flower-garden, now in all its midsummer beauty, from whence winding gravel-walks with heavy borders of box, allure you into the picturesque and luxuriant shrubberies, whose dwarfish proportions formed a pleasing contrast, shut in as they were by the noble oaks of Windsor Forest, which completed the picture. (p. 72)

The final sentence wraps up the description at the same moment as it wraps up the scene by imposing, retrospectively as it were, a frame upon it. But it is clear from the confident manner in which the scene is unfolded that the speaker/spectator has all along envisaged the garden as a visual image in which all the constituent features are available for simultaneous inspection. The simple arrangement, together with the harmony of house and grounds, preserves unity of composition, while within the frame there is the requisite variety and contrast.

Of special interest is the 'succession' of the scenes and their relation to the whole. This succession is based upon the principle of gradual transition: the idea that scenes should advance from the highly artificial and formal in the immediate vicinity of the house, towards semi-'natural' scenes in the more distant or irregular parts of the grounds.

In mid-century, this mixed or composite style was both popular (as Loudon observed[21]) and favoured by many garden theorists for its optimization of visual effects. The eye (and mind) of the spectator, initially excited by the effects of highly-coloured formal displays, is then relieved and rested by the more open and chromatically subdued prospect. In the case of Mr Cotherstone's garden, these horizontal effects are intensified by a 'pleasing' vertical contrast.

In many other fictional gardens, the advancement of the spectator's eye through a gradual succession of contrasting scenes is identified as the source of his aesthetically pleasing landscape experience. In *Wives and Daughters*, Elizabeth Gaskell describes the experience of the young Molly Gibson on the occasion of the garden party at Cumnor Towers. Molly is simultaneously pained and delighted by the brilliant scenes near the house, by the flower-beds, 'scarlet, crimson, blue, orange; masses of blossom lying on the greensward' (p. 12). The prospect affords her relief: 'Green velvet lawns, bathed in sunshine, stretched away on every side into the finely wooded park; if there were divisions and ha-has between the soft, sunny sweeps of grass, and the dark gloom of the forest-trees beyond, Molly did not see them; and the melting away of the exquisite cultivation into the wilderness had an inexplicable charm to her' (p. 12).

Later, she has a similar experience of landscape from an upstairs window of Hamley Hall, itself a visually appealing structure of old red brick. Molly sees 'A flower-garden right below; a meadow of ripe grass beyond, changing colour in long sweeps, as the soft wind blew over it; great old forest trees on one side; and, beyond them again, . . . the silver shimmer of a mere, about a quarter of a mile off' (p. 69).

It is interesting to compare the zonal structure of the scene available to Molly Gibson with the landscape upon which Aurora Leigh could gaze from the bedroom of her aunt's country house. By pushing her head out of the window, she had 'the privilege of seeing'

> First, the lime . . . past the lime, the lawn,
> Which, after sweeping broadly round the house,
> Went trickling through the shrubberies in a stream
> Of tender turf, and wore and lost itself
> Among the acacias, over which you saw
> The irregular line of elms by the deep lane
> Which stopped the grounds and dammed the overflow
> Of arbutus and laurel . . .
> Behind the elms,
> And through their tops, you saw the folded hills
> Striped up and down with hedges . . .[22]

What distinguishes the scenes unfolded in this description is their near inversion of the normal sequence from artificial to 'natural'. The garden immediately about the house is robbed of formality by the signifiers which render it a 'natural' landscape: 'sweeping', 'trickling', 'stream' and 'overflow'. The significance of the reversed succession is clarified a little further on when the speaker contrasts the wild and 'palpitating' landscapes of Italy with those of contemporary England, a 'nature tamed'.
In England

All the fields
Are tied up fast with hedges, nosegay-like;
The hills are crumpled plains, the plains parterres,
The trees, round, wooly, ready to be clipped,
And if you seek for any wilderness
You find, at best, a park.[23]

Presumably, the free-flowing forms of the garden serve to compensate for the visual deficiencies of a gardenized nature—a nature parcelled and tidily transformed by the packing projects of agrarian capitalism.[24]

To turn from Gaskell's treatment of garden landscapes in *Wives and Daughters* to Disraeli's presentation of them in *Coningsby* (1844), *Endymion* (1880), and (in particular) *Lothair*, is not to be greatly surprised. Both novelists privilege gardens enhanced by non-random internal differentiation, and by the fortuitous conditions of their situations. Both acknowledge the visual appeal of gardens with strong zonal structures. There are differences. Gaskell, who conceives of landscape in domestic and economic terms, stresses topographical continuities: gardens proper grade gently into the surrounding countryside. Disraeli's contrasts are more emphatic: his foregrounds more glaring, his backgrounds more savage. But neither novelist is as much concerned with the itemization of particular features as with the general effects of the whole. In Disraeli's case, these wholes are enormous. Brentham, home of Lady Corisande in *Lothair*, is a 'vast, ornate' palace rising from 'statued and stately terraces'.

> At their foot spread a gardened domain of considerable extent, bright with flowers, dim with coverts of rare shrubs, musical with fountains. Its limit reached a park, with timber such as the midland counties only can produce. The fallow deer trooped among its ferny solitudes and gigantic oaks; but beyond the waters of the broad and winding lake the scene became more savage. (p. 4)

Emphatic contrasts of colour and topography, yet within a cohesive visual structure, are still more striking in Disraeli's description of Lothair's own ancestral house of Muriel Towers. Its gardens are

> formed in a sylvan valley enclosed with gilded gates. The creator of this paradise had been favoured by nature, and had availed himself of this opportunity. The contrast between

> the parterres blazing with colour and the sylvan background, the undulating paths over romantic heights, the fanes and the fountains, the glittering statues, and the Babylonian terraces, formed a whole much of which was beautiful, and all of which was striking and singular. (p. 196)

Vernon Bogdanor has written that 'At Brentham and at Muriel, nature beyond the ordered confines of the house is savage and unfriendly'.[25] Bogdanor's coupling of adjectives is misleading, for Disraeli's use of 'savage', in its aesthetic applications, is always positive and commendatory. Nature may be savage, but it is also cooperative; it can be appropriated by the landscape gardener to complement his production.

Though Disraeli has often been cited as a champion of the blazing parterre characteristic of the High Victorian Display Garden,[26] it is clear from his fictional descriptions that his approval of brilliant effects is conditional upon their being offset by the subdued colours and irregular forms of the encincturing wildscape.[27] Had he been asked to justify the kaleidoscopic flower-bed of formal design, he might well have quoted Hibberd: 'Even when the garden slopes away to a splendid prospect of open country, flowers should embellish the foreground, not to draw the eye from natural scenes, but to combine happily the efforts of nature and art in the production of a living picture.'[28]

What Disraeli and Hibberd appear to share is a sense of the distinction between visual composition and mere visual impact, or the view that a garden can be highly colourful and of intricate design without necessarily being pleasing to the eye, and without combining 'happily the efforts of art and nature in the production of a living picture'.

As regards mere visual impact, Hibberd had two main targets. The first was the bedding-out system, which set the flower-garden ablaze for three months and kept it a 'dreary blank' for the remainder of the year. Hibberd was of the opinion that 'A few simple borders, well stocked with mixed herbaceous plants . . . would in many instances, afford more real pleasure and ever-changing interest than the most gorgeous display of bedding plants hemmed in between two glaring walls, or exposed on a great treeless, turfless place like the blazing fire at the mouth of a coal-pit.'[29]

Hibberd's other target was the 'Tudor' knot. In the middle decades of the century, some gardeners, searching for historical authenticity, revived features considered characteristic of Tudor gardens. One such feature was the intricate parterre filled with coloured earths and gravels. Hibberd had no time for them. He wrote: 'The working out of a great design in coloured earths and flower-beds is the most complicated and generally, the least satisfactory form of the parterre. It has this advantage, that during the winter it affords 'something to look at', and the corresponding disadvantage that nobody wants to see it.'[30]

In the concluding section of *Lothair*, which includes some of the most explicit comments on contemporary garden theory and practice to be found in Victorian fiction, the conversation of Disraeli's upper-class characters centres on 'modern gardens'. The views they express echo and endorse the sentiments of Hibberd and many other contemporary garden writers. The speakers are in a room at Brentham which looks out 'on a garden of many colours':

> 'How I hate modern gardens', said St. Aldegonde.
> 'What a horrid thing this is! One might as well have a mosaic pavement there. Give me cabbage-roses, sweetpeas, and wallflowers. That is my idea of a garden. Corisande's garden is the only sensible thing of the sort.'
> 'One likes a mosaic pavement to look like a garden,' said Euphrosyne, 'but not a garden like a mosaic pavement.'
> 'The worst of these mosaic beds', said Madame Phoebus, 'is, you can never get a nosegay, and if it were not for the kitchen-garden, we should be destitute of that gayest and sweetest of creations.' (p. 463)

The 'modern gardens' which St Aldegonde detests—elaborate, dazzling and declamatorily artificial—are far from prominent in Victorian fiction. Though many novelists appear to have assimilated the logic of the argument that a garden, as a work of art, ought recognizably to contrast with nature in the raw, their latitudes of acceptance—what they were willing to legitimate through favourable comments and descriptions—were reasonably narrow. As a rule, trim orderly arrangements of modest scale, flower-beds of mixed forms and colours, and designs highlighting internal variety and contrast, tend to fall within the parameters of acceptance; extreme formality and symmetry, elaborate geometrical beds of flaming and homogeneous plant materials, and predominantly architectural designs in which the free forms of nature are subordinated or excluded altogether, fall outside them.

Within this catalogue of proscriptions, one would logically have to place the Italian(ate) garden, in mid-century the most widely adopted of the architecturally-dominant historical styles. Christopher Thacker points out that the Italianate style came 'from the formal gardens of Italy, with a side-glance at Versailles'.[31] Provenance is pertinent here, for it was principally with reference to the prototypical models from which contemporary examples derived that Victorian novelists most clearly glossed the 'architectural' garden.

There are many references to 'Italian gardens' in Victorian fiction, but few are sufficiently developed to yield much in the way of attitudinal information. By contrast, Le Nôtre's work at Versailles defied perfunctory dismissal. Some Victorians were impressed by it, and sought to perceive its shadowy presence in contemporary English compositions.[32] Bulwer Lytton was one of the few novelists to venture a spirited defence of its derivatives. The narrator of *Eugene Aram* describes a Ducal garden with terraces, statues and fountains:

> It was one of those magnificent gardens, modelled from the stately glories of Versailles, which is now the mode to decry, but which breathe so unequivocally of the palace. I grant that they deck Nature with somewhat too prolix a grace; but is Beauty always best seen in *deshabille*? And with what associations of the brightest traditions connected with Nature they link her more luxuriant loveliness! (p. 93)

When Bulwer Lytton wrote this, the terraces of Shrublands had yet to be laid out, and the zenith of the High Display Garden in England was two decades away. Experience, perhaps, led him to revise his ideas, for in the later *Alice; or the Mysteries* (1838) he remarks, with reference to Ernest Maltravers's improvements to the gardens of Burleigh, that 'Nature was just assisted and relieved by Art, without being oppressed by too officious a service from her handmaid' (pp. 139–40).

For most Victorian writers, the Versailles gardens were neither stately nor glorious. Loudon declared them to be 'dreary beyond what can be imagined when they are not filled with company' since there was 'not a spot or corner in them to exercise the imagination, unless it be the orangery'.[33] Robinson was distressed by the 'indescribable emptiness of the scene'.[34] (As Edward Malins and Patrick Bowe explain, 'his dislike for the formal garden is linked with his advocacy of the landscape as the gardener's model . . .'.[35]) For Robinson, a dearth of the qualities most likely to appeal to painters of garden scenes and the subjugation of nature were concomitant demerits. The author of an article in the *Leisure Hour* of 1886 laid emphasis upon the latter. The gardens of Louis XIV formed, he wrote, 'a striking illustration of the French style, resembling their owner in irksome pomp and formality, and like him lacking the "touch of nature" which, in gardens or men, should never be wanting.'[36] It is to this 'want of the "touch of nature"' that imaginative writers most frequently directed attention. Here is how G. J. Whyte-Melville opens his historical novel, *Cerise: A Tale of the Last Century* (1866):

> In the gardens of Versailles, as everywhere else within the freezing influence of the *Grand Monarque*, nature herself seemed to accept the situation, and succumbed inevitably under the chain of order and courtly etiquette. The grass grew, indeed, and the Great Waters played, but the former was rigorously limited to certain mathematical patches, and permitted only to obtain an established length, while the latter threw their diamond showers against the sky with avenues stretched away, straight and stiff like rows of lately-built houses; and the shrubs stood hard and defiant as the white statues with which they alternated, and the very sunshine off blinding gravel glared and scorched as if its duty were but to mark a march of dazzling hours in square stone dials for the Kings of France'. (p. 1)

Nature, said Hibberd, ought in every garden to be 'robed, dressed, and beautified'; here it is straitjacketed by a rigid and suffocating formality. But, of course, this chilling passage cannot be read simply as an aesthetically motivated denunciation of excessive architecture and uncompromising axiality, for the gardens of Versailles as here described are a symbolic topographical reflection of their owner's absolutist ideology.

Though there were no Sun Kings and no gardens quite like Versailles in Victorian England, Whyte-Melville's judgemental description was not without contemporary relevance. There were among the affluent classes those who felt inclined to channel their considerable resources into a conspicuous display of wealth and power. And there were those who felt the need to counsel them against it.[37] Moreover, the dream of total environmental control, though no longer the expression of autocratic monarchy, was far from dead. Indeed, the view that nature itself was and ought to be controlled was central to the mid-Victorian belief in progress and to Gradgrindian versions of Utilitarian philosophy.

Perhaps the most striking thing about the opening paragraph of *Cerise* is its thematic similarity to the opening chapter (and many other parts) of Dickens's *Hard Times* (1854). The specific targets differ, but the equation of extreme formality with emotional frigidity and doctrinal inflexibility obtains in both. Like Louis XIV, though for dissimilar reasons, Gradgrind attempts to override or replace organic nature with a mathematical travesty of it. In the grounds of his house, that 'uncompromising fact in the landscape', geometric regularity rules (in both senses) the 'lawn and garden and infant avenue' (p. 10). The garden gives topographical expression to his 'botanical account-book' view of nature.

Like Dickens, Tennyson attaches negative meanings to gardens lacking a 'touch of nature'. His description of the gardens of the Women's College in *The Princess* (1847) is a case in point. On the face of it, their classical grandeur would appear to be poles apart from the barren geometricity of Gradgrind's garden. And yet, both are rigid (architecturally so in Ida's case); both betray their owner's want of 'natural' feelings and, by extension, their want of social sympathies. And in both, symbolic topographies help to define an attitude towards the theories of social progress they reveal or proclaim.

We first encounter Ida's gardens when the Prince and his companions in drag arrive at the College, and enter

> . . . through the porch that sang
> All round with Laurel, [which] issued in a court
> Compact of lucid marbles, bossed with lengths
> Of classic frieze, with ample awnings gay
> Betwixt the pillars, and with great urns of flowers.
> The Muses and the Graces, grouped in threes,
> Enringed a billowing fountain in the midst. (*TP*, p. 759)

Already the emphasis is upon stonework, statuary and architectural ornamentation, reinforced later by references to a marble bridge, a balustraded terrace and statues. The effects of this are not entirely negative. Some of Tennyson's contemporaries may have noted, in addition to some formal similarities between Ida's garden and those of newly-constructed Italianate gardens, a motivational similarity, for just as the latter served to channel classical impulses in a form acceptable to their Victorian owners,[38] so the gorgeous adornments of the College gardens serve as vehicles for the expression of Ida's noble aspirations. In regard to her inspirational statuary, the Princess herself declares that 'to look upon noble forms / Makes noble through the sensuous organism / That which is higher!' But the statues also 'stand as a metaphor of the bad metamorphosis brought about by the Princess's fixed attitudes and rigid adherence to a principle not fully in accord with the plastic impulses of nature.'[39] Statues also play a direct part in the action. One of the most blatantly symbolic moments in the poem occurs when the Prince is trapped between the two great garden portals of Art and Science. Thus, Tennyson appears to make use of the predominantly negative signification of abundant stonework, current at the time of the poem's composition, to imply an attitude towards the 'unnatural' inflexibility of Ida's social doctrines.[40]

Disraeli was probably the only Victorian novelist of any reputation persistently to have lavished description upon the grand and elaborate gardens of the Victorian upper-classes.[41] Among his many fulsome descriptions of aristocratic gardens, Beaumonoir in *Coningsby* and Brentham in *Lothair* contend for pride of place. In describing Brentham, Disraeli was almost certainly thinking of Trentham, the Staffordshire seat of the Dukes of Sutherland, and one of the most magnificent of the Italianate gardens constructed by Charles Barry (assisted, perhaps, by William Nesfield). Within Disraeli's version of it, are fountains, 'statued and stately terraces' and a flower-garden 'so glowing and cultured into patterns so fanciful and finished that it had the resemblance of a vast mosaic' (p. 1). Lothair's own estate of Muriel Towers (probably inspired by the remarkable gardens of Alton Towers) resembles Kubla Khan's pleasaunce extended to encompass the mighty chasm. But with all its diversity of romantic scenery, 'What charmed Lothair most . . . were the number of courts and quadrangles in the castle, all of bright and fantastic architecture, and each of which was a garden, glowing with brilliant colours, and gay with the voice of fountains or the forms of gorgeous birds' (p. 186).

Disraeli's enthusiasm for opulent, aristocratic gardens would not seem hard to explain. While many writers doubtless found them irritants to their democratic consciences, to Disraeli they were metonyms of a social order based on landed inheritance or, perhaps, 'representative symbols of that ordered society which Disraeli devoted his political life to preserve'.[42] Disraeli himself acquired Hughenden so that he might live the lifestyle of, and in the surroundings of, an English country gentleman; and by the time he came to describe Brentham, he had been a guest at some of the great country estates—Raby, Lowther, Ashridge, Woburn, and Stowe among them. His fictional descriptions were intended, no doubt, to imply his familiarity with the models upon which they were loosely based.

Whether Disraeli's predilection for showy display led him to exaggerate their opulence, is a matter for debate. Certainly, his emphasis upon glittering architectural splendour is an expression of his 'fascination with the ornaments of affluence' which 'always accompanied his rise through society'.[43] And it is also true that 'some contemporaries were quick to accuse Disraeli of a Jewish taste for tawdry decoration'. But 'in fact, Disraeli was hardly exaggerating the external pomp and show displayed by the great nobles of his day . . .'.[44]

On aesthetic grounds, Disraeli's attitude towards the magnificent display garden might best be characterized as one of fascination rather than of unqualified admiration. I mentioned earlier that Disraeli seems to approve of brilliant colour schemes and abundant stonework only when their effects are offset by more 'natural', open and reposeful vistas. This seems to be the case with Theodora Campion's estate of Belmont. The rear of this 'stately mansion' opens 'on a terrace adorned with statues and orange trees, and descending gently into a garden in the Italian style, in the centre of which was a marble fountain of many figures' (*Lothair*, p. 128). So far, all very formal. But then we were told: 'The grounds were not extensive, but they were only separated from the royal park by a wire fence, so that the scene seemed alike rich and illimitable' (p. 128). The beholder's sense of visual gratification appears to require this more expansive vista. One feels that Disraeli would have sympathized with the sentiments expressed by James Groom in an article entitled 'Draw-backs of Geometrical Gardens', which had this to say of the Italian garden: 'The system, though not wholly without merit, is too artificial in character to make any lasting impression. During the summer, it is, in fact, a gigantic bouquet, enclosed with stone edgings . . . and one instinctively turns to the fresh green turf, and the ever-welcome aspect of tree and shrub life for lasting enjoyment'.[45]

Disraeli was also sensitive to an excess of exuberant conceits. On beholding the gardens of Muriel Towers, Lothair murmurs, 'Perhaps too many temples' (p. 196), a charge often levelled at Alton Towers. The Rothschildean opulence of Hainault House gardens, in *Endymion*, is all too much for the attractively-presented Mrs Neuchatel. She much prefers the unpretentious gardens of the Rectory at Hainault. Taken together with Theodora Campion's reservations about the 'art-fulness' of Blenheim's formal gardens (*Lothair*, p. 99) and Lady Corisande's antipathies towards the intricate display garden, Mrs Neuchatel's rejection of architectural grandeur suggests that Disraeli was able to view the High Victorian Display Garden from a critical perspective.

An integral feature of Italian and grand display gardens was the elaborate and dazzling parterre. Its principal aesthetic function was to highlight expanses of turf, stonework and gravel paths. Because of the expense required to stock and maintain them, parterres were especially conspicuous in municipal gardens and the gardens of the upper classes. But they were not confined to such gardens. Many smaller gardens, during and long after the middle years of the century, boasted highly-coloured flower-gardens of regular or symmetrical design. Depending on space, tastes and resources, brightly-coloured annuals were crammed into tiny plots, packed into scattered flower-beds on the lawn or in ribbon-borders around its edge, or massed into a more elaborate arrangement to be viewed from a drawing-room or upstairs window.

Stimulated by (*inter alia*) the availability of suitable plant materials and the emphasis on artifice in garden design, 'barren geometry' (as Robinson dubbed it) became immensely popular in the middle decades of the period. We have only to turn the pages of the horticultural magazines published between the 1840s and 1860s to appreciate this. When the reaction to bedding-out set in, possibly as early as the mid-1860s,[46] its detractors, far from underplaying its importance, insisted tirelessly that its monopoly had still to be broken.

It is open to argument whether the bedding-system ever achieved the stranglehold that its opponents claimed. If it did not, then the imaginative writers of the period offer access to a less systematically distorted picture of contemporary garden practices than does Robinson in the pages of *The Garden*. What is certain, is that these garden writers could not have rifled literary texts to substantiate their claims. Put another way, we cannot recover from mid-Victorian fiction anything approaching an accurate idea of the popularity of the practices against which Robinson and his allies were to tilt, since Victorian novelists do not reflect contemporary manias in a welter of lovingly-detailed descriptions of kaleidoscopic flower-beds, geometric designs and massed plantings. With few exceptions, those novelists who do grant such features textual space are usually ambivalent if not adversely critical in the attitudes they imply towards them.

This is an interesting fact, but one not altogether easy to explain. Novelists must have known that geometric flower-gardens and carpet-bedding arrangements were popular, and at least some must have sensed the semiotic mileage to be gained from describing them. One can imagine, for example, a host of fictional contexts in which the description of a glaring, geometric flower-garden, liberally laced with pejorative epithets, might have served as a 'text' signifying, for example, the vulgarity and imaginative bankruptcy of the philistine bourgeoisie. Moreover, there must have been novelists for whom display gardens of massive scale and indubitable splendour offered irresistible opportunities for lavish and comprehensive presentation, and a chance to show off their botanical knowledge.

A rare example of the kind of thing I have in mind is Charlotte M. Yonge's highly particularized account of a High Victorian Display Garden in *Heartsease* (1854). As a social 'text', this garden is indicative of the wealth and expressive of the tastes of its owners—the respectable and wealthy upper-class Martindale family. Its initial effects upon Violet, the young and socially inferior wife of Arthur Martindale (the owner's younger son) are overwhelming:

> Violet held her breath. The grand parterre, laid out in regular-shaped borders, each containing a mass of one kind of flower, flaming elscholcias, dazzling verbenas, azure nemophilas, or sober heliotrope, the broad walks, the great pile of building, the innumerable windows, the long ascent of stone steps, their balustrade guarded by sculptured sphinxes . . . reminded her of prints of Versailles, by the sparkling fountains rising high in fantastic jets from its stone basin, in the midst of an expanse of novel turf, bordered by terraces and stone steps adorned with tall vases of flowers. On the balustrade stood a peacock, bending his blue neck, and drooping of his gorgeous train, as if he was 'monarch of all he surveyed'. (p. 22)

Violet is amazed to discover that there are at Martindale 'gardens' as well as the 'pleasure-ground' she took to be the gardens:

> There spread out before her a sweep of shaven turf, adorned with sparkling *jets d'eau* of fantastic forms, gorgeous masses of American plants, the flaming of the snowy azalea, the

> noble rhododendron, in every shade of purple cluster among its evergreen leaves; beds of rare lilies, purely white or brilliant with colour; roses in their perfection of bloom; flowers of forms she had never figured to herself, shaded by wondrous trees; the exquisite weeping deodora, the delicate mimosa, the scaly Himalayan pines, the feathery gigantic ferns of the southern hemisphere. (p. 36)

How might Miss Yonge's contemporary readers have responded to these descriptions? Not simply, one suspects, and certainly not upon purely aesthetic grounds, for in the conversational scenes in which they are embedded, the reader's attention is drawn ineluctably to the social determinants of aesthetic (landscape) experience. Violet's response—a kind of immobilizing awe—is determined not simply by the visual splendour and intensity of the scenes before her but by their very unfamiliarity: 'I did not know there could be anything so beautiful!' she exclaims. Though the Martindales regard the gardens with pleasureless indifference ('The natives never have any sport out of a showplace', says Arthur) or tedious disdain ('"It is simply a bore", said Theodora; "a self-sacrifice to parade"'), their responses seem no less socially motivated. The narrator's position is more ambivalent. She leaves no doubt that the Martindale gardens provide an opulent but joyless display of their owners' wealth but, in contrast to the Martindales, who seem capable only of responding to what the gardens signify, she attends also to what they are, to their inherent 'textual' properties. Hence, one finds here a degree of botanical specificity which surely exceeds the minimal functional requirements of the descriptive passages. At the same time, this referential attentiveness distinguishes the narrator's perspective from Violet's purely affective involvement. The narrator is able to impose upon the garden text a grid of differences because she is equipped with a specialized vocabulary which is simply unavailable to the socially unprivileged Violet.

Since the same gardens are assessed from three quite different perspectives, and since these do not correspond simply to a set of alternative aesthetic positions, it is by no means easy to decide how contemporary readers would have responded. If we assume, however, that their positions were aligned with the narrator's, it seems likely that they would have taken the view that, ultimately, the gardens fail *as* gardens because they succeed as show-places. They are visually intense, they 'parade' as they are intended to parade, but they are not fully integrated, visually gratifying compositions. The effects of individual features are powerful and impressive, but collectively these effects are homogenizing, and dysfunctional in that they militate against relaxed social intercourse. Plant material is various, but there are no marked contrasts and, in particular, little rest for the eye. In the terms supplied by one conceptual schema, all is prospect, nothing refuge.[47] Note especially how the piling up of details in paratactic units replicates both the internally differentiated but pictorially 'ungrammatical' structure of the garden text, and the accumulative effects by which the unfamiliar spectator is overwhelmed.

Of course, the narrator is impressed by the magnificence of the garden she produces in description; impressed, but not delighted. She doesn't decry such gardens, possibly because her 'weakness . . . for the stately houses of England'[48] precludes her from explicit deprecation, but mainly because her respectful tone and technical vocabulary are sufficient to gesture the reader towards the appropriate response: qualified admiration without genuine affection. Later in the century, another commentator points to the same limited response when he says that 'for a garden that was always and everywhere equally gaudy . . . you might entertain wonder, but you would hardly cherish affection.'[49]

As I have said, descriptions of display gardens of the Martindale ilk are rare in Victorian fiction. Where brightly-coloured flower-beds are not described with obvious distaste, they invariably form part of a balanced and differentiated composition. This is the situation in Gaskell's fiction. On the occasion of Mr Lennox's visit, the 'small lawn' of Helstone vicarage 'was gorgeous with verbenas and geraniums of all bright colours' (*North and South*, p. 60). But the brightness of the garden is emphasized only to contrast it with the faded interior and, in any case, the brilliance of the formal beds is offset by the 'peeping' honeysuckle and clustering roses. Exactly the same contrast, though on a grander scale, obtains at Cumnor Towers, where the flower-beds are both drained of artificiality by an image that redeems them as natural (they are 'masses of blossom on the greensward') and diminished as a cynosure by the 'inexplicable charm' of the wilder prospect (*Wives and Daughters*, p. 45). In the absence of a topographical contrast, it is less easy to determine the attitude implied. This is the case at Hamley Hall, where the drawing-room opens onto 'the prettiest bit of flower-garden in the grounds—or what was considered as such—brilliant-coloured, geometrically-shaped beds, converging to a sun-dial at the midst' (p. 99). The parenthetical disclaimer of authorial approval points in one direction; the fact that Molly Gibson borrows from the Hamley gardens the idea of laying out her own bed of scarlet geraniums, points in the other.

Another female novelist, Rhoda Broughton, describes many colourful gardens. Significantly, however, their colour tends to come from the mixing of various plant materials, and she evidently had a low opinion of massed plantings. Tucked away in one of her garden descriptions is the remark that 'the scentless flowers of the geraniums and calceolarias fills, without satisfying, the eyes'.[50] In his *Private Papers*, Gissing's Ryecroft also confesses an anathema for geometric flower-beds and for the glaring plants which fill them (p. 100). Gissing's occasional descriptions of small municipal flower-gardens are consistent with Ryecroft's attitude. In *Thyrza* (1887) we find a description of a small public garden in Lambeth—actually a converted graveyard. In summer, its bright flower-beds had little intrinsic beauty, and served merely to 'enhance the ignoble baldness of the by-way' (p. 25).

I have argued that a content analysis of Victorian imaginative literature would reveal little in the way of mirroring of or support for the emphatically artificial garden styles then in vogue. The inference would seem to be that imaginative writers were either unsympathetic to or unenthusiastic about highly formal arrangements in general and fashionable colour schemes of kaleidoscopic or homogeneous brilliance in particular. There is extensive evidence to suggest that they would have subscribed to the views of a contributor to *The Cornhill Magazine* who in the early 1870s lamented 'an undue tendency in these days towards too much uniformity and regularity in gardening', who said he liked to see 'a flower-bed with a variety of colours and forms in it—not a great patch of scarlet, or pink, or yellow, or purple', and who wished to 'encourage a style of natural wildness'.[51]

Much of this evidence is of a negative kind. For example, it is significant that most fictional flower-gardens of the more formal kinds are presented in only the most general terms. The absence of specificity is the hallmark of Trollope's flower-garden descriptions. As a rule, Trollope tells us where they are situated in relation to the house, how big they are, and whether or not they are of recent construction. But a single adjective—often 'trim', occasionally 'ugly'—is usually all we are given by way of description and evaluation. Trollope rarely proffers details regarding the number, shape and disposition of flower-beds, and he is generally unspecific about their contents. This cannot be put down to ignorance; Trollope was something of a gardener, and he sometimes displayed in his novels his knowledge of and interest in garden-related matters. Moreover, Trollope was attentive to the indicative and representational functions of gardens; descriptions of greater fleshiness could only have enriched their signifying possibilities. That he didn't produce more elaborate descriptions suggests, perhaps, that he didn't much care for the horticultural enthusiasms of many of his contemporaries; and that while he subscribed in theory to the principle of artifice, he was disinclined to endorse its working out in practice. If this is so, then his use of 'trim' is a strategy of evasion: it conceals more than it gives away.

The diction in which flower-gardens in fiction are generally cast is similarly untechnical and referentially indeterminate. The chances are that, had Victorian novelists been excited by bedding-out and its sister practices, they would have dipped into the special language register of its exponents. As it is, terms such as 'carpet-bedding', 'ribbon bordering', 'clock' and 'dial' gardens, 'cone beds' and 'select' (i.e. specialized) flower-gardens, occupy little or no textual space in novelistic descriptions. Instead, borders are described as 'sunny', beds as 'gay' or 'exquisite', and colour more frequently appears in 'bulk' than in the by no means synonymous in-term 'mass'. Furthermore, in the majority of fictional garden descriptions, the favourite bedding plants of the period, verbenas, calceolarias, lobelias, zonale geraniums, and strikingly-coloured 'foliage plants', are unnamed rather than overtly deprecated. Even Dickens, who 'loved all flowers, but especially bright flowers, and scarlet geraniums were his favourite of all',[52] only occasionally betrays his predilection in his writings.

This preference for exoteric, non-specialized and predominantly affective descriptive items appears to signal an orientation towards contemporary garden fashions that cannot easily be aligned with the orientation of the technical garden writers who supported and promulgated them. I intend to discuss the reasons for this more fully in the section on floral codes. Here it is necessary only to point out that any explanation must take account of the social and cultural as well as the aesthetic and horticultural significance of brightly-coloured fashionable flowers in highly regular arrangements. Put simply, if novelists and poets were disinclined to celebrate the most fashionable of contemporary garden practices, then it was not only because they found them imaginatively unappealing, but also because they had doubts about the social values and aspirations that these practices seemed to proclaim.

CHAPTER TWO

The Scented Garden

One of the qualities of gardens most conspicuously and persistently privileged in Victorian imaginative literature is the quality of odorousness. Throughout the poetry and fiction of the age, fragrance—or the lack of it—serves as an extraordinarily reliable index of general merit. Put baldly, if a garden is sweetly-scented, there is unlikely to be much wrong with it in other respects. Their insistence upon and unconcealed predilection for odiferous flowers placed imaginative writers—or, at least, their personas—in positions of opposition to some of the more popular horticultural practices of (in particular) the middle decades of the century. At least some writers were conscious of this and commented explicitly upon it.

It is fair to suppose that some writers stocked their imaginary gardens with fragrant flowers because, in part, fragrance is what they found most sadly wanting in the dazzlingly-coloured gardens around them. The staple flowers of the bedding-out system, including calceolarias, petunias, verbenas, scarlet salvias, dwarf geraniums and blue lobelias, were, in the main, low-growing (or, at least, unlikely to stray) and highly-coloured—that is, suitable for ornamentation, but not for filling the nostrils with agreeable perfumes. Since the massing of plants in showy colour schemes grew rapidly in popularity from about the mid-forties onwards,[1] stimulated by the influx of foreign plant materials, the hybridization of already available species (including dwarf varieties of 'older', straggling plants), and the introduction of greenhouses, in which huge numbers of tender annuals could be raised for wholesale use, brilliance of colour became the top requisite of the mid-Victorian garden.

A related reason that imaginative writers championed sweet-scented flowers is that they associated them with the cottage and old farmhouse gardens in which they continued to flourish—or so it was thought. In so doing, they subscribed to and, in this specific respect, may even have helped to write the crude version of garden history which posits that in the middle years of the century, odiferous hardy plants were ousted by exotic display plants from all gardens but those in which the owners were too poor or too wise to indulge in the excesses of bedding-out. Since nurserymen and seedsmen continued to stock and sell a great variety of plant materials, including hardy herbaceous plants, this reductionist version of garden history will not stand close examination.

Nonetheless, poets and novelists were tilting at odourless gardens long before William Robinson bewailed their ubiquity with characteristic exaggeration. In 1870 he wrote: '. . . a great mistake has been made in destroying *all* our sweet old border flowers' (my emphasis).[2] The association of fragrant flowers and out-of-fashion rural gardens is clearly established in a novel by Bulwer Lytton conceived when the bedding system was barely a twinkle in the nurseryman's eye. In *Kenelm Chillingly* he describes 'a pretty, quaint farmhouse' garden 'rich in those straggling old English flowers which are now-a-days banished from gardens more pretentious and infinitely less fragrant' (p. 91).

The connection between sweet-smelling flowers and the modest rural garden is cemented by virtually every other Victorian writer, and always in tones of approval and delight. The 'court' (i.e. the garden) of Hope Farm, principal setting in Gaskell's *Cousin Phillis*, is evidently so thick with scented vegetation that the young narrator, Paul Manning, 'fancied that [his] Sunday coat was scented for days afterwards by the bushes of sweetbriar and fraxinella that perfumed the air' (p. 12). Adam Bede's garden is no more than a 'patch' by the side of his cottage, but through the windows of his cottage 'the morning air brought with it the mingled scent of southernwood, thyme, and sweetbriar' (*Adam Bede*, p. 101). Dickens's Mr Boythorn has a larger but no less fragrant country garden: its 'smell of sweet herbs and all kinds of wholesome growth . . . made the whole air a great nosegay' (*Bleak House*, p. 247). Tennyson, too, highlights 'the English cottager's insistence on sweetness of scent'.[3] In *Aylmer's Field*, for example, Tennyson describes the labourers' cottages tended by Edith, each of which is festooned with fragrant growths. Of one, we are told,

> The warm-blue breathings of a hidden hearth
> Broke from a bower of vine and honeysuckle. (*TP*, p. 1165)

Rosetrees, jasmine, and a 'sea of gillyflowers' bedeck the other cottages.

Fragrant flowers constituted an integral element of the Victorian cottage dream—a fiction partly mediated, partly constructed, and sometimes exploded by novelists and poets. There are, for example, numerous moments in Victorian fiction when the perceived attractiveness of the humble cottager's existence —usually for characters who had never experienced anything like it themselves—is heightened by their consciousness of a delicious scent, real or fancied, drifting from some cottage garden. One such experience is presented by Mrs Oliphant in *Miss Marjoribanks*. It centres upon the politically ambitious and, at this moment, disconsolate Mr Cavendish, who is sauntering along a row of cottages in the small country town of Carlingford:

> By this time it was getting dark, and it was very pleasant in Grove Street, where most of the good people had just watered their little gardens, and brought out the sweetness of the mignonette. Mr Cavendish was not sentimental, but still the hour was not without its influence; and when he looked at the lights that began to appear in the parlour windows, and breathed in the odours from the little gardens, it is not to be denied that he asked himself for a moment what was the good through all this bother and vexation, and whether love in a cottage, with a little garden full of mignonette and a tolerable amount of comfort within, was not, after all, a great deal more reasonable than it looked at first sight. (pp. 67–8)[4]

In an age in which brilliance of colour seemed to many to take precedence over sweetness of scent, imaginative authors ascribed to odorous gardens an almost limitless number of virtues and positive environmental and experiential possibilities. Above all, they granted them the powers of restoration and revitalization traditionally associated with the countryside itself. The underlying assumption seems to be that only a garden that is both floriferous *and* odiferous is capable of engaging and gratifying *all* the relevant senses and, thus, of affording optimum conditions for therapeutic experiences. Oliver in *Oliver Twist* (1839) recovers his health and strength in the environs of the Maylies's country cottage, where he is surrounded by 'rose and honeysuckle' and 'garden flowers [which] perfumed the air with delicious odours' (p. 238). When Violet Martindale in *Heartsease* falls ill after the birth of her first child, she is sent away from the dazzling gardens of the family mansion to convalesce in a cottage on the Isle of Wight. The fragrance of myrtle, rose, honeysuckle, lilac, laburnum and clematis play an important part in her recovery (Part 2, ch. 4).

Sweetly-scented gardens invigorate the mind as well as the

body. When Maggie Tulliver in *The Mill on the Floss* (1860) is first 'launched into the higher society of St. Ogg's' after 'her years of privation', the 'intoxicating effect on her' comes partly from the 'new sense of leisure and unchecked enjoyment amidst the soft-breathing airs and garden-scents of advancing spring' (p. 370). The spiritual oscillations of the mourner in Matthew Arnold's 'Thyrsis' are both charted and regulated by the annual sequence of flowers in a country garden. 'When the year's primal burst is o'er' he is close to despair: 'The bloom is gone, and with the bloom go I'. Then he reminds himself that the garden is about to proffer a new and unparalleled peak of fragrance:

> Soon will the high Midsummer pomps come on,
> Soon will the musk carnations break and swell,
> Soon shall we have gold-dusted snapdragons,
> Sweet-William with its homely cottage-smell,
> And stocks in fragrant blow;
> Roses that down the alleys shine afar,
> And open, jasmine-muffled lattices. (*AP*, p. 541)

The anticipated feast of blooms, rich in colour and sweet of scent, is sufficient to restore his spirits.

Here, as elsewhere in Victorian poetry, the capacity to respond to the odorous life of the garden implies and impels a responsiveness to life itself. Its antithesis, olfactory insensibility, is typically symptomatic of a general state of enervating disengagement from life. Contrast, for example, the insentient speaker of Tennyson's early poem 'Youth', who sits among 'scentless flowers', unable to act in or upon the world he sees and hears revolve, with those more numerous moments in Tennyson's poetry in which flowers, heavy with scent, initiate or are intimately bound up with experience of a heady, exhilarating or mystical kind. Take as an instance the point in the inner frame story of *The Princess*, when the male intruders in the college gardens, having left the court,

> gained
> The terrace ranged along the Northern front,
> And leaning there on those balusters, high
> Above the empurpled champaign, drank the gale
> That blown about the foliage underneath,
> And sated with the innumerable rose,
> Beat balm upon our eyelids. (*TP*, p. 776)

This is a pure and exquisite landscape experience, not unfamiliar to the small minority of Victorians with privileged access to a terrace disposed to catch the scents of shrubs and roses.[5] For something altogether rarer, consider the much commented-upon section XCV of *In Memoriam*, in which Tennyson records his mystical, trance-like experience in the gardens of Somersby on a summer evening shortly before his departure from them. After the epiphanic evening, when 'The dead man touched [him] from the past', comes the 'doubtful dusk':

> And sucked from out the doubtful gloom
> A breeze began to tremble o'er
> The large leaves of the sycamore,
> And fluctuate all the still perfume,
>
> And gathering freshlier overhead,
> Rocked the full-foliage elms, and swung
> The heavy-folded rose, and flung
> The lilies to and fro, and said
>
> 'The dawn, the dawn', and died away;
> And East and West, without a breath,
> Mixt their dim lights, like life and death,
> To broaden into boundless day. (*TP*, p. 947)

Though critics vary in their interpretation of these stanzas (here taken from their informing context) almost all attach a very special significance to the perfumed wind. For James R. Kincaid, it is 'a symbol of transcendence of . . . intellectual uncertainty', a breeze that 'spreads sweetness and beauty everywhere'.[6] For W. David Shaw, 'the sacramental breeze and flowers . . . are an adjective of spirit, hiding the face of God even as they reveal his presence'.[7] Both appear to intimate this: that perfume privileges and permits a metaphysics of presence—permits, that is, a far more direct, unmediated and mysterious communion with the life of the garden than is possible through visual channels alone. As Richard J. Dunn, in a recent re-examination of section XCV, has rightly stressed, it is only when the poet becomes the 'receiver of multiple sensations'[8] that his senses are awakened to the powers of the natural world.

Though the perfumes of the Somersby vegetation, animated and released by the vocal breeze, clearly play some part in its statement-making function, there is, of course, no question of reducing the stanzas I have quoted to a piece of polemic about the putting-in-touch-with-the-spirit-of-nature possibilities of fragrant gardens. This is not to say that imaginative writers did not contemplate or draw attention to these possibilities, for they certainly did. Consider the episode in the late and short Gissing novel, *Will Warburton* (1905), in which Will, a city dweller, visits the family home in the country, and finds his sister in the kitchen garden early one morning. She is 'sparkling with pleasure [at] the heavy clusters of dark-green [bean] pods, hanging amid leaves and scarlet bloom'.

> 'Doesn't the scent do one good?' went on his sister.
> 'When I come into the garden on a morning like this, I have a feeling—oh! I can't describe it to you—perhaps you wouldn't understand — '
> 'It's as if nature were calling out to me, like a friend, to come and enjoy what she has done. I feel grateful for the things that earth offers me.' (p. 59)

The sentiment implied here and elsewhere in Victorian fiction is simple: scent is indispensable in a garden, for scent is nature's most direct way of hailing her human friends.

Odorous gardens are connected also with Proustian forms of temporal experience—with past times and the recollection of past times. The garden of childhood, particularly in its literal sense, can more easily be recalled or recaptured by the adult who in former times imbibed its associated scents. One writer has compellingly speculated that 'Odor has the power to evoke vivid, emotionally-charged memories of past events and scenes' probably because 'as children, not only were our noses more sensitive, but they were closer to the earth, to flower beds, tall grass, and the damp soil that gave it odors.'[9] This 'lesson' can be read in many Victorian poems treating of loss or childhood, and we can take it as a further point in favour of the fragrant garden. It is not an argument *for* the scented garden, still less an argument motivated by aesthetic or horticultural considerations, but rather a perception—that gardens are places with associations that we may wish to recall—that emerges naturally from the poetic contexts in which it is verbalized.

Scented flowers play a notable part in Matthew Arnold's poems of nostalgia and recollection. Amidst an austere mountain landscape and the general oppressiveness of the monastery, the speaker in 'Stanzas from the Grand Chartreuse' notices a

> garden, overgrown yet mild,
> See fragrant herbs are flowering there! (*AP*, p. 304)

Here 'the garden flowers suggest the theme of childhood explored elsewhere in the poem'.[10] In Arnold's 'The Youth of Man', the aging couple's memory of the past, as interpreted by the speaker, is dominated by the remembrance of a childhood spent in the sheltered seclusion of an old-fashioned garden retreat:

> . . . the castled house, with its woods,
> Which sheltered their childhood—the sun
> On its ivied windows, a scent
> From the gray-wall'd gardens, a breath
> Of the fragrant stock and the pink,
> Perfumes the evening air. (*AP*, p. 267)

(It is interesting to note that in his intelligent discussion of the Matthew Arnold 'tormented by the impermanence of experiences, feelings, and thoughts', J. Hillis Miller uses the following sentence to encapsulate Arnold's apprehension of the 'bad times' in which he lived: 'The flowers have no perfumes, and each man is an island cut off from his fellows.'[11])

Scents and memory are similarly linked in a number of Austin Dobson's poems. In a poem called 'Pot-Pourri', one of many by Dobson concerning garden-related experiences, it is the scent of vegetable matter in the garden in which the speaker is located that triggers his recollection of a happy youth, spent among 'old parterres / And "flowerful closes"' with a group of beautiful girls now dead. The poem begins:

> I plunge my hand among the leaves:
> (An alien touch—but dust perceives,
> Nought else supposes;)
> For me those fragrant ruins raise
> Clear memory of the vanished days
> When they were roses. (*DP*, p. 75)

Perfumed gardens are conspicuous also in Tennyson's recollection poems. For example, in *Recollections of Arabian Nights* the speaker finds refuge from the 'forward flowing tide of time' by succumbing to the anamnesic surge within him, and entering on an imaginary voyage which takes him through dream-like landscapes heavy with exotic perfumes of 'deep myrrh thickets' and other 'eastern flowers large' (*TP*, p. 207).

Here, as in conservatory scenes in Victorian fiction, fragrant exotics add considerably to a sense of sensuous other-worldliness. Though normally redolent of domesticity, odorous gardens are sometimes used to establish a fairy-world atmosphere freer and more heady than the atmosphere of the near-scentless bedded-out display garden. The 'sacrifice of incense' from 'sweet-briar, southern-wood, jasmine, pink and rose' in the Thornfield garden on Midsummer-eve contrives to create an atmosphere of paradise and unreality in or against which Rochester proposes to Jane in Chapter 23 of *Jane Eyre* (1847). A less famous but not dissimilar episode is described in Gissing's *The Nether World*. In the garden of a farmhouse in Essex, away from the oppressiveness of London, Sidney Kirkwood realizes for the first time his feelings of love for the young Jane Snowdon. In the garden are 'sunflowers and hollyhocks and lowly plants innumerable'. Their fragrance is such that he feels the 'flowers mingling with his blood and confusing him with emotion' (p. 168). It is by means of the dizzying, head-turning powers of scented flowers that the literary gentleman in *The Aspern Papers* (1888) hopes to solicit the cooperation of Miss Bordereau and her younger female companion. At an early stage in his quest, when his hopes are high, he confidently speculates that 'their door would have to yield to the pressure when a mound of fragrance should be heaped upon it' (p. 153).

The odorous garden has one other virtue to which nineteenth-century novelists frequently draw attention. That is its ability to invade the house, to bring the garden indoors. By implication through description and occasionally by explicit statement, Victorian imaginative writers in general subscribed to the idea, persistently averred by garden theorists, that a house and its garden should be as closely connected and as continuous as possible. They appear to have sensed that the most natural means of entwining the two environments was by encouraging the fragrance of the garden to waft into the house. Hence, the perceived attractiveness of scented gardens. Elizabeth Gaskell appears to have appreciated the benefits of minimizing or confusing the house–garden distinction. As W. A. Craik has observed, 'she has frequently set her scenes outdoors, or with that domestic mixture of in and out of doors which comes from open windows or changes from room to garden.'[12] The same can be said of Rhoda Broughton. In *Doctor Cupid* (1886) one of her doting male characters cherishes the 'fairest and most hopeless dream' of dining with the girl he adores 'in her own still house, amid the old and homely surroundings, with the summer evening tossing them in its lavish perfumes through the wide-opened windows' (p. 277).

Occasionally, invigorating odours emanate from coniferous

sources. Gissing appears to have appreciated the Victorian enthusiasm for conifers, and for what many believed to be their health-enhancing properties. The opening chapter of *A Life's Morning* (1888) includes a description of The Firs, 'a delightful house in the midst of Surrey's fairest scenery'. The scene is developed as follows:

> We find the [Athel] family assembling for breakfast at The Firs one delightful morning at the end of July. The windows in the room were thrown open, and there streamed in with the sunlight fresh and delicious odours, tonics alike of mind and body. From the Scotch firs from which the dwelling took its name came a scent mingled with wafted breath from the remoter heather, and the creepers about the house-front, the lovely bloom and leafage skirting the lawn, contributed to the atmosphere of health and joy. (p. 5)

If fragrant flowers could transport the garden into the house, they could also import the garden into dreary city apartments. During the course of the century, garden writers paid ever-increasing attention to the use of plants indoors; and in imaginative literature, a myriad scraps of description testify to the power of fragrant flowers to minimize differences between discrepant environments. Tennyson's painter-narrator acquires from his beloved gardener's daughter 'roses, moss or musk / To grace [his] City rooms' (*TP*, p. 518). Gissing's 'feminized' London apartments—among them, Miss Nunn's in *The Odd Women* (1893) and grandfather Snowdon's in *The Nether World*—are sweetened by the delicate scents of flowers which serve as substitute gardens.

Throughout the nineteenth century, then, poets and novelists persistently bore witness to the virtues of scented gardens and flowers, and consistently associated them with happy, invigorating and life-enhancing experiences. One effect of this must surely have been to foster or keep alive in the minds of many readers partialities and predilections which might not have found practical expression in their own horticultural enterprises. This curious discrepancy has recently been noted by Charles Van Ravensway:

> Victorian ladies professed a liking for delicate, modest, and fragrant plants, but the grounds landscaped in the new romantic style surrounding the boldly designed new Italian or Gothic-styled country villas included flower-beds intended as eye-catching ornaments amid the greensward.[13]

Did fiction writers do anything to bring attitudes and behaviour into closer alignment? Some of those writing in the 1870s and 1880s very probably did. That is, their descriptions and comments contributed something to the revival of interest in fragrant border and 'cottage' plants which those garden writers who reviled the pervasiveness of the bedding-out system placed high on their agendas. In 1883 William Robinson wrote:

> Of the many things that should be thought of in the making of a garden to live in, this of fragrance is one of the first. . . . Apart from the groups of plants in which all or nearly all, are fragrant, as in Roses, the annual and biennial flowers of our gardens are rich in fragrance—Stocks, Mignonette, Sweet Peas, Sweet Sultan, Wallflowers, double Rockets, Sweet Scabious, and many others. These, among the most easily raised of plants, may be enjoyed by the poorest cottage gardeners.[14]

In the previous year, William Morris had spoken out against the absence of scent in the flowers 'improved' by florists.[15] And three years after Robinson published *The English Flower Garden* (1883) Richard Jefferies opened *Amaryllis at the Fair* bemoaning that 'There are many grand roses, but no fragrance—the fragrance has gone out of life' (p. 201). By the 1880s, such remarks were commonplace in fiction and garden literature alike and, perhaps, redundant, since the sentiments they expressed had already been trumpeted in the much-acknowledged passage in *Lothair* concerning Corisande's garden.

Corisande's own garden practices are perfectly consistent with her 'theory, that flower-gardens should be sweet and luxurious, and not hard and scentless imitations of works of art' (p. 464). In the ancient garden over which she presides

> flourished abundantly all those productions of nature which are now banished from once delighted senses: huge bushes of honeysuckle, and bowers of sweet-pea and sweet-briar, and jessamine clustering over the walls, and gillyflowers scenting with their sweet breath the ancient bricks from which they seemed to spring. There were banks of violets which the southern breeze always stirred, and mignonette filled every vacant nook. (p. 464)

Disraeli had not always given such prominence to fragrance. His lavish descriptions of Walter Gerard's cottage garden in *Sybil* are almost devoid of specific references to scent, though the garden contained scented flowers. The conspicuous shift of emphasis (*Lothair* was published a full quarter-century after *Sybil*) is a measure, perhaps, of the degree to which, by 1870, fragrance had acquired an urgent and renewed importance for Disraeli and for his many sympathetic admirers in the gardening world.

Although I have abstracted fragrance for individual consideration, I have also endeavoured to suggest its connections with other textually privileged garden qualities, among them, old age and the absence of regimentation in the arrangement of plant materials. It is significant that in the imaginative literature of the period, the most frequently privileged garden qualities tend both to occur together and to be the qualities least conspicuous in gardens composed in the more egregiously fashionable styles of the time. It is to gardens that exhibit these qualities in aggregate that I now wish to devote attention.

CHAPTER THREE

Old-Fashioned Gardens

> The old gardeners, we are told, thought little of beauty, and chiefly of genera and species. Why, then, should the poet find that, with all its faults, the old garden stirs him in those depths which the modern one can seldom reach?[1]

So wrote Forbes Watson in 1872—and with considerable justification. Watson chose to illustrate his observation with quotations from the poetry of John Clare; he might just as easily have turned to any other nineteenth-century imaginative writer for textual support. Regardless of their attitudes towards modern gardens, the majority of novelists and poets betrayed a susceptibility to the charms of old and old-fashioned gardens, one effect of which was to afford readers with Watson's proclivities a repository of sustaining and inspiratory descriptions.

The privileging of gardens of, or reminiscent of, the past, was a rather complicated phenomenon. For one thing, different writers assigned the labels 'old' and 'old-fashioned' to gardens of different ages and styles. Very often these adjectives served not as precise historical tags at all, but as surrogates for bundles of intersubjectively recognized qualities and associations. Moreover, in literary texts 'old-fashioned' could signify either 'that which has endured' or 'that which has been lost'. Trollope, for example, tends to use 'old-fashioned' in the first sense, to stress historical continuity and tradition. Hence, he sometimes supplies ratifying details of age. Greshamsbury House (in *Dr Thorne*) is Tudor, while its gardens 'have been celebrated for two centuries' (p. 10). The fine old gardens of Carbury Manor House (in *The Way We Live Now*) date from the time of Charles II (Ch. 14). By contrast, in the many Victorian poems of recollection in which old gardens play an important part, the emphasis is usually upon temporal disjunction, and upon that which exists in memory only. In Edwin Coller's poem *Bessie and I*, the speaker's happiest memories are of his gambols in the 'quaint old garden' of his childhood. Similarly, in Will Carleton's *Death-Doomed*, the young man about to die on the gallows recalls 'The flowers that bloom in the dear old garden'.[2] In poems like these, what matters is the perception rather than the fact of age. Details of exact age are irrelevant, and might even ruin the sense of distance from the past.

When 'old-fashioned' is used in its historical (as opposed to its phenomenological) sense, the gardens invoked tend to be either of a remote past, or of a recent ('living memory') past. In Victorian literature, three historical styles are especially favoured: the enclosed medieval garden, the modestly formal country-house garden dating from (in particular) the seventeenth century, and the cottage or farmhouse garden of the early years of the nineteenth century, or a little before.

Victorian literature abounds in affectionate descriptions of cottage and cottage-like gardens. Most fall into one of three categories: those which are genuinely old; those which are of the recent past; and those which are old-fashioned in appearance and feeling, though not necessarily in age. An example of the first type is Overcombe Mill in Hardy's *The Trumpet-Major* (1880). It is a 'powerful presence in the novel',[3] and its history, like that of the ancient family of its owner, Miller Loveday, 'is lost in the mists of antiquity' (p. 10). Because of its role in the action of the novel, its features are disclosed bit by bit. The following passage reveals its main qualities:

> It was a quaint old place, enclosed by a thorn hedge so shapely and dense from incessant clipping that the mill boy could walk along the top without sinking in—a feat which he often performed as a means of filling out his day's work. The soil within was of that intense fat blackness which is only seen after a century of constant cultivation. The paths were grassed over, so that people came and went without being heard. The grass harboured slugs, and on this account the miller was going to replace it by gravel as soon as he had time; but as he had said this for thirty years without doing it, the grass and the slugs seemed likely to remain. (pp. 23–4)

There is little in this description for nostalgic temperaments to feed upon. The emphasis is upon the age and unalteredness of the garden, not upon its aesthetic merits. Though it is a garden *of* the past (the novel is set against the background of the French Wars), it is essentially timeless—afashionable rather than old-fashioned. By contrast, the old-fashioned garden has, by definition, some degree of historical specificity. This time-bounded quality is fundamental to its appeal.

The chief distinguishing characteristic of the old-fashioned fictional cottage garden is its abundant variety of vegetable life. It is not blatantly artificial, and evinces no fastidious division or chromatic uniformity of plant materials. (Recall that many Victorian gardens did, and prompted garden writers to express the opinion that look-alike bedded-out gardens 'are a poor substitute for the varied beauty of an old garden.'[4]) Rather, forms, scents and colours mix in disorderly but delightful confusion, and everything points to the maker's intuitive grasp of the painterly.

George Eliot wrote fondly of such gardens, and regretted what she took to be their virtual extinction. The picture of the very late eighteenth-century Hall Farm garden in *Adam Bede* is probably the most particularized garden description that Eliot ever produced. A similar garden is described in the story of 'Janet's Repentance'. It is the pride of the retired corn factor, Mr Jerome; the narrator is out to show why:

> The garden was one of those old-fashioned paradises which hardly exist any longer except as memories of our childhood: no finical separation between flower and kitchen-garden there; no monotony of enjoyment for one sense to the exclusion of another; but a charming paradisiacal mingling of all that was pleasant to the eye and good for food. The rich flower-border running along every walk, with its endless succession of spring flowers, anemones, auriculas, wall-flowers, sweet-williams, campanulas, snap-dragons, and tiger-lilies, had its taller beauties such as moss and Provence roses, varied with espalier apple-trees; the crimson of a carnation was carried out in the lurking crimson of the neighbouring strawberry beds; you gathered a moss-rose one moment and a bunch of currants the next; you were in a delicious fluctuation between the scent of jasmine and the juice of gooseberries. Then what a high wall at one end, flanked by a summer-house so lofty, that after ascending its long flight of steps you could see perfectly well that there was no view worth looking at; what alcoves and garden-seats in all directions; and along one side, what a hedge, tall, and firm, and unbroken like a green wall! (*Scenes of Clerical Life* (1858), pp. 232–3)

Like Hall Farm garden, Mr Jerome's has a fullness to which the comprehensiveness and specificity of the description do justice. But there is a difference. The Poysers's garden is fecund almost to the point of being feral. Its vegetables grow together in 'careless, half-neglected abundance'. Its flowers are 'all large and disorderly for want of trimming'. Its grass walks are uncut, and its rose trees 'looked as if they grew wild' (p. 188). Though equally fertile and fluid in texture, Mr Jerome's garden is the work of an artist, albeit an artless and unselfconscious one. We are not actually told so; subtle effects require subtle hints—and these are what we get. There is, for instance, the suggestion of a cannily unobtrusive colour motif: 'the crimson of a carnation was carried out in the lurking crimson of the neighbouring strawberry beds'. Still more subtle is the hint of synaesthetic manipulation in the 'delicious fluctuation between the scent of the jasmine and the juice of gooseberries'. Like the garden itself, the description ends with a 'green wall'—which strikes the perfect balance between natural freedom and aesthetic control.

Thus, for all its apparent spontaneity and profusion of plant forms, Mr Jerome's garden is not a work of raw nature, but a delicate work of art. It is an art which conceals art. As such, it contrasts with the blatant, unprepossessing artifice of mid-century garden styles, and Eliot draws attention to the contrasts. In her 'paradise' of the mid-1820s there is 'no finical separation between flower and kitchen-garden'. She follows this with the deictic 'there', leaving her readers to supply the suppressed 'as here'. And there is 'no monotony of enjoyment for one sense to the exclusion of another'—quite possibly an oblique swipe at the palling visual impact of bedding-out.

That old-fashioned gardens recall old-fashioned worlds is obvious enough, and has often been noted. What has not sufficiently been recognized is that the qualities of the gardens like Mr Jerome's—variety, simplicity, harmony, unforced abundance and the vegetable equivalence of natural generosity—are precisely the qualities which so many Victorians associated with pre-industrial England or, rather, with their highly selective, organic community model of it. Of all the old rural scenes the arts had to offer, that of the old-fashioned cottage garden afforded the most coherent, complete, and readily apprehensible symbolic version of the world it at once recalled, ratified, and rendered in miniature. It was also the most bounded and idyllic of these scenes, an image that bracketed off the complicating and discordant realities of agrarian capitalism and rural labour, with a potential for disguising material poverty as natural wealth.

George Eliot did not exploit this potential. She makes it clear that Mr Jerome has the time and the money to construct his 'old-fashioned paradise', and there is no reason to think that she thought it a microcosm of the pre-Victorian rural world. Many of her readers undoubtedly did. R. A. Forsyth, building upon the remark of a contributor to *Blackwood's Magazine* of 1881 who praised the novelist for 'preserving' the 'quiet, old-fashioned, easy going life of the last century', avers that among many of her readers, Eliot was 'greatly appreciated and praised for the accuracy and delineation of rural culture. Her pictures of English rural life in the 1820s were considered to be authentic reconstructions, and were admired nostalgically as much for this as for their being masterly works of art. Her descriptions of rural scenes and manners, so recently faded from English life, recalled past glories, and became a mean by which the tempo and extent of contemporary social change could be measured.'[5]

Fictional characters also have needs which images of old-fashioned gardens are able to gratify. In Dickens's *Little Dorrit* (1857), Mrs Plornish, the wife of a poor plasterer, lives in what is virtually an urban pigsty. To escape from or tolerate the drudgery of her existence, she has a scene-painter paint a mural on the wall that leads from her shop to her parlour. This 'little fiction' represents the exterior of a thatched cottage, about which old-fashioned flowers, 'the modest sunflower and the hollyhock were depicted as flourishing with great luxuriance' (p. 574). For Mrs Plornish, this 'wonderful deception' is nothing less than 'a perfect Pastoral . . . the Golden Age revived'. Dickens neither mocks her coping strategy, nor (here) protests about the social conditions which make it necessary. Instead, he draws attention to it by excessive exultation: 'No Poetry and no Art ever charmed the imagination more than the union of the two in this counterfeit cottage charmed Mrs Plornish' (p. 574).

Elizabeth Gaskell, too, acknowledges the fantasy-script possibilities of old-fashioned gardens—however incongruously transformed and two-dimensional they may be. In the miserable milliner's workshop, the young Ruth Hilton in *Ruth* (1853) finds comfort in the contemplation of a faded but still magnificent wall-drawing, on which is painted,

> with the careless, triumphant hand of a master—the most lovely wreaths of flowers, profuse and luxuriant beyond description, and so real-looking, that you could almost fancy you smelt their fragrance, and heard the south wind go softly

> rustling in and out among the crimson roses—the branches of purple and white lilac—the floating golden tressed laburnum boughs. Besides these, there were stately white lilies, sacred to the Virgin—hollyhocks, fraxinella, monk's-hood, pansies, primroses; every flower which blooms profusely in charming old-fashioned country-gardens was there, depicted among its graceful foliage, but not in the wild disorder in which I have enumerated them (pp. 6–7).

During the Victorian period as a whole, compensatory uses of images of the old-fashioned cottage garden were paramount. From fictional versions, readers with a rosy-eyed view of the recent past and a passion for the English countryside were able to derive the vicarious satisfactions they actively sought. But from about the 1860s onwards, old-fashioned cottage gardens were appropriated for more specific uses. Garden writers began increasingly to accredit them with a preservationist function. They saw the unspoiled cottage garden as a place of refuge for old garden plants, and applauded novelists and poets for keeping alive their names and charms. At the same time, these gardens came to be valued as models and sources of inspiration for all garden-makers. Artists, supporters of the Arts and Crafts movement, Old-England worshippers like Alfred Austin, and garden writers like William Robinson and (later) Gertrude Jekyll, were attracted to their simple designs, colour combinations, and dependence on hardy plants. The admirers of old cottage gardens were indebted to imaginative writers for inspiration, convenient frames of reference, and examples.

This debt was possible only because imaginative writers consistently turned their backs upon contemporary developments in cottage garden design. Even when they did not look back in their texts to a pre-industrial past, Victorian novelists continued to produce descriptions congruent with popular images of the old-fashioned cottage garden. Of course, this does not mean that they painted a wholly idyllic and mythical picture of cottage life. Most of the major novelists, including Eliot, Dickens, Kingsley, and Hardy, confronted their readers with demystifying depictions of the cottage idyll. The issue here is not whether the 'poet's picture of the cottage scene [was] fatuously unrealistic, untrue or unrepresentative'—what George H. Ford has termed the 'cottage controversy'[6]—but rather why they consistently privileged one kind of cottage garden style—that which seemed reminiscent of the past—to the neglect of more contemporary styles. Why, more specifically, did they not respond in a positive way to the major change that occurred about the middle of the century when 'many cottage gardeners copied their richer neighbours and switched from mixed planting to carpet bedding'?[7]

The obvious reason is that the survival of the cottage garden idea(l), both as an imaginatively compelling visual image and as a concentrated store-house of old-fashioned values, depended precisely upon its lack of modernity and sophistication. For novelists to have tricked out their fictional gardens with the fashionable geometric beds that came to characterize many actual cottage gardens, would have been to drain away the anachronistic charms that alone ensured their position within a signifying system of internally differentiated garden types. There are exceptions, but they only go to show the effects of weakening the opposition between the old and the new. In some of Bulwer Lytton's novels, for example, there are descriptions of old cottages which have had their traditional significations 'improved' away. For instance, quite early in *Night and Morning* (1841) there is a description of Fernside cottage, which is 'as rural and sequestered as if a hundred miles distant from the smoke of the huge city'. If this cues us to expect an ancient, time-forgotten haunt, then we are in for a disappointment.

> Though the dwelling was called a cottage, [its owner] had enlarged the original modest building into a villa of some pretensions. On either side of a graceful and well-proportioned portico stretched verandas, covered with roses and clematis; to the right extended a range of costly conservatories, terminating in vistas of trellis-work which formed those elegant alleys called roseries, served to screen the more useful gardens from view. The lawn, smooth and even, was studded with American plants and shrubs in flower, and bounded on one side by a small lake, on the opposite bank of which limes and cedars threw their shadows over the clear waves . . . It was one of those cottages which bespeak the ease and luxury not often found in more ostentatious mansions'. (pp. 30–1)

That many of Bulwer Lytton's readers would have found this attractive is beside the point. The point is that its appeal is quite obviously not that of the old-fashioned cottage garden. As I have said, most novelists steered clear of describing modern or modernized cottage gardens decked out in the most blatant of contemporary styles. That they did so without a striking loss of artistic integrity, without incurring charges of unrepresentativeness and myth-making, and without violating mimetic expectations, is attributable to their selective choice of subjects. Most fictional cottage-type gardens are either situated in remote country districts where, it could reasonably be assumed, horticultural innovations had failed to penetrate, or else acclaimed for their very lack of typicality.

I should like to cite some familiar examples. None pre-dates the effective influence of bedding-out by more than thirty years; some, in theory, might have been affected by it. The most temporally remote are the 'old-fashioned gardens' of Raveloe in George Eliot's *Silas Marner* (1861). At the time of Eppie's wedding, their 'great lilacs and laburnums . . . showed their golden and purple wealth above the lichen-tinted walls' (p. 156). At this point in the novel, Eliot is harking back to the 1820s or early 1830s. Had the novel concluded in mid-century, it seems fair to assume that she would have described them in much the same way.

When Hardy describes the gardens of Casterbridge, he is thinking of the late 1840s, but the gardens themselves are much older. They are visible 'through the long, straight, entrance passages' that connect the 'old-fashioned fronts' of the houses with their 'older than old-fashioned backs'. They are 'mossy gardens . . . glowing with nasturtiums, fuchsias, scarlet geraniums, "bloody warriors", snap-dragons, and dahlias, this floral blaze being backed by crusted grey stone-work remaining from a yet remoter Casterbridge than the venerable one visible in the street.'[8] Hope Farm in Gaskell's *Cousin Phillis* is similarly unaffected by contemporary garden fashions, and has all the undisciplined plenitude of the old cottage garden. It was 'so full of flowers that they crept out upon the low-covered wall and horse-mount, and were even to be found self-sown upon the turf that borded the path to the back of the house' (p. 12).

The garden of Dickens's Mr Boythorn is a rather different case. It is not, strictly speaking, a cottage garden, and it has what appear to be some modern 'improvements'. But again the emphasis is upon age, abundance, and a pleasing absence of regimentation—the definitive characteristics of the fictional cottage garden. Here is Esther Summerson's fulsome account in *Bleak House*:

> He lived in a pretty house, formerly the parsonage house, with a lawn in front, a bright flower-garden at the side, and a well-stocked orchard and kitchen-garden in the rear, enclosed with a venerable wall that had of itself a ripened ruddy look. But, indeed, everything about the place wore an aspect of maturity and abundance. The old lime-tree walk was like green cloisters, the very shadows of the cherry-trees and apple-trees were heavy with fruit, the gooseberry-bushes were so laden that their branches arched and rested on the earth, the strawberries and raspberries grew in like profusion, and the peaches basked by the hundred on the wall. Tumbled about among the spread nets and the glass frames sparkling and winking in the sun there were such heaps of drooping pods, and marrows, and cucumbers, that every foot of ground appeared a vegetable treasury. . . . Such stillness and composure reigned within the orderly precincts of the old red wall that even the feathers hung in garlands to scare the birds hardly stirred; and the wall had such a ripening influence that where, here and there high up, a disused nail and scrap of list still clung to it, it was easy to fancy that they had mellowed with the changing seasons and that they had rusted and decayed according to the common fate (pp. 247–8).

Even in later nineteenth-century works of fiction there are descriptions of cottage gardens, the old-fashioned appearance of which is legitimated on the grounds of geographical remoteness. There is a simple, rather stock, example in Gissing's short story, 'A Victim of Circumstances'. The main events take place in an 'out-of-the-way place' in Somerset in 1869. The hopeful young artists of the story live in 'one of a row of simple cottages, old and prettily built; in the small garden were hollyhocks, sunflowers, tall lilies, and other familiar flowers blooming luxuriantly, and over the front of the house trailed a vine' (p. 6). However, in novels of the 1860s and onwards, the recusantly unfashionable cottage or farmhouse garden is more often explained in terms of the peculiar tastes of its owner. This is the legitimating strategy adopted by Meredith and Jefferies. In *Rhoda Fleming* (1865) Meredith tells us that Mrs Fleming 'cherished the old-fashioned delight in tulips' and other such flowers, but forfends the charge of unrepresentativeness with the remark that 'perhaps her taste may now seem questionable' (p. 2). To reinforce the point, the narrator points out that Mrs Fleming's neighbours were critical of her unorthodox tastes. Likewise, in *Amaryllis at the Fair*, Jefferies glories in the idiosyncratic and anachronistic character of Farmer Iden's garden:

> No other garden was planted as Iden's garden was, in the best of old English taste, with old English flowers and plants, herbs and trees. (p. 290)

Iden's garden, Jefferies suggests, deviates from the contemporary country garden norm, though he does not define the particular norm he has in mind.

Though wonderfully productive gardeners, Mrs Fleming and Farmer Iden are conspicuously impractical and inefficient in other respects—as critics of Meredith and Jefferies have not been slow to point out.[9] While in debt to the grocer, Mrs Fleming 'would squander her care on poppies', and 'could not see' that her gardening activities 'drained' and 'distracted' the farm, and 'most evidently impoverished' her husband (p. 7). Iden is no more practical. He is 'like the great engineer who could never build a bridge, because he knew so well how a bridge ought to be built' (p. 342). His inability to manage his affairs takes its toll on his wife, and strains their life together.

But it is because of, not in spite of, their impracticality that Mrs Fleming and Iden are the authors of uncommonly 'poetic' old-fashioned gardens. In other words, there is a direct link between their inefficiency on the one hand, and their old-fashioned tastes and feelings on the other.

To grasp the significance of this link is to understand why the majority of cottage and farmhouse gardens in Victorian literature are untouched by modern 'improvements'. For within the Victorian cultural context, 'efficiency' came to be associated with utility and pragmatic modern methods, 'inefficiency' with an older, less rigorously systematic, and altogether more homely and 'human' system of values. Translated into garden terms, 'efficiency' suggested that sophisticated and progressive character of modern horticulture, 'inefficiency' the antique quaintness of the picturesque.

Many Victorians were acutely conscious of this opposition, which they experienced as a contest between the competing claims of the head and the heart. I believe it to be true that while practical Victorians approved of modern advances, 'their affections were still with things past or passing',[10] though George Eliot didn't see it quite like this. In 'Amos Barton' she observes that

> the well-regulated mind, which unintermittingly rejoices in ... all guarantees of human advancement ... has no moments when conservative-reforming intellect takes a nap, while imagination does a little Toryism by the sly revelling in regret that dear, old, brown, crumbling, picturesque inefficiency is everywhere giving place to spick-and-span new-painted new-varnished efficiency, which will yield endless diagrams, plans, elevations, and sections, but alas! no picture (*Scenes of Clerical Life*, pp. 3–4).

Other novelists made the same point more pithily. In *Clergymen of the Church of England*, Trollope observed: 'In seeking the useful, we are compelled to abandon the picturesque' (p. 28). In *Barchester Towers* he places—physically and symbolically—the 'inefficient' Mr Harding in the 'antiquely picturesque' gardens of his beloved Hiram's Hospital, and manoeuvres Eleanor Bold and Mr Arabin into the equally old-fashioned gardens of Ullathorne. Mr Arabin opines:

> 'There is something about old-fashioned mansions, built as this is, and old-fashioned gardens, that is especially delightful.' 'I like everything old-fashioned', said Eleanor; 'old-fashioned things are so much the honestest.' (II, 231)

Hardy's view of old-fashioned things was more complex, but in *The Dorsetshire Labourer* he remarks, sententiously, that 'progress and picturesqueness do not harmonize'.[11] Hardy puts this thesis to work in his novels—in *The Mayor of Casterbridge*, in particular. Michael Henchard, who conducts his corn business by 'the rugged picturesqueness of an old method' is pitted against the efficient improver, Donald Farfrae.

And then there is Dickens. No other Victorian novelist did more to validate 'old-fashioned' as an affective term of implosive compactness. In Dickens's early works (*Oliver Twist, Nicholas Nickleby* and *Pickwick Papers*) 'the word "old-fashioned", applied to Pickwick, Brownlow and the Cheerybles, among others, is given a particularly positive, connotative value, equivalent to virtuous, cheerful, generous and sincere rolled into one. Since the past was paradise, anything old must be good.'[12]

There is one more point to make about old-fashioned inefficiency: somehow—to a degree—it worked. At least, Victorians who cherished the past supposed or liked to believe that it did.

Pickwick muddled through. Hamfisted Henchard built up a thriving business by 'rule o' thumb'. The old-fashioned cottage garden of fiction provided a synecdoche of a world that had achieved unforced abundance. The charm of the recent past was heightened by the miracle that it had worked at all.

R. D. Blackmore, whose passion for fruits and flowers, and unbusinesslike mind, invites comparison with fictional gardeners like Mrs Fleming and Iden,[13] marvelled time and again at the success achieved by 'inefficient' gardeners of the past. Consider the following passage from his novel, *Alice Lorraine*:

> Master Martin Lovejoy [a fruit grower in the Vale of Medway] had, in the month of October 1812, as fine a crop of pears as ever made a fountain of a tree.
>
> For the growers of old did not understand the pruning of trees as we do now. They were a benighted lot altogether, proceeding only by rule of thumb, and the practice of their grandfathers . . . and yet they grew as good fruit as we do! They had no right to do so; but the thing is beyond denial.[14]

For many Victorians, then, the term 'old-fashioned garden' suggested the delightfully abundant cottage or farmhouse garden of, or reminiscent of, the recent rural past as they perceived it. The majority of Victorian novelists shared and consolidated this particular historical sense of the term. In so doing, and irrespective of their wishes and intentions, they helped to shape and maintain the fiction of a paradisiacal world scarcely more remote than their readers' earliest memories.

But for some imaginative writers, this was not nearly remote enough. To those with a medievalizing imagination, 'old garden' evoked something altogether more distant—conceptually as well as temporally—than the cosy cottage garden.

In the early novels of Bulwer Lytton and Disraeli, the descriptions of medieval gardens are in part an expression of the aristocratic fashion for picturesque Gothic, and a reactionist idealization of the feudal past. Two remarkably similar examples are the quadrangle gardens of Godolphin Priory in Bulwer Lytton's *Godolphin*, and Cadurcis Abbey in Disraeli's *Venetia* (1837). The latter is 'an ancient Gothic building', formerly an abbey, but for two centuries 'the principal dwelling of an old baronial family'. In the inner court of the Abbey is 'a curious fountain, carved with exquisite skill by some gothic artist in one of those capricious moods of sportive invention that produced those grotesque medley's for which the feudal sculptor was celebrated' (p. 8).

As they wander in the garden of a modern villa at Richmond, Lord Cadurcis and Venetia encounter 'a marble fountain of gigantic proportions and elaborate workmanship, an assemblage of divinities and genii, all spouting water in fantastic attitudes'. Plantagenet Cadurcis comments: 'Old days . . . are like old fountains at Cadurcis, dearer to me than all this modern splendour' (p. 315).

The old baronial or memorial garden was one synecdoche of the Middle Ages, but its currency was historically circumscribed. It belongs very largely to the neomedievalism of the 1830s and 1840s, and to Disraeli's Tory and tinsel view of the medieval paradise in particular. In general, later medievalists placed less emphasis upon the patriarchal social structure of the Middle Ages and, consequently, less emphasis upon the gardens of its most palpable physical symbols. Like the gardens of Trollope's Miss Thorne in *Barchester Towers*, post mid-century irruptions of this feudalistic neomedievalism tend to be quaint or bizarre.

In and after the 1850s, artists and writers 'discovered' more inspiratory images of the medieval garden—in particular, the medieval pleasure garden as portrayed in illuminated manuscripts such as the fifteenth-century *Roman de la Rose* (1485).

For the Pre-Raphaelites, and for writers like Ruskin and Morris, whose medieval social nostalgia was characterized by a marked anti-industrialism and a stress on the ugliness and joylessness of modern life, the medieval pleasure garden—bright and orderly, rich yet simple—was a peculiarly expressive symbol of the lost 'gothic Eden'.[15] It was associated not with the abbey or the festive great hall, but with the cathedral or workshop, and with Ruskin's and Morris's model medieval man—the anonymous craftsman whose art was pleasurable labour. Moreover, for Morris, it brought to mind a time when the elements of the cultural landscape were as integrated and unfragmented as art and labour, when town and country interpenetrated, and when the non-coercive spirit in which natural materials were subjected to human architecture made it possible to welcome the intrusion of wild flowers into well-kept gardens. In his youth, Morris channelled his celebratory response to the pre-Renaissance past into his description of a medieval garden; it appeared in the *Story of the Unknown Church*, first published in the *Oxford and Cambridge*

Magazine of 1865. The narrator, appropriately enough, is a master mason:

> The old Church had been burned, and that was the reason why the monks caused me to build the new one; the buildings of the Abbey were built at the same time as the burned-down Church, more than a hundred years before I was born, and they were on the north side of the Church, and joined to it by a cloister of round arches, and in the midst of a cloister was a lawn, and in the midst of that lawn, a fountain of marble, carved round about with flowers and strange beasts; and at the edge of this lawn, near the round arches, were a great many sun-flowers that were all in blossom on that autumn day; and up many of the pillars of the cloister crept passion-flowers and roses. Then, farther from the Church, and past the cloister and its buildings, were many detached buildings, and a great garden round them, all within the circle of the poplar trees; in the garden were trellises covered over with rose, and convolvulus, and the great-leaved fiery nasturtium; and specially all along by the poplar trees were there trellises, but on these grew nothing but deep crimson roses; the hollyhocks too were all out in blossom at that time, great spires of pink, and orange, and red, and white, with their soft, downy leaves. I said that nothing grew on the trellises by the poplars but crimson roses, but I was not quite right, for in many places the wild flowers had crept into the garden from without; lush green briony, with green-white blossoms, that grew so fast, one could almost think that we see it grow, and deadly nightshade, La bella donna, O! so beautiful; red berry, and purple, yellow-spiked flower, all growing together in the glorious days of early autumn. (*MSW*, pp. 275–6)

The emphasis here is upon the richness of the garden. Morris believed that every garden should be 'rich', but it is important to be clear about what he meant by this. He did not mean opulent, for he despised the bedded-out garden with its showy display of social wealth, and in his lecture on 'Art in the Future' (which Robinson printed in *The Garden*[16]), he exprobated 'luxury', and called instead for 'honesty and simplicity . . . two virtues much needed in modern life'. Nor did Morris apply 'rich' to the fecundity of nature in the raw. As Nicholas Gould has explained, 'Morris did not want a natural world, totally free from human influence: he was not a man for wilderness. He loved England, a land without "great wastes overwhelming in their dreariness, great solitudes of forests, terrible untrodden mountain-walls". His ideal was a comfortable symbiosis between man and nature.'[17]

For Morris, 'rich' meant bristling or, to use a term of Ruskin's, 'quick-set'—but always as a metaphor for, or within the context of, joyful and spontaneous human labour. Morris was heavily influenced by Ruskin's essay on 'The Nature of Gothic' (in *Stones of Venice* (1853)), in which Ruskin 'praised Gothic workmanship because it was always energetic and luxuriant . . .'.[18] Significantly, when Morris spoke about gardens he always coupled 'rich' with 'orderly'. It was the orderliness of the medieval garden that he tried to replicate in the gardens of his own homes. With the assistance of Philip Webb in the early 1860s the Red House at Upton was 'spaced formally into four little square gardens making a big square together; each of the smaller squares had a wattled fence round it, with an opening by which one entered, and all over the fence roses grew thickly'.[19] Later, at Kelmscott in Hammersmith, Morris fashioned the garden into 'separate spaces' described by old clipped yew hedges, and there were also trellises over which grew raspberries, 'so that they look[ed] like a medieval garden'.[20]

Morris also liked the rich but never glaring colours of the medieval pleasure garden. This is evident from his description of the garden in *The Unknown Church*, which one critic has termed 'very Pre-Raphaelite in its detail and its feeling for primary colours'.[21] The garden described in the first twelve lines of 'Golden Wings' (from *The Defence of Guinevere* (1858)) is also strong in elementary colours:

Midways of a walled garden,
 In the happy poplar land,
 Did an ancient castle stand,
With an old knight for a warden.

Many scarlet bricks there were
 In its walls, and old grey stone;
 Over which red apples shone
At the right time of the year.

On the bricks the green moss grew,
 Yellow lichen on the stone.
 Over which red apples shone;
Little war that castle knew. (*MSW*, p. 424)

Yeats considered these lines the finest description of happiness he knew.[22] But the poem as a whole is anything but happy; it 'belongs to the chivalric world, but it moves inexorably from the beautiful mood in which it opens',[23] for 'Golden Wings' is the story of the 'Fair Jehane de castel beau', who, despairing of finding the lover for whom she calls in song, commits suicide, while her castle is stormed and destroyed. The final lines of the poem fully justify the assertion that 'Golden Wings' 'does not belong to a romantic dream of the Middle Ages—but presents a quite different vision of that period':[24]

> The apples now grow green and sour
> Upon the mouldering castle-wall,
> Before they ripen there they fall;
> There are no banners on the tower.
>
> The draggled swans most eagerly eat
> The green weeds trailing in the moat;
> Inside the rotting leaky boat
> You see a slain man's stiffen'd feet. (*MSW*, p. 431)

'Golden Wings', then, prompts us to consider the question of how Morris's predilection for the enclosed medieval garden was related to his vision of the Middle Ages in general. To put it simply, did Morris idealize the medieval pleasure garden because of or in spite of its historical determinations? Probably both. He associated it with all that he admired in the medieval world. As the product of an art ancillary to Gothic architecture, it was for him, as for Ruskin, 'the organic expression of the faith, values, and talents of the European peoples'.[25] But Morris did not idealize the Middle Ages as a whole, for he was sensible not only of the period's beauty and simplicity, but also of its brutality and turbulence—to which the castle garden in 'Golden Wings' falls victim. Moreover, as is clear from *The Dream of John Ball*, 'Morris associated his revival of crafts not with the social structure of the Middle Ages, but with the revolt against it'.[26]

But it is clear also that Morris was delighted and inspired by the sheer forms and appearance of medieval gardens, responses which did not require him to endorse the culture from which they derived. And because he could envisage the medieval garden extricated from its less appealing contextual determinations, Morris was able to construct his own gardens on medieval lines and, in *News from Nowhere*, imagine a socialist Utopia thickly scattered with medieval-looking gardens, but without the enclosing walls of the original versions.

The medieval pleasure garden that Morris and the Pre-Raphaelites helped to make familiar, provided one of the models for the revival of interest in the old-fashioned formal garden during and after the 1860s. Other models were provided by formal gardens of a less remote past, including the small trim gardens associated with the red brick architecture of the 1630s and, more generally, trim formal gardens of the seventeenth century and early eighteenth century. These were especially favoured by gardeners of the so-called 'Free Classic' or 'Queen Anne' movement which burgeoned in the 1870s and 1880s. In his illuminating study of the Queen Anne garden, Mark Girouard notes that its exponents reacted against the two main traditions of mid-Victorian gardening: the formal Italianate garden, and the 'gardenesque' garden. They 'accepted and enjoyed formality, but only the modest formality of the "old-fashioned" gardens of the late seventeenth and early eighteenth centuries. They preferred clipped hedges and topiary to temples and balustrades, and borders of "old-fashioned" flowers to parterres of bedded-out ones.' Girouard goes on to point out that the Queen Anne garden 'was inspired more by painters, poets, and architects than by professional gardeners',[27] and mentions, among others, Tennyson, the late Pre-Raphaelites, and William Bell Scott, whose sonnet sequence *The Old Scotch House* (c. 1874) includes a sonnet commemorating an old-fashioned garden in Ayrshire.

Mid- (and later) Victorian literature offers many approving descriptions of modestly formal old-fashioned gardens. Some are specifically intended to symbolize old-fashioned values and traditions, particularly those associated with the conservative English gentry. Trollope's Carbury Manor House, in *The Way We Live Now*, has 'that thoroughly established look of an old country position', and its large gardens are 'screened from the road by a wall ten feet high', and include 'yew and cypresses said to be of wonderful antiquity' (p. 129). Trollope presents it as a pocket of resistance, as aloof from and impervious to ephemeral fashions in garden design as is its owner, the 'dependable' Roger Carbury, from the ugly materialism by which he is surrounded.

Other old-fashioned gardens of unpretentious formality are associated with a more personal past. Gaskell's Ruth Hilton returns with Mr Bellingham to Millham Grange, the 'picturesque' home of her childhood, and shows him the little garden she has often spoken about. It is 'pretty' and 'old-fashioned'. 'There was a sunny border just under the windows, and clipped box and yew-trees by the grass plot, further away from the house; she prattled again of her childish adventures and solitary plays' (*Ruth*, p. 49). Doubtless many of the writers and artists who gave an impetus to the revival of the old-fashioned garden drew, like Ruth Hilton, upon their own early experiences of old gardens that had survived unscathed the swingeing effects of successive garden fashions. This seems to have been the case with Kate Greenaway, whose book illustrations of the 1870s and 1880s, to *The Quiver of Love* (1876), *Under the Window* (1879), *Mother Goose or The Old Nursery Rhymes* (1881), and *Marigold Garden* (1885) depict trim, symmetrically patterned little old-fashioned gardens sporting dwarf trees in tubs and neat rows of tulips and other flowers. Though her depiction of garden foliage owed much to her training in ornamental design, the original inspiration for and love of old-fashioned gardens can perhaps be traced to her childhood experiences in the large backgarden of her mother's millinery shop, and in the farmhouse garden in the Valley of the Trent, in which she spent many happy days in the 1850s. Like other enthusiasts of old-fashioned gardens, she tried to invest her own imaginative work with something of the enchantment she herself had discovered. Ruskin praised Kate Greenaway's work because he believed that 'her flowers and young children restored the element of fantasy and beauty fast disappearing from industrial England'.[28]

Perhaps one indication of the mounting interest in old-fashioned formal gardens at this time is their description in the works of writers not in themselves directly connected with the formal garden revival. The stylistic diversity of these fictional gardens anticipates, even if it is not directly connected with, the tolerance and historical eclecticism which came to characterize turn-of-the-century garden design. And it is further evidence of the sympathy shown by imaginative writers throughout the Victorian period towards garden styles not easily accommodated within the mainstream traditions of contemporary garden design.

Four examples will have to suffice. The first is from Wilkie Collins's novel, *The Evil Genius* (1886). In Chapter 9 the narrator provides details of the gardens of the old Scottish mansion of Mount Morven, one of the main settings in the novel. At the limits of its lawn there are two paths. One leads to a grassy walk and, thence, to a thick shrubbery—a very typical Victorian feature. The other path leads to something more interesting and unusual: 'a quaintly pretty enclosure, cultivated on the plan of the old gardens at Versailles, and called the French garden' (p. 75). 'Quaintly pretty' implies approval, modest formality and, perhaps, old age, though towards the end of the century gardens were again being constructed on the French plan.

At the same time, there was an even greater upsurge of interest in Dutch and topiary gardens. An appealing fictional example is Dr Fitzpiers's garden in Hardy's *The Woodlanders* (1887):

> The cottage and its garden were so regular in their plan that they might have been laid out by a Dutch designer of the time of William and Mary. In a low dense hedge was a door, over which the hedge formed an arch, and from the inside of the door a straight path, bordered with clipped box, ran up the slope of the garden to the porch, which was exactly in the middle of the house-front, with two windows on each side. Right and left of the path were first a bed of gooseberry bushes; next of currant; next of raspberry; next of strawberry; next of old-fashioned flowers; at the corners of the porch being spheres of box resembling a pair of school globes. Over the roof of the house could be seen the orchard on yet higher ground, and between the orchard the forest-trees, reaching up to the crest of the hill. (pp. 140–1)

The age of Fitzpiers's garden is difficult to determine. It looks old, but Hardy tells us that it is 'comparatively modern'. He doesn't tell us *who* constructed it. He may have had in mind one of the early- or pre-Victorian champions of topiary. But since Fitzpiers's dwelling lies plumb in the wooded heartland of rural Wessex, it seems more likely that Hardy had in mind the traditional craftsmanship of the country gardener oblivious or indifferent to the vicissitudes of garden fashions.

At any rate, Fitzpiers's garden would have delighted contemporary enthusiasts of the old (late seventeenth-century) formal topiary garden, and slightly later advocates like J. D. Sedding, Inigo Triggs, and E. S. Prior. Significantly, Hardy conflates his description of house and garden, thereby suggesting that they are constructed on a single architectural plan, which in turn provides the spatial continuity and order so dear to the formal gardeners. The axial path divides as it holds together the discrete, symmetrically-patterned plots of fruit-bushes and flowers, and its 'clipped box' makes the garden seem an extension of the 'small, box-like cottage'. Moreover, the ornamental topiary work is offset by more 'natural' and useful elements, while the whole is embedded in an 'undressed' landscape of fruit and forest trees. These features should have appealed to gardeners like Gertrude Jekyll who sought a reconciliation of the formal and the freer or more 'natural' approaches to garden design.

A still less pretentious old-fashioned formal garden is described in Tennyson's *Enoch Arden*. Behind Philip Ray's dwelling

> Flourished a little garden square and walled:
> And in it throve an ancient evergreen,
> A yew tree, and all around it ran a walk
> Of shingle, and a walk divided it. (*TP*, p. 1147)

Internal evidence suggests that this simplest of small formal gardens dates from well before the end of the eighteenth century. There is nothing remarkable about it; but readers who admired such gardens for what Gertrude Jekyll called their 'homely dignity',[29] and perhaps modelled their own gardens upon them, may have been struck by its simple geometrical plan and its ancient evergreen, just as topiary enthusiasts picked up the detail of the 'peacock-yewtree' mentioned elsewhere in the poem.

My final example is Corisande's garden in Disraeli's *Lothair*. Before describing it, Disraeli accounts for its survival:

> When the modern pleasure-grounds were planned and created, notwithstanding the protest of the artists in landscape, the father of the present Duke would not allow this ancient garden to be entirely destroyed, and you came upon its quaint appearance in the dissimilar world in which it was placed, as you might some festival or romantic costume upon a person habited in the courtly dress of the last century. It was formed upon a gentle southern slope, with turfen terraces walled in on three sides, the fourth consisting of arches of golden yew. (p. 464)

As we soon discover, the garden is stocked with 'all those productions of nature which are now banished from once delighted senses'—Disraeli mentions a dozen kinds of old-fashioned flower—and with two other living features thought typical of ancient country gardens: peacocks and bee-hives.

To garden writers of the 1870s and 1880s, Corisande's garden was the most interesting and important garden in contemporary fiction. It is not hard to see why. It appeared at exactly the right time to attract attention. Robinson's first really influential book, *The Wild Garden*, was published in the same year (1870); his magazine, *The Garden*, followed on its heels. As the revolt against 'barren geometry' and carpet-bedding gathered momentum, garden theorists began to cast around for models of the kinds of garden they wished to see revived or established. Disraeli proffered them a paradigm, while Corisande's theory, 'that flower-gardens should be sweet and luxuriant, and not hard and scentless imitations of works of art', was entirely consonant with their own. Moreover, Corisande's garden survived, not in some sequestered rural spot but, remarkably, in the very midst of a modern display garden of stupendous grandeur. The incongruity of this juxtaposition, and the peculiarity of the garden itself, was painful, yet at the same time heartening, to those who sought a radical shift of emphasis in garden design.

I wish to conclude this chapter with some remarks about 'old-fashioned' flowers, and the part imaginative writers played in reflecting, maintaining and, in some cases, consciously promoting, interest in them.

Contrary to what some historians of the visual arts appear to suggest, novelists, poets and artists did not suddenly discover old-fashioned flowers at some time around the 1860s. Nor was the taste for these flowers confined to writers associated with the Arts and Crafts movement, and to those who spoke up for the old-fashioned formal garden. The enthusiasm for old-fashioned flowers burgeoned, but did not begin, in the latter part of the century. Consider the following passage from Emily Eden's highly successful comedy of manners, *The Semi-attached Couple*, published in 1860, but written some thirty years earlier:

> When Lord Teviot despatched his letters, he found [his wife] in her garden; not one of the old-fashioned gardens, full of roses and honeysuckles, and sweet peas, suggestive of the country, and redolent of sweetness—but in a first rate gardener's garden, every plant forming part of a group, and not to be picked or touched on any account; all of them forced into bloom at the wrong time of the year; and each bearing a name that it was difficult to pronounce, and impossible to remember. (p. 77)

In this fascinatingly precursive passage, Emily Eden not only betrays her fondness for old garden flowers with pronounceable names, but also rehearses some of the principal objections to the gardenesque garden and to modern horticulture made familiar by a later generation of garden writers. The point to stress here is that the taste for old-fashioned flowers was by no means either narrowly sectional or historically specific.

Even so, there is no denying the intensification of interest in old-fashioned flowers in the latter decades of the nineteenth century. There were, concomitantly, three significant qualitative developments.

First and foremost, the enthusiasm for old-fashioned flowers became increasingly purposive as the century progressed. Many imaginative artists either inspired, or more directly participated in, efforts to re-establish the status of flowers eclipsed by those more suited to carpet-bedding. Juliana Ewing's story *Mary's Meadow* was (in part) dedicated to just this project. The excitement it aroused led to the idea of forming a 'Parkinson society' (after John Parkinson, author of the first major British work on the pleasure garden, *Paradisi in Sole Paradisus Terrestris* (1629)); one of its main objects was 'to search out and cultivate old garden flowers which have become scarce'.[30] (The Natural History and Gardening Society of Bedford Park, formed at the same time, 1883, had precisely the same object.[31]) Morris was an even more influential advocate of old-fashioned flowers; it was through Morris that 'the Arts and Crafts garden inherited an affection for English cottage plants, such as sunflowers and stocks'.[32] Morris's commitment to old-fashioned flowers was heightened by, and, in part, a response to, his acute distaste for carpet-bedding and the 'over-artificiality' of florists' flowers.

In addition to having fairly specific causes and goals, the movement to revive interest in old garden plants in the second half of the Victorian period was also decidedly collaborative in character. It can properly be called a movement because poets, painters, architects and book illustrators collaborated in and shared a collective perception of the projects in which they were engaged. Their tastes were shaped by similar values (simplicity as opposed to elaborateness and ornamentation for its own sake); they favoured the same kinds of garden flowers, and the same sources of literary and artistic inspiration. As Girouard points out, Tennyson was much admired in Pre-Raphaelite circles, as was Blake, who influenced the later style of Rossetti, the art work of Walter Crane, and Art Nouveau.[33] Both poets probably influenced the floral preferences of later Victorian imaginative artists.

One of these artists was Walter Crane, whose series of flower books was clearly informed by and produced within a framework of common interests and influences. Some of the designs in *Flora's Feast: A Masque of Flowers* (1889)—Crane's first and most successful flower book—suggest the influence of Blake (one page is headed 'Lilies turned to Tigers'), and indicate a Pre-Raphaelite and Tennysonian attention to the details of plant forms. His second book was *Queen Summer of the Tournay of the Lily and the Rose* (1891). The floral opposition, and the theme of a tournament of floral suitors for the favour of Queen Summer, again recalls Tennyson (in particular, *The Idylls of the King*). The medieval style, 'a kind of decorated Gothic',[34] may also owe something to Pre-Raphaelite subjects, and to Morris, with whom Crane was closely associated both professionally and politically. In 1893 Crane furnished the decorations for Margaret Deland's *Old Garden and Other Verses*, and six years later produced *A Floral Fantasy in an Old English Garden*, the cover design of which depicts symmetrically placed and severely simple Art Nouveau trees in tubs, with what appear to be rectangular hedges and topiary peacocks. The design would doubtless have pleased the architect and formal garden exponent, J. D. Sedding, with whom Crane came into contact during his (Crane's) periods as president of the Arts and Crafts Society (1888–90; 1895–1915).

Finally, the revival of interest in old-fashioned flowers was distinguished by a certain selectivity of plant materials. Though all old-fashioned flowers were favoured, if not always for themselves, at least for the values they were thought to symbolize, a few were positively idealized. Chief among them was the sunflower. Walter Hamilton observed in 1882, that the sunflower is 'as distinctively the badge of the true Aesthete as the green turban is among the Mohammedans'.[35] Oscar Wilde once claimed the credit. He told *Punch* (New York, January 1882): 'I believe I was the first to devote my subtle brain-chords to the worship of the sunflower.'[36] His claim seems weak, however. Rossetti, Burne-Jones, and Morris had popularized the plant in the 1850s and 1860s, taking their inspiration, perhaps, from Blake's brief poem, and from the two instances in which Tennyson speaks of the sunflower: in *Song*, 'A spirit haunts the year's last hours', and *In Memoriam*, CI.

Like the tall madonna lily—exalted by the aesthetes—and the

more widely popular hollyhock, the sunflower was markedly different from the plants which stocked the parterres of contemporary display gardens, not only in its historical and literary associations, but also in its towering form. At least some of the later Victorian poets discerned in its physical characteristics associations of an old-fashioned nobility. Swinburne was one of these poets. I shall close this section by quoting part of 'The Mill Garden' section of his long poem *A Midsummer Holiday*:

Stately stand the sunflowers, glowing down the garden side,
Ranged in royal rank arow along the warm-grey wall,
Whence their deep disks burn at rich midnoon afire with pride,
Even as though their beams indeed were sunbeams, and the tall,
Sceptral stems bore stars whose reign endures, not flowers that fall.[37]

CHAPTER FOUR

The Picturesque Garden

According to Christopher Hussey, 'the picturesque became the nineteenth century's mode of vision'.[1] Certainly, the word itself appears frequently and prominently in Victorian fiction, in essays, letters, and journals, and in the voluminous technical literature on gardens, architecture, and the visual arts. But what a purely statistical analysis of the term does not reveal is its semiotic complexity.[2] It is this which makes the picturesque an infuriatingly difficult concept to explicate.

Some things are certain. First, it is clear that picturesque scenery and picturesque modes of perception appealed to many Victorian novelists. Second, there can be little doubt that in applying the term not only frequently but freely, such writers as Disraeli, Charlotte Brontë, Elizabeth Gaskell, and George Eliot reflected and reinforced the interests of many of their readers and, at the same time, participated in the process of diluting and diffusing the significations of the term itself. And third, we know that at least some novelists, including Dickens and Eliot, were conscious of the dangers to socio-moral attitudes of certain kinds and certain applications of the picturesque. Their misgivings must be seen as contributions to a wider critical interrogation of the picturesque, conducted from aesthetic, social, and ethical points of view.

For some curious reason, very little has been written about the picturesque in relation to Victorian literature.[3] Perhaps Christopher Hussey's dismissive assertion that after Scott 'only second-rate writers continued . . . to be conscious of the picturesque',[4] has been given far more credence than it deserves. Perhaps it has also been too widely assumed that imaginative writers ceased to take an interest in parks and gardens built in the picturesque tradition because the tradition itself 'ceased to dominate garden landscape design after the early nineteenth century'.[5] Whatever the reasons, the subject has been neglected, but quite undeservedly so.

As far as possible, I wish to confine my discussion to picturesque *gardens*, though a narrow focus is not always possible nor, given the multiplicity and inter-relatedness of picturesque phenomena, always desirable.

The picturesque garden was an eighteenth-century development. Its most vocal exponents were two Herefordshire landowners, Richard Payne Knight and Uvedale Price, whose *bête noire* was the Brownian pastoral garden (which, to make things more confusing, has also been labelled 'picturesque'), with its stock devices of 'clumps' and 'belts' of trees scattered on gently undulating turf. For Knight and Price, the qualities to be sought in landscapes—irregularity, ruggedness, surprise, and fidelity to (untamed) nature—were precisely those qualities which lent themselves to pictorial representation; and in the late eighteenth century and after, gentlemen of fashion with the means to travel in search of pictorially composed scenes, looked at landscapes with models derived from their favourite painters: Claude Lorrain, the Poussins, Salvator Rosa, and seventeenth-century Dutch artists.

This eighteenth-century cult was channelled into nineteenth-century literature in various ways, though not without some significant modifications and developments. It was kept alive partly because it had and produced the right modish associations: with medievalism, antiquarianism, and associationism.

The historical, philosophical, and emotional connections between the picturesque and the Gothic revival have often been acknowledged. J. Mordaunt Cook has described the picturesque as 'the essence of Gothic taste',[6] and Kenneth Clark has called it 'an amplification of the mood of the Gothic poets'.[7] Alice Chandler also has traced the origins of the Gothic revival to the picturesque,[8] while Edward Malins has noted that the picturesque came into the Victorian period through the landscapes and architecture of the eighteenth century, when it meant precisely a 'mixture of historical and pictorial', with particular reference to 'mossy cells, old castles on cliffs, and gloomy pines . . . a ruin, ivy-clad and mouldering', and all that was especially 'capable of being illustrated in painting'.[9]

Like the Gothic, the picturesque, together with landscape gardening in general, was brought into the nineteenth century through its connections with associationist philosophy. The main associationist treatise on aesthetics, *Essays on the Nature and Principles of Taste* (1790), was the work of the Scottish rationalist, Archibald Alison, who held that beauty is not intrinsic to objects, but exists in the mind of the beholder. Alison has much to say on the picturesque, which for him, as apparently for Knight and later for Loudon, was a subdivision of the Beautiful, not an alternative aesthetic category. The picturesque objects he instances as 'familiar to everyone's observation' include old towers in the middle of deep woods, bridges flung across chasms beyond rocks, and cottages on precipices. He writes: 'If I am not mistaken, the effect which such objects have on everyone's mind, is to suggest an additional train of connections beside what the scene or description itself would have suggested; for it is very obvious that no subjects are remarked as picturesque which do not strike the imagination by themselves.'[10]

From the first, then, picturesque scenery was valued not simply as an end, but as the means to an end. Picturesque parks with their striking contrasts, their desuetude inspiring romantic melancholy, and their signs of age and decay had 'a power to stimulate in the viewer a piquant mixture of painful and pleasurable impressions and associations';[11] and the ladies and gentlemen who retired to the sham ruins they had erected in their parks and gardens 'were presumably helped by them to meditate more seriously on change, mortality, and time'.[12] Since the picturesque love of ruins naturally encouraged the 'habit of seeing landscapes through past associations', and 'the valuation of places according to their connections with a presumed or inferred history',[13] the picturesque was also connected with antiquarianism, nostalgia for the past, and rejection of the present.[14]

Historical conditions in general, and industrialization in particular, did much to ensure the survival of picturesque predilections and associations, especially among those early Victorians who looked back to a 'happier' past—historical or mythical, their country's or their own—and who turned to landscape scenes to reflect on what has been called 'the battle of ideal beauty against time and man's vandalous nature'.[15]

Unsurprisingly, descriptions of picturesque gardens of the grander kinds are prominent in the early novels of Bulwer Lytton and Disraeli, both of whom gave romantic treatment to aristocratic subjects. The high-born heroes of Bulwer Lytton's novels—meditative, restlessly introspective, sensitive to history, and indifferent to conventional social ambitions—are temperamentally predisposed to picturesque parks. Ernest Maltravers is a good example. At one moment in the novel, the titular hero decides to flee 'the gay metropolis' for his ancestral home of Burleigh, in which he will spend the next two years virtually in solitary confinement. His arrival, 'one lovely evening in July' is described as follows:

> What a soft, fresh delicious evening it was! He had quitted his carriage at the lodge, and followed it across the small but picturesque park alone and on foot. He had not seen the place since childhood—he had quite forgotten its aspect. He now wondered how he could have lived anywhere else. The trees did not stand in stately avenues, nor did the antlers of the deer wave above the sombre fern; it was not the domain of a grand seigneur, but of an old, long-established English squire. Antiquity spoke in the moss-grown palings, in the shadowy groves, in the sharp gable-ends and heavy mullions of the house, as it now came in view, at the base of the hill covered with wood—and partially veiled by the shrubs of the neglected pleasure ground, separated from the park by the invisible ha-ha. There gleamed in the twilight the watery face of the oblong fish-pool, with its old-fashioned willows set at each corner—there, grey and quaint, was the monastic dial—and there was the long terrace walk, with discoloured and broken vases, now filled with orange or the aloe, which, in honour of his master's arrival, the gardener had extracted from the dilapidated green-house. The very evidence of neglect around, the very weeds and grass on the half-obliterated road, touched Maltravers with a sort of pitying and remorseful affection for his calm and sequestered residence. (p. 217)

Disraeli's attachment to the picturesque is suggested by many passages in his novels of the 1830s and 1840s. One example is the description of the fictional St Genevieve in *Coningsby* (1844). It captures, as David Rubenstein has remarked, 'the picturesque, romantic style favoured by many early Victorian architects of country houses (though opposed by others) . . .'.[16] Rubenstein points out that St Genevieve was in reality Garendon Hall in Leicestershire, an eighteenth-century Palladian house, remodelled on Gothic lines by E. W. Pugin in 1866, though the original plans had been drawn up by Pugin senior in 1841. In the same novel is Beaumanoir, probably a fictionalized version of the picturesque Deepdene, estate of the wealthy supporter of the Young England movement, Henry Hope, with whom Disraeli often stayed. For Disraeli, it almost certainly suggested the romantic aspirations, and the concern with past traditions, of the Young England movement itself.

Perhaps Disraeli's most exuberant and romantic picturesque

park is Armine, described in *Henrietta Temple*, which was published in the same year (1837) as *Ernest Maltravers*:

> In one of the largest parks of England there yet remained a fragment of a vast Elizabethan pile, that in the old days bore the name of Armine Place. . . . It was now thickly covered in moss and ivy which rather added to than detracted from the picturesque character of the whole mass. . . . Long lines of turreted and many windowed walls, tall towers, and lofty arches, now rose in picturesque confusion on the green ascent . . .
>
> Armine Place, before Sir Ferdinand, unfortunately for his descendants, determined in the eighteenth century on building a feudal castle, had been situate in famous pleasure grounds, which extended at the back of the mansion over a space of some hundred acres. The grounds in the immediate vicinity of the buildings had of course suffered severely, but the far greater portion had only been neglected; and there were some indeed who deemed, as they wandered through the arbour-walks of this enchanting wilderness, that its beauty had been enhanced even by this very neglect. It seemed like a forest in a beautiful romance; a green and bowery wilderness where Boccaccio would have loved to woo, and Watteau to paint. So artfully had the walks been planned, that they seemed interminable, nor was there a single point in the whole pleasaunce where the keenest eye could have detected a limit. Sometimes you wandered in those arched and winding walks dear to pensive spirits; sometimes you emerged on a plot of turf blazing in the sunshine, a small and bright savannah, and gazed with wonder on the group of black and mighty cedars that rose from its centre, with their sharp and spreading foliage. The beautiful and the vast blended together; and the moment you had beheld with delight a bed of geraniums or of myrtles, you found yourself in an amphitheatre of Italian pines. A strange exotic filled the air: you trod on the flowers of other lands; and shrubs and plants, that usually are trusted only from their conservatories, like sultanas from their jalousies to sniff the air and recall their bloom, here learning from hardship the philosophy of endurance, had struggled successfully even against northern winters, and wantoned now in native and unpruned luxuriance. Sir Ferdinand, when he resided at Armine, was

> accustomed to fill these pleasure-grounds with macaws and other birds of gorgeous plumage; but these had fled away with their master, all but some swans which still floated on the surface of a lake, which marked the centre of this paradise. (pp. 10–11)

Needless to say, this description owes little to Disraeli's first-hand observations of picturesque parks. In fact, Disraeli would have been hard-pressed to find real-world models of sufficient grandeur, for few such gardens were constructed. (The grounds of Scotney Castle, Kent, created from 1835 by Edward Hussey and W. S. Gilpin, are a rare approximation.) Nonetheless, it is interesting for two reasons. First, because it expresses one form of the picturesque ideal, which might be termed the aristocratic or magnificent picturesque to distinguish it from the rural or homely picturesque. Second, because it illustrates, for Disraeli's purposes, the perfect compatibility of picturesque subjects and attitudes with earlier, more traditional images of enchanting topographies. For what we have in the description of Armine is a fantasy script pastiche, a flamboyant medley of literary and artistic landscape images: from medieval romance, from Milton's Eden (strongly echoed in 'wantoned' and 'luxuriance'), from early eighteenth-century French landscape paintings, from images of the exotic East—within an exaggeratedly romanticized version of the aristocratic picturesque ideal.

It is important to note that Armine, like Burleigh, is not of recent construction. It is an ancient park, fortuitously neglected, and so picturesque by default rather than by design. This gives it the 'right' (i.e. genuine) historical associations, important because the picturesque was 'largely an appeal to the landed aristocracy's sense of heredity and ownership, particularly now that it was found pleasing actually to *possess* one's park by riding or promenading through it . . .'.[17] The emphasis on old age also enables Disraeli to avoid any suggestion of the too-obviously contrived or the sham, and hence of guilt by association with Gilpin who advocated deliberate destruction for picturesque effects—to the embarrassment of his Victorian successors.

This insistence upon authenticity is evident also in descriptions of picturesque ruins and their gardens. Such places are especially prominent in early Victorian novels. One example is in Bulwer Lytton's *Godolphin*, the events of which span the years between the Prince Regent and the Reform Bill of 1832. The picturesque ruins of Godolphin Priory, ancient seat of the Godolphin family, are initially described from the point of view of two female tourists—Lady Erpingham and the beautiful Constance Vernon, heroine of the story:

> The scene as they approached was wild and picturesque in the extreme. A wide and glassy lake lay stretched beneath them: on the opposite side stood the ruins. The large oriel windows—the Gothic arch—the broken, yet still majestic column, all embrowned and mossed with age, were still spared, and now mirrored themselves in the waveless and silent tide. Fragments of stone lay around, for some considerable distance, and the whole was backed by hills, covered with gloomy and thick woods and pine and fir. (p. 27)

There is nothing counterfeit about these ruins. They include a genuine Elizabethan garden: a smooth green lawn, surrounded by shrubs and flowers, ornamented in the centre by a fountain and, a little to the right, an old-monkish sundial, the whole designed to be viewed from a small room above. When Constance encounters Percy Godolphin at the ruins, she exclaims upon their 'romantic and picturesque beauty'. Percy, though by no means impervious to its venerable associations, points out that the place is now fit only for sight-seers; his impecunious father is forced to live in a cottage in the grounds. And when Lady Erpingham remarks that 'It wants nothing but a few deer', Percy provides her with a simple lesson in land economics: 'it is not,' he says, 'for the owner of a ruined priory to consult the aristocratic enchantments of that costly luxury, the Picturesque' (p. 31).

Costly (and destructive) it was. Perhaps Bulwer Lytton was thinking of Gilpin, who said that to turn 'a piece of Palladian architecture' into 'picturesque beauty . . . we must beat down one half of it, deface the other, and throw the mutilated members around in heaps. In short, from a *smooth* building we must turn it into a *rough* ruin.'[18]

Gilpin's prescription and Uvedale Price's fascination with associations of pain and humiliation would seem to confirm the assertion that the whole cult of the picturesque was in some sense 'a sadomasochistic pleasure in vandalism, dismemberment and ugliness.'[19] This may be true of the cult in the eighteenth century, but the pleasure of painful perceptions is much less in evidence, and more complex where it does occur, in Victorian fiction. This is partly because of the insistence upon genuine picturesque ruins, and hence, upon authentic emblematic significance. As Wilkie Collins comments in *Blind Love* (1890): 'Age is essential to the picturesque effect of decay: a modern ruin is an unnatural and depressing object' (p. 32). In particular, ruins stimulate the socially responsible visitor to question the relations between past and present, and provide the atmosphere in which he can ponder the social problems of the day.

These are the functions which the picturesque ruins of Marney Abbey serve for the disenchanted aristocratic hero of Disraeli's *Sybil* (1845). The place itself is similar to Godolphin Priory:

> The desecration of a spot once sacred, still beautiful and solemn, jarred on the feelings of Egremont. He sighed and turned away, followed a path that after a few paces led him into the cloister garden. This was a considerable quadrangle, once surrounding the garden of the monks; but all that remained of that fair pleasaunce was a solitary yew in its centre, which seemed the oldest tree that could well live, and was according to tradition, more ancient than the most venerable walls of the Abbey. (p. 68)

It is through his musings in Marney Abbey that Egremont gropes towards a realization that the poor are a separate 'Nation', a nation created by working-class resentment of aristocratic power without responsibility; and it is here that he first encounters the two men who are to play such a large part in his subsequent development: Walter Gerard and Stephen Morley.

Sybil is a novel of the 1840s, and partly about the social problems of an industrial era; and yet Disraeli has his hero ponder these problems in the picturesque ruins of a monastic garden. There is nothing incongruous about this, for it was largely the Industrial Revolution and the changes it brought about—in landscape, in social relations, in sentiments and consciousness—which guaranteed the persistence of picturesque attractions in the Victorian period. Even so, it would be misleading to lay too much stress on the particular emphases of Bulwer Lytton and the young Disraeli, for it was not the cloister, or the neglected park of the landed ruling class which provided the principal subjects of picturesque interest in Victorian fiction, but rather the sketchable country scene and the modest cottage garden. Through their attraction to these subjects, Victorian novelists played an instrumental part in domesticating, miniaturizing and, sometimes, in sentimentalizing a concept originally associated in its sublimer aspects with the very antithesis of cosy rurality.

These processes were well under way by the 1830s and 1840s, a period that has been described, albeit in lyrical and transcendental terms, as the 'perfect pastoral moment' when 'the impulse from a vernal world which had been renewed by Romanticism met with the new industrialization and the urbanization of early Victorian years. . . . On the one hand was the sense of a complex and sophisticated culture, of pressing national problems, and, on the other, of an older and greener world which was rapidly fading away but had not yet altogether been lost.'[20] The impetus for the homely picturesque was provided by the desire to capture pictures of 'an older greener world' not yet dead (if it had ever existed![21]) on the part of writers unable or unwilling to acknowledge the harsh realities of agrarian capitalism and, in some cases, happy to arrange rural life into a cosy idyll.

Cottage and farmhouse gardens furnished perfect subjects for the picture-making descriptions of the prose idylls, revived and developed between the 1820s and 1840s, and popular for long after. Mary Mitford's *Our Village*, written between 1824 and 1832, was one of the first and most influential of the prose idylls or sketches. (It is sub-titled 'Sketches of Rural Characters and Scenery'.)

Most of the cottage gardens Miss Mitford describes are 'pretty'. 'Pretty' is one of her favourite adjectives; of one garden—the 'old place' from which she was wrenched—she uses the word three times. In her sketches, 'pretty' modifies or implies 'picture'. Of the gardens of Hillhouse she declares: 'What a pretty picture they would make; what a pretty foreground they do make to the real landscape!' (p. 21).

The gardens of her village are pretty pictures by virtue of their size, form and contents. The majority are reasonably small, and some are miniature. Though they vary in shape, each is discrete; collectively, they have the requisite irregularity, and resemble a group of 'close-packed' 'islands' (p. 3). Each is well-stocked, and the majority are immaculately tended and visually pleasing.

Historically and conceptually, Miss Mitford's notion of the picturesque cottage garden is proto-Victorian. On the one hand, she anticipates and possibly influences the domestication and Anglicization of the picturesque in Victorian literature through her definition of the typically homely English cottage. This is evident by contrast in her response to the atypical, to Tom

Cordery's 'uncouth and shapeless cottage' which stands in a wooded defile:

> It is a scene which hangs upon the eye and memory, striking, grand, almost sublime, and above all, eminently foreign. No English painter would choose such a subject for an English landscape. . . . It might pass for one of those scenes which have furnished models to Salvator Rosà.[22]

On the other hand, she preserves the received distinction between the artlessly picture-like, or what I have termed the homely picturesque, and the self-consciously picturesque—a distinction which has all but collapsed by mid-century. Hence, she uses 'picturesque' sparingly and with specific reference to cottages constructed by wealthy landowners for the express purpose of having something fancy to look at.

If, as seems certain, Miss Mitford shaped the picturesque preferences of her many Victorian readers, she did so in favour of the artless artistry of the homely cottage garden, and to the detriment of the picturesque both in its excessively embellished and in its tumbledown forms. What of the descriptions themselves? Miss Mitford's presentation of country life as a whole is cosy, selective and 'cleverly unspecific'.[23] Overall, her depictions of cottage gardens contribute to the warm glow; but individually they are neither mawkish nor idealized. In contrast to the eighteenth-century lover of the picturesque 'bent upon discovering not the world as it is, but the world as it might have been had the Creator been an Italian artist of the seventeenth century',[24] Miss Mitford appears to describe what she has seen rather than what she should like to have seen. Hence, she describes not only the pretty but the downright ugly and messy (the poacher's garden, for instance). Hence, her descriptions are particularistic; individuality and variety are the qualities she most admires and adduces.

One of the interesting differences between *Our Village* and William Howitt's *Rural Life of England* (1838)—the two are frequently coupled—is Howitt's freer, less discriminating use of 'picturesque'. This has something to do with the broader scope of Howitt's book: it purports 'to present to the reader a view of the Rural Life of England at the present period, as seen in all classes and all parts of the country' (p. viii). But it is attributable also to the fact that Howitt, like Southey before him, uses the idyllic country cottage as a contrast to the dwellings of the industrial poor:

> There is not a more beautiful sight in the world than that of our English cottages, in those parts of the country where the violent changes of the time have not been so sensibly felt. There, on the edges of the forests, in quiet hamlets and sweet woody valleys, the little grey-thatched cottages, with their gardens and old orchards, their rows of beehives, and their porches clustered with jasmines and roses, stand . . . and give one a poetical idea of peace and happiness which is inexpressible . . . and it is the *ideal* of these picturesque and peace-breathing English cottages that have given the origin to some of the sweetest paradises in the world,—the cottages of the wealthy and the tasteful. (pp. 411–12)

Howitt interweaves with his encomiums on the country cottage comments upon the troubles and sufferings of the country labourers, so that the whole 'hovers uncertainly between the realistic and the picturesque view of the countryside and its inhabitants'.[25] In applying the picturesque as he does—to almost any pretty cottage, and to countless other country scenes—Howitt pushes it towards one of its dominant functions in Victorian literature: as the locus for a cluster of intersubjectively recognized concepts, values, and myths. Under the pressure of its many significations and associations, the earlier, more specific and comparatively trivial referents of 'picturesque'—the *cottage orné* and the *point de vue*—were progressively subsumed. That they constitute but a minor part of the domestic picturesque, and even distract from its larger meanings, is a point that Howitt himself developed from his observation that there is more to cottage life 'than ever inspired the wish to build cottage ornés, or to inhabit them' (p. 410).

Early- and mid-Victorian fiction is fairly packed with descriptions of picturesque country dwellings and their gardens. Here are three examples. The first, from *Henrietta Temple*, is a description of the farmhouse encountered by Ferdinand Armine on Ducie Common. The second is Gaskell's description in *Ruth* of Milham Grange, childhood home of Ruth Hilton. (It is followed in the text by a description of the pretty old-fashioned garden at the rear of the Grange.) And the final passage, from Charlotte Brontë's *Shirley* (1849), is the word-picture of Shirley's house of Fieldhead:

Its picturesque form, its angles and twisted chimneys, its porch covered with jessamine and eglantine, its verdant homestead, and its orchard rich with ruddy fruit, its vast barns and long lines of ample stacks, produced altogether a rural picture complete and cheerful. (p. 135)

It was a house of afterthoughts; building materials were plentiful in the neighbourhood, and every successive owner had found a necessity for some addition or projection, till it was a picturesque mass of irregularity—of broken light and shadow—which as a whole gave a full and complete idea of a 'Home'. All its gables and nooks were blended and held together by the tender green of the climbing roses and young creepers. (p. 45)

If Fieldhead had few other merits as a building, it might at least be termed picturesque: its irregular architecture, and the grey and mossy colouring communicated by time, gave it a just claim to this epithet. The old latticed windows, the stone porch, the walls, the roof, the chimney-stacks, were rich in crayon touches and sepia lights and shades. The trees behind were fine, bold, and spreading; the cedar on the lawn in front was grand, the granite urns on the garden wall, the fretted arch of the gateway, were, for an artist, as the very desire of the eye. (p. 160)

In Brontë's description, the focus is primarily upon the first-order significations of 'picturesque'. In other words, the narrator draws attention to 'picturesque' as a label for pictorially-appealing physical and surface characteristics.[26] But in the first two descriptions, 'picturesque' acts also as a stimulus word for a chain of associated concepts and expressive values. These second-order significations include rural plenitude, age and the idea of growth by gradual and unplanned accretion, homeliness, purity, tranquillity, and the perfect commingling of nature and architecture.[27]

Milham Grange and the farmhouse in *Henrietta Temple* are 'complete'—as pictures, and as pictorial representations of an ideal mode of rural existence. All three dwellings are irregular, an essential spatial quality of picturesque gardens and architecture, but significant also for what it connotes: an emotional expressiveness opposed to the logic and symmetry of the rationalism evinced by the village laid out in regular rows, and the too-evidently planned garden of geometric design.

Because of its multiplicity of positive significations, the picturesque provides the paradigmatic frame of reference in many descriptions of fictional houses and gardens; their demerits are measured in terms of how they deviate from or fall short of the picturesque ideal. The rectory garden of Dr Marsham in Disraeli's *Venetia*, though not without its attractive features, 'was altogether a scene as devoid of the picturesque as any that could well be imagined; flat, but not low, and rich, and green, and still' (p. 52). Thorpe-Ambrose, one of the principal physical settings in Wilkie Collins's *Armadale* (1866), is negatively defined in terms of its absence of picturesque associations:

> Nothing picturesque, nothing in the slightest degree suggestive of mystery and romance, appeared in any part of it. It was a purely conventional country-house—the product of the classical idea filtered judiciously through the commercial English mind. (p. 160)

The same might be said of the Italian and various other gardens of Thorpe-Ambrose through which the reader is whisked perfunctorily by the narratorial guide.

It would be easy enough to cite scores of similar descriptions, since there is scarcely a Victorian novelist who does not invoke the picturesque at moments when it seems necessary either to affirm its reality in specific instances, or to have some mythic yardstick by which to measure the distance between what is and what was or might have been.

At the same time, the cult of the picturesque did not go unchallenged. By mid-century, it was evident to discerning novelists that 'picturesque' did not so much denote a class of objects with an invariant set of distinguishing characteristics, as a particular, fundamentally aestheticist, mode of perception. It was equally obvious to them that this mode of perception had its dangers. It could be superficial. It could sentimentalize. It could make pictures of pigsties. Hence, Victorian novels bristle with comments and accounts specifically intended to mock, demystify and discourage the practice of making pictures when the effects of that practice were morally reprehensible and socially undesirable.

George Eliot was especially alert to the deleterious consequences of uncritical picture-making. She was not against the cult of the picturesque as such.[28] Her target was, rather, the lover of the picturesque who derived visual gratification from the hovels of the poor, and whose picture-making practices 'transformed' country life into a pretty fiction or myth. Her principal concern was to render explicit the conditions under which this fiction could be maintained. She specifies three prerequisites. The first is the observer's physical separation from the object of his picturesque perceptions. She was not the first writer to recognize this precondition. When George Eliot was just a child, Macaulay had pilloried Robert Southey for his hill-top view of some traditional labourers' cottages. This viewpoint, Macaulay had suggested, made it possible for Southey to entertain the belief that 'the body of the English peasantry . . . lived in substantial or ornamental cottages, with boxhedges, flower gardens . . . and orchards'.[29] George Eliot's service was to formulate the enabling possibilities of physical disengagement in a general principle. In *Daniel Deronda*, she stated: 'Perspective, as its inventor remarked, is a beautiful thing. What horrors of damp huts, where human beings languish, may not become picturesque through aerial distance' (p. 114).

For Eliot, physical disengagement implied social, moral and imaginative disengagement. Only an observer oblivious or indifferent to the poverty concealed by the floral façades of tumbledown cottages, and imbued with what she called 'cockney sentimentality',[30] and what Ruskin termed the 'lower picturesque ideal' could delight in making pictures of pigsties. Eliot's views ran on parallel lines to Ruskin's, whose aesthetic and moral critique of the picturesque in *Modern Painters* IV (1856) shaped her own. Though Ruskin thought the lower picturesque ideal 'an eminently heartless' one, he did not entirely condemn the lover of the lower picturesque, whom he characterized as 'kind-hearted, innocent of evil, but not broad in thought; somewhat selfish, and incapable of acute sympathy with others', misguided and in need of 'humane' rather than of 'artistic' education (*RW*, VI, 21).

This is the kind of person Eliot has in mind when in *Middlemarch* (1871–2) she prefaces her description of the ironically named 'Freeman's End' with the following remark: 'It is true that an observer under the softening influence of the fine arts which makes other people's hardships picturesque, might have been delighted with the homestead called "Freeman's End".' When she describes the cottage (its owner is the miserly Mr Brooke) Eliot concentrates upon externals: the chimneys 'choked with ivy', the shutters 'about which the jasmine-boughs grew in wild luxuriance', and 'the mouldering garden wall with hollyhocks peeping over it [which] was a perfect study of highly mingled subdued colour . . .' (p. 291). We are given no specific account of what life inside the cottage was like, though it must have been squalid.[31] Eliot was testing her readers; if they accepted her presentation of its surface appearance, they failed.

Eliot's third precondition for heartless picture-making was the over-generalized or ideal-typical frame of reference. It was possible, she believed, for a 'heartless' observer to produce a dishonest picture of a cottage and its garden, irrespective of his physical point of view, if he was bent on reconstructing actual landscapes according to a normative model. Like Ruskin and the Pre-Raphaelites, with their preference for particular truths over general ones, Eliot 'preferred a sense of unique place and abundant local detail in landscape descriptions'.[32] In her review of *Modern Painters*, she wrote:

> The truth of infinite value that he [Ruskin] teaches us is realism—the doctrine that all truth and beauty are to be attained by a humble and faithful study of human nature, and not by substituting vague forms, bred by imagination as the mists of feeling, in place of definite substantial reality.[33]

In *Felix Holt* (1866), we find a picturesque description which exemplifies perfectly Eliot's attention to particular details:

> The Rectory was on the other side of the river, close to the church of which it was the fitting companion: a fine old brick-and-stone house, with a great bow-window opening from the library on to the deep-turfed lawn, one fat dog sleeping on the door-stone, another fat dog waddling on gravel, the autumn leaves duly swept away, the lingering chrysanthemums cherished, tall trees stooping or soaring in the most picturesque variety, and a Virginian creeper turning a little rustic hut into a scarlet pavilion. (p. 208)

Eliot's novels are crammed with similar descriptions, and justify the claim that 'she raises the picturesque to the dignity of an intellectual system'.[35]

Though no novelist contributed more than Eliot to the moral critique of the picturesque, there were many who echoed and endorsed her sentiments. For example, Disraeli anticipated her strictures on the enabling (or disabling) possibilities of aerial distance. In *Sybil* he describes the rural town of Marney from two perspectives. He begins with a prospective view, from which Marney, 'surrounded by meadows and gardens, and backed by lofty hills' appears 'delightful' (p. 68). This 'beautiful illusion' is shattered when the observer approaches Marney and discovers the disease-ridden hovels of the labourers' dwellings. Much later in the century, Meredith in *Sandra Belloni* (1886) provides an ironic comment on the misconceptions of privileged observers; on the evidence of 'the cottage children whose staring faces from the garden porch and gate flashed by the carriage windows', Adela Pole declares to her sisters 'that a country life was surely the next thing to Paradise' (p. 10). And there is at least a hint of disdain in Bulwer Lytton's reference in the opening chapter of *Night and Morning* to 'those luxurious amateurs of the picturesque who view Nature through the windows of a carriage and four' (p. 1).

The stereotypic image of the picturesque cottage, for which George Eliot had little sympathy, is mocked in Gaskell's *North and South* by Mr Lennox when Margaret Hale offers him a description of Helstone hamlet:

> 'There is a church and a few houses near it on the green—cottages, rather, with roses growing all over them.'
> 'And flowering all the year round, especially at Christmas—make your picture complete', said he.
> 'No', replied Margaret, somewhat annoyed. 'I am not making a picture, I am trying to describe Helstone as it really is. You should not have said that.'
> 'I am penitent', he answered. 'Only it really sounded like a village in a tale rather than in real life.'
> 'And so it is', replied Margaret eagerly. 'All the other places in England that I have seen are so hard and prosaic-looking, after the New Forest. Helstone is like a village in a poem—in one of Tennyson's poems.' (p. 9)

Most cottages fell short of the picture-like ideal. A few, like Helstone, approximated to it. But it was hard even to take these seriously for, as Mrs Gaskell seems to suggest, the very pervasiveness of picturesque myths had made it virtually impossible for any intelligent and socially responsible Victorian to be anything other than sceptical and critical.

Dickens, like Eliot, was both, and knew well that the observer's picturesque was likely to be the occupant's pigsty. As Will Fern in *The Chimes* (1844) reminds Sir Joseph and his guests: 'there ain't weather in picters, and maybe 'tis fitter for that, than for a place to live in'.[36] This was Dickens's view. He wrote to Forster in 1845: 'I am afraid the conventional idea of the picturesque is associated with such misery and degradation that a new picturesque will have to be established as the world goes onward.'[37]

The most direct and unsparing attack on heartless picture-making in Victorian fiction, is that launched by 'Mark Rutherford' in *Catherine Furze* (1893). He begins with a highly detailed account of a labourer's cottage. He then proceeds as follows:

> Miss Diana Eaton, eldest daughter of the Honourable Mr Eaton, had made a little sketch in water-colour of the cottage. It hung in the great drawing-room, and was considered most picturesque.
>
> 'Lovely! What a dear old place!' said the guests.
>
> 'It makes one quite enamoured of the country', exclaimed Lady Fanshawe, one of the most determined diners-out in Mayfair. 'I never look at a scene like that without wishing I could give up London altogether. I am sure I could be content. It would be so charming to get rid of conventionality and be perfectly natural. You really ought to send that drawing to the Academy, Miss Eaton.'
>
> That we should take pleasure in pictures of filthy, ruined hovels, in which health and even virtue are impossible, is a strange sign of the times. It is more than strange; it is an omen and a prophecy that people will go into sham ecstasies over one of these pigstyes so long as it is in a gilt frame; that they will give a thousand guineas for its light and shade—light, forsooth!—or for its Prout-like quality, or for its quality of this, that, and the other, while inside the real stye, at the very moment when the auctioneer knocks down the drawing amidst applause, lies the mother dying from dirt fever; the mother of six children starving and sleeping there—starving, save for the parish allowance, for the snow is on the ground and the father is out of work. (pp. 313–14)

I have devoted a lot of space to the myth of the picturesque cottage, and to the parts played by novelists in its promulgation, interrogation and demystification; and rightly so, for it was through their contributions to what Ford has called 'the cottage controversy'[38] that the bulk of these writers signalled their interest in the idea of the picturesque garden. What they all seem to have appreciated was the immensely important part played by the cottage garden in encouraging and, from one point of view, permitting and legitimating, the practice of picture-making. For without their gardens and their floral façades, many pretty cottages, both in and out of fiction, would have stood out as eyesores, resistant to the pictorializing operations of even the most determined seeker of picturesque beauty. This is a point that Nathaniel Hawthorne made explicit. In his *English Note-Books* (1883), he recorded his impressions of some ancient cottages scattered about a modern villa in a suburb of Liverpool: 'These cottages are in themselves as ugly as possible, resembling a large kind of pigsty; but often, by dint of the verdure on their thatch and the shrubbery clustering about them, they look picturesque.'[39]

At the same time, Victorian writers did not confine either their critical appraisal of the picturesque, or their application of the term itself, to the country cottage garden. This is particularly true of garden writers, though novelists also played a part in extending both the significations of 'picturesque', and the scope of the critique of the picturesque garden which centred principally upon the relations between gardening and painting.

During the first half of the nineteenth century, a number of garden theorists saw the need to re-think these relations. Most believed that too close an identification of the two arts flattered neither. Firstly, they acknowledged the limitations of a picture-based garden aesthetics. Loudon, himself a landscape painter, admitted that 'no comparison between the powers of landscape-painting and those of landscape-gardening can be instituted, that will not evince the superior powers of the former'. The gardener 'may and ought to aim for the highest degrees of beauty which his own imagination, the genius of the place, and the views of the owner, will admit; but let him not proceed with, or hold out to the world, mistaken views of what his art can or cannot perform.'[40] Secondly, most garden theorists objected to the hegemony of the picturesque in practice. An anonymous contributor to the *Quarterly Review* of 1842 complained of the 'encroachments which the natural and picturesque styles have made upon the regular flower gardens'. He castigated, also, the abuse and misapplication of the label itself: 'this unfortunate word "picturesque" has been the ruin of our gardens. Price himself never dreamt of applying it, in its present usage, to the plot of ground immediately surrounding the house. His own words are all along in favour of a formal and artificial character *there* in keeping with the mansion itself.'[41] Complaints about the physical encroachments of the picturesque were not uncommon even in the 1820s. In 1829, George M'Leish wrote: 'Of all the artificial scenery, a flower-garden should be the least disfigured by any kind of ruggedness.'[42]

This unhappy situation had come about, Loudon believed, because too many gardeners had mistakenly assumed that picturesque beauty was the only beauty to be aimed at in the laying out of grounds. In his review of Sawrey Gilpin's *Practical Hints in Landscape-Gardening* (1832)—a book which set out to put into practice the ideas of Price—Loudon wrote: 'There are various other beauties, besides those of the picturesque, which ought to engage the attention of the landscape-gardener; and one of the principal of these is, what may be called the botany of trees and shrubs. . . . Mere picturesque improvement is not enough in these enlightened times: it is necessary to understand that there is such a character of art as the gardenesque, as well as the picturesque.'[43] Elsewhere, he distinguishes the picturesque style, 'as an art of design and taste', from the gardenesque style, 'as an art of culture'.[44]

As a plantsman, Loudon was concerned with the science as well as with the art of gardening. In neglecting science, gardeners who recognized only picturesque styles were behind the times, as well as blind to other sorts of beauty. One such beauty was the beauty of 'convenience'. Loudon appreciated that the picturesque garden, though pleasing to the eye, could be inimical to comfort and use. He was all for the appropriation of gardens to man, and would have endorsed the view of one of his contributors, that 'we must engraft upon our own romantic harshness something that will accord better with the equipment of the interiors of our residences . . .'.[45]

By mid-century, arguments in favour of the plantsman's garden, the regular flower-garden, and the garden of convenience, were largely redundant. Gardens in the gardenesque and architectural styles had been firmly established, and where picturesque irregularity was admitted, it was more often than not reserved for remoter parts of the grounds. Many fictional gardens conform to this pattern.

To complicate matters, by the 1850s, 'picturesque' was being increasingly applied to any garden which pleased the eye of the onlooker. In part, this reflected continued uncertainties over nomenclature. 'Picturesque' was popular because it afforded a label of convenience—exoteric, intersubjective, and connotatively richer than alternative stylistic labels. Moreover, as anxieties abated over the territorial encroachments of the rugged picturesque, and with the repeated affirmation of the principle that *all* gardens are to some degree necessarily artificial, mid-century theorists were able to expose the picturesque/gardenesque opposition as an essentially false dichotomy. As the *Quarterly Review* of 1855 put it: 'The principle of the picturesque, properly understood, should be applied to the arrangement of the most formal garden, not less than to the treatment of the most romantic scenery.' Since all gardens should please the eye, and since there was no place in a beautiful garden for negligence either 'studied or unstudied', the term 'picturesque' could serve 'to denote any kind and every degree of beauty.'[46]

In Victorian fiction it came close to fulfilling this function. Indeed, if novelists as a whole contributed anything really positive to the fate of the 'picturesque' as a signifier, it was in the direction of extending its reverberative range. Well-tended rectory gardens and thoughtfully laid out villa gardens were almost as likely to be lauded for their picturesque attractions as were homely cottage gardens and romantic rural landscapes. In *Lothair*, Disraeli takes the term to its referential limits—and, perhaps, beyond—when he sums up the private garden of Blenheim as 'ornate yet picturesque' (p. 99).

Some novelists extended or canalized the denotations of 'picturesque' in more particular directions. In *In the City of Flowers* (1889), Emma Marshall describes a row of towering fir trees that lead to the old manor of Cruttwell Court. She writes: 'Nothing could be more picturesque than the far-stretching avenue, as the sun pierced the dark plumes of the firs, and shot bright beams of golden light across the drive, at the farther end of which the house was seen' (p. 10). George Eliot's partiality was for 'pretty bits' of landscape. Like a latter-day Scott, Wilkie Collins reserved the term largely, though not exclusively, for old Scottish manors and their grounds: for Mount Morven in *The Evil Genius*, for Swanhaven in *Man and Wife* (1870). He opposes the latter to the 'monotonous' and 'perfectly common-place English scenery' of the 'perfectly common-place English country seat' of Hall Farm (p. 230).

Other novelists 'imported' the picturesque. Both Henry James and George Gissing pushed back their readers' horizons through their scene-setting descriptions of Roman gardens—versions of the picturesque a long way removed from home-bred varieties.

In *Roderick Hudson*, James describes the 'mouldly little garden house', the 'high stemmed pines', and the other features which contributed to the 'magical picturesqueness' of the immense gardens of the Villa Ludovisi (p. 78). He expands upon these impressions in two essays written at about the same time (spring 1874). As the first of these essays suggests, the gardens of the Villa Ludovisi are, for James, impressively picturesque though markedly un-English in their constituent features and in the visual experience they offer.

> The stern old ramparts of Rome form the outer enclosure of the villa, and hence a series of picturesque effects . . . The grounds are laid out in the formal last century manner; but nowhere do the straight black cypresses lead off the gaze into vistas of a more fictive sort of melancholy . . . [Nature leaves you] nothing to do but to lay your head among the anemones at the base of a high-stemmed pine and gaze crestward and skyward along its slanting silvery column.[47]

In a short story entitled 'The Ring Finger', Gissing describes, with greater attention to detail though in very similar terms, the 'varied beauty and picturesqueness' of the garden of the Villa Medici.

> Along the terrace, great pines, leading the gaze upward; and slim trunks of eucalyptus, with leafage flashing white in the sun-glare; amid the green lawns and cropped box hedges, a dreaming palm, winter-touched with yellow. In front, the medieval pleasure-house; behind, the ramparts of the old world's fallen majesty.[48]

There is little textual evidence to suggest that fiction writers recognized, let alone worried over, the incursions of the picturesque—whether territorial or linguistic—about which some garden writers had been so testy. But there are some indications that they sympathized with the Loudonian sentiment that the picturesque garden, as conceived by its eighteenth-century exponents, was not the be-all and end-all in landscape design. For example, it is significant that even the wild and romantic beauty of Armine Park in *Henrietta Temple* could not, apparently, gratify all the needs of its owners, for they take the step of calling in an expert gardener to construct a flower-garden in the vicinity of the house. Trollope and other novelists were, it would seem, in favour of trim gardens about the dwelling place to ensure the functional interconnectivity and the visual harmony of house and grounds. In the novel, *The Belton Estate* (1866), where Trollope does describe a picturesque park in the eighteenth-century vein, the park of Belton Castle, he stresses its resistance to human appropriation: it is lovely to look upon but depressingly unproductive. And when in *Ayala's Angel* (1881) Trollope describes Drumcaller, a picturesque cottage on the side of Loch Ness, it is the discomfort of the place that he emphasizes. It was an 'inconvenient rickety cottage', perched 'on the edge of a ravine, down which rushed a little stream'. 'It was also a beautifully romantic spot.' 'Those who knew the cottage of Drumcaller were apt to say that no man in Scotland had a more picturesque abode, or one more inconvenient' (pp. 169–70).

On the 'evidence' of the language of landscape in Victorian poetry, Pauline Fletcher concludes that there was 'a steady decline in the cult of the picturesque' associated with a decline of interest in mere scenery and a movement away from 'the wilder and more rugged types of romantic scenery' towards 'men and society'.[49] This conclusion is not entirely invalid, for as a cult, the picturesque not only declined in the Victorian period, but was also interrogated from a variety of perspectives. But what Fletcher ignores (possibly because she confines herself almost exclusively to the language of poetry) are the processes by which 'picturesque' became steadily detached from its provenance in an eighteenth-century cult. As 'picturesque' became increasingly drained of its referential specificity and increasingly severed from its association with 'a descriptive vocabulary which predetermines what is to be seen and valued',[50] it acquired an increasingly wide currency and an extension of its range. Far from rejecting 'picturesque' because of its cultish associations, many novelists exploited and enhanced its felicitous connotations, relocated it within the humanized landscape,[51] and applied it, it would seem, to just about any garden for which they hoped to elicit a positive response.

CHAPTER FIVE

Imaginative Literature and Garden Consciousness

In this chapter, I wish to confront the question I have tried to keep in my sights throughout the preceding chapters: in what ways, and to what extent did Victorian novelists and poets influence the thinking of contemporary garden enthusiasts?

The first thing to establish is whether they *tried* to exert an influence, or whether the implication of conscious intent is misleading. The main problem here is deciding what to consider as evidence of persuasive intent. Of potential relevance are the more or less explicit authorial comments on garden theory and practice with which Victorian fiction is peppered. Bulwer Lytton, Trollope, George Eliot, Rhoda Broughton, Charlotte Yonge, George Gissing and many other novelists interrupt the narrative flow or protract descriptions to express opinions on what a garden should or should not be. Many of these observations are, arguably, dispensable interpolations serving no significant textual function. When Trollope lists the features that are *not* found in John Grey's garden, because they are 'beauties of landscape, and do not of their nature belong to a garden', he is not so much presenting the reader with information directly relevant to the object he is describing, as voicing an opinion he expects his readers to share or to consider. The very gratuitousness of the authorial intrusion is indicative of such a purpose.

Fictional characters also proffer opinions on gardens and gardening, usually in exchanges with other fictional characters. But their opinions are generally inadmissible as evidence of persuasive intent since we cannot normally be certain that they reflect the author's attitudes, or that they are meant to affect the attitudes of garden-minded readers. Their intended functions, including those of characterization, may be quite different. The same uncertainties pertain to descriptions of gardens in which the author's views may appear to be either manifest or smuggled in. We can make judgements about the garden styles he or she appears to favour and disfavour; we cannot convert these judgements into declarations of desired attitudinal or behavioural effects.

Perhaps there are some relatively minor exceptions. Mrs Ewing's garden writings for children, whatever their aesthetic merits, are barely disguised exercises in proselytism. The relations between Morris's lectures and essays on gardens, and the gardens he idealizes in his imaginative writings, are unmistakably incestuous. The same can be said of the writings of R. D. Blackmore. And then there are the garden books of Alfred Austin, *The Garden That I Love* (1896), and *In Veronica's Garden* (1897), leisurely discourses on Austin's favourite subject—gardens in general, and his own secluded and informal garden in particular—though they also include poetic interludes, and what *The Times* described as 'genial colloquies'.[1] Though informal in style and confidential in tone, they bristle with forcefully expressed opinions, sufficiently strident to suggest that the author is out to instruct and convert as well as to charm and please.

If there is limited evidence of persuasive intent, there is still less to indicate that imaginative writers were effective in influencing the horticultural practices of their garden-minded readers. (Again, Morris may be the one notable exception.)

For these reasons, it is generally more valid to think in terms of the effects (as opposed to the effectiveness) of fictional descriptions and comments or, better still, perhaps, to shift the focus from a sender-oriented to a receiver-oriented perspective of literary discourse, so as to identify the uses to which garden-minded readers put these descriptions and comments.

Even these approaches present problems, the chief of which is tracing changes or continuities in garden design to the presumed predilections of imaginative writers. In general, we are compelled to speculate on the basis of textual 'evidence' alone. In effect, this means identifying the ideas and precepts available to Victorian garden enthusiasts conversant with contemporary fiction. The ideas that they would have been hard pressed not to have encountered include the following: that the attractiveness of a garden does not normally depend upon its size; that gardens tended by their owners tend to be more delightful than 'gardeners' gardens'; that gardens which appeal only to the eye are inferior to those which engage all the relevant senses; and that old-fashioned gardens possess charms only seldom matched by fashionable modern gardens.

It is likely, also, that poets and novelists did something to arouse their readers' interests in gardens, and that their descriptions and encomiums served to keep alive interest in the plants and gardens squeezed out by the devotees of contemporary fashions. Garden writers frequently plundered literary texts for illustrative and supportive material, though some of their favourite authors—including Shakespeare, Milton, Cowley and Crabbe—were not Victorian. In addition, many garden writers overtly acknowledged the valuable part that imaginative writers played in promoting a love of gardens and gardening. The following panegyric is typical:

> The poets, blessings on them! have done more to awaken a love of nature and of flowers; and to cherish a taste for horticulture, than all the professional horticulturalists.[2]

The implication here—a very important one—seems to be this: that the poet's power to enthuse is based upon resources of power different from but more potent than those of the professional horticulturalist. The poet stimulates by virtue of his ability to reward the reader with imaginatively appealing descriptions, though the reader's sympathetic identification with the poet is also a salient factor. By contrast, the power of the professional gardener is based upon his horticultural expertise, and upon the amateur's acceptance of it. The corollary is that while the writing of the professional horticulturalist has the power to affect the cognitions of garden-minded readers, the poet has the edge when it comes to arousing interests and emotions. If Victorian garden essayists were correct in their assumption that the uses and effects of imaginative 'garden' literature were primarily non-utilitarian and non-instrumental, then it follows that the direct effects of fictional descriptions upon garden practices were likely to have been negligible or non-existent, though they may have fostered a 'taste for horticulture' and heightened what can only, though inadequately, be termed garden-consciousness.

There is a good deal of truth in this—as I hope to show with reference to the uses and effects of Tennyson's 'garden' poetry. But there are also complications. In the first place, Victorian garden writers were less scrupulous than modern literary theorists in distinguishing between fictional gardens and gardens in the 'real' world. Their apparently implicit faith in the mimetic nature of imaginative literature led them to refer to fictional gardens as though they were ontological facts accessible to physical inspection rather than textual constructs. So although they granted that fictional gardens were peculiarly effective in generating interests and feelings, they tended to ascribe these powers simply to the 'fact' that they were more delightful or exemplary versions of the gardens that existed in the physical world.

In the second place, it is conceivable that imaginative 'garden' literature had effects and uses for garden-minded readers comparable to the effects and uses of technical garden literature. It may have provided a fund of practical ideas and models, formed, reinforced or channelled the attitudes and tastes of readers with a calculative and instrumental orientation, in much the same way as did technical garden books and manuals. (As I shall show in the following chapter, there is evidence to suggest that in the latter decades of the nineteenth century, 'garden' poets were accorded much the same status as old garden authorities like Bacon, Gerard, and Parkinson). To assume, for want of concrete evidence to the contrary, that the effects of fictional descriptions were exclusively affective and amorphous may be seriously to underestimate its perceived use value.

In one or two instances, there is sufficient documentary evidence to link a particular garden description with a specific set of attitudinal and/or behavioural changes. Disraeli's description of Corisande's garden in *Lothair* is perhaps the most striking case. As I have already pointed out, the publication of *Lothair* coincided with a tide of change in the gardening world. The reaction against bedding-out and highly formal geometric gardens in the mid-Victorian mode could only have enhanced the perceived attractiveness of Corisande's old-fashioned garden. Many garden writers latched onto Disraeli's description, elevated it to an exemplar, and sometimes alluded to it as though it existed in fact. There are references to it in Robinson's magazine *The Garden*. In an article entitled 'The *Graphic* on Flower Gardening'—another diatribe against the practice of making small suburban gardens 'doleful places' empty between 'crocus time and bedding out'—the unnamed author rues that 'too many . . . of Bacon's favourites are almost confined to old-fashioned gardens like the Lady Corisande's in "Lothair".'[3]

It is remarkable how swiftly Corisande acquired an almost mythical status as the Alcinous of later Victorian fiction. When in 1885 Bright referred to 'her garden of every perfume',[4] he did so in the confidence that her name was a sufficient referent in itself. Even less motivated garden-minded readers sang the praises of her garden. After his first reading of *Lothair*, Thomas Longman wrote to Disraeli:

> . . . permit me to say that the grace and refinement of the concluding chapters has much struck me. The atmosphere of cultivated mind and manner pervades the whole story, and is as delightful, and refreshing, as the air of those charming old gardens full of roses, wallflowers, and sweet peas, that you describe, and not the less because all perfectly natural, though nature appears in her most graceful mode.[5]

Some garden writers went so far as to suggest that Disraeli's description had a direct impact on contemporary horticultural practices. Just two years after the publication of *Lothair*, H. W. Sargent had this to say:

> Though this [the Italian] style still has many advocates, yet the tide has commenced to turn and is slowly rolling back to the good old herbaceous borders of the past. Mr. Disraeli, in his charming description of Corisande's garden, in *Lothair*, has perhaps contributed to this change.[6]

If Disraeli *did* contribute to the change, then it was because *Lothair* attracted plenty of attention, being the first novel by an ex-Prime Minister of Britain.

If any imaginative writer had an impact on garden-minded readers, then it was Tennyson, who made extensive use of the garden as symbol, setting, image and theme. Tennyson himself was an enthusiastic practical gardener, and he took a keen interest in trees and flowers.[7] His own gardens occasioned comments, and many of his visitors recorded their impressions of them;[8] his garden at Farringford was one of the more remarked-on private gardens in Victorian England. Some gardeners held it up as a model of the 'careless order'd garden';[9] George Milner considered it a skilful example of 'the blending of unobtrusive gradations by the artificial with the natural'.[10] Gardens also played an important part in Tennyson's social, personal and imaginative experiences; in turn, his garden-related experiences found their way into his poems.[11] Significantly, Tennyson often imaged poetry and poetic processes in terms of gardens and gardening.[12]

In spite of all this, Tennyson's poetry probably made only a slight impression upon the *ideas* of garden designers and theorists. Unlike, say, Morris, Tennyson did not write prescriptively about gardens; there is no evidence that he ever made fully explicit his idea of what a garden should be. Only in one poem, the early

Amphion, did he allude unmistakably to contemporary horticultural practices.

Nevertheless, Tennyson was widely regarded as 'the most garden-conscious of all Victorian poets',[13] and the one Victorian poet significantly to have heightened garden-consciousness. Esteemed, absorbed, and textually redistributed, not only by technical garden writers but by poets, novelists, and painters, Tennyson was made into the most quoted 'garden' writer of the age. The reasons for which he was quoted suggest the ways in which he affected garden-consciousness.

The notion of garden-consciousness is difficult to define and, in terms of the psychological and imaginative processes involved, hard to pin down. Tennyson's 'garden' poetry, for example, appears to have worked upon receptive readers in subtle ways, slipping easily into their minds, and sometimes resurfacing only in response to specific stimuli. Garden writers were forever testifying to its almost subliminal resonance. For example, when Henry Arthur Bright wrote about spring flowers, the subject brought to his mind the crocus that '"broke like fire" at the foot of the three goddesses, whom poor Oenone saw on Ida'.[14] When the Rev. B. G. Jones wrote a piece on roses, his first thought was Tennyson. His article opens with the following lines:

> The flower ripens in its place
> Ripens, and fades, and falls, and hath no toil
> Fast-rooted in the fruitful soil.[15]

Such were its insinuating effects, that only at moments of reproducing Tennyson's 'garden' poetry were some Victorians conscious ever of having consumed it—and sometimes not even then. Alfred Austin had to have it pointed out to him that his 'favourite phrase' (which also furnished the title for his most successful book) came from two of the best-known lines in the *English Idylls*:

> Not wholly in the busy world, nor quite
> Beyond it, blooms the garden that I love.

Austin comments:

> What an insidious way with it has beautiful verse, creeping without effort, and without observation on one's own part, into one's heart, and dwelling in our memory, like some fair, winsome, indispensable child. Of course I have for years known *The Gardener's Daughter*, yet I was unaware, till

> accurate Veronica reminded me, that the phrase 'The Garden that I love', is thus to be found there. (p. 22)

If the more or less passive assimilation of resonant phrases from Tennyson's poetry intensified garden-mindedness, the more active uses to which it was put directed and structured it. Garden-conscious Victorians were able to use it to articulate their own experiences and states of mind—either those directly connected with gardens, or those which Tennyson poetically structured in garden terms. As an example, consider the famous 'Farewell to Somersby' section of *In Memoriam* (CI), in which Tennyson's sense of time passing, and his feeling of regret and finally of resignation, are registered by a predominantly autumnal garden landscape. Here are stanzas one, two and five:

> Unwatched, the garden bough shall sway,
> The tender blossoms flutter down,
> Unloved, that beech will gather brown,
> This maple burn itself away;
>
> Unloved, the sun-flower, shining fair,
> Ray round with flames her dusk of seed,
> And many a rose-carnation feed
> With summer spice the humming air; . .
>
> Till from the garden and the wild
> A fresh association blow,
> And year by year the landscape grow
> Familiar to the stranger's child. (*TP*, p. 954)

Leaving Somersby 'is not just a matter of leaving home, but also a separation of the poet's thoughts and feelings from the familiar landscape with which he associated them.'[16] Each of the first four stanzas begins with a word which emphasizes separation: 'Unwatched', 'Unloved', 'Unloved', 'Uncared for'. In the rest of the description, the poet focuses upon the natural forms of the garden he has lovingly observed and which he recalls wistfully in careful, botanical terminology.

Within a few years of the publication of *In Memoriam*, Section CI became, in effect, the standard poetic structure through which to articulate the experience of parting from a garden of familiar and pleasing associations. Elizabeth Gaskell borrowed it for Margaret Hale's farewell to Helstone in Chapter 6 of *North and South*. George William Curtis chose it for his memorial to the great American garden writer, A. J. Downing.[17]

That Tennyson was seen as the pre-eminent garden poet of the age is evident from the uses to which he was put by other writers. Some of the garden scenes and garden-related experiences he wrote about acquired an almost mythical or archetypal status. For example, *Audley Court* became almost a by-word for picnicking in the grounds of an untenanted country house. In Tennyson's poem, the lawn beside the porter's lodge of the abandoned Audley Court provided the setting for the singing contest between Francis Hale and the narrator. When Charlotte M. Yonge, in *The Pillars of the House* (1893), came to relate the episode in which the poor clergyman, Mr Underwood, brought his frail wife and many children from the dirty town of Bexley to the 'extensive plantations and exquisite vistas' of the untenanted Centry Park, she explicitly acknowledged her frame of reference. The relevant chapter (2) is headed 'The Picnic' and opens with the following lines from *Audley Court*:

> There, on a slope of orchard, Francis laid
> A damask napkin wrought with horse and hound,
> Brought out a dusky loaf that smelt of home,
> And, half cut-down, a pasty costly-made,
> Where quail and pigeon, lark and leveret lay,
> Like fossils of the rock, with golden yolks
> Imbedded and injellied; last, with these,
> A flask of damask of cider from his father's vats,
> Prime, what I knew.

When Victorian writers sought an image of the enclosed garden, a garden to which access was strictly controlled, it was to the gardens of the women's college in *The Princess* that they sometimes turned. There is an episode in Emma Marshall's novel, *In the City of Flowers*, in which a young man is asked to join some ladies in the garden of a country house. The man replies:

> I did not know whether I might set my foot on this enchanted ground. It is, I know, a forbidden territory, like the garden of Princess Ida. (p. 12)

The gardens of Ida's college were associated not only with the principle of exclusion, but also with poetry, romance, and the delightful landscape experience of the male intruders. It is these associations that Henry James evokes in *Roderick Hudson*. On the verge of his departure for Italy, Roderick breaks out in a snatch of song from *The Princess*, which Rowland Mallet later echoes when his experience of landscape from the Belvedere in the garden of the Villa Ludovisi in Rome leads him to declare that it 'looked like the prospect from a castle turret in a fairy tale' (p. 79).

The least attractive garden that Tennyson ever described was probably also the most prototypically influential: the monotonous, rotting, wasteland garden of Mariana's moated grange. To account for this we need to consider its functions within the text as well as its details. In contrast to, say, the rose-garden in *The Gardener's Daughter*, or the cottage gardens in *Aylmer's Field*, the garden in *Mariana* is, as a garden or a verbal picture of a garden, intrinsically uninteresting. The 'glooming flats', the 'blackened waters' and 'blackest moss', the pear-tree unhinged from the gable-wall, and the single poplar, 'all silver-green with gnarled bark', are either an embodiment or a secretion of the perceptually overwhelming consciousness of the maiden. 'All the landscape images . . . are designed to lead us into a state of consciousness; they are not there for their own sakes.'[18]

That *Mariana* is a superb example of what John Stuart Mill called Tennyson's 'power of *creating* scenery, in keeping with some state of human feeling; so fitted to it as to be the embodied symbol of it',[19] helps to explain why Mariana's garden became the master script for many other fictional gardens. Dickens, who read and enjoyed Tennyson's poetry, was fascinated by the mood-scape garden of the blighted bride.[20] Harry Stone suggests that the rank and neglected garden of Miss Havisham's Satis House has a precursor in 'The Bride's Chamber'. The moss was allowed 'to accumulate on the untrimmed fruit-trees in the red-walled garden, the weeds to over-run its green and yellow walls'.[21] There is also the description of the red-brick mansion on the outskirts of the small market town where Scrooge had gone to school as a boy, of which 'the whole impression and half the details, come from Tennyson's "Mariana"'.[22] Later anti-garden or wasteland garden poems—Swinburne's *A Forsaken Garden*, for example—may also owe something to *Mariana*.

Tennyson's poem served not only as a model for rotting garden poems, but also as a negative model for delightfully abundant and visually pleasing gardens. This has something to do with Tennyson's method of description.[23] The subject matter is also important, for the details of Mariana's garden can function as objective correlatives of her emotional and spiritual condition only because they negate, distort and parody the myths and ideals which constitute the poem's implicit frames of reference. The primary frame of reference is the pastoral myth of a Golden Age. One can find in *Mariana* 'bitterly distorted' references to beauty, order and hope, an inversion of the 'usual image of comedy and the pastoral'. The opening lines 'give a parody of beauty that is ordered and controlled.... The image of man as master of nature's beauty is thrown against that of man as victim of nature's anarchy.'[24]

The parodic pastoral landscape is cognate with another negated paradigm: the country house and garden estate as a symbol of historical continuity, order and community. In *Mariana*, the historical continuity function of the country house is subverted by the substitution of the normative model of temporal processes—gradual, 'natural', organic—with one in which all distinctions between past and present are grotesquely collapsed. Similarly, Mariana's isolation and social dislocation provide a mocking counter-symbol to the social collectivity function of the country house, in which ordinary social affairs are transformed into ritual enactments of community.

Fictional descriptions which seem to 'derive' from *Mariana* in topic and technique reaffirm the ideals that Tennyson's poem negatively transforms. An example is Dickens's account of Mr Boythorn's garden in Chapter 18 of *Bleak House*, where the emphasis is upon venerable 'vegetable treasury'. Like Mariana's garden, Mr Boythorn's has a wall in which are lodged disused nails and scraps of list. But these are the products, not of unnatural corrosion and stagnation, but of 'ripening influence', and 'it was easy to fancy that they had mellowed with the changing seasons and that they had rusted and decayed according to the common fate' (p. 260). Morris's 'Golden Wings' probably also 'derives' from *Mariana*. Morris's poem opens with a description of an enclosed medieval garden, old, colourful and abundant, the converse of Mariana's garden, and the perfect synecdoche of an apparently organic and stable community. But by the end of the poem it has suffered the same terrible fate as the castle community. Morris's description of its rankness and decay hints strongly at the textual prototype he may have had in mind.

Tennyson's attention to details, so evident in his description of Mariana's house and garden, is a characteristic of his garden poetry in general, and one of the reasons he was so frequently quoted by contemporary garden writers to illustrate or support the points they made. The author of an unsigned article in *The Floral World* (1867) observes that some of 'our hardiest and cheapest trees and shrubs . . . die gloriously . . . to justify that sublime passage in "In Memoriam", where he speaks of

—Autumn laying here and there
A fiery finger on the leaves'.[25]

Tennyson's acuity as a botanical observer made it possible for Ruskin to take snatches from Tennyson's poetry to illustrate his own observations in *Proserpina*. For instance, in his discussion of the thorn, Ruskin borrows the following lines from the 'Ode on the Death of the Duke of Wellington':

Thou shalt see the stubborn thistle bursting
Into glossy purples, which out redden
All voluptuous garden roses. (*RW*, XXV, 295)

Having in him 'the ingredients of both landscape painter and field naturalist',[26] Tennyson was in a peculiarly strong position to sensitize the perceptions of his readers to details of the natural world. The experience of Mr Holbrook, the 'Old Bachelor' in Gaskell's *Cranford*, who confessed that though he had lived all his life in the country he had not realized that ash buds were black till 'this young man [Tennyson] comes and tells me' (p. 42), could not have been unique.

Because he observes closely, describes carefully, and, to use Ian Fletcher's nice phrase, 'anxiously botanizes',[27] Tennyson was (and is) compared with the Pre-Raphaelites. In 1870 Karl von Elze wrote:

> Mr Tennyson's Nature differs from Byron's as a flower-piece by Von Huysum, or an English Landscape by Creswick differs from a Salvator Rosa or a Caspar Poussin. In the elaborate minuteness of his finish he may be compared to the painters of the pre-Raphaelite school, who . . . convert their backgrounds into foregrounds, and make you look more at the roses and apple-blossoms than at the damsels who are embowered in them.[28]

Tennyson's foregrounding technique was appreciated by his nature- and garden-loving readers:

> Tennyson, like Millais in his Pre-Raphaelite phase, rewarded his public with an attention to natural detail that was almost biological. It was what the middle-class public demanded. They themselves, only half a century ago, had belonged to the countryside, and in their urban world of exile, they

> wanted reminders of the imaginary demi-paradise. In faultless images, Tennyson provided them.[29]

Tennyson's garden poetry furnished artists no less than writers with subjects, techniques, and frames of reference for their own 'picturesque delineation of objects'. Millais's *Mariana*, in which the garden encroaches threateningly upon the casement of the moated grange, is possibly the best-known example. The swirling, lashing floral forms depicted in Burne-Jones's *Briar Rose* series of pictures, produced between 1870–90, recall passages from the 'Sleeping Princess' section of Tennyson's *The Day-Dream*, 'a poem that Burne-Jones would certainly have known, as it was included in Moxon's illustrated edition of Tennyson's poems published in 1857'.[30]

A single line from a Tennyson poem could offer inspiration and the tag for a 'garden' painting. When Sir John William Inchbold exhibited his *Mid-Spring* at the Royal Academy in 1856 he accompanied it with a one-line quote from Tennyson: 'You scarce can see the grass for flowers.'[31]

While Victorian artists drew inspiration from Tennyson's garden poetry, garden theorists drew encouragement from it. Two of the most prestigious and prolific garden writers, Shirley Hibberd and William Robinson, found in Tennyson's poetry what they were looking for and, more importantly perhaps, an absence of what they were not looking for. What they were not looking for was the poetic celebration of the bedding system. Fortunately for them, they didn't find it; they found, instead, descriptions of old-fashioned, traditional flowers disposed in visually appealing arrangements. There is surely significance in the fact that Hibberd opened his 'Introduction' to *The Amateur's Flower Garden* by quoting the famous 'Maud has a garden of roses' stanza of *Maud* (in which two other long-established flowers, lilies and passion-flowers, also figure), and then promptly proceeded to complain of the 'constantly increasing tendency to superficial glare and glitter in garden embellishment, to the neglect of more solid features that make a garden interesting and attractive . . . all the year round.'[32] Like Hibberd, Robinson claimed Tennyson as an ally in the battle against bedding-out. In *The Wild Garden*, Robinson quoted four lines from *Amphion* which, he claimed, articulated a widely-shared opinion that 'a pretty plant in the wild state is more attractive than any garden denizen:

Better to me the meanest weed
That blows upon its mountain,
The vilest herb that runs to seed
Beside its native fountain.'[33]

Tennyson was probably the chief, but by no means the only, Victorian imaginative writer to be put to illustrative and supportive uses by contemporary garden theorists and enthusiasts. These uses seem to suggest that novelists and poets most potently influenced garden-enthusiasts, if often unwittingly, in two major directions: first, in reflecting and promoting their garden-mindedness; second, in preserving or keeping alive an interest in those qualities and features of gardens eclipsed by the more prominent contemporary fads and practices. In the light of the evidence available, it is possible only to conclude that the direct impact of imaginative literature on actual garden practices was generally negligible, beyond accurate measurement, or arguable only in specific instances.

PART TWO

CHAPTER SIX

Floral Codes

Victorian Britain was characterized by industrial and commercial expansion, and by an unprecedented rate of urban development. In spite of, and partly because of, these processes, a great many Victorians, including many imaginative writers, were flower-oriented. More people than ever before spent their leisure time growing and displaying plants. Developments in plant breeding, together with the influx of imported exotics, ensured the availability of an unprecedented variety of plant materials. Advances in glass-house engineering and the repeal of the tax on glass (in 1845) made it possible to construct more efficient greenhouses and hot-houses, which in turn permitted or encouraged the production of huge quantities of plants for bedding-out.

Quantitative measures of the Victorian flower boom are less interesting and less significant than the qualitative dimensions of what might be called the Victorian flower culture. Indeed, the emphasis on numbers—of plants, and of plant enthusiasts—distracts from the complexity, diversity, and fragmentation of that culture. Many Victorians were flower-minded, but flower-mindedness and flowers themselves meant different things to different people.

Percipient observers commented upon this heterogeneity. Some, like John Ruskin and Juliana Ewing, fashioned their observations of the disparate ways of knowing and relating to plants into evaluative classifications of flower enthusiasts. Ruskin's is rather depressing. In *Frondes Agrestes* (1874) he dilates on the thought that 'flowers seem intended for the solace of humanity'. Then he ponders upon the actual state of things:

> Yet few people really care about flowers. Many, indeed, are fond of finding a new shape of blossom, caring for it as a child cares about a Kaleidoscope. Many, also, like a fair service of flowers in the greenhouse, as a fair service of plate on the table. Many are scientifically interested in them, though even these in their nomenclature, rather than the flowers; and a few enjoy their gardens. . . . But, the blossoming time of the year being principally spring, I perceive it to be the mind of most people, during that period, to stay in the town. (*RW*, VII, 115–16)

Mrs Ewing's classification, though addressed to children, is a more elaborate version of Ruskin's. She identifies four types: those who 'like to have a garden . . . and like to see it gay and tidy, but who don't know one flower from the next'; scientists 'acquainted with botany and learned in horticulture' for whom 'every garden is a botanical garden'; those who 'fully appreciate the beauty and scent of flowers' but 'who can't abide to handle a fork or meddle with mother earth'; and those who, like herself, 'love not only the lore of flowers, and the fragrance of them, and the growing of them, and the picking of them, and the arranging of them, but also inherit from Father Adam a natural relish for tilling the ground from whence they were taken and to which they shall return'.[1]

All of these types are represented in Victorian imaginative literature and, broadly speaking, each has a value equivalent to that which Ewing gives it. So, for example, fictional gardeners who cherish flowers for their own sakes tend to be more positively and warmly evaluated than those who look upon plants merely as botanical specimens. In one respect, however, the literary representation of flower enthusiasts corresponds neither to Ruskin's nor Ewing's breakdown of types. Neither of these writers gives any indication of relative numbers. By contrast, in contemporary fiction, scientifically-interested flower enthusiasts are greatly outnumbered by those whose interests lie elsewhere. Thus, imaginative literature tends to lead away from rather than towards Ruskin's conclusion that 'few people really care about flowers'.

Nonetheless, Ruskin, Ewing, and the majority of imaginative writers were attitudinally at one, especially with regard to the scientifically-inclined enthusiast—who fares rather badly all round. Ruskin is not emphatically deprecatory in the passage quoted above; but elsewhere he speaks of the 'great difference between the botanist's knowledge of plants, and the great poet's or painter's knowledge of them. The one notes their distinctions for the sake of swelling his herbarium, the other, that he may render them vehicles of expression and emotion.'[2]

As a rule, the erudite botanists of Victorian fiction are minor characters whose proclivities are damned rather by faint praise than by explicit criticism. They are given a negative stress by the functions they serve—many are foils to genuine or ingenuous flower-lovers—and by the arcane codes in which they indulge. For example, in *Wives and Daughters*, Molly Gibson's innocent response to the flowers in the conservatory of Cumnor Towers forms a contrast to Lady Agnes's 'more scientific taste'. Lady Agnes 'expatiated on the rarity of this plant, and the mode of cultivation required by that, till Molly began to feel very tired and then very faint' (p. 45). Similarly, in *Heartsease*, Violet's delight at the flowers in the Martindale gardens is opposed to the chilly insouciance of the floriculturally knowledgeable Theodora.

At the opposite pole to the scientific gardener is the 'genuine' flower-lover. He grows his own plants—for pleasure rather than profit—and develops a close attachment to them. He cares little for mere display, still less for change for the sake of change. His art is one of imagination, not one of imitation or 'improvement', though he never forgets his partnership with nature. He cares more for sentiment than for professional expertise, more for simplicity than for sophistication, more for variety than for uniformity.

A further hallmark of the genuine flower-lover is his ability to make things grow without recourse to modern 'improving' or forcing practices. His primary skills are intuitive or acquired informally from grassroots experience, as it were, rather than received from books or formal instruction. Like the titular hero of Tennyson's *Amphion*, who moved nature at his pleasure, and 'left a small plantation' 'wherever he sat down and sung', there is something almost magical about his powers. The dejected speaker of Tennyson's poem laments that modern horticulturalists have lost this magic. They depend instead upon knowledge culled from horticultural manuals, which is both a symptom of and a response to living in a 'brassy age' in which conditions are unpropitious for any kind of creative activity. As Tennyson's speaker makes plain, book learning is no substitute for native genius:

> But what is that I hear? a sound
> Like sleepy counsel pleading;
> O Lord!—'tis in my neighbour's ground,
> The modern Muses reading.
> They read Botanic Treatises,
> And works on Gardening through there,
> And Methods of transplanting trees
> To look as if they grew there.

The withered Misses! how they prose
O'er books of travelled seamen,
And show you slips of all that grows
From England to Van Diemen.
They read in arbours clipt and cut,
And alleys, faded places,
By squares of tropic summer shut
And warmed in crystal cases.

But these, though fed with careful dirt,
Are neither green nor sappy;
Half-conscious of the garden-squirt,
The spindlings look unhappy.
Better to me the meanest weed
That blows upon its mountain,
The vilest herb that runs to seed
Beside its native fountain. (*TP*, p. 687)

The 'natural' gardeners in Victorian literature are conspicuously more successful than the 'withered Misses'. Some are expert botanists who have managed to retain a fruitful and innocent rapport with nature. Eugene Aram is one, as evidenced by his capacity to instil in others a love of gardening and flowers. Another is Glastonbury, the multi-talented scholar in Disraeli's *Henrietta Temple*, whom the Armines invite to construct for them a rich and beautiful flower-garden. We are told that 'under his auspices the garden of the fair Constance soon flourished' (p. 19), and he is frequently pictured in the company of his beloved plants.

Other genuine flower-lovers are more firmly placed, both socially and within the Victorian horticultural fraternity. For example, Sergeant Cuff in Wilkie Collins's *The Moonstone* (1868) is anything but a Bohemian scholar. He is a professional man who grows flowers to gratify the needs which his occupation cannot fulfil. But where roses are concerned, he combines a prosaic concern for practicalities and a high level of erudition with a touching, almost childlike affection for the flower that blooms everywhere in his own cottage garden. This mixture of pragmatism, science, and honest sentiment comes out strongly in the following passage:

> 'Ah, you've got the right exposure here to the south and south-west', says the Sergeant, with a wag of his grizzled head, and a streak of pleasure in his melancholy voice. 'This is the shape for a rosery—nothing like a circle set in a square. Yes, yes; with walks between all the beds. But they oughtn't to be gravel walks like these. Grass, Mr Gardener—grass walks between your roses; gravel's too hard for them. That's a sweet pretty bed of white roses and blush roses. They also mix well together, don't they? Here's the white musk rose, Mr. Betteredge—our old English rose holding up its head along with the best and the newest of them. Pretty dear!' says the Sergeant, fondling the Musk Rose with his lanky fingers, and speaking to it as if he was speaking to a child. (p. 95)

Although there are other Sergeant Cuffs in Victorian literature—other broadly middle-class characters for whom a scientific or improver's interest in plants is perfectly compatible with a personal attachment to them—the majority of 'genuine' flower-lovers are humble farmers and country cottagers. Some are in a position to eschew modern horticultural practices; many country labourers, as opposed to the middle-class occupants of country cottages, are not. The rural labourer may grow flowers for love, or from a spirit of poetic communion with nature; this is the explanation implied in many cottage garden descriptions. But some have no choice. Lacking the means and the education to garden scientifically, or with the self-conscious sophistication of the better-off, they either garden for love, or not at all.

This is something like the case with Meredith's Mrs Fleming in *Rhoda Fleming*. The wife of an indigent Kentish farmer, she pours all her energies into the flower-garden of which she has sole charge. Her floral displays are famed, and she has 'gained a prize at a flower show for one of her dahlias'. She spends money on her garden, but it is money which her husband can ill afford. Her economic resources are clearly limited, and the effects of her 'unrivalled garden' are achieved in spite of rather than because of them. What she brings to her gardening activities, and what places her poles apart from the pragmatic and profit-minded horticulturalist, is an irrepressible imaginative vitality. Her garden 'gave vivid sign of youth'. 'The joy of her love for it was written on its lustrous beds as poets write. She had the poetic passion for flowers' (p. 2).

Of all the genuine flower-lovers in Victorian literature, none is more 'natural' than farmer Iden in Richard Jefferies's *Amaryllis at the Fair*. To scrape a living he plants potatoes—methodically, but with tender solicitude: 'had he been planting his own children he could not have been more careful' (p. 203). For *farmer* Iden, nature is the combatant with whom he has constantly to struggle. For Iden the gardener, nature offers a spiritual partnership, the issue of which is marvellous prodigality:

> Flowers, and trees, and grass seemed to spring up wherever Iden set down his foot: fruit and flowers fell from the air down upon him. It was his genius to make things grow—like sunshine and shower; a sort of Pan, a half-god of leaves and boughs, and reeds and streams, a sort of Nature in human shape, moving about and sowing Plenty and Beauty. (p. 309)

The avatar of Pan (or Amphion), Iden is the antithesis of the sophisticated Victorian horticulturalist. His language declares his lineage. He spoke of garden products 'with a simplicity of language that reminded you of Bacon and his philosophy of the Elizabethan Age.'

'Iden in a way certainly had a tinge of the Baconian culture, naturally, and not from any study of that author, whose books he had never seen. The great Bacon was, in fact, a man of orchard and garden, and gathered his ideas from the fields' (p. 220).

It is not hard to see why Jefferies should have emphasized Iden's intuitive, mystical, experiential kind of competence. Jefferies spurned book learning, and his view of Nature as a vital force approximated to the Wordsworthian view. If his field-level focus on man in nature, and his repudiation of urban and urbane culture set him apart from many other Victorian writers, he was not alone in celebrating a floricultural competence based not upon textual study, but upon direct experience and imaginative engagement. That this may have been the only kind of competence possible for the educationally and economically disadvantaged rural labourer appears not to have disturbed the scores of minor writers who applauded the cottager's knowledge of plants. Typical of this sentimental approval are the following stanzas from Mary Howitt's mid-century poem, *The Poor Man's Garden*:

> He knows where grow his wall-flowers,
> And when they will be out;
> His moss-rose, and convolvulus
> That twines his poles about.

He knows his red sweet-William;
  And the stocks that cost him dear,—
That well-set row of crimson stocks,—
  For he bought the seed last year.

And there, before the little bench,
  O'er shadowed by the bower
Grow southern-wood and lemon thyme,
  Sweet-pea and gilliflower;

And pink and clove-carnations,
  Rich scented, side by side;
And at each end a hollyhock,
  With an edge of London-pride.[3]

Between the extremes of the scientific gardener and the genuine lover of plants, there are various grades of flower-enthusiasts. Towards one group of floricultural 'improvers', imaginative and garden writers alike were generally sympathetic. These were the amateur cultivators, who spent what time and money they had on bringing their favourite flowers (often the 'old favourites') to the highest states of perfection.

According to contemporary observers, many of the most devoted amateur flower-specialists were rural labourers and factory workers rather than affluent middle- or upper-class gardeners.[4] Late in the century, Alfred Austin picks out for special commendation the exhibits of a railway mechanic whose particular pride is a giant *Echeveria* of exceptionally hearty growth.[5]

But in Victorian fiction, the majority of amateur flower-specialists are well-to-do ladies. The works of Charlotte Yonge provide a number of examples. In the opening pages of *The Heir of Redclyffe* (1853), she captures the excitement of Amy Edmonstone who, having cultivated a camellia, 'a perfect blossom, so pure a white, and so regular!' declares herself 'proud of having beaten mamma and all the gardeners' (p. 2). There are also examples in Thackeray's novels, including Madame de Florac in *The Newcomes* (1855), who 'won prizes at the Newcome flower and fruit shows' (p. 626).

Some garden writers had doubts about flower shows, fearing that amateurs might neglect their gardens in order to secure prizes and reputations with their choicest specimens. There is little suggestion of this in Victorian fiction. Mrs Fleming's garden is a joy to behold; Madame de Florac's is 'pretty'. And Amy Edmonstone's solicitude for flower-show exhibits does not lessen her respect for 'undressed' flowers. On taking cuttings of a wild rose to transplant at Hollywell House, she says: 'I don't know that the grand roses will be equal to these purple shoots and blushing buds with long whiskers' (p. 132).

The amateur flower-specialist was one thing; the professional horticulturalist or floriculturalist, driven by commercial imperatives and/or a preoccupying concern for botanical 'progress', was another. In imaginative literature, the latter are conspicuous by their relative absence, as are the institutional infrastructures by which they were supported. Where professional 'improvers' are given textual space they are, with few exceptions, coolly received. In Trollope's *Orley Farm*, for example, the narrator informs us that about the 'commodious, irregular, picturesque, and straggling' Orley Farm stand ancient fruit trees, 'large, straggling trees, such as do not delight the eyes of modern gardeners; but they produced fruit by the bushel, very sweet to the palate, though probably not so perfectly round, and large, and handsome as those which the horticultural skill of the present day requires' (II, 7; 8). Though Trollope does not explicitly condemn horticultural authorities for setting exacting critical standards, he hints very strongly that their standards are arbitrary, and vitiated by the positivistic assumption that bigger necessarily means better. Perhaps he had in mind the horticultural societies. But more likely Trollope was thinking of what R. D. Blackmore was later to call the [commercial] 'middle-men'. In a letter to *The Times* (22 Sept. 1894) Blackmore wrote: 'These [middle-men] know little concerning the merits of this or that variety, but call for something large and showy, and, above all, something whose name they know.'

Needless to say, the flower-consciousness of the Victorians did not develop spontaneously. Rather, it was generated, often purposively, by a variety of institutions, practices and texts. Since different institutions tended to channel flower-consciousness in different directions, the nature of an individual's interest in flowers was in part determined by the sources of influence to which he was predominantly exposed. Nursery firms and other commercial enterprises, some of substantial capital investment, endeavoured to extend the range of floral interests and, in particular, to stimulate interest in what was novel and 'improved'. The horticultural press, the proliferation of which is a principal fact of Victorian garden history, tended also to stress the flower-consciousness of the progress-minded plantsman. This tendency was particularly prominent in the middle decades of the century, though throughout the period, technical garden literature was multifarious and by no means exclusively technical in content. In magazines specifically directed at gardeners, and more so in general interest magazines as different as *Blackwood's*, *The Quarterly Review*, *The Leisure Hour*, and *The Quiver*, articles on the dynamics of contemporary floriculture included or nestled among philosophical morsels concerning the moral and poetic qualities of plants. At the very least, these pieces suggested alternative notions of flower-consciousness to those predicated upon the 'science' of improvement.

For many Victorians, the most compelling of these alternatives issued from religious institutions and from particular Christian writers. Through sermons on flowers, printed tracts on the same themes, and books on the language of flowers imbued with Christian imagery, religious writers promoted a floral ideology based upon an emblematic interpretation of nature, and encouraged their readers to dwell upon the eternal verities of flowers as opposed to their strictly botanical properties or merely quotidian uses.

The belief that flowers are vehicles for transcendent truths is expressed by one of Trollope's more effusive female characters, Ugolina in *The Three Clerks* (1858). Responding enthusiastically to the flowers on display in Chiswick Gardens, she professes that 'they convey to me the purest and most direct essence of that heavenly power of production which is the sweetest evidence which Jehovah gives us of his presence. . . . They are the bright stars of his handiwork . . . and if our dim eyes could read them aright, they would whisper to us the secret of his love' (p. 302).

From this point of view, the ability to make sense of the meanings of flowers ought in principle to be exoteric and widespread, since plant meanings could be thought to be transparent to anyone with the necessary set of commonly held religious convictions. And, indeed, Victorian garden literature bristles with statements proclaiming the transparency and universality of floral codes. The following are typical: 'Flowers speak a universal language, and they need no introduction beyond their loveliness';[6] '"the language of flowers" has no need to be taught in books; it is understood in all lands, by sage and savage, bound and free'.[7]

What these statements deny or fail to acknowledge is the cultural determination of floral codes. If, as many Victorians believed, flowers have collective, pre-established significations by virtue of their divine ontogenesis, then these are always smothered by more local, historically specific meanings. Certainly within the Victorian cultural context, flowers and groups of flowers acquired, to a greater or lesser extent, recognized significations as various as the culture from which they emerged.

The most stable, fixed, and formalized of these codes was floriography, or the 'language of flowers' proper, in which flowers were conceived as 'emblems of thoughts and sentiments ... invested with a language of their own'.[8] Middle-class Victorians took great delight in reviving the language of flowers, as the numerous flower books published in the period testify. Each book has the same basic format: a list of plant names arranged alphabetically and, next to each plant name, the sentiments customarily assigned to it. The floral alphabet is often followed by a section on the poetry of flowers, and/or prefaced by an account of the rules of grammar governing the language of flowers. According to Robert Tyas: 'The first rule in the language of flowers is, that a flower, presented in an upright position, expresses a thought; to express the opposite of that thought it suffices to let the flower hang down reversed.'[9]

In spite of its extensive vocabulary and rather formidable syntax, there was every incentive for the educated Victorian to learn the language of flowers. Its users could exchange messages without the use of words, and without, moreover, the degree of explicit commitment involved in the making of verbal propositions. This must have been of particular advantage to those constrained by upbringing and bourgeois social conventions from disclosing their feelings more openly. (Eric Maple has noted that Victorian Valentine cards often carried a 'secret' message in the form of a prominently depicted posy of flowers.[10]) Furthermore, the language of flowers was respectable, and conferred status and respectability upon those conversant with it. An 'interest in flower language lent an air of modest feminine erudition to the lady gardener, at the same time allowing her to mingle dreams of romance with more prosaic gardening concerns'.[11] A competence in floriography was considered a prestigious social accomplishment which accentuated the femininity of the woman and revealed the virtue in the man. If a man is blind to beautiful landscapes, suggested Praed's 'A Letter of Advice' in 1828,

> If he knows not the language of flowers,
> My own Araminta, say 'No!'[12]

The enormous popularity of the language of flowers derived

largely from two apparently quite different tendencies. One was an escapist impulse; floriography was a cultivated parlour game which afforded a diversion from the ugliness of urban life and the tedium of humdrum social routines. It was allied to the widespread use of flowers for decoration, ornamentation, and consolation, by means of which the countryside was imported indoors, and to the many hundreds of sentimental flower poems scattered throughout the popular magazines of the period. In spirit it was playful rather than serious. Its heirs were the book illustrations of Kate Greenaway in the 1870s and 1880s—which Ruskin praised for restoring the elements of fantasy and beauty fast disappearing from industrial England—and of Walter Crane in the 1880s and 1890s, in which plant names are interpreted freely and imaginatively.

The other tendency was emblematic and typological. As an expression of the desire to discover the deeper meanings of plants, the enthusiasm for the language of flowers was itself an expression of the impulse to revive a symbolic world picture. The impetus came from various quarters. Religious writers encouraged the emblematic interpretation of nature for the lessons it imparted to mankind. The Flower Sermons preached by the Rev. W. M. Whittemore and others—to which all the worshippers carried flowers—appear to have been simplified versions of the Tractarian theory of 'vertical correspondences'. This was the theory that 'any object in nature must have a concealed affinity with every other object in nature, lateral correspondence, because all objects form part of the vertical correspondence between nature and God'.[13] It was derived by Keble (in *The Christian Year* (1827)) from the world-model of living emblems promulgated in seventeenth-century devotional writings—themselves a rich source of flower symbols.

Ruskin and some of the Pre-Raphaelites also embarked on the search for the deeper symbolic meanings of flowers. That they found such meanings is suggested by the typological interpretations that Holman Hunt and others produced for pictures, and by numerous statements and descriptions of Ruskin's, ranging from the emphatically unambiguous ('The grass and flowers are types') in *Modern Painters IV* to the more extended explorations in *Proserpina* (1875–6). Ruskin's starting point was close observation and a precise recording of natural details. In this sense, his method, like that of Hunt and Millais, and like the approach often taken by Tennyson and George Eliot, was 'scientific'. This has been taken as evidence of a reconciliation of the 'new scientific interests of the nineteenth century and the outmoded concept of types'.[14] But Ruskin's frame of reference was quite different from and irreconcilably opposed to that of the empirical scientist. His perception was always informed by a moral and imaginative vision and his 'scientific method inclines to devotion rather than analysis'.[15] His contempt for the 'vile industries and vicious curiosities of modern science' (*RW*, XXV, 56), his refusal to countenance investigations into the reproductive functions of plants, his distrust of and infrequent references to contemporary botanical 'authorities', and his antipathy to the Darwinian idea that nature was in a state of constant flux, all point to his fundamental opposition to the mechanistic science of his day.

Virtually every Victorian who sought an emblematic interpretation of flowers believed in the abiding and immutable truths expressed by the natural forms, and struggled to tease out the moral significance of every detail of a plant's form. They differed principally in terms of their willingness and ability to discover meanings outside a strictly biblical framework. Ruskin's vision, particularly in *Proserpina*, was shaped by art and mythology as well as by the Bible, and the typologies of artists were generally more inventive and subjective than those of religious writers. Mrs Loudon's 1848 account of Christ's Passion as displayed by the Blue Passion Flower (*Passiflora Caerulea*) is a good example of an emblematic reading within a conventional scriptural framework:

> The leaf they expound to be the spear which pierced His side; the twined threads of red and white which form the crown of the flower were supposed the symbol of the lashes of the whip tinged with blood; the fire encircling stamens the crown of thorns; the pistils the column to which our Lord was bound; the three divisions of the stigma the three nails used in the crucifixion.[16]

The Victorians' enthusiasm for the language of flowers is evident in contemporary literature. Poems were dedicated to it, including Thomas Hood's 'The Language of Flowers'[17] and Leigh Hunt's 'Love-Letters Made of Flowers'.[18] It is explicitly mentioned in a number of literary texts[19] and, more importantly, it illuminates many others. A number of scholars have argued that it contributes to the seemingly cryptogrammatic design of Browning's *Pippa Passes*.[20] Floral alphabets have been shown to provide the key to many of Christina Rossetti's poems.[21] Tennyson's floral oppositions, and his use of the flower symbolism of classical mythology, have long been recognized as more than merely decorative in function. In addition, there are the countless moments in Victorian fiction where characters give and receive a gift of flowers—selected, perhaps, for their symbolic values. One of M. E. Braddon's heroines receives a gift of blue violets—flowers customarily associated with faithfulness. The donor calls it a 'hero's emblem'.[22] In Gaskell's *Ruth*, Mr Bellingham presents the young Ruth Hilton with a 'snowy white' camellia, ostensibly in gratitude for her 'dexterous' work on Miss Duncombe's dress (p. 17). Since the white camellia is a symbol of perfected loveliness, Bellingham's choice of flower is, at the very least, felicitous and suggestive. Such was the popularity of the language of flowers, that Victorian writers could work on the supposition that their cultivated readers had some acquaintance with it. Lacking this competence, most modern readers are likely to assume that the choice of plant names in Victorian poems and novels is either random or merely subjective.

In many respects, the language of flowers proper was quite different from most other Victorian floral codes. For one thing, its vocabulary and rules of use were written down, which made it comparatively formalized, and meant that it had to be learned by rather formal means. For another, it was not firmly anchored in contemporary horticultural practices and did not emerge from the signifying operations performed upon it; that is, it was independent of the meanings assigned informally to flowers by flesh-and-blood Victorians. This ought theoretically to have rendered it incompatible with floral codes of much greater historical specificity, and dependent upon what phenomenologists would probably call 'commonsense' knowledge. In practice, many Victorians were able to entertain simultaneously and with no apparent discomfiture the notion that the significations of plants were, in one sense, fixed and achronic, and in another sense, culturally contingent. This curious case of double-think betrays conflicting desires: on the one hand, an enormous reluctance on the part of many Victorians to relinquish the consoling belief that nature is a source of abiding truths; on the other, a desire to make the evidence to the contrary still more compelling by releasing the semiotic potential of plants held in check by the language of flowers. Unfettered by the rigid constraints of the floral alphabets, plant names could be used to signify (*inter alia*) moral values, social status, and social group identities—no small gain for those in the business of mapping the cultural terrain. This includes Victorian imaginative writers, who were instrumental in the mediation, construction, and negotiation of floral codes.

Various sets of factors played a part in determining the conventional, widely agreed meanings which plants came to acquire for the Victorians. One of the principal determinants was 'age'—which turned largely upon the distinction between 'old favourites' and newly imported exotics, hybridized plants and other prized cultivars. The latter were usually expensive and often showy; not surprisingly they functioned as indices of social status and material wealth. Some Victorian novelists exploited these significations. Exotics of Babylonian splendour make manifest the almost fabulous affluence of some of Disraeli's fictional aristocrats. As we have seen, Charlotte Yonge's *Heartsease* includes a description of an upper-class display garden brimful of exotics and costly American plants.

Some plants were only ephemerally expressive of wealth. The fate of the tulip is a case in point. At the height of the tulip mania in England (between about 1830 and 1850), affluent fanciers paid anything up to £150 for a single rare bulb.[23] As the less common varieties of tulips became cheaper, and so more widely available, their significations became commensurately more variable. By the end of the century they had all but ceased to function as social signs of wealth, and garden writers were free to debate their more 'personal' qualities. Alfred Austin discerned in them displeasing associations of 'eighteenth-century correctness',[24] while 'Elizabeth', the author of *Elizabeth and her German Garden* (1898), considered them 'the embodiment of alert cheerfulness and tidy grace' (p. 71).

Other plants were similarly democratized. In 1853, an anonymous garden writer declared that he was 'pleasantly surprised to see in the gardens of the poor . . . plants which a very few years ago we could only have expected to find in gardens of some pretensions'. He mentions in particular 'showy dahlias' and 'hardier varieties of the fuchsia'.[25] This trickling-down process diminished rather than nullified the indexical significations of exotics and 'quality' plants; most remained real or vestigial signs of material wealth.

By contrast, the connotative values of these plants had to be fought for. This struggle for the mastery of plant meanings was not the cultural expression of a class struggle so much as a tussle between those who occupied different ideological positions within the dominant value-system. For the commercial middle classes, exuberant exotics were indubitable symbols of triumph and progress—their own and their country's. Giant plants brought back from distant lands were the palpable signs of entrepreneurial efficiency as well as colonial power. That they could be made to flourish in artificial environments, themselves created by British engineers, showed that nature itself could be controlled.

In marvelling at exotics, the industrial middle classes and progressive upper classes were marvelling at themselves and their own achievements. How else can we explain the extraordinary public interest generated by Paxton's successful cultivation of the remarkable South American water-lily *Victoria Regia* or, more accurately perhaps, by the attention it received from the middle-class press?[26] Its prodigious size and vigorous growth seemed perfectly to symbolize the confidence, energy and expansionist ambitions of the classes who lionized Paxton in the years immediately preceding the Great Exhibition.

That imported exotics acquired their positive connotative values largely from and by their association with the rising middle classes helps to explain why they were less favourably encoded by those whose conservative sympathies made them critical of parvenu capitalists and their flamboyant status symbols. The identification of exotics and showy bedders with brazen social upstarts is implicit in comments denouncing new plants for their lack of pedigree and breeding. One writer lamented that 'some prime old favourites . . . have lost their place in the parterre to make room for the upstart *parvenus* of vaunting propagators'.[27]

In the novels of Anthony Trollope, exotics are semiotically akin to foreigners and imperfect gentlemen of dubious or unknown origins. With Tory grandiloquence and the backing of an ancient lineage, the young Frank Gresham in *Framley Parsonage* asserts that he would 'sooner have one full-grown oak standing in its pride alone . . . than all the exotics in the world' (p. 100). Old oaks, like true gentlemen, cannot be whistled up by wealth alone. Nor can they be brought into conservatories on 'great barrows'—as are the exotics at Gatherum Castle at the behest of Lady Glencora in Trollope's *The Prime Minister* (1876). To her husband, the Duke of Omnium, they have about them a repulsive look of 'raw newness' (p. 211).

Trollope's reluctance to assign positive values to exotics was by no means unusual. The majority of Victorian imaginative writers displayed an enthusiasm for old-fashioned flowers that they rarely exhibited for newer and 'improved' plants. What they appear to have sensed, though rarely made explicit, was that the apparent displacement of old favourites by fashionable annuals and imported newcomers provided a paradigmatic case of the displacement of the old cultural system by the new. As it was generally perceived, the old cultural system had as its core the organic rural community, of which the cottage garden provided an imaginatively compelling synecdoche. As synecdoches of the cottage garden, old-fashioned plants were powerful reminders of a world that was quickly passing—if it hadn't already passed.

To some extent, then, hollyhocks, sunflowers, larkspurs, pinks, pansies, lupins, and the other plants generally considered old-fashioned were positively accented for the values their names were thought to symbolize. But their peculiar qualities also played some part in the way they were encoded. According to their champions, the old favourites appealed to all the relevant senses. They usually combined handsome colour with sweetness of scent, and they also had 'interesting' forms. In addition, their beauty was not of the transitory kind. Hence, for the majority of novelists and poets, and for garden lovers who did not despise them for their intractability or their 'vulgar' associations—they were often referred to as 'poor men's flowers'—old-fashioned plants held the positive connotations of plenitude, variety, individuality, and the kind of stability equivalent to homeliness.

By contrast, bedding plants such as verbenas, scarlet geraniums and calceolarias had only bright colour, ornamentation, and docility to recommend them. To the advocates of the old favourites, and of the omnium-gatherum garden styles with which they were associated, bedders spoke of homogeneity, ephemerality, and the absence of 'personality'. These negative connotations were accentuated by (con)textual factors. As the name implies, bedders were normally planted in massed arrangements for maximum visual impact. For Forbes Watson and the later Victorians who shared his views, this inevitably involved the 'subjection of the imaginative, or higher, to the sensuous, or lower, element of flower beauty'.[28] Since they were not individuated and had little staying power, bedding plants could not be regarded as 'old friends on whose coming we can rely, and who, returning with the recurring season, bring back with them pleasant memories of past years'.[29] As Mrs Oliphant suggests in one of her fictional garden descriptions in *Miss Marjoribanks*, they were merely 'tenants-at-will', whereas the old perennials always looked thoroughly 'at home' (p. 188). And being at home, probably in long established herbaceous borders, 'friendly perennials', as E. M. Braddon pointed out in *A Lost Eden* (1904), 'ask so little of the gardener' (p. 74). Bedding annuals always asked so much.

Plants commonly defined as 'old' and 'traditional' acquired felicitous significations for other reasons. Imaginative writers and those with little taste for 'modern' gardens considered exotics and bedders to be more artificial than the plants they threatened to displace. Though very few Victorians argued that a garden should pretend to be an unworked patch of raw nature, many believed that mid-century horticultural practices abused the principle of necessary artifice. As a derogatory term, 'artificial' was applied both to the physical disposition of plants and to their mode of cultivation. The detractors of carpet-bedding condemned what they saw as the over-regulation and 'unnatural' patterning of plants. Robinson dubbed it 'barren geometry'; one of his allies called it 'horticultural tailordom'.[30] Shirley Hibberd, who perceived in the glaring colours and mechanical designs of bedding displays (some took the shape of wheels and the like) a visual echo if not a symbolic reminder of the industrial practices by which they were supported, likened them to 'manufactories' and to 'the blazing fire at the mouth of a coal-pit'.[31] He might almost have been thinking of the garish townscape of Dickens's Coketown in *Hard Times*, and of Gradgrind's own unnatural flower-garden where mathematical regularity rules the 'lawns and garden and an infant avenue' (p. 10).

'Artificial' was applied also to plants 'forced' by hot-house cultivation, and by the 'improving' practices of florists and scientifically-minded horticulturalists.

Though pampered exotics figure prominently in conservatory scenes in Victorian fiction—where they add considerably to the atmosphere of fairy-tale other-worldliness—the prevailing tone of the hot-house imagery in Victorian literature is decidedly unflattering. Grown by force, exotics signify the false. In George Gissing's novels, hot-house plants invariably suggest some form of artificiality or false display. Paula Tyrell in *Thyrza* 'looked the most exquisite of conservatory flowers'. By way of clarification, the narrator tells us that she was 'entirely . . . a child of luxury and frivolous concern. Exquisite as an artistic product of Society, she affected the imagination not so much by her personal charm as through the perfume of luxury which breathed about her'

(p. 133). In *Demos* (1886), Adela Waltham's 'strange new emotion, the beginning of a self-conscious zeal' for Richard Mutimer's socialist ideas, is 'an enthusiasm forced into being like a hothouse flower' (p. 187), and so destined to early atrophy. And in *A Life's Morning*, we find the following lines in the passage describing Emily Hood's devotions at the grave of her parents: 'Close at hand was a grave on which friends placed hot-house flowers, sheltering them beneath glass. Emily had no desire to express her mourning in that way; the flower of her love was planted where it would not die' (p. 265). Swinburne uses forcing-house imagery in an essay in which he praises two of D. G. Rossetti's lyrics, 'Troy Town' and 'Eden Bower'. 'There is', he writes, 'a strength and breadth of style about these poems also which ennobles their sweetness and brightness, giving them a perfume that savours of no hotbed, but of hill flowers that face the sea and sunrise; a colour that grows in no greenhouse, but such as comes with morning upon the mountains.'[32] A similar comparison, distinguishing the genuine article from the product of pampered artifice, appears also in Charlotte Brontë's *The Professor* (1857), when William Crimsworth declares to Hunsden that the sweetness of Frances 'my little wild strawberry . . . made me careless of your hot-house grapes' (p. 313).

If only obliquely, the pejorative significations of hot-house flowers may seem to imply a negative view of forcing-house cultivation, which recalls Ruskin's more explicit protestations against the deleterious practice of pampering to improve. In *Modern Painters III* (1856) he writes:

> The exalted or seemingly improved condition, whether of plant or animal, induced by human interference, is not the true and artistical idea of it. It has been well shown by Dr. Herbert that many plants are found alone on a certain soil or subsoil in a wild state, not because such soil is favourable to them, but because they alone are capable of existing on it, and because all dangerous rivals are by its inhospitality removed. Now if we withdraw the plant from the position, which it hardly endures, and supply it with earth, and maintain about it the temperature, that it delights in; withdrawing from it, at the same time, all rivals, which, in such conditions, nature should have thrust upon it, we shall indeed obtain a magnificently developed example of the plant, colossal in size and splendid in organization; but we

> shall utterly lose in it that moral ideal which is dependent on its right fulfilment of its appointed functions. (*RW*, IV, 170–1)

Ruskin detested hot-houses (he once described the Crystal Palace as a 'cucumber frame' [*RW*, XXXV, 47]) and vilified 'the vile and gluttonous modern habit of forcing' (*RW*, XXVIII, 182). But he also believed that plants could be unnaturally overdeveloped even under seemingly more natural conditions. In one of his earliest published articles he wrote:

> A flower-garden is an ugly thing, even when best managed: it is an assembly of unfortunate beings, pampered and bloated above their natural size, starved and heated into diseased growth; corrupted by evil communication into speckled and inharmonious colours. . . . (*RW*, I, 156)

William Morris also had a good deal to say about the 'over-artificiality' of florists' flowers, and he was especially dismissive of plants 'which are curiosities only, which Nature meant to be grotesque, not beautiful, and which are generally the growth of hot countries, where things grow over quick and rank' (*MW*, XXII, 89–90). He argued that such plants should be confined—or consigned—to botanical gardens. Morris was vituperative on the subject of carpet-bedding (he called it 'an aberration of the human mind' [ibid.]) and 'was appalled by everything he called "horticulture" between inverted commas, either Romantic or baroque, shrubberies and rockeries.'[33]

For both Ruskin and Morris, the mindless pursuit of floricultural novelties was of more than local significance. Both writers construed it as an index of cultural degeneration under the conditions of industrial capitalism. In the second volume of *Modern Painters* (1846) Ruskin remarked that 'we see every day the power of general taste destroyed . . . by the vain straining of curiosity for new forms such as nature never intended', as in 'the delight of horticulturalists in the spoiling of plants' (*RW*, IV, 161). Morris regarded the commercial florist's 'way of dealing with flowers' as an apt illustration of that 'change without thought of beauty, change for the sake of change, which has played such a great part in the degradation of art in all times' (*MW*, XXII, 87–8).

Like Jefferies, who opened *Amaryllis at the Fair* with a lament for the old roses which for him had quite different significations from modern varieties, Morris illustrated his case against the florists by charting the declining fortunes of the rose. In so doing, he joined the chorus of a small band of contemporary rose enthusiasts who 'protested against the wholesale neglect of the old roses', while the Victorian 'world in general . . . looked upon the roses of former days as experiments discarded in the search for progress'.[34]

Does this assertion hold true of other 'old plants'? Did the Victorian 'world in general' emphasize the significations of newer and 'improved' plant species? The answers to these questions depend partly upon the texts we consult. There are at least two good reasons for drawing heavily upon the 'evidence' of literary texts. First, the majority of (at least) mid-Victorian novelists inhabited substantially the same cultural community as their readers; hence, fiction offers access to the dominant floral codes of the age, though it also challenges some of them. Second, the evidence of imaginative literature provides a valuable alternative to the vulgar version of Victorian garden history—promulgated initially by opponents of the bedding system—according to which bedders monopolized Victorian flower gardens until finally superseded rather late in the century by (i) more 'natural' uses of plants, and (ii) modestly formal gardens constructed with old-fashioned models in mind.

Some old favourites may have been pushed to one side by bedders and exotics in the middle decades of the century. But their prominence in imaginative literature suggests that the positive significations of old-fashioned plants were maintained and even enhanced. Even at the height of their popularity, bedders failed to attract the wealth of felicitous associations evoked by such plants as the sunflower and hollyhock. *The Floral World* of March 1862 illuminatingly revealed that 'annuals are grown everywhere, and almost everywhere condemned. They are variously pronounced 'trashy', 'flimsy', 'unsatisfactory', and 'not worthy of a place in my garden'. But the condemnation is never pronounced till some time in July, when most of the popular kinds of hardy annuals go out of bloom.'[35] This ambivalence is registered in virtually every issue of *The Floral World* in the 1860s. Readers were apprised of the latest developments in the cultivation of bedding-plants; at the same time, they were urged not to be carried away by them.

That Shirley Hibberd (editor of *The Floral World*) should have blown hot and cold is significant and not altogether surprising. He knew that many of his readers enjoyed a great splash of colourful bedders, and that they relished also the connotations of progress, fashion-consciousness, and middle-class respectability these plants conveyed. And at least one part of him was committed to floricultural innovations—hence, for example, his enthusiasm at the introduction of 'strikingly coloured foliage' bedders.[36] Yet Hibberd also sensed that for a growing number of his contemporaries, bedding displays spoke too loudly of mid-century complacency, vulgarity, and misdirected energy.

In the last thirty years of the century, Hibberd's circumspect admonitions escalated to the unrestrained denunciations of William Robinson and a host of less famous garden writers who fulminated hyperbolically against what they perceived as the 'tyranny' of the bedding system. The war against the bedders was accompanied by an upsurge of interest in, and respect for, old-fashioned 'cottage' plants, and more natural and less sophisticated uses of plants in general. The impetus came, as previously noted, from various pressure groups: from gardeners associated with the so-called 'Queen Anne' movement in architecture and design; from the advocates of the 'wild' garden; from the followers of the Arts and Crafts movement; from the painters, photographers, and 'Old England' worshippers who went in search of cottage scenes and other representative bits of the rural past; from critics of culture, like Ruskin and Morris; and from poetic and fictional models of old-fashioned gardens, including Corisande's garden in Disraeli's *Lothair*, which acquired an almost mythological status in the 1870s and 1880s.

The renewed reverence for old-fashioned flowers can be explained in two ways. The more obvious explanation is that many later Victorians, particularly among the upper middle classes, attempted to distance themselves from the ugliness of the present—epitomized by the meretricious glare of bedding displays—by resurrecting the beautifully simple symbols of the pre-industrial past. The less obvious and more radical explanation is that the canonization of 'cottage' garden plants was motivated by a perceived need to shore up, revitalize and purify the imaginatively bankrupt floral culture of the philistine bourgeoisie.[37] It was thought in some quarters that the middle classes, though economically dominant, were culturally impoverished—as their monomania for the imaginatively sterile and crassly ostentatious bedding system clearly showed. Their cultural refurbishment could come about only through the assimilation and appropriation of vital elements from the apparently untainted and flourishing floral cultures of the 'junior' or tradition-bearing classes: from the old-fashioned gardens of genuine rural labourers and farmers, from the gardens of more genteel cottagers and, where they survived, from the Corisande-type gardens of the gentry and the aristocracy.

Although this Arnoldian project was never explicitly formulated, the sheer volume of anti-bedding literature of a scourging and reformatory kind is itself enough to suggest that the inadequacies of the bedding system were conceived in cultural as well as in horticultural terms. As its shrewder critics hinted, the quick turnover of large quantities of plants, produced under what amounted to factory conditions, too clearly betrayed the material preoccupations of its principal subscribers. One anonymous writer candidly confessed that 'few gardeners cultivate the plants they like' because 'they are obliged to conform to horticulture *de convenance*, as their customers are compelled to make *marriages de convenance*'. Commercial imperatives, he suggested, were responsible for the production of 'bedding-out stuff by the train-load and the milliard'.[38]

That most of the critics of bedding out advocated more 'natural' uses of plants and cottage garden models, suggests that their ultimate objective may have been the cultural refinement of the privileged classes. For one of the great merits of the old-fashioned cottage garden was that it appeared to speak more of natural wealth than of material wealth. Similarly, in the so-called 'wild garden', and in the modestly formal old-fashioned garden, the connection between these two forms of wealth was suggested rather than trumpeted.

The struggle to confer status upon more 'natural' uses of plant materials often took the form of giving fresh accents to old labels. In mid-century, 'trim' was frequently applied as a term of commendation to bedding arrangements and to other highly regulated uses of flowers. In *The Wild Garden*, Robinson gave 'trim' a pejorative twist; many other garden writers followed suit, though some re-directed the term to formal gardens with clipped yews and tidy walks.

While 'trim' became a more dubious term of approval, 'wild' and 'weeds' were positively reappraised. Having averred that 'hap-hazard' flower-beds are 'more picturesque' than regular and uniform ones, a contributor to *The Cornhill* wrote:

> I am not sure that if I were allowed to have my own way, I should not rather encourage a style of natural wildness. Often the fairest and sweetest things come up by chance. I

> have, indeed, a sort of partiality for what the gardener calls 'weeds'. It is not easy, indeed, to determine the exact point at which the domain of 'weeds' ends and that of 'flowers' commences. My gardener not only calls, but treats as weeds what I regard as very beautiful flowers.[39]

'Weeds' and (comparatively) wild gardens had many champions in the latter decades of the century. Several novelists of the time reflected this; the novels of George Meredith, for example, suggest very little affection for the more conventional and respectable garden flowers, but rather a predilection for wild flowers and 'weeds'. His sympathetically-presented characters identify imaginatively with such plants. Mrs Fleming violates conventions of context by bringing poppies into her garden; to her neighbours this love of 'weeds' is a sure sign of moral perversity. Clara Middleton in *The Egoist* (1879) values more highly the bouquet of wild flowers presented to her by the young Crossjay than the 'oppressive load' of Sir Willoughby's formal flower garden. The titular heroine of *Diana of the Crossways* (1885) tells Mr Dacier that she is

> 'reluctant to take the life of flowers for a whim. Wild flowers, I mean. I am not sentimental about garden flowers: they are cultivated for decoration, grown for clipping.'
> 'I suppose they don't carry the same signification', said Dacier. . . .
> 'They carry no feeling,' said she. (p. 153)

The speaker in the long poem *Love in the Valley* (1883) expresses an almost identical sentiment:

> Prim little scholars are the flowers of her garden,
> Trained to stand in rows, and asking if they please.
> I might love them but for loving more the wild ones. (*MP*, p. 233)

And in a poem entitled 'The Wild Rose', the speaker leaves little doubt that he prefers the 'superbly shy' wild rose to the roses of the garden—'Her queenly sisters enthroned by art' (*MP*, p. 564).

The attempt to canonize modest and traditional 'cottage' flowers also involved the simplification and demystification of plant names. One of the chief reasons Ruskin produced *Proserpina* was to reform the nomenclature of plants, or what he called 'the vulgar and ugly mysteries of the so-called science of botany' (*RW*, XXV,

200). Robinson and his followers argued that English plant names were more democratic and infinitely less pretentious than Latin ones.[40] Similarly, Miss Mitford contended that 'one is never thoroughly sociable with flowers till they are naturalized as it were, christened, provided with decent, homely, well-wearing English names'. She claimed to be distressed by the 'heathenish appellations' of the 'true connoisseur'.[41]

The belief that esoteric nomenclature had the effect of alienating the gardener from what ought to have been the objects of his affection, appears to have weighed heavily upon later champions of old-fashioned flowers. They may also have sensed that the special languages spawned by various categories of middle-class flower cultivators were deleterious to their interests of achieving cultural dominance in the horticultural sphere. Since arcane codes were generally inaccessible to all but a socially and educationally advantaged minority, they were socially divisive, and militated against the formation of a truly common flower culture spearheaded by a truly responsible and sympathetic middle class.

Whether or not the campaigners for a democratic nomenclature were ideologically motivated, they certainly recognized that there was a linguistic rift between the esoteric and 'unpronounceable' names of 'gardeners' plants, and the familiar names of the 'poor man's' or amateur's plants. Narrowcast plant codes may have developed as an inevitable accompaniment to a predominantly scientific interest in plants; they may have been generated as a means of regulating 'access' to the social classes they came to identify. They undoubtedly had the effect of excluding the educationally disadvantaged.[42] This was evident, for example, at the height of the fern craze in the mid-1850s. The significations of ferns themselves were various, ambivalent, and dependent upon context, connoting everything from rococo elegance to romantic melancholy, from wholesomeness and natural freshness to moral fervour and kill-joy sobriety. (Mr Slope's 'strongest worldly passion was for ferns'.[43]) But the taxonomic codes of the fern enthusiasts were singularly cabalistic. The young heroine of *Heartsease* is made acutely conscious of her ignorance and humble origins when she is proffered a 'beautifully illustrated magazine of horticulture—whilst the other [upper-class] ladies talked about the fernery, in scientific terms, that sounded like an unknown tongue' (p. 32). In *Glaucus* (1855), Charles Kingsley wrote:

> Your daughters, perhaps, have been seized with the prevailing 'Pteriodomania', and are collecting and buying ferns, with Ward's cases wherein to keep them . . . and are wrangling

> over unpronounceable names of species (which seem to be different in each new fern-book they buy), till the Pteriodomania seems to be somewhat of a bore. (p. 4)

The mid-century fern specialists were but one of a host of Victorian sub-collectivities differentiated partly in terms of their floral allegiances. Various groups and movements appropriated particular flowers as badges of identity. The Pre-Raphaelites and Aesthetes were identified by their reverence for sunflowers and lilies (and the tall madonna lily in particular); Girouard suggests that these may have been chosen to symbolize physical love and spiritual love respectively.[44] Other plants played an important part in signalling differences between groups occupying different social spaces. In the later decades of the century, the rhododendron and other foreign shrubs were much in evidence in suburban villa gardens; for Richard Jefferies and others they were emblematic of sudden riches.[45] Other shrubs and trees served to symbolize gradations of status within suburbia. In London suburbs, as Gissing well knew, plane trees and horse chestnuts were among the signifiers of the really well-to-do; limes, laburnums and acacias signified suburban residents of middle incomes; the absence of trees denoted wage-earners.[46]

Finally, a brief mention must be made of the ideologically motivated functions of floral codes and discourses within the Victorian cultural context. This is a big and important subject; here, some remarks of a general nature will have to suffice.

Contrary to popular belief, 'flower power' was not an invention of the hippy youth cult movement of the 1960s. Many Victorians were convinced that flowers had power to influence almost every area of human life, and many sought to extend this influence. These writers, most of them members of the educated middle classes, emphasized primarily the 'innocence' of flowers and of the activities connected with them. But some of the uses to which they wished flowers to be put, and the more covert functions of Victorian floral ideology, were anything but politically innocent. Though the advocates of flower power sought to purify and humanize the values of the dominant classes, they rarely sought to challenge them. Quite the reverse. What, for example, was the ultimate target audience that countless garden writers had in mind when they spoke of the value of fostering an interest in flower cultivation? An anonymous contributor to *The Gardener's*

Chronicle of 1861 was quite explicit: 'It is certainly most desirable to cultivate a taste for flowers among the working classes.'[47] No reasons are given for this opinion, though the writer almost certainly assumed that flower cultivation would keep working people from the brutalizing influence of the ale-house and/or divert their minds and energies from politically 'dangerous' activities. In an article entitled 'The Influence of Flowers', an anonymous contributor to *The Saturday Magazine* declared that the principal advantage 'derived from a fondness for this pursuit' (flower growing) is that 'it attaches men to their homes; and on this account every encouragement should be given to increase a taste for gardening, in general, in country towns and villages.' He argued also that flower cultivation 'promotes civilization, and softens the manners and tempers of men'.[48] Whatever the conscious intentions of this writer, his (or her) article reads suspiciously like an attempt to maintain the status quo by inducing consent for middle-class values. This deliberate or unwitting propaganda is still more apparent in texts directed specifically at working-class city-dwellers. As Robert Harling has noted, 'Touching anecdotes of the love of the *lower orders* for their flower-boxes were recorded in the introduction to manuals for city gardeners;' 'such tales were of the greatest possible aid to the industrialists in the great unspoken crusade to make millions of slum dwellers contented with their lowly lot in life'.[49]

Less specific, probably less conscious, but far more pervasive in their effects, were the ideological aspects of flower-oriented discourse specifically concerned with women. Through texts proclaiming their fondness for, association with, and equivalence to, flowers, the decorative and domestic functions of women were persistently naturalized. Victorian garden literature bristles with linguistic sexism and sexist distinctions. The following comments from Henry Burgess's *The Amateur Gardener's year-book* (1854) are fairly representative:

> The retiring habits of ladies make them turn to flowers with an almost instinctive love, and dispose them to fill up their spare moments in tending and training these ornaments of their homes.[50]

Though men may appreciate flowers, he says, 'female taste is more pure'. The 'gentleman amateur is more attached to novelty . . . but the lady will find pleasure in attending to old favourites'. He adds: 'the gentler sex is more easily pleased, and less easily discouraged by the results of garden operations'.[51]

Books specifically directed at women gardeners, and articles dealing exclusively with women and flowers, were by no means uncommon. William Robinson himself produced a piece entitled 'Ladies' Flowers' which opened with the following remark: 'Ladies' Flowers! The name sounds odd. Surely *all* flowers have hitherto been beloved of ladies.'[52]

In Victorian imaginative literature, women are frequently presented in the company of flowers in such a way as to heighten their femininity, and in terms suggesting a metaphorical exchange value between human and vegetable forms. Like the plants they lovingly tend, 'ladies' are 'naturally' delicate, ornamental, wholesome, pure, and submissive, performing for their husbands and lovers the same civilizing and refining functions which flowers perform for people in general. Explicit comparisons between women and flowers are not uncommon. Witness Rhoda Broughton's 'shamelessly sentimental' use of the metaphor of the rose to describe the heroine of *Red as a Rose is She* (1870). Having described a pot 'brimming over' with freshly plucked roses, the narrator says:

> But the freshest, the sweetest, the largest of the roses is not in the beanpot with the others; it is on a chair by itself; there are no dew-tears on its cheek, it has no prickles and its name is Esther.[53]

In Charles Reade's *It is Never Too Late to Mend* (1856) the narrator sketches one of the 'little garden scenes' enacted by George Fielding and his sweetheart, Susan Merton, before George is compelled to seek his fortune in Australia. Susan presents the poor farmer with a marigold, which she despises for its gaudiness, and subsequently a 'lovely clove-pink' which she has carefully nurtured. Though he admits to being 'not so deep in flowers' as Susan, George professes a preference for the pink. He moralizes as follows:

> I see flowers that are pretty, but have no smell, and I see women that have good looks, but no great wisdom or goodness when you come nearer to them. Now the marigold is like those lasses, but the pink is good as well as pretty, so then it will stand for you, when we are apart . . . (p. 67)

Gender construction, sexual politics and flower imagery are more than usually interlinked in a major mid-century poem that specifically addresses the 'woman question': Tennyson's *The Princess*. In the story of the poem's inner frame, the metaphor of woman as flower is advanced as an enlightened alternative to the reactionary metaphor of woman as 'game', and as a moderate alternative to the extreme feminist position. Though the shrieking sisters of the poem (Lilia in the Prologue, Ida in the tale) are given ample opportunity to present their case for separatist development and the abolition of marriage as an institution, they must contend with the gender definitions imposed upon them by the dominant (male) discourse of the poem that codifies divergent female types in floral terms. These prove more difficult to resist than the blatantly sexist image of woman as game.

This is evident even in the Prologue. Lilia, the spirited modern girl, speaks about women's rights and wrongs, and fulminates against men and the 'conventions' that 'beat' women 'down'. Because she recognizes their nature, she can deal with the overtly patronizing gestures of her father, Sir Walter, as she demonstrates when she 'shook aside / The hand that played the patron with her curls' (*TP*, p. 747). But she has also to struggle against the voice of the male narrator who tells her story and defines her as 'A rosebud set with little wilful thorns' and as a 'little hearth-flower' (p. 748). Even the connotations of her name run counter to her ideal self-concept.

The female characters of the story she inspires are similarly fixed into subordinate positions by the floral metaphors of a man-made code. Having internalized that code, or lacking a language untainted by its sexual ideology, even the feminists of the story unwittingly perpetuate it. Lady Psyche (admittedly the most 'feminine' of Ida's satellites) calls her baby girl, Aglaia, 'my flower' and 'my little blossom' (p. 803). When Ida addresses her as 'Pretty bud! / Lilly of the vale' (p. 823) she unconsciously echoes the Prince's description of her as 'the lily-shining child' (p. 793). Lady Blanche's daughter, Melissa, combines the innocent passivity of one female type with the beauty and potential passion of the other: hence she is at one time both 'lilylike', 'rosy blonde' and 'clad like an April daffodily' (p. 768). The male narrator describes the students who packed the long hall of the Women's College as 'beauties' who 'glittered like a bed of flowers' (p. 771).

Ida herself is assailed by floral metaphors from her male admirers. Cyril informs her that the Prince worships her as his 'one rose in all the world' (p. 760)—though she has donned a white robe to signal her repudiation of the sexual stereotype implied by the image of the red rose. Her brother, the semi-articulate Arac, labels her 'the flower of womankind' (p. 809). In some sense this image 'sums up ... the pattern of growth and development which produce this flower, this essence toward which change has been directing its energies'.[54] Yet Ida herself explicitly rejects the model of unbroken, fixed and predetermined development implied by the flower image. At the height of her feminist convictions, she insists upon a necessary rupture between childhood and womanhood. Gerard Joseph, whose reading runs smoothly with the grain of the poem's preferred meaning, says that Ida's desire 'to lose the child, assume the woman' is 'immature'.[55] From a feminist position, however, Ida's ambition is born of a perception to which she is later blinded by her capitulation to the role of wife, mother and moral guide: the perception that the bud-into-flower image of gradual and continuous growth serves to make unthinkable the idea of radical, self-determining change.[56]

In a great many Victorian imaginative texts, the sustained identification of women with flowers is a principal means by which female characters are constructed and defined. A particularly good example is Browning's presentation of the Duchess in *Colombe's Birthday* (1853). Colombe is associated with flowers almost from her first appearance, and the flower imagery gathers increasingly intense and complex meanings as the play unfolds.[57]

The deployment of flower imagery in Victorian imaginative literature should also be understood as a technique for both complying with and circumventing the taboo on the overt acknowledgement of female sexuality. The sexual ideology of the Victorian middle classes demanded sexual restraint, especially in imaginative literature produced for family consumption. One novelist who was highly conscious of, and possibly constrained by, 'respectable' notions of the permissible was George Meredith. As a consequence, Meredith drew heavily upon flower symbols and other natural images to allude tactfully to the physical desires of women and to sexual relations generally. Consider, for instance, the much-discussed scene in *The Egoist* in which Clara Middleton peers down at Vernon Whitford stretched out under the double-blossom cherry tree:

> ... still with a bent head, she turned her face to where the load of virginal blossom ... showered and drooped and clustered as thick as to claim colour.... From deep to

> deeper heavens of white, her eyes perched and soared. Wonder lived in her. Happiness in the beauty of the tree pressed to supplant it, and was more mortal and narrower. Reflection came, contracting her vision and weighing her to earth. Her reflection was: 'He must be good who loves to lie and sleep beneath the branches of this tree'. She would rather have clung to her first impression; wonder so divine, so unbounded . . . but the thought of it was no recovery of it; she might as well have striven to be a child. (I, 135)

Clara's moment of irrepressible sexual awakening is clinched when Vernon peers up and they are fleetingly locked in an implicitly sexual 'embrace' tempered and mediated, as it were, by the 'dazzling blossom' that 'circled' Clara's head (I, 136). Here, as elsewhere, Meredith hints more strongly at the physical nature of women than do most of his contemporaries. Imaginative writers in general either denied the existence of female sexuality or sanitized it by displacement into symbolic representations. This point can be illustrated with reference to the symbol of the rose.

Though the rose has multiple significations, three are outstanding: beauty, transience and sexual passion. In most of the enormous number of Victorian poems in which the rose is symbolic of glorious but transitory female beauty, sexual connotations are conspicuously suppressed. A thoroughly typical example is 'The Gardener's Daughter' by W. C. Bennett, which appeared with no fewer than four other 'Rose' poems in the same volume of *The Quiver*. As in so many similar verses, the starting point of Bennett's poem is the coupling 'rose'/'Rose', which conflates the identities of flower and woman. The first two stanzas run:

> Rose among roses sweet,
> Flower fresh and fair
> As any bloom you meet
> Clasped in June air;
> Fitly your beauty's flush
>   To many summer shows
> Blush fair to fairest blush,
>   Rose sweet to rose.
>
> Ah, as with soft gloved hand
>   You pluck each flower,
> Think how old Time's quick sand
>   Flows, hour on hour;
> Roses bloom, roses pass,

Pity 'tis true!
So, through time's wasteful glass
Speed your hours too.[58]

For the few writers prepared to confront the sexuality of women, the rose afforded a relatively blatant but permissible symbol of the explicitly unspeakable. The floral opposition or pairing of white lily (for purity) and red rose (for passion) is recurrent in the poetry of Tennyson. It occurs in *The Princess*, is prominent in *Maud* (1855), and figures at its most emblematically patterned in a momentous scene in the idyll of *Balin and Balan* (1872–3), involving a chance encounter between Lancelot and Guinevere in an enclosed Camelot garden. The garden has a 'walk of roses' 'crost' by a 'walk of lilies' (*TP*, p. 1583). 'Lancelot implicitly asserts his will to chastity' by taking the walk of lilies, and by disclosing his vision of a 'maiden Saint' who stood 'with lily in hand'.[59] By contrast, Guinevere chooses the 'range of roses', and declares her preference for the 'garden rose/Deep-hued and many-folded' (p. 1583). As a contemporary reviewer was quick to point out, the rose 'is a fitting emblem of the voluptuous, passionate Queen.'[60]

Hardy was less reticent even than Tennyson when it came to releasing the sexual connotations of the rose. 'Hardy's deeply sensuous response to his female characters shows . . . in his fondness for bathing his admired women in shades of red and pink'; 'Tess, as she epitomizes the peak of Hardy's flower comparison device, is also the quintessence of Hardyesque rosy glow.'[61] Early in *Tess of the D'Urbervilles* (1891) she appears as 'a rosy warming apparition' with 'roses in her breast; roses in her hat; roses and strawberries in her basket to the brim' (p. 67). More than once we are told of her 'flower-like' mouth and her 'deep red lips'.

As for liking flowers, there is scarcely a romantic heroine who does not express in word or deed or both a passionate fondness for flowers. Indeed, flowers are one of the very few things for which the conventional heroine of mid-century fiction is expected to feel passion, as opposed to mere affection. This is not to say that less conventional heroines are immune to the passion. Kate Chester, 'the first in a line of [Rhoda Broughton's] self-willed heroines whose passionate nature gets them into trouble'[62] is, we are told in *Not Wisely, but Too Well* (1884), a 'ripe' woman with none of 'the emaciated prettiness of young ladies' (p. 107). Yet she also confesses to her lover, Dale Stamer, that 'flowers are one of the very few weak points in my character' (p. 107). Even feminists, like Rhoda Nunn in Gissing's *The Odd Women*, are susceptible to the charms of flowers. Of her Chelsea apartment we are told that 'the numerous bunches of cut flowers, which agreeably scented the air, seemed to prove the student a woman' (p. 30).

In one way or another, the flower-loving heroine is usually rewarded for her floral devotions. It may heighten her feminine attractions in the eyes of a suitor: this is the effect that Henrietta Temple's love of plants has upon Ferdinand Armine. It may bring her compliments of a more direct kind—as Disraeli's Sybil discovers when she is visited by a group of noble women who congratulate her upon her floral pursuits (*Sybil*, p. 233). It may even bring her tangible material benefits. Miss Pawker, one of the young women in M. E. Braddon's *Just As I Am* (1880), is employed as a lady's companion largely on the strength of her professed fondness for flowers (p. 69). That women especially are open to the influence of flowers is the supposition upon which the *belles lettristic* 'hero' of *The Aspern Papers* devises his strategy for beguiling the Misses Bordereau into permitting him access to the 'sacred relics' of his literary idol. With *fin de siècle* exuberance he declares:

> I cling to the fond fancy that by flowers I should make my way—I should succeed by nosegays. I would batter the old woman with lilies—I would bombard the citadel with roses. Their door would have to yield to the pressure when a mound of fragrance should be heaped upon it. (p. 153)

His possibly disingenuous confession to Miss Tina—'It's absurd, if you like, for a man, but I can't live without flowers' (p. 138)—makes explicit an assumption almost universal in Victorian literature: that it is women, not men, who have a natural and privileged affinity with flowers.

The point is reinforced in countless ways. Authorial comments draw attention to it, as when Hardy in *Far From the Madding Crowd* (1874) has this to say regarding Bathsheba's attempts to repair the damage done to Fanny's grave by the water-spouting gargoyle: 'Bathsheba collected the flowers, and began planting them with that sympathetic manipulation of roots and leaves which is so conspicuous in a woman's gardening, and which flowers seem to understand and thrive upon' (p. 346). And then there is the satisfaction that heroines derive from tending their plants—or simply from knowing what they are called. The speaker in Browning's *The Flower's Name* (1844) recalls the occasion when the 'she' of the poem 'stooped over' a flower and, 'with pride to make no slip' told him 'its soft meandering Spanish name' (*BP*, p. 436).

But these examples seem trivial when compared to those fictional heroines whose minds have been thoroughly colonized by flower and garden consciousness. One such heroine is the titular protagonist of a generically indescribable piece by Thomas Hood entitled *Mrs Gardiner* (1843).[63] Though nominally a story (its subtitle is 'A Horticultural Romance') *Mrs Gardiner* is a comic, seam-prominent, digressionary sketch of an apparently eccentric suburban housewife who breathes, thinks and speaks in floricultural terms. Hood introduces her to his 'Gentle Readers' as 'a woman after your own hearts—for she is a Gardiner by name and a Gardiner by nature' (p. 168). Her peculiarity is that she

> speaks the true 'Language of Flowers', not using their buds and blossoms as symbols of her own passions and sentiments, according to the Greek fashion, but lending words to the wants and affections of her plants. Thus, when she says that she is 'dreadful dry, and longs for a good soaking', it refers not to a defect of moisture in her own clay, but to the parched condition of the soil in her parterres: or if she wishes for a regular smoking, it is not from any unfeminine partiality to tobacco, but on behalf of her blighted geraniums. . . . But this identification of herself with the objects of her love was not confined to her plants. It extended to every thing that was connected with her hobby—her garden implements, her garden-rails, and her garden-wall. (p. 169)

Preposterous and idiosyncratic as she may seem to be, Mrs Gardiner is in fact neither an oddity nor a 'phantom'. Seeming to anticipate cries of incredulity from his readers, Hood insists that she is 'real' and 'substantial'—that she may be seen 'any day . . . employed in her horticultural and floricultural pursuits' (p. 168). In other words, Hood asks his readers to believe that Mrs Gardiner is an exaggerated portrait of an actual early Victorian type: a suburban housewife of 'limited ways and means' (p. 170) for whom gardening is not just an all-absorbing occupation but the only reality her spoken language mediates or constructs. This susceptibility of the individual (female) consciousness is, or so Hood implies, a logical development or accompaniment of the process by which horticultural interests have become diffused within the social hierarchy. It is notable, however, that while *Mrs Gardiner* opens with an extensive catalogue of garden-lovers of both sexes, it is a woman who exemplifies the most complete internalization of the gardening experience.

Between *Mrs Gardiner* and *The Portrait of a Lady* there are 38 years and at least as many technical and programmatic dissimilarities. Even so, James's Isabel Archer does have one thing in common with Mrs Gardiner: the tendency to experience the world and the self in garden terms. True, she is not besotted with the actual practice of horticulture, and her public speech is not habitually spiced with horticultural locutions. But as many critics have observed, James not only repeatedly manoeuvres his heroine into garden settings, but also attempts to render the diastolic-systolic rhythms of her consciousness by means of spatial metaphors in general and by the symbol of the garden in particular.[64] Moreover, the imagery by which the contractions and dilations of Isabel's mental life are registered is justified by Isabel's psychological disposition:

> Her nature had, in her conceit, a certain garden-like quality, a suggestion of perfume and murmuring boughs, of shady bowers and lengthening vistas, which made her feel that introspection was, after all, an exercise in the open air, and that a visit to the recesses of one's spirit was harmless when one returned from it with a lapful of roses. (p. 80)

Horticultural metaphors also provide a currency for Isabel's narrated monologue, as here where she is meditating upon her husband:

> Her mind was to be his—attached to his own like a small garden-plot to a deer-park. He would rake the soil gently and water the flowers; he would weed the beds and gather an occasional nose-gay. It would be a pretty piece of property for a proprietor already far-reaching. (p. 432)

Isabel Archer is not Everywoman, and it would be crass to contend that her presentation is a simple instance of the ideological practice of validating a culture-specific image of woman by equation with flowers and gardens. Though James appears to have had greater sympathy with traditional than with feminist conceptions of women, and though he 'is interested in the way his women think and feel, not in the fundamental injustice of their situation',[65] the horticultural imagery by which he characterizes the experience of his heroine is motivated by aesthetic and psychological considerations rather than by 'political' ones. Still, the fact remains that Isabel Archer is a female character and, to my knowledge, no nineteenth-century novelists writing in English treated the consciousness of any of their major male characters in terms so persistently derived from gardens. I take this to be a fact of some significance.

I remarked earlier that some Victorian commentators tended to disesteem a purely scientific interest in flowers. In practice, however, only women were actively discouraged or prevented from the serious study of what was tellingly termed by some 'promiscuous biology'. 'A girl was expected to love flowers and animals, but to know nothing of biology, particularly of its darker side.'[66] The principal reasons for this are stated with alarming candour by a minor character in Charles Reade's *A Woman-Hater* (1874)—perhaps the only Victorian novel purposively to expose the iniquity of the situation. When an articulate and intelligent young woman, Miss Garrett, has the gall to apply to a university to study medicine, a high-ranking male official pontificates as follows: 'Woman's sphere is the hearth and the home: to impair her delicacy is to take the bloom from the peach: she could not qualify for medicine without mastering anatomy and surgery, branches that must unsex her' (p. 150).

When Miss Garrett is finally admitted, she is not allowed to study botany with the male students. Her fellow student, the feminist Miss Gale, is struck by the absurdity as well as by the injustice of the situation:

> we might have gathered blackberries with them in umbrageous woods, from morn to dewy night, and not a professor shocked in the whole Faculty; but we must not sit down with them to an intellectual dinner of herbs, and listen, in their company, to the pedantic terms and childish classifications of botany, in which kindred properties are ignored. Only a male student must be told publicly that a foxglove is *Digitalis purpurea* in the improved nomenclature of science. . . . (p. 155)

Not that Miss Gale has any respect for male-constructed botanical classifications: she dubs them 'puerile and fanciful'. It is simply that she is convinced that 'the sexes will never lose either morals or delicacy through courses of botany endured together' (p. 156).

A Woman-Hater is exceptional in its interrogation of the

institutional practices by which women are denied access to scientific discourses relating to flowers. Victorian fiction in general serves by acquiescence the myth that rationalizes these practices: that is, the myth that opposes male 'reason' to female 'intuition' (or feeling),[67] by the logic of which women are deemed constitutionally unfit for intellectual enquiry, and in need of protection from the harsh truths which science uncovers. By the same (il)logic, they are deemed to be blessed by nature with an instinctive love of and affinity with flowers.

Very occasionally, this dichotomy of female intuition and male intellect is foregrounded in its totality—as it is in the very title of Wilkie Collins's *Heart and Science* (1883). Collins's novel is virtually a counterblast to *A Woman-Hater*; its 'overall protest is against the exaltation of the head at the expense of the heart'.[68] The protest is made concrete, in part, through the characterization of the novel's Jezebel, the Gradgrindian Mrs Gallilee. The reader is asked to believe that Mrs Gallilee has been made hard and callous by her monomania for science. One proof of this is her view of flowers. She calls them 'superfluities', cares nothing for their beauty or for their powers to refresh and delight, hires a 'florist's man' to arrange her house-plants, but lights up at the thought of dissecting them. Since she is also money-conscious, she appreciates their uses as status symbols, and on one occasion spends lavishly on a 'profusion of splendid flowers' (p. 143) to impress her wealthier sister. The implied unnaturalness of her 'protoplastic point of view' (p. 106) is heightened by contrast with the floral interests of the gentle lawyer, Mr Mool, who combines an enthusiasm for botany with a genuine love of flowers, and who regards dissection as 'murderous mutilation' (p. 172).

Heart and Science does not indicate the ways in which Mrs Gallilee has acquired what the novel encodes as a perverse interest in plants. This omission is of more than local significance, for the sexual ideology highlighted in flower imagery generally entails the suppression of those parallels between women and flowers which bear directly upon the conditions under which both are 'grown'. Much flower imagery implies that women of the dominant social classes resemble flowers most exactly in the way they are brought up. Like conservatory exotics, they are reared for brief but glorious, husband-attracting show in stultifying and debilitating environments. This is precisely the image used by John Stuart Mill in *The Subjection of Women* (1869), where he argues, in effect, that women are made into, not born, flowers.

If upper-class women are frail, nervous and emotionally fraught, then it is only because 'a hot-house and stove cultivation has always been carried on of some of the capabilities of their nature, for the benefit and pleasure of their masters'.[69]

One of the few Victorian heroines permitted not only to recognize the subjection of women but also to articulate it in the imagery by which that subjection is typically mystified and sweetened, is George Eliot's Gwendolen Harleth in *Daniel Deronda*. Before her marriage, Gwendolen is asked by Grandcourt whether she intends always to live at Offendene. Gwendolen replies:

> I don't know. We women can't go in search of adventure. . . . We must stay where we grow, or where the gardeners like to transplant us. We are brought up like the flowers, to look as pretty as we can, and be dull without complaining. This is my notion about the plants: they are often bored, and that is the reason why some have got poisonous. (p. 98)

On the face of it, Gwendolen appears to harbour no illusions about her own fate. Since she is a woman, she must also be a plant: static, dependent, pretty and uncomplaining. But it is clear from her *thinking* at this stage that she expects to avoid the usual fate of upper-class women. Her self-comparisons with plainer plants (her younger sisters), the reactions of others to her, and her showy, forcing-house school education have imbued her with a 'sense that so exceptional a person as herself could hardly remain in ordinary circumstances or in a social position less than advantageous'. She also feels 'ready to manage her own destiny' (p. 27).

It seems probable that under the pressures of the situation, Gwendolen gives utterance to what she has been programmed to accept, if not to think in the terms she does. Ironically, her scenario has greater personal application than she realizes. Equipped chiefly with charm and the ability to captivate, she does indeed become 'a beautiful but harmful plant, misusing its powers of attraction'.[70]

One of the effects that Gwendolen's speech makes possible is that of renewing the reader's attentiveness to the flower imagery used elsewhere in *Daniel Deronda*. For example, with reference to the Archery Meeting at Brackenshaw Park, the narrator poses the following rhetorical question: 'What could make a better background for the flower-groups of ladies, moving and bowing and turning their necks as it would become the leisurely lilies to do if they took to locomotion?' (p. 72). Read with Gwendolen's speech in mind, this flower image invites a less automatic response and a less innocent construction than it is otherwise likely to receive.

Nonetheless, the defamiliarizing force of the speech should not be overestimated. Although Gwendolen brings into prominence the idea that women in her position have their destinies determined for them, there is no suggestion here that she thinks of this as anything other than natural and inevitable. Nevertheless, the estranging effects of her speech do draw attention to the potentially deleterious consequences of treating women as flowers. From a critical perspective, this is at least a step in the right direction, particularly since the mass of flower imagery in Victorian literature tends to beautify the plant-like destinies of women. Even a novelist as sympathetic to women as Hardy uses flower comparisons to suggest that women can expect 'a short life, but a gallant show'.[71]

Gwendolen's speech bears interesting comparison with the following passage from Ouida's *Moths* (1880):

> When gardeners plant and graft, they know very well what will be the issue of their work; they do not expect the rose from a bulb of garlic, or look for the fragrant olive from a slip of briar; but the culturers of human nature are less wise, and they sow poison, yet rave in reproaches when it breeds and brings forth its like. 'The rosebud garden of girls' is a favourite theme for poets, and the maiden, in her likeness to a half-opened blossom, is as near purity and sweetness as a human creature can be, yet what does the world do with its opening buds?—it thrusts them in the forcing house amidst the ordure, and then if they perish prematurely, never blames itself. The streets absorb the girls of the poor; society absorbs the daughters of the rich; and not seldom one form of prostitution, like the other, keeps its captives 'bound in the dungeon of their own corruption'. (p. 117)

Like Gwendolen, Ouida's narrator challenges floral discourse and the social practices with which it is associated. In the novel as a whole she is overtly critical of 'the marriage-market, the education and wasted lives of upper-class girls [and] the legal position of the unhappily married woman'.[72] She draws a daring parallel between the commodity values of upper-class and working-class girls, and shows none of Ruskin's inclination in 'Of Queens'

Gardens' (1865) to cloak prostitution in the sentimentality of flower language.[73] At the same time, she appears to accept without question the identification of women with plants, and all that this implies about their moral beauty and social ductility.

Does anyone benefit when women are raised to be as delicate and submissive as flowers? One novelist to have addressed himself to this question was Thackeray. The conclusions reached in his fiction are complex and ambivalent, but in *The Newcomes* at least, no one seems to gain in the long run. Lady Clara suffers an unhappy marriage after she is 'sold' by her parents and 'bought' with 'a fine country-house with delightful gardens, and conservatories' (p. 582). And when, to the misery of everyone, Rosa Newcomes dies at the age of twenty-six, the narrator comments: 'So this poor little flower had bloomed for its little day, and pined, and withered, and perished' (p. 838). The tone seems fatalistic, but Thackeray's target, as the context makes clear, is the parent who exploits the flower-like meekness of a daughter for which he is in any case primarily responsible.

In *Pendennis* (1850) Thackeray applies the flower image to marriage itself:

> Damon has taxes, sermon, parade, tailors' bills, parliamentary duties, and the deuce knows what to think of; Delia has to think about Damon—Damon is the oak (or the post), and stands up, and Delia is the ivy or the honeysuckle whose arms twine about him. Is it not so, Delia? Is it not in your nature to creep about his feet and kiss them, to twine around his trunk and hang there; Damon's duty to stand like a British man with his hands in his breeches pocket, while the pretty fond parasite clings round him? (pp. 628–9)

Variants of the horticultural image of marriage, most inviting women to identify with the role of dependent and decorative wife, would not have been unfamiliar to Thackeray's contemporary readers. Doubtless, some would have found nothing either exceptional or exceptionable about his rhetorical enquiry. But 'pretty fond parasite' seems to imply a male perspective, and hints at the ambivalence, the mixture of kudos and resentment, which many middle-class husbands felt about supporting economically unproductive wives. At the very least, the passage from *Pendennis* permits the construction that status-conscious husbands are the victims as well as the victors of their own sexual politics.

Occasionally, then, Victorian imaginative writers express some awareness, and even criticism, of the darker implications and effects of woman-flower equivalences. Much more frequently, however, they re-affirm these equivalences and the sexual ideology to which they are tied. Their contributions to one of the dominant sexual myths of the age can have been nothing short of massive.

CHAPTER SEVEN

Gardens, Landscapes and Nature

The significance of the garden in Victorian literature has in part to be understood in terms of its relations of equivalence. Since it is generally cognate with the domestic world—the sphere of paramount interest in nineteenth-century fiction as a whole —'garden' discursively associates with words like 'house', 'home', 'leisure' and 'marriage'. But its significance is explicable also and perhaps primarily in terms of its relations of opposition. Of relevance here is the structuralist postulation that meaning inheres—if it inheres at all—not in signs but in the differential relations between them. 'Garden' signifies by virtue of its positions with networks of differentiated 'landscape' signifiers.

I say 'positions' rather than 'position' because the meanings and connotations of 'garden' vary according to the ways in which it is used within different discourses. Thus in some texts it is virtually identical with 'nature'; in others, it breaks semantically from it to nestle among words denoting the world of social construction.

How can we account for these shifting relations? As a starting point we might take the observation that 'nineteenth-century authors define the ontology of Nature variously'.[1] 'Nature' meant different things to different writers; so, presumably, did 'garden'. Nor did the Victorians as a whole have any consensual concept of nature. Hence, 'nature' in Victorian literature may carry a variety of significations, and given the complex cultural conditions of the period, this is precisely what we should expect.

The expansion of urban and industrial landscapes, and the pressures and perplexities of city life, ensured the persistence of 'nature' as a romantic honorific for the countryside and for landscape scenery having the power to refresh, revitalize and give visual delight. In this sense, 'nature' is closely related to the cult of ruralism, and to a 'nostalgia for a lost world of peace and companionship, of healthy bodies and quiet minds'.[2]

But 'nature' was bound also to be more negatively accented by writers who found it impossible to worship nature with the enthusiasm of the Romantic poets. Matthew Arnold is a case in point. Arnold valued 'gentle' landscapes, and saw in gardens, glades and dells a partial and temporary solution to certain human problems. The speaker of 'Lines Written in Kensington Gardens', for example, finds in his 'long open glade' a peaceful retreat from the social furor of the engirdling city. What he does not find, and what Arnold can never quite achieve, is an 'enhanced sense of participation in the life of nature'.[3] From a human standpoint, Arnold's relative certainties are generally depressing. Nature's steadfastness—the theme of, for instance, 'The Youth of Nature' and 'The Youth of Man'—reminds us only of our otherness from it; the instinctual harmony with nature possible in the joy and innocence of childhood gives way in adulthood to estrangement, and lingers merely as a remote Wordsworthian memory.

Two things in particular made the worship of nature a difficult matter for many Victorian writers. Firstly, many lacked faith in the divinity or immanent powers of nature, and were convinced of the fundamental separateness of man (the perceiving subject) and nature (the observed object). They did not see nature as a source of transcendent truths or, if they did, they could not normally apprehend these truths by an exercise of the imagination. Secondly, there was the disabling influence of Victorian science. Darwin and the earlier evolutionists had seemed to suggest that nature was 'red' rather than 'green', competitive and antagonistic rather than co-operative and charitable. They also drew attention to the mutability and the invisible processes of nature, and not (as had the Romantics) to its grand, static and apparently timeless visible structures. Both suppositions—that nature was probably amoral, and that nature was a material world in flux—encouraged what might be called the botanical hand-book view of nature as 'just a collection of discrete things, all jumbled up together, with no pattern and no hierarchy'.[4]

On the one hand, then, 'nature' serves as a warmly-accented synonym for the beneficent countryside. Generally speaking, the garden in Victorian literature is identified with the more positive qualities ascribed to the countryside, and frequently functions as a synecdoche of, or surrogate for, nature in its pastoral and generous modes. Its antitheses are the city—the negation or subjugation of nature—and the wilderness—nature in its sublime, threatening and least co-operative modes.

On the other hand, 'nature' is more negatively accented when it implies a philosophic or scientific frame of reference. (There are exceptions to this generalization, most notably in the writings of Meredith and Swinburne.) As a rule, the garden is remote from 'nature' in its abstract and cheerless senses. Indeed, it seems likely that the garden appealed to Victorian writers partly because it suggested a means of evading, suspending or positively redefining the discomforting intimations of nature conceived as purely materialistic or 'red in tooth and claw'. Certainly, in the majority of garden descriptions, the appetitive aspects of nature are absent, firmly under human control, or, as in some of Browning's poems and a great many cottage garden descriptions, heartening manifestations of the earth's irrepressible exuberance and spontaneity. Moreover, gardens legitimized the botanical hand-book view of nature, and offered comfort to those who, like Arnold and Tennyson, were forced to accommodate it. It may have been disquieting to think of nature in general as a collection of disparate things with no esemplastic force to interanimate them. But *gardens* could properly be regarded as special cases, since they *are* assemblages of plants and trees, and since their designs *are* imposed rather than naturally occurring. Their features can be itemized in the manner of a botanical catalogue or on the basis of organizing principles that do not entail a sense of nature as 'more deeply interfused'. To take just one example: in Browning's 'The Flower's Name', the account of the garden is organized in terms of the speaker's imaginative reconstruction of the movements of a woman through it. If there is any interanimating force at work, it is the spirit not of nature but of the woman whose 'dear mark' the speaker strains to make out on each of the flowers she touched (*BP*, p. 436).

Like many other Victorian garden poems and fictional garden descriptions, 'The Flower's Name' is not about nature, but about (in part) natural things in a domestic or humanized landscape. Moreover, these natural things acquire their significance not from their ontological connections with nature conceived as a material system or spiritual force, but from their associations with people, places, and experiences. This orientation betrays a set of post-Romantic convictions regarding nature and human relations with it. If nature as a whole is inscrutable and probably indifferent to human needs and interests, at least the natural objects of gardens can be known and made meaningful by their peculiar associations for particular individuals. If nature cannot be relied upon to offer spiritual sustenance and moral enlightenment, gardens at least can offer a kind of friendship and partnership. If the analysis of nature is sometimes corrosive, direct engagement with flowers and gardens delights, refreshes and cultivates the heart. (Charles

Kingsley's advice was to 'Feed on Nature [but] do not try to understand it.'[5])

These convictions surface almost everywhere in Victorian literature. They are implicit, for example, in the countless farewell-to-garden passages in fiction, each of which discloses a character's emotional investment in a garden long considered a personal friend. They come closer to the surface in the 'garden' books of Alfred Austin and 'Elizabeth' (E. M. Russell), in which nature, now thoroughly personified, is simply and comfortably construed as a superior kind of gardener—or 'senior partner' as Austin has it. A good many fictional characters are restored to physical or spiritual health not through their contemplation of nature in the abstract, but through their exposure to gardens and the knowable natural things they contain.

The distinction I am pressing here, between a theorized concept of nature and the concretization of nature in complaisant particulars, informs and helps to account for the dozens of garden-as-refuge poems produced in the Victorian period. It can be traced, for example, in two superficially similar poems: Arnold's 'Lines Written in Kensington Gardens', and the much anthologized 'A Garden Song' by Austin Dobson.

The opening stanza of Arnold's poem places the speaker within a framed and finite garden landscape:

> In this lone, open glade I lie,
> Screened by deep boughs on either hand;
> And at its end, to stay the eye,
> Those black-crowned, red-boled pine-trees stand. (*AP*, p. 269)

In the immediately succeeding stanzas, the speaker supplies an inventory of the sights and sounds which animate the scene: bird-songs, sheep-cries, 'blowing daisies', 'fragrant grass', a stray child or two. Because of its 'endless, active life', its 'peace for ever new', its clearness and freshness, the glade compares favourably with the 'mountain sod', a vignette of which is the subject of stanza five. Although the speaker is an observer of rather than a participant in the life of the glade—his 'harmony with nature' is 'modest, mundane, unmystical, unquestioning'[6]—his sympathies are with it, and its peacefulness soothes him. He is as close to knowing the things of the garden as he can get. That he nonetheless experiences a sense of alienation, a lack, is a measure of his perceived separateness from the spirit of nature—the 'calm soul of all things' to which he prays in the concluding lines.

'A Garden Song' might crudely be described as a simplified version of 'Lines'. What in particular makes it more simplified—and thus more typical of the garden-as-refuge poems strewn in the pages of popular Victorian magazines—is the simple opposition of peaceful garden and noisy world; 'nature', the complicating third term, is conspicuous by its absence. The poem is, admittedly, packed with the names of natural things; but consider the first stanza:

> Here, in this sequestered close,
> Bloom the hyacinth and rose;
> Here beside the modest stock
> Flaunts the flaring hollyhock;
> Here, without a pang, one sees
> Ranks, conditions, and degrees. (*DP*, p. 178)

The 'sequestered' close shuts out disturbing intimations of nature—its anarchy, its amorality, its troubling mysteries—as effectively as it shuts out the distant 'sounds of toil and turmoil'. The flowers of the garden, nameable and therefore knowable, are agreeably humanized with the epithets of an implied social code. And with equal anthropocentric assurance, the garden 'text' is presented as an innocuous mirror image of the hierarchical social structure it seems at the same time almost to naturalize.[7]

The speaker's certitude—the tone of which persists throughout the poem—issues from his sense of inhabiting a known and graspable world of natural things that behave predictably and in accordance with human interests. 'Here', the confident indicative, abounds. Even the seasons are contained and personified (they 'run their race') within the walls of the enclosed garden. And although, like Arnold's 'Lines', the poem ends with an invocation, this is not to the mysterious 'soul of all things', but to the resident *genius loci*, the congenial 'garden-god' (*DP*, p. 178).

Thus far, I have attempted to determine the significance of the garden in Victorian literature by examining its complex relations with 'nature'. I now wish to focus more specifically upon the garden as a landscape, since its significations must also be understood in terms of its position within a topographical system based upon qualitative landscape distinctions.

In contrast to the Romantics' predilection for heights—'the terrifying reaches of Shelley's Mont Blanc, or even of Wordsworth's Snowdon'—'Victorian fiction typically lives at low altitudes'. 'The literature of manners, of social order and social accommodation—the Victorian novel—found its metaphors not in wild and extreme Nature but by the glowing hearth and in the cultivated fields'. And 'the great mythic seat of innocence is not the craggy mountain but the garden'. In other words, Victorian novelists 'tended to place happiness in bounded human landscapes'.[8] A recent study of the language of landscape in Victorian poetry makes a similar division of poetic landscapes, distinguishing between 'antisocial' landscapes of isolation and retreat—'the great primeval wildernesses of mountain, sea, and forest'—and 'social landscapes'—gardens and other landscapes expressive of commonality and social values. Though it may be that 'the garden is the most complex and ambiguous of all landscapes', and that some gardens 'are created specifically for the antisocial purposes', 'to a certain extent it might be said that the Victorians retreated from the mountains into the [?] garden'.[9]

It can be said, then, gardens are prominent in Victorian literature chiefly because they displaced nature in its wilder forms as the principal sources of poetic inspiration, and because gardens were semiotically more appropriate to the functions that literary landscapes were required to serve. It is true, at least, that most Victorian writers modified, lost confidence in, or actively repudiated the attitudes towards natural scenery that they inherited. There were a number of reasons for this.

There was, first of all, a general decline in what might be termed the touristic perspective. More accurately, there was a reluctance on the part of some socially conscious Victorians to endorse the notion of a 'pure' aesthetics of landscape, a notion that could be maintained, they believed, only by those for whom the spectator was absolved of social responsibilities and moral obligations. For Ruskin, George Eliot and others, the habit of seeing nature as merely something 'out there' was the penchant of the aristocratic sightseer or writer whose determination to wrest aesthetic pleasure from a 'sublime' or 'picturesque' landscape implied indifference to the misery of its human inhabitants or, at the very least, a wilful disengagement from the world of human affairs.

Certain kinds of gardens could also be viewed touristically; but since they bore the imprint of human construction and occupation, it was considerably more difficult for the spectator to confine his attention to mere scenery. It was this inevitable presence of what the eighteenth-century advocates of the picturesque would have regarded as 'noise' in the landscape, rather than a sudden cessation of interest in raw nature or of the gratifications to be derived from viewing it, that induced Victorian novelists and poets in general to transfer their picture-making operations from mountains to gardens. For gardens and garden-flecked landscapes afforded them the opportunity of indulging touristic proclivities with relative impunity from the charge of heartless detachment, irrespective of their sensitivity to the moral and social dimensions of landscapes.

The retention but topographical redirection of the touristic perspective is evident in the opening chapters of some of George Eliot's novels, *Felix Holt* and *The Mill on the Floss* in particular, but still more obtrusive in a number of less famous novels. An excellent example is *A Year at Hartlebury*, a piece of political fiction, published in 1834 and written, as we now know, by Benjamin Disraeli in collaboration with his sister, Sarah.[10] It opens with an invitation from the narrators in their role of tourist-guides:

> Gentle reader, wander with us awhile, along the banks of this tranquil river, as it winds its course through this verdant valley, and we will show you a fair scene. (p. 1)

The location is a rural lowland, and 'fair' prepares the reader for a prospect altogether remote from the wild and rugged. It begins with the conventional imperative:

> Behold a rural green, encircled by cottages and embosomed in wood-crowned hills. Each humble dwelling stands in the midst of a garden rich in vegetable store, and gay with the many-coloured tulip, the garden crocus, and its slanting thatch is covered with the fragrant honeysuckle. . . . The green gradually ascends the side of the narrow valley, and, on the right on a sloping lawn, gay with laburnums, lilacs, and syringa, stands a low irregularly built house with gable ends and tall chimneys. It is the Parsonage; its porch is covered with ivy, and its large projecting windows are clustered with brilliant scarlet flowers of the Pyrus japonica. On the lawns, and separated from the garden only by a light iron fence, stands a very small church mantled with ivy. It is sheltered from the North by a rich dark plantation of firs and yews, while around are scattered humble but neat graves of the peaceful villagers. A road winds round the upland

> green to the wide gates of the mansion-house, an ancient Elizabethan Hall. (p. 1)

This is picturesque scenery with a small 'p', the kind that came to appeal to country-starved Victorians, glad enough to partake of vicarious sightseeing, though not with an aristocratic connoisseur as a guide.

Of the succeeding seven chapters of *A Year at Hartlebury*, no fewer than four begin with similar, if more localized, scenic descriptions in which gardens are the dominant landscape features. Only one chapter (Chapter 8) introduces the reader to 'picturesque beauties' that are even remotely reminiscent of eighteenth-century touristic descriptions:

> Amid the wildest scenery of Bohun Park, you suddenly come to a small rustic gate. Pass through it a few yards, and a magical scene is before you. The ground seems to have opened at your feet; you look over the heads of the tallest trees upon a green and bowery glen, nearly surrounded by precipitous banks covered with towering trees growing one above the other. At the furthest point these banks gradually slope down, and form a natural opening. (p. 27)

But even the wild and romantic scenery of Bohun Castle has its social uses: it provides the scene for a picnic party from Hartlebury.

The Disraelis doubtless considered it an advantage to live a stone's throw away from enchanting castle scenery, though the Hartlebury locals were not the only people to avail themselves of the beauties of Bohun Park. We are told that it 'was a regular show place', and that 'few travellers came within twenty miles of it that were not induced to stay on their way'. And not because it was a picturesque ruin: 'the splendid pile bore no marks of devastation—scarcely of neglect' (p. 28). Bohun, though welcoming, is sufficiently uncluttered with sightseers to offer the genuine seeker after landscape experience an adequate substitute for the pleasure of gazing upon rugged natural scenery.

This suggests a further reason for the decline of interest in mountain scenery: for the majority of Victorians and for many fictional characters as well, such landscapes were either too inaccessible or by no means inaccessible enough. Those who retained the inclination to wander lonely as clouds in (say) the Lake District or the Alps, were frequently frustrated by the number of other 'clouds' who were there for other purposes. 'The poet or painter could no longer enjoy the mountains in solitude, but must share them with boisterous groups of tourists and mountaineers.'[11] The trend towards thronging the mountains for non-aesthetic purposes intensified in the course of the century, so much so that by the 1890s some of the best-selling romantic novelists, including Mrs Hoare, were setting their stories in snowy, peaked Tyrolean landscapes.[12] Ironically, then, private gardens and even public ones sometimes afforded greater opportunities for solitary experiences than the more popular 'wildernesses'—which helps explain the prominence of the garden-as-a-retreat motif in Victorian literature.

Even so, the option of actively avoiding wild landscapes was the prerogative of a privileged minority. Mountains, being so remote from the places in which the majority lived and worked, could never have met their needs for recreation and scenery. Whatever their preferences, most people had to be content with tamer surrogates—public parks, the countryside and, usually for the better-off, private gardens. Victorian fiction abounds in accounts of occasional trips to the 'middle landscape' (that is, the countryside between the polarities of city and wilderness).[13] Victorian literature 'swarms with characters obeying a powerful centrifugal impulse urging them away from the city'[14] and, it should be added, an equally powerful centripetal impulse compelling them to remain in or return to their gardens. Elizabeth Gaskell was aware of the strength of both impulses. A substantial portion of her first published story, *Libbie Marsh's Three Eras* (1847) is devoted to Libbie's Whitsun outing to Dunham Park, which had for years been 'the favourite resort of the Manchester work people. . . . [Its] scenery presents such a complete contrast to the whirl and turmoil of Manchester: so thoroughly woodland, with its ancestral trees (here and there lightning blanched); its "verduous walls"; its grassy walks leading far away into some glade.'[15] *Mary Barton* (1848) opens with a similar episode: an account of the Bartons' holiday excursion to Green Heys fields. Had the events of the novel been set a few years later (in the late 1840s, for example) the outing might well have been to the newly constructed Peel Park, one of the 'people's parks'.

An account of a similar excursion is given by Charlotte M. Yonge in *The Pillars of the House*. Here the dependants of a poor city curate leave the 'smoky' town of Bexley, and head for the nearest green space: the park of an untenanted country mansion. The scene recalls that of the picnickers in Tennyson's *Audley Court* who hold their singing contest 'on a slope of orchard' on the garden estate of an abandoned country house. Perhaps she also had in mind the outer frame of *The Princess*, the setting of which is the 'broad lawns' of the socially-conscious Sir Walter Vivian who, on this occasion at least, has made his park accessible 'to the people', in this case the members of the local Mechanics' Institute.

The strength of the centripetal impulse is exemplified, in Gaskell's *North and South*, by Margaret Hale's attachment to the garden of Helstone vicarage, which impels her to revisit it long after her move to Milton Northern.

Some critics have made much of Dickens's complicity in or unwitting perpetuation of 'middle landscape' myths: the myth of the countryside as an Edenic world of pastoral innocence; the myth of the regenerative country- or semi-rural garden. But gardens and fields are important places in Dickens's novels primarily because they are the only restorative environments accessible to characters most in need of refuge and escape. *Little Dorrit* offers an example. With her father in the Marshalsea, Amy Dorrit's only chance of a change of scenery comes every other Sunday with her trip to 'some meadows and green lanes' where she 'picked grass and flowers to bring home' (p. 70). Wemmick's return each evening to his suburban garden at Walworth may enable him to shake off the Little Britain cobwebs; in any case, the garden and miniature castle are the only recuperative spaces available to him. As Dickens appreciated, the suburban garden was enormously important to the 'regular City man', not because it was the only landscape supremely well fitted to gratify his recreational requirements, but because the commuter's daily rhythms, together with the frictional effects of distance, conspired to narrow down the range of functional alternatives. This is not to say that the City gentleman regarded his precious garden as no more than a convenient substitute for the 'real' thing—for nature in the wild. He may well have concurred with the sentiment expressed by one of Wilkie Collins's characters, Benjamin Rondel in *The Fallen Leaves* (1879), that there is no need to venture outside London to experience the beauties of nature since they are all there in Finsbury Square 'carefully ordered and arranged' (p. 2).

This is claiming a great deal for the reorientation of nature to man-made circumstances—more, perhaps, than most Victorians would have been willing to grant. But they would have accepted the implication: that nature 'ordered and arranged'—'dressed' as garden writers were wont to put it—is more acceptable, in both senses, than nature in its naked state. The point has been made that 'for the Victorians, nature generally functions as an anomalous symbol having the irreconcilable features of beauty and cruelty', and that it was 'viewed for the most part as an indifferent rather than a beneficent force'.[16] For many Victorians, however, the wildscape was neither beautiful nor merely indifferent to human interests; rather, it was unequivocally ugly and brutal.

Scientific discoveries may have strengthened this view, but its pervasiveness had more to do with the (Christian) belief that the wilderness was 'uncivilized' rather than ontologically autonomous. Nature might be brutal—but not irremediably so; civilized people could make parts of it benign and a testimony to the goodness of God. It has been argued that 'because of the expanding material wealth that resulted from the ingenious harnessing of natural forces' in the Victorian period, 'the idea of Optimism in a divinely-controlled, rational universe tended to be replaced by that of PROGRESS in an industrialized environment'.[17] But for many Victorians, God and man were not at strife, since progress in the form of environmental domination could be construed as the perpetration of God's will to civilize (i.e. Christianize) apparently godless landscapes and people. To the evangelically inclined, the association of the wilderness with the heathenish was confirmed by the reports of missionaries and explorers who attested to their encounters with 'brutal' people living in 'brutal' surroundings. Lord Kaimes touched upon this association in an article in *The Saturday Magazine*:

> Rough uncultivated ground, dismal to the eye, inspires peevishness and discontent: may not this be one cause of the harsh manners of savages?
>
> A field richly ornamented, containing beautiful objects of various lands, displays in full lustre the goodness of the Deity, and the ample provision he has made for our happiness. . . . Other fine arts may be perverted to excite irregular, and even vicious, emotions; but gardening, which inspires the purest and most refined pleasures, cannot fail to promote every good affection.[18]

Kaimes's views were reaffirmed by innumerable other Victorian writers equally keen on transforming wildscapes into gardens, and no less convinced of the refining effects of gardening. These views find echoes, as well, in contemporary imaginative literature.

The transformation of a wild country into a civilized garden is the cultural project rehearsed in Tennyson's *Idylls of the King*. Arthur himself is presented as 'the bringer of civilization to a barbarous people'.[19] Like a head gardener newly appointed to a huge unkempt estate, his first mammoth task is to carve edenic clearings in a wasteland ruled by heathens and wild beasts. His mission does not end there, for having successfully created a garden, he has then to extirpate the weeds of evil and chaos from the very realm he has civilized. In an important speech to Geraint, he illustrates the insidiousness of habit and custom in specifically horticultural terms:

> The world will not believe a man repents:
> And this wise world of ours is mainly right.
> Full seldom doth a man repent, or use
> Both grace and will to pick the vicious quitch
> Of blood and custom wholly out of him,
> And make all clean, and plant himself afresh.
> Edryn has done it, weeding all his heart
> As I will weed this land before I go. (*TP*, p. 1574)

When Arthur embarks on a weed-plucking expedition, the narrator reinforces the metaphorical equivalence of horticulture and the progress and purification of civilization:

> and as now
> Men weed the white horse on the Berkshire hills
> To keep him bright and clean as heretofore,
> He rooted out the slothful officer
> Or guilty, which for bribe had winked at wrong,
> And in their chairs set up a stronger race
> With hearts and hands, and sent a thousand men
> To till the wastes, and moving everywhere
> Cleared the dark places and let in the law,
> And broke the bandit holds and cleansed the land. (*TP*, p. 1575)

Here, as elsewhere in the *Idylls*, 'green' language serves the seemingly paradoxical function of naturalizing the cultural control of nature; 'Arthur's insistence upon a perfect nature is indistinguishable from the imposition of unnatural (i.e. cultural) constraints to curb the ferocity of natural impulses.'[20] Nonetheless, it is Arthur's view of 'uncooked' nature as 'the hostile environment against which man must defend his spiritual identity'[21] that the poems consistently emphasize. Those who are sympathetic to

Arthur's mission as 'gardener' are accorded positive 'horticultural' qualities. Thus Gareth first travels to Camelot dressed like one of the 'tillers of the soil'; Lynette dubs him 'the flower of kitchendom'. Those who wilfully oppose and subvert the cultural experiment have nature—but not the narrator—on their side. Vivien, who may be taken to represent the 'threatening natural world',[22] is a wanton, writhing serpent: 'wily', 'lissome', and 'snake'-like; Mordred is a 'Green-suited' creepy-crawly. When he scales the wall of Guinevere's garden 'to spy some secret scandal if he might', he is caught in the act by Lancelot,

> and as the gardener's hand
> Plucks from the colewort a green caterpillar,
> So from the hall wall and the flowering grove
> Of grasses Lancelot plucked him by the heel,
> And cast him as a worm upon the way. (*TP*, p. 1726)

The essential point here is that Arthur's gardenizing crusade is motivated by and predicated upon broadly the same notion of progress and the same positivistic assumptions upon which Victorian garden theorists constructed their non-mimetic garden designs:

> Why should we imitate wild nature? The garden is a product of civilisation. Why any more make of our gardens imitation of wild nature, than paint our children with woad, and make them run about naked in an effort to imitate nature unadorned? The very charm of a garden is that it is taken out of savagery, trimmed, clothed and disciplined.[23]

The association of wildscapes with brutality, and gardens with civility and refinement, is suggested in other ways in Victorian literature. Gardening is closely associated with other 'cultivating' activities—notably with reading. In the novels of Wilkie Collins and others, the nearness of libraries to gardens or garden rooms hints at their functional equivalence. The *Quarterly Review* of 1884 specified gardening and reading as the principal 'amusements' of country life.[24] Fictional correlatives conflate the two activities in pictures of privileged country-house dwellers reading and reclining in immaculately tended gardens—recurrent models of gracious living. Furthermore, fictional scholars often double up as knowledgeable gardeners: Eugene Aram, Glastonbury (in *Henrietta Temple*), Father Coleman (in *Lothair*). The *belles lettristic* 'hero' of *The Aspern Papers* confesses a 'horticultural passion' (p. 153);

Charlotte Brontë's M. Emanuel 'had a taste for gardening' (p. 398); and to judge from his books, Alfred Austin did nothing but read, write and garden and converse on all three. The catalogue of cultivated cultivators is vast.

Still more compelling illustrations of the humanizing and refining influence of gardening are provided by working- or lower-middle-class fictional gardeners whose lives are ruthlessly segmented into work and non-work. Wemmick's gardening activities are in part an expression of the finer feelings and creative impulses he is compelled to contain in Little Britain. Wilkie Collins's Sergeant Cuff is a similar case; if anything, his personality is even more strikingly divided than Wemmick's. As the 'illustrious thief-taker' he is taciturn, impassive and impenetrable; these behaviours, like Wemmick's 'post-office' mouth, are functional adaptions to a working environment in which spontaneous displays of sentiment are all but proscribed. But in the presence of his precious roses, Cuff confesses his capacity for 'fondness', and babbles with the contentment of a child at play. When questioned about his 'odd taste', he explains:

> If you will look about you (which most people won't do) . . . You will see that the nature of a man's taste is, most time, as opposite as possible to the nature of a man's business. Show me any two things more opposite one from the other than a rose and a thief, and I'll correct my taste accordingly—if it isn't too late at my time of life. (p. 89)

Richard Jefferies's farmer Iden in *Amaryllis at the Fair* is an equally dichotomous figure. Forced to seek a meagre living from a meagre soil, he can see in nature only a harsh antagonist: 'Nature never plants—nature is no gardener—no design, no proportion in the fields' (p. 317). Iden's work inevitably makes him hard, insensitive and coarsely materialistic. When his daughter gambols over to him, breathless with excitement at having discovered the first daffodil of spring, he can manage only a gruff and bruising rebuke: "Flowers bean't no use on; such trumpery as that; what do 'ee want a messing about arter thaay?" (p. 203). Yet when he looks at the flower with a gardener's eye, he no longer regards it as a useless inedible luxury. There is even a remarkable alteration of 'his pronunciation from that of the country folk and labourers amongst whom he dwelt to the correct accent of education' (p. 204). Gardening releases in him all those felicitous feelings that potato planting compels him to suppress.

As his grossness dissolves, so also do the tensions that lacerate his interpersonal relationships, and there is 'billing and cooing and fraternizing, and sunshine in the garden over the hedge of lavender' (p. 240).

In general, mid-century fiction avoids extremes—both geographical and (with the exception of so-called sensation fiction) experiential. Implicit in this orientation towards familiar social worlds is the assumption that 'ordinary' human experience, like realist fiction itself, is imperilled when it passes the boundaries of the known and knowable humanized landscape. As a consequence, the antithesis of brutalizing wildscape and civilizing garden tends to be blunted or merely implied. The obvious exception is *Wuthering Heights*, in which an isolated, provincial house of fortress-like stolidity, exposed to the tumult of the elements and surrounded by an unreclaimed wildscape of moors and marsh, stands in physical and symbolic opposition to a conventional country mansion, distanced and cushioned by parklands and gardens from nature in the raw. The characters at home in the landscapes encircling these houses also share their distinctive characteristics. This may be a schematic simplification, but no qualifications can spirit away the reader's sense of a fundamental topographical dichotomy of exposed wildscape and enclosed park.

It is worth drawing attention to a salient fact about the critical reception of *Wuthering Heights*; when the novel first appeared, it was, first and foremost, grist to the mill of those who subscribed to the most vulgar version of environmental determinism. The reviewer for the *Athenaeum* wrote: 'The brutal master of the lonely house on "Wuthering Heights" . . . has doubtless had his prototype in those uncongenial and remote districts where human beings, like the trees, grow gnarled and dwarfed and distorted by the inclement climate.'[25] Other early critics were equally attentive to the brutalizing effects of the moors, but also curiously inattentive to the environmental influence of the more humanized landscapes in the novel. For example, the reviewer for the *Britannia* lamented that 'There are no green spots in it on which the mind can linger with satisfaction.'[26] Since there most certainly *are* such spots in *Wuthering Heights*, the blindness of the early critics to them suggests that they were intent upon venting their antipathy towards unreclaimed nature and towards what they supposed to be the deleterious effects of wildscapes upon those who exposed themselves to them.

Had old Mr Earnshaw been a moral reformer, he might have set Heathcliff to work in the garden of the Heights in a bid to nurture his latent finer qualities. And he might well have deemed it folly to loose him upon a landscape so harsh that it could serve only to exacerbate his 'native' savagery. The calvinistically and evangelically inclined were apt to favour gardening among the young as a means of inculcating the virtues of self-discipline, submission to authority, and individual responsibility. A régime owing something to this attitude is described in *Jane Eyre*. Behind the walls of the garden of Lowood School—walls that excluded any wider prospect—were 'scores of little beds; these beds were assigned as gardens for the pupils to cultivate, and each bed had an owner' (p. 80). The regimentation of these flower beds suggests that they are there to regulate the behaviour of the pupils, not to awaken in them an interest in nature. For Brocklehurst, the manager and treasurer of Lowood School, nature is a thoroughly negative model. As he declares, the girls are there to be drilled into 'Grace', 'not to conform to nature' (p. 96).

Many earnest, middle-class Victorians shared the conviction that 'uncooked' nature cannot improve morals and manners since it is itself rude and in need of correction. Words like 'training' and 'cultivation' were often used in ways which conflated their literal (i.e. horticultural) and figurative senses. Reflecting this habit, one of Mrs Henry Wood's characters, Lady Augusta in *The Channings* (1862), dilates upon the value of cultivation:

> God's laws everywhere proclaim it. . . . Look at the trees of our fields, the flowers of our parterres, the vegetables of our gardens—what are they, unless they are pruned, dug about, cared for? It is by cultivation alone that they can be brought to perfection. (p. 443)

Similarly, Mrs Gatty's *Parables from Nature* is very largely a diatribe against the anarchy of nature untrained. One of the parables, entitled 'Training and Restraining', tells the story of a Wind—here the personification of 'wicked' wild nature—that gleefully seeks to arouse the frustrations and dissatisfaction of the flowers in 'a pretty villa garden' by drawing attention to the restraints imposed upon them by the gardener. With the assistance of the anarchic Wind, the flowers rebel against submission, with the result that they perish or grow wild. The daughter of the gardener draws a moral lesson from the sight of the fallen rebels. Addressing her mother, she says:

> I quite understand what you have so often said about the necessity of training, and restraint, and culture, for us as well as for flowers, in a fallen world. The wind has torn away these poor things from their fastenings, and they are growing wild whichever way they please. I know I should once have argued, that if it were their *natural* mode of growing it must therefore be the best. But I cannot say so, now that I see the result. They are doing whatever they like, unrestrained; and the end is, that my beautiful GARDEN is turned into a WILDERNESS. (pp. 54–5)

Small trace here of that 'Rousseauistic faith in the goodness of human nature and the spontaneous flowering of the moral sentiments, so long as they are uncorrupted by the "evil" influence of civilization and unrestrained by authoritarian discipline'.[27] The Victorians may have inherited the 'cult of noble emotions' from the Romantics, but most conventionally-minded Victorians were more likely to work on the supposition that savages are ignoble precisely because they have missed out on the benefits of corrected or civilized nature. To be civilized, savages, reprobates and children require gardens rather than mountains.

This view was given official endorsement in the Report of the Parliamentary Committee on the Labouring Poor of 1843, which pointed out: 'Many striking instances have been stated . . . where the possession of an allotment has been the means of reclaiming the criminal, reforming the dissolute, and of changing their whole moral character and conduct'.[28] There was indeed a long-established practice, in the more enlightened reformatory institutions, of giving criminals and idlers gardens to tend. In Charles Reade's *It is Never Too Late to Mend* (1856), the narrator describes the effects of an all too brief spell of gardening upon a prisoner (Robinson) whose other assignments are meaningless and cruel. The garden itself 'was inclosed within walls of great height, and to us would have seemed a cheerless place for horticulture, but to Robinson it appeared the garden of Eden. . . . Robinson drove the spade into the soil with all the energy of one of God's creatures escaping from system back to nature' (p. 107).

Like Reade, Dickens often depicted gardening as a potentially redemptive and revivifying activity, and advanced it from philanthropic rather than from puritanical motives. In the *American Notes* (1842) he relates the story of a prisoner in a Pennsylvanian penitentiary whose debilities earned him the right to work in the prison garden. Like Robinson, he 'went about the new occupation with great cheerfulness' (p. 111). Then one day the garden gate opened magically before him and he returned to the outside world. Perhaps Dickens took this for an apologue, for by the mid-1840s gardening as a means of rehabilitation and re-entry into the wider world was looming large in his plans for an Asylum for Fallen Women. In a letter to Angela Burdett Coutts—the philanthropist who inaugurated and funded the project—he wrote: 'The cultivation of little gardens, if they be no bigger than graves, is a great resource and a great reward. It has always been found to be productive of good effects wherever it has been tried.'[29] Dickens hoped that each woman would be offered a garden of her own.

A number of Dickens's fictional characters are restored and comforted either by gardening, or simply by the prospect of it. Old Mr Wickfield in *David Copperfield*, a broken lawyer but a 'reclaimed' man, travels almost daily to occupy himself in his garden 'a couple of miles or so out of town' (p. 841). In *Little Dorrit*, John Chivery's sustaining idea of 'pastoral domestic happiness' is a scrap of the Marshalsea, transformed by 'a trellis-work of scarlet beans and a canary or so' into 'a very Arbour' (p. 212). It is highly significant, in this context, that none of Dickens's characters finds the quality of his or her life improved by direct contact with the wildest natural scenery and, indeed, Dickens's narrators consistently negate the belief that happiness is to be found among the solitudes of mountains and other barren landscapes.

Like many of his contemporaries, Dickens could respond in a positive way to rugged scenery, but only as a touristic spectator, and never with any Wordsworthian sense of communion with the natural world. The travel books (but not, significantly, the novels) are thick with 'picturesque' perceptions, and contain some generally unremarkable descriptions of beautiful scenery, even including a few which exalt the awesome serenity and power of the natural world. For example, Niagara Falls is described as a 'tremendous spectacle', an 'Image of Beauty' with 'nothing of gloom or terror about it'.[30] The nearest novelistic equivalent is probably Esther Summerson's account in Chapter 18 of *Bleak House* of a storm in the park of Chesney Wold, in which 'the power of nature is associated with the Christian myth of creation'.[31] Nonetheless, Dickens was basically a fair-weather sightseer who liked his landscapes to assume a friendly countenance. He was appalled by the 'unutterable solemnity and dreariness' of Vesuvius at sunset, though he had enjoyed the 'same' scene under the sunny skies of daytime. He was delighted by the 'elegance and neatness' of the villa gardens of Cincinnati, but dispirited by the desolation of the Mississippi flood-plain, and oppressed by the 'barren monotony'[32] of the prairies. 'When Dickens travelled west to the frontier and was confronted by the raw, untamed power of nature, he was quite simply terrified.'[33] When he came to give the experience fictional expression in *Martin Chuzzlewit* (1844) he stressed the almost antediluvian character of the American wilderness. Of the ironically named settlement of 'Eden'—almost certainly inspired by Dickens's sight of Cairo, Illinois, in 1842—he wrote: 'The waters of the Deluge might have left it but a week' (p. 377).

Dickens had come to accept that there was no such thing as an intrinsically virtuous natural environment and, hence, no possibility of a return to primal innocence. The Kent marshes where Pip spent his childhood are a far cry from the American wasteland, but they too are bleak and oppressive, and Dickens presents them as no more or less virtue-inducing than London.

The wildest natural landscapes, by contrast, acquire consistently negative accents. Dickens uses 'Nature at its wildest (as, for instance, in the death of Steerforth) to act out passions not legitimate within society',[34] and almost always makes mountains the sites of extreme and dangerous action. There is an example of this in *No Thoroughfare* (1867), the late story Dickens wrote with Wilkie Collins: 'The villain, Obeneizer, spent his childhood in the mountain gloom; and in the Simplon pass he reveals his villainy to the hero and almost succeeds in killing him.'[35] Moreover, Dickens's characters almost never find mountains exhilarating or elevating. It is significant that the only character in *Little Dorrit* with a taste for such scenery is the evil Blandois, who declares: 'I love and study the picturesque in all its varieties' (p. 258).

The Dorrits themselves find their Alpine tour anything but productive of picturesque experiences. Their ascent to the Great St Bernard leaves them panting after shelter from the 'searching cold'. Above the lower slopes of the Swiss Alps, all is 'barrenness and desolation' (p. 432). The soil, like the wine, is 'hard' and 'stony'. Only in the lower, 'softer regions' is nature hospitable and refreshing. Amy discovers that the mountains are less real than 'the old Marshalsea room'; they are 'visions' which 'might melt at any moment' (p. 463). For William Dorrit, similarly, the Alps do not offer 'a new kind of transcendence; rather they are a bad dream, an unreality that makes a worse prison than the one before.'[36]

When David Copperfield journeys to Switzerland it is to recover his health and spirits. But the Alpine peaks can do nothing positive for him; like the Dorrits, he is unable to shed the burden of the recent past. 'If those awful solitudes had spoken to my heart,' he says, 'I did not know it. I had found sublimity and wonder in the dread heights and precipices, in the roaring torrents, and the wastes of ice and snow; but as yet, they had taught me nothing else' (p. 814). David's recovery is contingent upon his descent to the lowlands. When he comes down to the 'clustered village in the valley' he finds not only Agnes's heartening letters but also the 'softening influence' of peaceful landscapes, and the 'human interest' from which he 'had lately shrunk' (p. 815).

In Dickens's novels, then, the distinction between hard and soft landscapes is very marked. Soft landscapes occur more frequently and are presented more positively. Few of Dickens's characters turn to more rugged landscapes for stimulation or transcendence and, because of their states of mind, rarely find it when they do. On the other hand, many of his characters have needs which soft landscapes—gardens and bits of benign countryside—are peculiarly fitted to supply: refreshment, restoration, tranquillity and protection. Hence, many of his domestic havens, like the Asylum for prostitutes, have a rural or semi-rural setting: the Maylies's cottage at Chertsey, for instance, or the Meagles's cottage at Twickenham—though the latter is a more ambivalent case. This does not mean that Dickens described the countryside in consistently idyllic terms.[37] His rural 'Edens' are havens, not heavens. The Maylies's cottage garden offers Oliver what he needs: security and a certain degree of freedom. But it is not the perfect antithesis of the subterranean city world from which he has been rescued. The 'rose and honeysuckle which *cling* to the cottage walls, and the ivy which *creeps round* the trunks of the trees' are 'images of enclosure rather than of complete openness.'[38]

Though Dickens never lost faith in the restorative powers of pleasant pastoral pockets, he came to realize the insufficiency, even the partial impotency, of rural 'Edens', and except in the early novels, incorporates his most resilient and efficacious garden spaces within rather than outside the urban community.

In reflecting these modifications to the Wordsworthian view of nature and its place in the lives of ordinary people, Dickens was responding to a set of social conditions quite different from those which had obtained in the early years of the century. Wordsworth 'was able to remove himself from that "monstrous anthill on the plain"', London. Dickens knew that his own role, his world, his relation to his readers had unalterably changed: the "common haunts of the green earth" could not really be expected to fasten on the hearts of a public of novel-readers.'[39] Conscious of his close relationship with middle-class readers, appreciative of their expectations from literature and life, and aware that they did not commune with nature in the manner of a Wordsworth or a Keats, Dickens offered his readers vicarious access to surrogates of Eden consonant with the interests and aspirations of his characters and readers alike. This is a major reason that 'edenic' landscapes in the novels of Dickens and his contemporaries more often take the form of gardens than of mountains.

I have tried to show that the identity of the garden in Victorian literature is established largely in terms of its differential relations to 'wild' landscapes. The garden is closely identified both with 'soft' nature and with culture; it frequently functions as a surrogate for the gentle English countryside, but it is also granted refining and civilizing powers.

Though reasonably valid in general terms, this summary is vitiated by an oversimplified account of wild nature and its significance in Victorian literature. 'Wild' as an epithet for landscape and scenery has, in fact, widely varying applications and connotations. Some of these *are* pejorative, particularly when the landscapes signified are vast, unhumanized and perceived as threatening. It is these negative uses of 'wild'—'wild' as in 'wilderness', for example—that make it possible to identify Tennyson, Browning, Swinburne, Arnold, and Thomson as the precursors of the twentieth century 'wasteland poets', and to discuss how and why they 'used wasteland imagery with great effectiveness to express their melancholy moods.'[40] But 'wild' can also imply a positive evaluation, and appears in contexts which connect it with, rather than oppose it to, the garden.

There are two main explanations for these varying uses of 'wild'. The more obvious one is that the adjective is assigned to a diversity of topographical and botanical forms. The more important one is that many Victorians responded to wild nature with understandable ambivalence. They saw that it could be threatening and, therefore, something to overcome or avoid. But some, particularly in the latter part of the century, also realized that wild nature itself was threatened with attrition or emasculation by the increasing human powers of environmental control. From the latter perspective, the wildscape was seen as something to cherish and protect against the encroachments of city and cultivated landscapes alike. Many writers sensed that the garden had a part to play here. Though incapable of serving as a proper surrogate for wild nature, the garden could at least accommodate, within an unmistakably humanized framework, vestigial elements of nature's wilder forms and processes.

Phineas Fletcher, the narrator of Mrs Craik's mid-century novel, *John Halifax, Gentleman* (1857), declares that his ideal garden is one that is 'half trim, half wild'. He has in mind the 'dear old-fashioned garden' of 'fruits, flowers, and vegetables living in comfortable equality and fraternity, none being too choice to be harmed by their neighbours, none esteemed too mean to be restricted in their natural profusion' (p. 175). Fletcher's notion of wildness may be cosy and limited—'half trim' clearly operates as a qualifier—but at least it overrides his partiality for order and constraint. He concludes his detailed description of an instance of the kind of 'half wild' garden he loves by affirming its superiority to 'the finest modern pleasure-ground' (p. 175).

Fletcher's preferences are far from idiosyncratic. Many fictional characters are made to sing the praises of carelessly ordered, over-brimming cottage gardens, or of gardens that approximate to the pleasantly chaotic profusion of nature in the wild. That this is the kind of garden 'one rarely sees now-a-days' suggests also that the half wild garden is associated with the past, and usually with a sentimentalized and romanticized view of the past. The myth of a pre-industrialized world where man and nature had lived in near-perfect harmony is basic to another popular version of the half trim, half wild garden. This is an 'Old World' garden in which the process of humanization has long since taken place, and where nature has been able gradually to reassert itself. Victorian magazines contain numerous poems about once trim gardens made wild and picturesque by neglect. 'The Deserted Garden' by Julia Goddard begins:

Beyond the woods, yet half by woods inclosed
A tangled wilderness of fair growth lay;
A spot where dreaming poets might have dosed
Into the dawning of a fairy day;
For in its desolation wild reposed
Something that pointed to a past more gay,
Since here and there one found the lingering trace
Of caresome hands in the neglected place.

In one sense, the wildness of the garden speaks sadly of what has long since passed away. In another, it ratifies the spirit of the past, and makes it possible for the speaker vicariously to experience that spirit, to 'weave a tale of mystery to the last; / And in the old deserted garden bowers / Find fairer blossoms than 'mongst tended flowers.'[41]

Of course, 'The Deserted Garden' and the many mawkish poems like it are predicated upon a view of nature as romantic and picturesque rather than as Darwinian and appetitive. Doubtless they reflect the tastes of those middle-class Victorians with a propensity to use nature as an anodyne. Even so, the nostalgia evident in such poems seems to betray anxieties about the over-'civilizing' of nature in the name of Progress, and expresses a desire to find reassuring evidence of nature's irrepressibility and mystery. (It is worth noting that Goddard's poem appears on the same page of *Chambers's Journal* as an article on the improvident destruction of 'indigenous forests'.)

The half trim, half wild garden, then, takes two basic forms: trimness and wildness occurring together, and trimness turning into wildness. In Victorian literature, both forms hint at 'solutions' to the paradox they imply: that gardens are opposed to wild nature, but in a period of unprecedented urbanization and environmental domination must also help to keep it alive. Even many of the most highly manicured gardens in Victorian fiction contain token 'wildernesses', which may suggest the desire to smuggle into gardens acceptable echoes of the wildness they otherwise exclude.

Without at least a nod in the direction of the wildscape, the garden stands in peril of losing those very qualities which connect it with the natural world and distinguish it from the merely social. Most English authors were to some degree cognizant of this; and many gardens of English nineteenth century fiction are endowed with sufficient vestiges of natural landscapes to retain a semblance of wildness. On the other hand, some so closely resemble the commercially productive cultivated landscape as to be scarcely distinguishable from it. This is true of the garden landscapes in Gaskell's *Wives and Daughters*. 'Far from being a romantic breezy novel of the countryside, *Wives and Daughters* never looks at scenery without seeing economic value. Nature does not provide a sense of release but entails responsibilities and financial rewards.' The garden estate of Cumnor Towers 'is a landscape that is planted with money and flourishes accordingly.'[42] Lawns, flower-beds and hot-houses place an almost infinite physical and psychic distance between the observer in the grounds (Molly in Chapter 2) and the 'dark gloom of the forest-trees beyond' (p. 12). The park of the Hamleys is still more economic, being devoted to 'meadow-grass, ripening for hay' (p. 69).

Gardens like these are the confederates of commercial civilization rather than bulwarks against its expansion. Thus, in the nineteenth century, cultivated landscapes as well as cities could be 'perceived as enemies of pristine nature'[43] since both were expanding at the expense of the wilderness. Most writers could not but be aware of this. Matthew Arnold's walks in the Oxfordshire countryside certainly made Arnold aware that one effect of agrarian capitalism was the literal marginalization of wild nature—as the following stanza from *Thyrsis* clearly shows:

> I knew the slopes; who knows them if not I?
> But many a dingle on the loved hill-side,
> With thorns once studded, old, white-blossomed trees
> Where thick the cowslips grew, and far descried
> High towered the spikes of purple orchises,
> Hath since our day put by
> The coronals of that forgotten time;
> Down each green bank hath gone the ploughboy's team,
> And only in the hidden brookside gleam
> Primroses, orphans of the flowery prime. (*AP*, p. 544)

The survival of wild nature was threatened also by the exportation of 'city' values into the countryside—a process most visible in the appropriation and construction of garden estates by *nouveaux riches* industrialists. Far from assisting the survival of the wildscape, these egregious products of urban culture collaborated in its very demise. No Victorian understood this better than Hardy and, with the possible exception of Lakelands in Meredith's *One of Our Conquerors* (1891), there is no better example of the 'imported', anti-wild garden than that of The Slopes in *Tess of the d'Urbervilles* (1891). Hardy describes The Slopes as 'a country-house built for enjoyment pure and simple, with not an acre of troublesome land attached to it beyond what was required for residential purposes, and for a little fancy farm kept in hand by the owner, and tended by a bailiff' (p. 42). Like Victor Radnor's Lakelands, the newly erected 'seat' of the d'Urbervilles is a red brick blot on the green landscape from which it rises 'like a geranium bloom' (p. 42). With its extensive lawn, its ornamental tent, its gravel sweep, glass-houses, and fashionable evergreens, the garden of The Slopes betrays its complicity with the worlds of city and commerce. And lest we should miss the point, we are told: 'Everything looked like money—like the last coin issued from the Mint' (p. 43). The unnaturalness of The Slopes is emphasized by its contrast to the adjacent Chase, 'a truly venerable tract of forest, one of the few remaining woodlands in England of undoubted primeval date' (p. 42).

The Slopes, then, is a kind of *urbs rure*; instead of accommodating the wildscape it suppresses and assaults it. Moreover, its garden, though 'bright, thriving, and well-kept' (p. 43) is not imaginatively compelling. It lacks those qualities of scenery—openness, vitality, irregularity, even a degree of harshness—that most appealed to Victorian authors who had a true and therefore unsentimental knowledge of the landscapes which inspired them. The Brontës are obvious examples. The thoroughly trim garden left Charlotte cold—as she clearly indicates in a letter to G. H. Lewes. She remarks that she finds in Jane Austen's *Pride and Prejudice* 'a carefully-tended, highly cultivated garden, with neat borders and delicate flowers; but no glance of a bright, vivid physiognomy, no open country, no fresh air, no blue hill, no bonny beck'. She confesses that she 'should hardly like to live with her ladies and gentlemen, in their elegant but confined houses.'[44]

Not surprisingly, most of the positively presented gardens in Charlotte Brontë's novels possess elements of wildness, and are surrounded by 'unspoilt' natural scenery. The house in which William Crimsworth of *The Professor* finally settles is in 'a sequestered and rather hilly region whose verdure the smoke of mills had not yet sullied'. At the bottom of its 'sloping garden there is a wicket, which opens upon a lane as green as the lawn, very long, shady, and little frequented' (p. 352). The garden is, in fact, quite literally made out of the stuff of the surrounding wildscape, for it is 'chiefly laid out in lawn, formed of the sod of the hills, with herbage short and soft as moss, full of its own peculiar flowers' (p. 351). The 'picturesque' garden of Shirley's Fieldhead in *Shirley* (1849) is contiguous with the wild scenery at the narrow end of the Hollow where there is a 'wooded ravine' and, running through it, a mill-stream 'struggling with many stones, chafing against rugged banks, fretting with gnarled tree-roots, foaming, gurgling, battling as it went' (p. 300). Even Mr Rochester's estate of Thornfield in *Jane Eyre* has affinities with the wildscape. In its ground is 'an array of mighty old thorn trees, strong, knotty, and broad as oaks' (p. 131) which gives the place its name and redeems it from smoothness. In addition, the tree-filled garden near the house merges into the 'lonely fields' from which it is separated only by a sunken fence.

Anne Brontë's apparent landscape predilections are similar to Charlotte's and, like hers, shaped by personal experience of untamed Yorkshire scenery. In her very Wordsworthian poem 'Memory', the speaker calls to mind the flowers of her infancy. All are flowers of 'Green fields and waving woods'.[45] As she walks in miserable solitude about the countryside of Horton Lodge (where she is governess), Agnes Grey in the work of the same name also longs 'intensely' not for garden flowers, but 'for some familiar flower that might recall the woody dales or green hill-sides of home' (p. 103).

Perhaps Anne Brontë's most explicit rejection of the trim in favour of the wild garden comes in the poem 'Home'. The speaker stands in the grounds of a 'mansion high'. Its garden is

> fair and wide,
> With groves of evergreen,
> Long winding walks, and borders trim,
> And velvet lawns between;

But this neatly cultivated garden can do nothing to alleviate her homesickness, and so she prays to be restored to

> that little spot,
> With gray walls compassed round,
> Where knotted grass neglected lies,
> And weeds usurp the ground.[46]

In these works of the Brontës, the half wild garden is one that is congruent with the surrounding countryside—countryside that is wild but not bleak or inhospitable. For a later, post-Darwinian generation of writers, the half wild garden is distinguished not only by its scenery, by what Charlotte Brontë would have called its 'physiognomy', but also by its ecology—in particular, by the ceaseless, irrepressible activity of its animal and vegetable life. Two of the principal representatives of this generation are Meredith and Hardy. There are significant differences between their works, but they share an intense, physical receptivity to wilder English landscapes, assimilation of the Darwinian theory of evolution, and the struggle-for-existence view of nature that this theory entails.

If Meredith's works have a message to impart it is that the spiritual well-being of humanity is contingent upon its communion with the Earth. It is from the Earth that man has derived his faculties and desires: his craving for the life of the senses, his rationality ('man's germinant fruit'[47]), his capacity for selfless action and moral conscience. Only by recognizing his kinship with the natural world can man as a species evolve through social progress.

There is nothing either gloomy or coldly scientific about the evolutionary naturalism that Meredith espouses. As one anonymous reviewer remarked, 'if Mr. Meredith sings Evolution, he sings it in a lyrical rapture, and with a thrill of personal ecstasy'.[48] Nature for Meredith is 'an active and benevolent principle that reveals to man his kinship with the rest of creation and that teaches him to order his private, public and political life'.[49] But there is a proviso: nature teaches only those who are prepared to 'read' its signs; Meredith sensed that many of his contemporaries were not. His own mature nature poetry (that published after c. 1880) offers a reading of Earth from the perspective of a kind of sanguine Darwinian semiotician. His fiction offers (to speak reductively) misreadings of nature, and a checklist of the reasons for them: egoism, sentimentality, suppression of sensual life, and conventional, exploitative and expansionist forms of social organization.

Meredith appears to regard the garden as one of those places in which human beings display the extent (if any) of their receptivity to, and fellowship with, the natural world. In truth, his works are only occasionally enthusiastic about gardens of any description, preferring the open countryside. In his own lifetime he was famed for his thirty-five-mile hikes across the hills of Surrey and Hampshire from which some 'aspiring writers took the idea that fresh air and natural scenery were the necessary complements to the creative process'.[50] Meredith's works also imply that the signs of wild nature are richer than those of the garden. In 'Love in the Valley', the speaker responds only tepidly to 'prim' garden flowers and their comparatively narrow discourse. 'I might love them', he says, 'but for loving more the wild ones' because the wild ones 'tell me more' (*MP*, p. 233).

Nonetheless, a garden teeming with living things that had invited themselves in but were happily tolerated was for Meredith a healthy sign of human communion with nature. He describes such a garden in 'Change and Recurrence':

I stood at the gate of the cot
Where my darling, with side-glance demure,
Would spy, on her trim garden-plot,
The busy wild things chase and lure.
For these with their ways were her feast;
They had surety no enemy lurked.
Their deftest of tricks to their least,
She gathered in watch as she worked.

When berries were red on her ash,
The blackbird would rifle them rough,
Till the ground underneath looked a gash,
And her rogue grew the round of a chough.
The squirrel cocked ear o'er his hoop,
Up the spruce, quick as eye, trailing brush.
She knew any tit of the troop
All as well as the snail-tapping thrush.

I gazed: 'twas the scene of the frame,
With the face, the dear life for me, fled.
No window a lute to my name,
No watcher there plying the thread.
But the blackbird hung pecking at will;
The squirrel from cone hopped to cone;
The thrush had a snail in his bill,
And tap-tapped the shell hard on stone. (*MP*, p. 361)

Here, without a trace of revulsion or perturbation, is Meredith's version of the Darwinian world in homely miniature. Only a poet who had 'wholeheartedly absorbed and accepted the Victorian scientific world view'[51] could have written about the rapacity of nature within the context of an affective revisitation poem. The garden isn't pretty, but then 'only the sentimentalist, that typical

Meredithian butt, would require of Nature the smooth charm of human society.'[52]

Gardens which possess the 'smooth charm of human society' come in for some rough treatment in Meredith's fiction. More than simply dull to the nature-worshipper, they are signs of the hubristic folly man exhibits when he tries to 'raise a spiritual system in antagonism to Nature'.[53] Throughout *The Egoist*, but particularly in the portrait of Sir Willoughby Patterne, nature and the human ego are polarized. In seeking the 'Arcadian by the aesthetic route' (I, 12), Sir Willoughby abjures the natural. His estate, a 'flat land' held in by 'hedges and palings', is the topographical correlative of his 'art of life' (I, 146), a philosophy he can exemplify only by ruthlessly enclosing the lives of those he gathers about him. Like its owner, Patterne estate is impeccably groomed and superficially charming. But Clara Middleton (here the author's mouthpiece) finds its prettiness 'overwhelming'. She confesses to Laetitia Dale on their walk across the park: 'It is very pretty; but to live with, I think I prefer ugliness. I can imagine learning to love ugliness. However young you are, you cannot be deceived by it. . . . I would rather have fields, commons' (I, 183).

Even Sir Willoughby cannot entirely dispose of ugliness or, what amounts to the same thing, unruly fecundity. Nature kicks back when 'civilization' flexes its muscles; as Meredith expressed it, 'Nature abhors precociousness, and has the habit of punishing it.'[54] Sir Willoughby's curse is the dryadical Crossjay, the unextirpatable weed in whom nature is 'very strong'. When it is time for his lessons, he has to be 'plucked out of the earth, rank of the soil, like a root' (I, 34). The mountain is another symbol of wild, free nature that will not be denied. Clara and Vernon Whitford, the alpinist, at first discuss the Alps, and finally escape to them. With this pair lies 'hope for the future, potential fertility and growth in the world'.[55]

In contrast to Sir Willoughby, Victor Radnor, the successful businessman hero of *One of Our Conquerors*, pursues an Idea that does not exclude nature but rather 'represents a means of achieving the ideal of reconciling society to nature'[56]—though it is forever slipping from Victor's conscious grasp. Society refuses to sanction Victor's unorthodox relationship with Nataly, his mistress; he realizes that society is not 'in the dance with nature' (p. 435). But Victor's Lakelands venture—his scheme for scoring a victory over society and of securing a respectable future for his illegitimate daughter, Nesta—betrays the extent of his entanglement with society. Lakelands is a grandiose, hurriedly-constructed country estate, 'a stately pleasure dome indeed' with 'the botanical and human flowers protected and nurtured under the glass of the conservatory'.[57] Even Nataly's dream place—a 'real nest' in the country where she can 'strike roots' (p. 48)—would have been closer to an honest communion with nature than the gardens of Lakelands, tricked out as they are with every fashionable feature that money can provide (see pp. 81–4).

Clearly Meredith's works convey much more than the notion of a simple dualism between garden and wild landscape. He would have argued that the appetitive aspect of nature, the scourge of the totter-kneed sentimentalist, is as necessary a counter-force to atrophy in the garden as it is in natural landscapes and in man himself. It is suggested in *The Woods of Westermain* that 'blood' must join 'brain and spirit' 'for true felicity' (*MP*, pp. 201–2). In a garden, the vitality immanent in plants and the like must be read for its lessons, and yet directed and governed by human rationality (or 'brain').

A great deal has been written about Hardy's presentation of nature and the countryside, but very little specifically about the gardens in his novels and poems. The obvious reason for this is that his woods, heaths, and hills have a physical vastness and an imaginative intensity that dwarfs or eclipses the (generally) modest gardens with which they are dotted. But there is a further and perhaps more interesting reason: the typical Hardian garden pleads for no special attention because it is essentially a miniature version of the landscape in which it is situated. Its flora may be different, but it is subject to the same natural processes and inhabited by the same kinds of creatures. Only by dint of human effort is the garden prevented from reverting to the wilderness. Even then, if it is a living garden, it must partake of the active life of nature.

In Hardy's works the garden, just as much as the wood or the heath, is a site of struggle—objectively, between nature and man, and subjectively, between competing views of nature: the beneficent, Romantic view, and the Darwinian view of struggle intensified by random choice. These struggles, expressed at a global level in Hardy's treatment of dominant landscapes, are distilled in miniature in garden descriptions. Consider the modulation (from 'beautiful' to 'writhing') in Hardy's account of Henchard's garden in *The Mayor of Casterbridge*:

> They locked up the office, and the young man [Farfrae] followed his companion through the private little door which, admitting directly to Henchard's garden, permitted a passage from the utilitarian to the beautiful at one step. The garden was silent, dewy, and full of perfume. It extended a long way back from the house, first as lawns and flower-beds, then as fruit gardens, where the long-tied espaliers, as old as the old house itself, had grown so stout, and cramped, and gnarled that they had pulled their stakes out of the ground and stood distorted and writhing in vegetable agony, like leafy Laocoöns. (pp. 102–3)

When Hardy wishes to suggest gentle domesticity and nature's 'simple proximity to village life',[58] his descriptions incline towards the beneficent view of nature. But even here, itinerant or indigenous insects serve as the guarantors of wild nature's animating presence. Thus, in *The Trumpet-Major*, Miller Loveday's grassed-over paths 'harboured slugs' (p. 84); 'plodding bees' and 'gadding butterflies' are among the 'animate things that moved amid' the gardens of Welland in *Two on a Tower* (p. 174); and in *Under the Greenwood Tree*, the happy symbiosis of country folk and nature is reflected in the micro-life of the cottage gardens:

> It was a morning of the later summer-time; a morning of lingering dews, when the grass is never dry in the shade. Fuchsias and dahlias were laden till eleven o'clock with small drops and dashes of water, changing the colour of their sparkle at every movement of the air; and elsewhere hanging on twigs like small silver fruit. The threads of garden spiders appeared thick and polished. In the dry and sunny places, dozens of long-legged crane-flies whizzed off the grass at every stage the passer took. (p. 171)

More often in Hardy's garden scenes, the Darwinian perspective is dominant. When Mrs Smith in *A Pair of Blue Eyes* (1873) inveighs against the 'horrid Jacob's ladders' in her cottage garden, it is to the intractable fecundity of nature that she draws attention:

> Instead of praising 'em, I am mad wi' 'em for being so ready to grow where they are not wanted. They are very well in their way, but I do not care for things that neglect won't kill. Do what I will, dig, drag, scrap, pull, I get too many of

> 'em. I chop the roots: up they'll come treble strong. Throw 'em over hedge; there they'll grow, staring me in the face like a hungry dog driven away, and creep back again in a week or two the same as before. (pp. 258–9)

Other scenes exemplify the observation that Hardy 'seems at times to have had an almost perverse delight in destroying the convention of a happy, pretty, gentle rural world, where the only vile thing is man'.[59] The park of Lady Constantine's Great House in *Two on a Tower* (1882) is smothered by nature at its nastiest:

> A fog defaced all the trees of the park that morning; the white atmosphere adhered to the ground like a fungoid growth from it, and made the turfed undulations look slimy and raw. (p. 55).

Even the sunny suburban garden can expect to fall victim to the predations of nature and time. This is the theme of Hardy's poem 'During Wind and Rain'. In each of the four stanzas, a convivial and vigorous scene of the past is abruptly terminated by the speaker's wailing refrain upon the effects of change and decay. The middle two stanzas run:

> They clear the creeping moss—
> Elders and juniors—aye,
> Making the pathways neat
>   And the garden gay;
> And they build a shady seat . . .
>   Ah, no; the years, the years;
> See, the white storm-birds wing across!
>
> They are blithely breakfasting all—
> Men and maidens—yea,
> Under the summer tree,
>   With a glimpse of the bay,
> While pet fowl come to the knee. . . .
>   Ah, no; the years O!
> And the rotten rose is ript from the wall.[60]

The best known and by far the most discussed of Hardy's gardens—the neglected garden at Talbothay's through which Tess in *Tess of the d'Urbervilles* is drawn by the entrancing strains of Angel's harp—is also the one that most closely approximates to Darwin's 'tangled bank'. The following paragraph has received the most critical attention:

> The outskirts of the garden in which Tess found herself had been left uncultivated for some years, and was now damp and rank with juicy grass which sent up mists of pollen at a touch; and with tall blooming weeds emitting offensive smells—weeds whose red and yellow and purple hues formed a polychrome as dazzling as that of cultivated flowers. She went stealthily as a cat through this profusion of growth, gathering cuckoo-spittle on her skirts, cracking snails that were underfoot, staining her hands with thistle-milk and slug-slime, and rubbing off upon her naked arms sticky blights which, though snow-white on the apple-tree trunks, made madder stains on her skin; thus she drew quite near to Clare, still unobserved of him. (p. 158)

Reactions to this passage vary widely. Some, perhaps the majority, of commentators feel that the overriding impression is one of unqualified nastiness. A typical response declares that all the living things of the garden are 'whitish, cold and drearily insubstantial, yet thoroughly unpleasant in their mere existence'.[61] A more ambivalent and positive reaction senses 'some general vague corruption' in the symbolism of the decaying garden, but realizes also that it is the 'sticky objectionableness of Nature' that makes 'our senses come alive'.[62] Similarly, it has been noted that 'the conventional response (of revulsion) invited by concepts like "rank", "offensive smells", "spittle", "snails", "slug-slime", "blights", "stains", etc., is insistently checked by an alternative note which runs through the landscape, a note of celebration of the brimming fertility of the weeds and the keen sensations they afford.' The overgrown garden is an apt image of 'unconstrained nature', and 'reminds us of the wild, exuberant, anarchic life that flourishes on the dark underside, as it were, of the cultivated fertility of the valley.'[63]

In other words, a degree of disagreeableness is an integral part of nature's virility, or the price to be paid for permitting its expression. Better mildly unpleasant fecundity than the amicable impotence of a garden laundered of the wildness that anchors it in nature. *The Return of the Native* (1878) contains passages of similar implications. The farmers of Egdon, we are told, smile to see the landscape fashioned into 'square fields' that 'look like silver gridirons':

> But as for [Clym] Yeobright, when he looked from the heights on his way he could not help indulging in a barbarous satisfaction at observing that, in some of the attempts at

> reclamation from the waste, tillage, after holding on for a year or two, had receded again in despair, the ferns and furze-tufts stubbornly reasserting themselves. (p. 205)

Hardy's visceral sympathies, I suspect, are with Clym rather than with the cultivators. And many of Hardy's readers may well have been heartened rather than disturbed by his aggressively unromantic descriptions of potent gardens—in much the same way that the speaker in Browning's 'Sibrandus Schafraburgensis' is impishly delighted to observe 'live creatures' 'frisking and twisting and coupling' upon the scholarly book he had deposited in the crevice of a garden tree (*BP*, p. 439). Unmoored from an ever-receding wildscape, they sought for reassuring signs of nature's resilience. Given the circumstances that led in the late nineteenth century to 'a sudden and sustained flowering of societies and committees for protecting and preserving pieces of old England from urban and industrial depredations',[64] a 'realistic', even a Darwinian interpretation of the natural world was palatable and possibly more comforting than the gentle 'word painting of Nature' turned out 'not so much from Nature's seers as from her showmen'. Havelock Ellis remarks that, in reading Hardy, 'we are conscious of the voice of one who has worshipped at the temple's inner shrine'.[65]

There is certainly little evidence to suggest that Hardy's early readers were perturbed by his unsentimental presentation of gardens and other landscapes. Writing in 1887, R. H. Hutton found the Hintock woods the 'only really pleasant part'[66] of *The Woodlanders*, and yet, they 'are not described as green, fresh and growing but as sinister, hostile and dark'.[67] If the Victorians found Meredith's 'manly' attitude towards nature 'tough, vigorous, and enduring',[68] they could scarcely have found Hardy's less so.

I am not, of course, suggesting that Hardy set out to reassure his readers that nature was alive and well. Nor do I wish to imply that Hardy blurred the garden/non-garden distinction because he was really just another nature-worshipper at heart, though canny enough to veil it by a hard-hitting blend of Darwinian biology and Schopenhauerian pessimism. With some exceptions, the gardens in Hardy's works interpenetrate with natural and wilder landscapes because they are not exempt from nature's laws. They flourish and decay, are nasty or pleasant, not because nature for Hardy is whimsical (benevolent on occasions, malevolent on others) but because it is indifferent to man.

A summary of the main points of the argument in this chapter may not be out of place.

The prominence of gardens in Victorian literature has much to do with the declining imaginative and inspirational potency of wilder, natural landscapes, and with the rejection or modification of the aesthetic interests responsible for their earlier exaltation. The Romantic enthusiasm for (untamed) nature attenuated. Veneration of sublime mountain scenery came to many to seem a misdirection: a recherché cult tempting individuals to dissipate socially useful energies in the self-indulgent pursuit of aesthetic experience and solitary heroics—posturings incompatible with the prevailing social orientation of nineteenth-century fiction. For other reasons, gardens came to be privileged as the antithesis of the wildscape: less brutal, less 'heathenish', more 'civilized' and 'civilizing', less likely to place the perceiver in the role of mere spectator, more obviously a surrogate for the absent or disappearing countryside, physically more accessible, socially more accommodating, psychically more congenial.

At the same time, gardens were invested with the more positive qualities of wild nature—plenitude, vitality, and spontaneity—that the agrarian development of the countryside and the spread of urban influences were threatening to eliminate. Many writers sensed that the tame garden is also a lame garden, an ineffectual counter-image to the city, and sometimes even complicitous with it. Stronger antidotes seemed necessary. Hence the celebration of the half wild garden, sometimes shown as romantically beneficent, sometimes as riotously, even unpleasantly, exuberant. Some writers, rooted in wilder English landscapes, retained a passion for untamed natural scenery and the kinds of gardens that most closely resembled it. Some absorbed Darwinism, and infused their gardens with the life force of virile nature. (Swinburne takes this to extremes: some of the gardens in his poems are actually emptied, decimated and reduced to death-like stasis by the grand, elemental forces of nature.[69]) A few, though firmly anti-romantic in their attitudes towards nature, and with no great love of the wilderness, favoured the retention of pockets of wildscape within garden landscapes. Morris is a case in point. His vision of post-revolutionary England is of a garden containing tracts of forest valued both for their beauty and utility. In fact, in *News from Nowhere*, Morris comes close to exposing the wildscape/garden distinction as a false dichotomy or, more precisely, as a bifurcation emphatic only in capitalist societies where gardens are mostly private property, and the countryside is *apparently* 'open' and 'free'. In the variegated landscape of his socialist utopia, gardens blend harmoniously with fields and forests, villages and clean, green cities. England is filled with gardens; but England is itself a garden, since human beings are in control of nature and yet very much a part of it. The old distinctions are dead.

But they were not dead in the England in which Morris himself lived, which is why the gardens in Victorian imaginative literature often seem to suggest ideal middle landscapes between the extremes of wildscape and city, combining and reconciling the merits of each. The middle landscape ideal is central to, say, the physical and symbolic topography of *Hard Times* in which Dickens 'idealizes neither the chaotic growth of a wholly natural forest nor the ordered mechanism of a wholly artificial city, but the ordered growth, the blend of pattern with spontaneity, exemplified by a cultivated field or garden'.[70] This ideal seems also to triumph at the end of *Wuthering Heights* when Hareton Earnshaw and Catherine Heathcliff make for themselves a garden which couples something of the vitality of the nearby moors with the gentle domesticity of the enclosed gardens of Thrushcross Grange. And as I have pointed out in preceding chapters, versions of the 'half trim, half wild' garden are among the more positively presented garden types in Victorian imaginative literature as a whole.

In conclusion, I return to the point I made at the start of this chapter: in Victorian literature there is no simple or consistent pairing, oppositional or otherwise, between 'garden' and 'nature', or between 'garden' and 'landscape' terms to which it is paradigmatically related. 'Garden' carries many, sometimes contradictory, significations, some of them previously carried by other 'landscape' terms, and through their presentation of gardens, Victorian writers also articulate their attitudes towards landscape scenery and the natural world.

CHAPTER EIGHT

Gardens and Cities

In Victorian imaginative literature, garden/city relationships are complex, varied and variously defined. To identify the principal permutations is also to determine the 'answers' offered by novelists and poets to questions addressed more directly by town planners, social reformers, and others concerned with the problems of an unprecedented rate of urban growth: Can humanized nature survive, with or without human assistance, in city environments? If so, can it help to make urban existence tolerable, even comfortable—and for whom? If not, what can or should be done about it? Four main models of the relationship can be identified. The order in which they are presented hints—but no more than that—at their historical ascendancy.

The first can be represented by the formulation 'the city and the garden'. In some respects this is a variant of the more familiar opposition of town and country. The syntax of both formulations—polarized nouns about an adversative 'and'—mimes the position it articulates: that the (industrial) city is irreconcilably opposed to the *topos* from which it is distinguished environmentally, morally, and in every other way. We have seen that in nineteenth-century literature 'country' and 'garden' are frequently tied to the same pastoral myths, frequently connote similar positive qualities, and frequently gratify similar personal needs. But the terms are not entirely synonymous, and for writers who wished to insist upon a simple dichotomy between rural England and industrial England, 'garden' is sometimes the preferred term. One reason for this is obvious: when used as a pastoral metaphor, 'garden' inevitably defines the country as something to look upon and enjoy rather than as something from which to derive a living—in short, as landscape rather than as land. The effects of this are to make the country seem ideal and idyllic, to direct attention to its otherness from the city, and to mask its social and economic realities. Moreover, since 'garden' has a literal as well as a figurative significance, to equate 'country' with 'garden' is also to equate the rural landscape with a particular kind of enclave within it and, because 'country' also has a double sense, with England itself.

The idea that 'real' England was old, rural England, and that pre-industrial England was a garden, was at the heart of the anti-urban bias of much nineteenth-century literature, and fondly nourished in the writings of many visitors from abroad. A recent study of Anglo-American travel literature comments:

> The most recurrent image used to describe England in nineteenth-century American travel literature was that of the garden. The American was impressed by the sheer number and variety of the gardens that he found in England; he was even more impressed by the fact that the whole country was 'groomed', 'finished', 'completed' to the point that it could be described as 'the very garden of the world'. There was, so far as he could see, no wilderness at all. . . . The domesticated, tamed quality of the landscape induced a sense of unreality. At the same time, it encouraged a selective vision that excluded anything that was ugly or disruptive: 'I used to think the gardens never ended', Nadal wrote, 'but lay side by side the island through, and that the sea washed them all round'.[1]

British writers who shared the American tourist's predilections, even if they could not take comfort in his selective perceptions, tended to image the industrial city as a corrupted garden. There are patterns of miscultivated field and corrupted garden imagery in Dickens's presentation of Coketown,[2] a town of 'savages' and unnatural red and black. Wilkie Collins called London a 'house-forest';[3] numerous other detractors of the metropolis called it a 'wilderness'.[4]

Some Victorian writers had another reason for emphasizing the city/garden antithesis: they found that the garden had advantages over the country as a counter-image to the oppressive industrial city. That is, they sensed that the garden afforded a more specific, more focused and potentially more realizable model of innocence and tranquility upon which the inner eye could fix its yearnings. The anti-urban sentiments evident in the works of writers as different as Ruskin, Gissing, and M. E. Braddon can be traced in part to their recollections of actual, vividly remembered childhood gardens.

The 'nexus and emblem'[5] of Ruskin's early childhood was the garden of his parents' 'rustic eminence' at Herne Hill. In Chapter 2 of *Praeterita* (1885–9) he recalls precisely its dimensions, its contents, and his experiences within it. From these details, and not from hazy impressions of a generalized rural topography, he constructs his subtly qualified version of the myth of edenic childhood. Like Ruskin, M. E. Braddon spent her formative years in a rustic suburb of London: Camberwell of the 1850s. In the three novels in which she recalls it,[6] it takes the form of a sizeable, well-stocked garden, such as she had known, and 'such as' (she wrote in 1904) 'no one could hope for nowadays within five miles of London'.[7]

Gissing's case is somewhat different. As a boy, his affection for the countryside about the industrial town of Wakefield was stronger than that for the utilitarian town garden rented by his parents. Yet he knew that when city-dwellers dream of a rural retreat, their dream generally assumes a specific if hand-me-down form. Those of meagre means may set their sights no higher than a modest allotment garden, a place like that of the Cartwrights in *A Life's Morning*, 'laid out with an eye less to beauty than to usefulness' (p. 107). The well-heeled and socially ambitious hanker after the ancestral country retirement they have never known. In *The Whirlpool* (1897) Alma Frothingham's well-to-do ideal is

> one of those picturesque old places down in Surrey—quite in the country, yet within easy reach of town; a house with a real garden, and perhaps an orchard. (p. 368)

Gissing probably intends here to mock such aspirations—but he fully acknowledged the conditions which gave rise to them.[8] Before him, Gaskell, Dickens, and a host of minor novelists had attested to their sustaining power. Fictional 'evidence' tends to support the contention of one mid-century reviewer that the longing to possess a garden is 'the universal wish of the human heart', and especially intense in the garden-less city dweller, who

> dreams of ending his days in a cottage festooned with honeysuckle and sweet jasmine, and of growing the simple flowers which pleased his boyhood.[9]

In its most extreme and reductionist form, the city/garden antithesis is founded on the belief that, at least for the mass of working people, the industrial city is a place of unmitigated misery, ugliness, and degradation, and a breeding ground of social and political unrest. In most early and some later Victorian versions of the formulation, the power and ideology of the 'millocracy' (i.e. the industrial bourgeoisie) are held responsible for urban evils, though working-class political activity exacerbates these conditions. The only solution envisaged for society in general is a return to the 'past' conceived in conservative, idealized, and sometimes glutinously sentimental terms as a world of pastoral peace and stable social formations. The only solution for the individual is to stay away from the manufacturing town or, if he is unlucky enough to be penned within it, to withdraw to the country.

It is difficult to tell how many novelists subscribed in full to this particular definition of the situation. What is certain is that only a very few novels depict flight from the city as the only satisfactory strategy for survival. Among those who present such escape in favourable terms are one or two of the novelists who first probe 'the Condition of England' question in the late 1830s and 1840s.

One such writer is the Tory and ultra-Protestant evangelical Charlotte Elizabeth Tonna. Her *Helen Fleetwood* (1841)—the first English novel centrally concerned with the plight of industrial workers—documents the rapid destruction of a simple rural family after their migration to the manufacturing centre of Manchester. The novel is an unrelenting assault upon the social and political anarchy and the moral debilitation wrought by industrialism. Notwithstanding two very salient facts—firstly, that Widow Green and her brood of granddaughters (including the adopted Helen Fleetwood) are dispossessed of their land in a country village; and secondly, that they are lured to Manchester by the fraudulent pamphlets glamorizing city life put about by parish guardians intent on shirking their obligations to the poor—the preferred model here is an idealized notion of the country:

> There are districts in the land still retaining much of the primitive character of English rusticity—places where the blight has not come; where the demoralising swarm of railway excavators has never alighted, nor the firebrand of political rancour scattered its darkening smoke, nor the hell-born reptile of socialism trailed its venomous slime. (p. 238)

For the nation at large, the only solution mooted here is 'the re-establishment of the spirit of Christian brotherhood';[10] but elsewhere she suggests as a more practical palliative the reverse migration of industrial workers to rural allotment gardens. *The Perils of the Nation* argues that 'the poor, helpless, day-labourer, just subsisting on seven shillings per week' would become 'at once sober, frugal and most industrious' if given 'half an acre of land, at a moderate rent.'[11] Interestingly enough, moderate Chartists also favoured allotment gardens for the independence they would give to individual workers.

Disraeli's *Sybil*, which relates the social conditions of early-Victorian England to the state of national politics, the class struggle, and the history of Chartism, is an altogether more ambitious project than *Helen Fleetwood*. A selective reading might suggest that Disraeli's novel was operating within the same conceptual framework—the simple opposition of industrial city and rural garden—as that of Mrs Tonna. With bluebook accuracy infused with imaginative intensity, he exposes the working and living conditions of a multiplicity of labouring groups in the industrial centres of northern England: among them, the miners of a despoiled countryside, the factory operatives of Mowbray (which may be a fictional conflation of Skipton and Huddersfield), and the metal workers of Wodgate, 'the ugliest spot in England . . . where a tree could not be seen, a flower was unknown' (p. 188). Though there are local variations, the industrial poor are in general degraded by a miserable and unhealthy environment, brutalized by tyrannical manufacturers and (at Wodgate) by *soi disant* proletarian 'aristocrats', and easy prey to Chartist agitators and violent malcontents. Conditions in the capital are scarcely better. As Sybil discovers, London outside 'the dainty quarters of the city' (p. 364) is a dingy labyrinth crawling with criminals and ruffians.

As a contrast, Disraeli presents the stone cottage and teeming country garden of Sybil and Walter Gerard—a modern place but of medieval simplicity:

> Its materials were of a fawn-coloured stone, common in the Mowbray quarries. A scarlet creeper clustered round one side of its ample porch; its windows were large, mullioned, and neatly latticed; it stood in the midst of a garden of no mean dimensions, but every bed and nook of which teemed with cultivation; flowers and vegetables both abounded, while an orchard rich with the promise of many fruits—ripe pears and famous pippins of the north and plums of every shape and hue—screened the dwelling from that wind against which the woods that formed its background were no protection. (pp. 154–5)

If it was Disraeli's intention to suggest as an alternative to industrialism the 'thinking' peasant's revivification of the medieval ideals of beauty, simplicity, and human harmony with the natural world, then the Gerards' cottage garden, and the idyllic Vale of Mowe in which it is situated, is the symbol of this alternative. It is here in the Vale of Mowe that the aristocratic hero of the novel, Charles Egremont, assumes the name of Mr Franklin, rents a place with 'a little garden', enjoys a 'delicious' existence amid 'clustering orchards and gardens of flowers and herbs' (p. 203) and delights in enlightening conversation with the Gerards and Stephen Morley. Later in the narrative, when Walter Gerard has become deeply involved with Chartist extremists, Sybil 'sighed for the days of their cottage and garden'—'touching images of the past' (p. 349) that have their historical equivalents in Disraeli's nostalgic images of 'Merry England'.

Obviously, there is much more to *Sybil* than the opposition of ugly city and beautiful garden. But even to take undue account of this contrast may result in a misreading, for however compelling the mode of existence the cottage garden represents, it does not escape the complexities and ambiguities which riddle the novel as a whole.[12]

In the first place, the Gerards' cottage is in no sense a representative symbol of rural peace and beauty. Gerard himself is a factory worker, not a farm labourer; and far from idealizing the country, the novel draws attention to the contrast between its beautiful image and its miserable reality. The rural town of Marney has more slum dwellings, more disease, and more penurious inhabitants than any of the industrial towns in the novel. Its residents are displaced farm workers, expelled from their cottages by landowners intent on exempting themselves from 'the maintenance of the population' (p. 63). The fortunate few who are still employed obtain but 'scant remuneration' and are forced to endure a 'weary journey' to 'reach the scene of their labour' (p. 63). Not even the 'social problem' novels of Charles Kingsley, *Yeast* (1848) and *Alton Locke* (1850), do more than *Sybil* to dispel the belief that industrial towns have a monopoly of hardship and misery.

In the second place, Disraeli's propaganda is not directed against towns and industrialism as such, but rather at the exploitation of factory workers by socially irresponsible capitalists, without whom Chartism would be otiose. In *Coningsby* he goes as far as to say that 'A great city . . . is the type of some great idea' (p. 161); and nowhere in *Sybil* does he suggest repatriating urban workers to country cottages and gardens like that of the

Gerards. Unwittingly, perhaps, he betrays the fact that Sybil's garden—Sybil calls it her 'cloister'—is the privileged shelter in which she is able to maintain the fiction that society is divided neatly between the oppressors and the oppressed. Only when she ventures beyond it does she realize that the working class is not homogeneous, that some factions of it are violent and rough, and that some aristocrats are good and well-intentioned. Her father and the scholarly Owenite Stephen Morley are never entirely contented with their cottage garden existence. For them it is associated with talk rather than with action. It is a curious irony that the Gerards' garden—presumably their symbol of home—is the work of Morley, whose socialist convictions centre upon his detestation of the 'domestic principle'. Home for him is a 'barbarous idea' because 'home is isolation' and 'therefore anti-social'. 'What we want', he says, 'is community' (p. 225).

Community, of a different sort, is also what Disraeli's hero desires: a community of interests between capital and labour, existing within a graded class structure, and organized by a revitalized aristocracy who accept the social obligations encumbent upon the privileged. And this is why the ideal in *Sybil* is not the Gerards' cottage and garden but the model factory and village of Mr Trafford—one of the rare employers with 'gentle blood', 'old English feelings', and a genuine concern for the welfare of his employees. Trafford's concept of community embraces the concept of home, for

> He knew well that the domestic virtues are dependent on the existence of a home, and one of his first efforts had been to build a village where every family might be well lodged. (p. 212)[13]

His employees are 'proud of their house and little garden, and of the horticultural society, where its produce permitted them to be annual competitors'. Trafford's own house stood 'in the midst of the village, surrounded by beautiful gardens, which gave an impetus to the horticulture of the community' (p. 212). The message is clear: if all employers were like Trafford, then no industrial worker would yearn for a cottage and a garden in the country.

It is worth noting that the concluding pages of Charlotte Brontë's *Shirley* provide a decidedly more ambivalent perspective on the model village as a solution to the social and environmental problems of the industrial proletariat. Having weathered the storm of Ludditism, having been softened through experience and the influence of Caroline Helstone, the once cold-hearted industrialist Robert Moore feels able to deal more benevolently with his employees. His intention, partly fulfilled forty years on from its conception in the years of the Napoleonic Wars, is to 'root up the copse' at Fieldhead and fill the 'barren Hollow with lines of cottages, and rows of cottage gardens' (p. 508). From a Disraelian perspective, this paternalistic project is progress indeed. But Caroline's reaction is one of horror: 'You will change our blue hill-country air into the Stilbro' smoke atmosphere' (p. 508). Her frame of reference is endorsed by the nostalgic image of the Yorkshire countryside before the Industrial Revolution with which the novel closes.

Mary Barton, the first of Elizabeth Gaskell's industrial novels, seems also to give positive emphasis to the environment of the countryside over that of the industrial town. However, the contrast beween them is never allowed to detract from larger concerns, while the garden-as-escape motif is not so much discredited as unchallenged and quite literally pushed aside, for the novel is framed by images of pastoral idyll at its outermost fringes. It opens with a memorable description of 'Green Heys Fields', the beautiful spot accessible to Manchester cotton operatives on holiday excursions. Here there is a farm house surrounded by a little garden

> crowded with a medley of old-fashioned herbs and flowers, planted long ago, when the garden was the only druggist's shop within reach, and allowed to grow in scrambling and wild luxuriance—roses, lavender, sage, balm (for tea), rosemary, pinks and wallflowers, onions and jessamine, in most republican and indiscriminate order. (p. 2)

The novel closes with an image of the rural Canadian home of Mary and Jem Wilson. The reader is invited to picture a cottage, surrounded by a homely garden, with orchards stretching beyond it.

Between these pastoral poles, attention is overwhelmingly fixed upon the industrial town of Manchester, and upon the lives and conditions of its working-class inhabitants. The countryside, gardens, flowers—these things are scarcely whiffed. The narrator's assertion that 'there are no flowers in Manchester' (p. 110) is given the lie only twice: first, by the 'geraniums, unpruned and leafy' (p. 13) that sit on the window-sill of the Bartons' home, and symbolize their relative prosperity at the start of the story; second, by the flowers that decorate the 'almost' country house of the wealthy Carsons. Here they symbolize self-indulgent luxury. The mill-owner's daughter, 'little Miss Extravagance', is willing to pay half a guinea for a single rose; for her 'Life was not worth having without flowers' (p. 73). Significantly, her eulogy on flowers follows jarringly upon the description of the starving Davenports and their filthy, fever-ridden, subterranean hovel. Miss Carson's brother Henry woos Mary with the roses he sends to brighten her dingy rooms.

For the unemployed 'workers' of Manchester in the 'Hungry Forties', flowers and gardens are simply irrelevant, not because their living conditions have made them gross and insensitive (quite the reverse), but because their 'comforts' necessarily take the more practical forms of tea, bread, and Cumberland oatcake.

Since Gaskell accepts that the industrial city is here to stay, and that the sufferings of industrial workers will persist until and unless the social classes can be reconciled by the spirit of fraternal love—the solution to which the latter part of *Mary Barton* unconvincingly points—she resists the temptation to offer rural retreat as a generally available solution to the problems of the urban poor. That this may have been a temptation is suggested by her account of the genesis of *Mary Barton*. 'Living in Manchester, but with a deep relish and fond admiration for the country,' she writes, 'my first thought was to find a frame-work for my story in some rural scene.'[14] Though she chose instead to write 'A Tale of Manchester Life', she could not completely exorcise her love (and seemingly romantic view) of the countryside. Traces of it are evident in her Methodistical model of fortitude, Alice Wilson, a first generation 'townie' who refuses the appellation, and feeds upon her memories of a happy childhood in a Cumberland cottage.

What must be stressed, however, is that 'Gaskell's faith in the beauty of nature to restore people to their better selves and to reinstate a feeling of harmony, community, co-operation and wholeness,'[15] leads her to suggest only two practical forms that 'escape' can realistically take. The first is the occasional excursion into the countryside, represented by the trip to 'Green Heys Fields', one or two other references to 'operatives sallying forth for a breath of country air', and, more lyrically, by the account of the Whitsuntide outing in *Libbie Marsh's Three Eras*. Its function is Wordsworthian: the storing up of happy memories 'to haunt in greenness and freshness many a loom and workshop and factory with images of peace and beauty' (p. 468). The second is the complete and irrevocable break, not only with the industrial town but also with the society and nation of which it is a part. With the final scene of *Mary Barton* specifically in mind, Raymond Williams comments: 'We can see in the industrial novels of the mid-nineteenth century how the idea of emigration to the colonies was seized on as a solution to the poverty and overcrowding of the cities.'[16] The more conventional 'solution'—withdrawal from the city to a country cottage existence—is the one escapist strategy that Gaskell's novels refuse to endorse.

One of the differences between *Mary Barton* and Gaskell's second and only other industrial novel, *North and South*, is the greater topographical variety of the latter. There are four locales in *North and South*, but the keenest juxtaposition is between the New Forest hamlet of Helstone and the industrial town of Milton Northern. 'At first a naïve contrast seems set up between the paternalistic south, full of sunny charm and the traditional values of English culture, and the struggling, brutal north, an "unhealthy, smoky, sunless place", whose ungenteel values are work and profit.'[17] Gradually, however, the reader, together with the heroine Margaret Hale, is compelled to participate in the interrogation of the schematic opposition implicit in the novel's title. This involves the realization that life in a small country house and garden is not, in spite of its obvious environmental attractions, a self-evidently preferable alternative to life in an expanding industrial city.

Helstone is defined and judged from a number of perspectives, only some of which make it seem idyllic. On Margaret's return to Helstone from London in Chapter 2, the narrator describes both the general countryside about the vicarage, and the vicarage garden itself, in terms suggesting beauty and enchantment. Lennox, the up-and-coming London lawyer with conventional if slightly mocking attitudes towards the country, pictures Helstone as a pastoral fiction where roses bloom all year round and life is 'exquisite' and 'serene'. He attempts to woo Margaret in the sunny garden, and enjoys with the Hales a feast of golden pears gathered and eaten in the garden. But within the vicarage things are less rosy. The interior is dingy and threadbare, Mr Hale's contentment is clouded by his religious doubts, and Mrs Hale complains that Helstone is 'one of the most out-of-the-way places in England' (p. 17).

Margaret's experience of Helstone is more complex, and her attitudes towards it neither fixed nor entirely consistent. She derives intense pleasure from its scenery, is heartbroken when she has to leave the vicarage garden, and continues to think of it as home long after her move to Milton. She dilates enthusiastically on its beauty to the dying Bessy Higgins, and defends the pre-industrialized south in general as a place of 'less suffering' than the industrial north.

Nonetheless, she comes increasingly to view it in a more critical light. On her final return visit to Helstone, she is disappointed to find the vicarage garden much changed, and is disenchanted by other changes as well. This subjective disillusionment involves or leads to a more objective reappraisal of the relative merits of the north and south, so that when the despairing Nicholas Higgins thinks of leaving Milton for the south, she dissuades him in the following terms:

> You would not bear the dullness of the life; you don't know what it is; it would eat you away like rust. Those that have lived there all their lives, are used to soaking in the stagnant waters. They labour on, from day to day, in the great solitude of steaming fields—never speaking or lifting up their poor, bent, downcast heads. The hard spadework robs their brain of life; the sameness of their toil deadens their imagination; they don't care to meet to talk over thoughts and speculations. . . . What would be peace to them, would be eternal fretting to you. (p. 364)

This speech suggests that Margaret has learned to differentiate between life in a country garden and life on a working farm. It shows also that she has distilled an important lesson from her experience of Milton: that in spite of its general ugliness, the suffering of many of its people, the open hostility between mill-owners and their employees, and the immorality of unbridled economic individualism, the industrial town has one supreme virtue: energy. It is this which renders stultification impossible, and holds out the hope of social progress in the form of class reconciliation.

In Gaskell's industrial novels, then, there is no symbolic scaffold erected upon the simplistic division of England into country and city, and nostalgia for the countryside and country gardens is always kept firmly in check. For example, though it leads to the disruption of small rural communities and their attractive garden landscapes, the installation of the railway—the supreme symbol of industrial progress—is allowed to intrude even in Gaskell's 'country' fiction: *Cranford*, *Cousin Phillis*, and *Wives and Daughters*.

By the mid-nineteenth century, few novelists of any note were prepared to suggest that the problems of the industrial and urban poor could be remedied by flight to a country garden or, less specifically, by a 'return' to a pre-industrial past. Yet a great many fiction writers still found it possible to evade the kinds of issues which Gaskell's industrial novels confront, and so hence to say nothing of consequence about the environmental needs and aspirations of the urban working classes.[18] Those writers who at least glanced at the situation generally subscribed to some weaker form of the city/garden formulation. That is, they captured the yearnings of the urban poor without suggesting how they might be fulfilled, or presented the idea of flight from the city as an unrealized and probably unrealizable possibility. One example of a 'purely imaginary' flight from the city is that of the sempstress in Thomas Hood's 'The Song of the Shirt' (1844) who, while plying her needle in a miserable city attic, yearns 'to breathe the breath / of the cowslip and the primrose sweet'.[19] In Eliza Cook's poem, 'The City Artisan', the speaker is a city dweller for whom 'A dog-rose hedge, a cottage door, / Still linger in my wearied brain'.[20] The same theme recurs in innumerable lyrics by many other minor Victorian poets: 'The Children's Cry' by Clement Scott,[21] for example, and 'A City Flower' and 'The Simple Life' by Austin Dobson.[22] Still other writers, while accepting that people with gardens can live contentedly in towns, acknowledge the superiority of country gardens and rural existence. When in *John Halifax, Gentleman* John Halifax and his family remove from their urban house and garden in Norton Bury to their country home at Longfield, Phineas Fletcher comments: 'For pretty as our domain had grown, it was still in the middle of a town, and the children, like all naturally-reared children, craved after the freedom of the country' (p. 184).

This brings me to a consideration of the second model of city-garden relations: what one may term the 'garden-in-the-city' model, though in its more ambitious forms it comes close to resembling the garden city ideal. The garden-in-the-city concept in Victorian literature tends to be as firmly anti-urban as the city/garden dichotomy, but differs from it in taking as its starting point the recognition that gardens can and should improve the living conditions of urban dwellers—firstly, because the city cannot be made to disappear; and secondly, because permanent withdrawal from the city and its influence is an impracticable solution for all but a tiny and privileged minority.

It is in the novels of Dickens—regarded developmentally rather than collectively—that the paradigmatic shift from a garden *versus* the city model to a garden *in* the city one is most thoroughly explored.

Though Dickens never quite shrugged off his pastoral frame of reference, it is only in the early works, the *Pickwick Papers* and *Oliver Twist* in particular, that flight from the city is presented as a strategy likely to bring about human growth and regeneration. In *The Old Curiosity Shop*, flight is identified with death itself, but even in *Oliver Twist* there are hints that Dickens is edging towards the perception that the influence of the city is pervasive and inescapable. It requires the intervention of middle-class altruists with money to whisk Oliver from London to a garden retreat in the country; yet even in the 'free world' of the Maylies's cottage Oliver is not entirely safe. The episode in which Fagin and Monks appear to Oliver in a waking dream can be taken 'to imply that no matter how far you retreat from the rottenness you can never get right away from it'. Moreover, this

> is an idea that Dickens plumbs in novel after novel and always with an increasing subtlety and range of imaginative grasp, so that by the time he came to *Little Dorrit* the noble air of freedom is itself merely a dream and there can be no pastoral retreat which images freedom from the city's spreading corruption.[23]

In other words, Dickens moved firmly if reluctantly towards the perception that the modern city is not a self-contained place but a space virtually coextensive with social reality itself. Unable or unwilling to envisage a comprehensive reconstruction of urban society, whether sociopolitical or environmental, Dickens apparently came to accept that individuals could experience regeneration only within the city. This does not mean that Dickens came to purvey a romantic image of the city and of the place of humanized nature within it—quite the reverse. As one critic speculates, 'a detailed study of Nature's victories and defeats in Dickens's city would very probably reveal a slow degradation or elimination of the *rus in urbe*, and the gradual emergence of a totally de-naturalized city.'[24] Coketown is completely 'unnatural'; the London of *Great Expectations*, *Little Dorrit* and *Our Mutual Friend* is polluted and prison-like and, as Little Dorrit sums it up, 'large', 'barren' and 'wild' (pp. 169–70). Nor are the gardens that survive this comprehensive urbanization necessarily untainted by it. Unless they represent an intention to combat the physical and psychical homogenization of the urban environment, Dickens's city gardens partake of the general contamination. One thinks of the St Albans brickmakers' hovels in *Bleak House*, with their 'miserable little gardens before the doors growing nothing but stagnant pools' (p. 106); of the 'square court-yard' before Mrs Clenham's house in *Little Dorrit*, 'where a shrub or two and a patch of grass were as rank (which is saying much) as the iron railings enclosing them were rusty' (p. 31); and of the 'little slip of a front garden' at Panck's Pentonville lodging-house, 'where a few of the dustiest leaves hung their dismal heads and led a life of choking' (p. 296).

What it means to speak of Dickens's incorporation of pastoral powers of renewal within the city is that Dickens had sufficient faith in the inextinguishability of 'natural' human values—the values mythically associated with an ideal rural world—to make some of his most thoroughly urban characters the most conspicuous purveyors of these values. Imagination, goodness and fellow-feeling enable them both to act upon and to accommodate themselves to 'unnatural' city conditions or 'to *reinvest* the alien man-made world with its original meaning as an intentional world'.[25] There is a long line of such characters: among them, the Cheerybles, the Nibbles, the Traddles, the Toodles, the Bagnets, the Plornishes, and John Chivery. As in the case of the Plornishes, who create the illusion of a cottage garden in their urban home, or the crippled boy in *Nicholas Nickleby* (1839) who displays in his back-attic window a remarkable 'double wall-flower' blooming in 'a cracked jug, without a spout' (p. 514), their reinvestment of the alien city suggests an intuitive grasp of the Ruskinian principle that nature must be built into the architecture of the modern city in order to compensate for the loss of human fellowship. Such green spots are not just minor modifications to the urban environment but also sites of human affection designed to 'foster a more satisfying sense of community'.[26]

The essence of the view to which Dickens increasingly gravitated is that the survival of nature in the city is inextricably linked to the survival of urban dwellers with 'pastoral' values. Other writers express a less contingent version of the garden-in-the-city model.

In its simplest and most negative form, this model emerges in fictional descriptions of city gardens which serve merely as buffer zones against the ugliness and clamour of the physical environment. A characteristic example occurs in Wilkie Collins's early novel *Basil* (1852). From a window at the rear of his father's dreary London residence, Basil peers out upon

> a strip of garden—London garden—a close-shut dungeon for nature, where stunted trees and drooping flowers seemed visibly pining for the free air and sunlight of the country, in their sooty atmosphere, amid the prison of high brick walls. But the place gave room for the air to blow in it, and distanced the tumult of the busy streets. (pp. 41–2)

A similar yet slightly more equivocal example is Hardy's description of a garden area of Bede's Inn in *A Pair of Blue Eyes*. It focuses upon a sycamore tree visible from the window of Henry Knight's apartment. In October, the narrator observes,

> We notice the thick coat of soot upon the branches, hanging underneath them in flakes, as in a chimney. The blackness of these boughs does not at present improve the tree—nearly forsaken by its leaves as it is—but in the spring their green fresh beauty is made doubly beautiful by the contrast. Within the railings is a flower-garden of respectable dahlias and chrysanthemums, where a man is sweeping the leaves from the grass. (pp. 141–2)

Though Hardy grants the flora a degree of positive value, the figure of the polluted tree is hardly a sanguine sign of nature's capacity to survive in the city. Fortunately for Victorian readers seeking in fiction more consoling affirmations of nature's resilience, many imaginative writers subscribed to a stronger version of the city/garden model, produced more positive readings of the garden elements of urban 'texts' and

> made it a habit, it appears, to emphasize, magnify and glamourize the natural or rustic features still perceptible in the urban environment. The result is that the Victorian city, as described by many authors, resembles a vast conservation area, an assemblage of green spots and secluded nooks, complete with flowers, butterflies and bird-songs.[27]

'Green spots' are generally of two kinds. First, there are the older, more 'passive' and least purpose-built of the city's gardens. These include pastoral nooks and other vestiges of an essentially pre-industrial era, now largely forgotten and nestling inconspicuously within the labyrinthine structure of the expanding city. They furnish the subject matter of a welter of magazine articles which treat of the 'myriad-sided picture of [London] life'[28] with nostalgic enchantment. As editor of *Household Words*, Dickens himself probably approved the publication of one such piece entitled 'Left Behind'. The author guides his readers to the sequestered gardens of the metropolis, such as those of the Temple and the Inns of Court, 'quiet nest[s], more delightful for being in the heart of London's vitality' which 'seems to have been preserved in these busy days as needful harbours against the roar and storm of the main streets'.[29] These words echo Dickens's own description of the Temple in Chapter 15 of *Barnaby Rudge*, where the emphasis is upon the 'dreamy dullness of its trees and gardens' and its 'clerkly monkish atmosphere' in contrast to the 'tumult of the Strand or Fleet Street' (p. 113).

Throughout his writing career, Dickens showed a fascination for the sequestered pockets of (his version of) the metropolis. In a strictly formal sense, some of them are thoroughly unpastoral. In fact, the term 'secluded nooks' is used first in *Pickwick Papers* of the old London coaching inns like that of White Hart Inn 'which have escaped the rage for public improvement and the encroachments of private speculation' (p. 118). Similarly, in *Nicholas Nickleby* the city square in which the Cheerybles' warehouse is located 'has no grass but the weeds which sprang up round its base' (p. 468). The chief function of this 'desirable nook in the heart of a busy town' is not to create an illusion of the countryside but to reduce the din of the city to a 'distant hum' (p. 468). Nonetheless, Tim's City Square is more garden-like in atmosphere and a more tranquil refuge than the city gardens to which it stands symbolically opposed: explicitly, to 'the gravel walks and garden seats of the Squares of Russell and Euston' (p. 468); implicitly, perhaps, to the 'melancholy little plot of ground' behind Ralph Nickleby's house in Golden Square. The latter contains only deformed living things: 'a crippled tree', a 'rheumatic sparrow', and 'stunted everbrowns' (p. 8).

But some of Dickens's sequestered city gardens are suggestive of the countryside and a beckoning rural past. In *A Tale of Two Cities* (1859), Doctor Marette's retirement is a 'very harbour from the raging streets' and evokes a time when the district around Soho was more 'country' than 'town' (Ch. 6). The following description from *The Mystery of Edwin Drood* (1870) is evidence that Dickens made effective use of the *rus in urbe* motif to the very end of his novel-writing career:

> Behind the most ancient part of Holborn, London . . . is a little nook composed of two irregular quadrangles, called Staple Inn. It was one of these nooks, the turning into which out of the clashing street, imparts to the relieved pedestrian the sensation of having put cotton in his ears, and velvet soles in his boots. It is one of these nooks where a few smoky sparrows twitter in smoky trees, as though they called to one another, 'Let us play at country', and where a few feet of garden-mould and a few yards of gravel enable them to do that refreshing violence to their tiny understandings. (p. 112)

Most of Dickens's secluded pastoral pockets are the fortuitous accidents of urban history. They have survived because, secreted within the urban matrix, they have escaped the attention of planners and builders. But they are also the potential casualties of urban encroachment. This vulnerability, which helps to account for their imaginative resonance, also limits the contribution they can make to the ruralization of the city environment. Since many writers took the view that nature can survive in the city only if imported or assisted by people, the green spots they celebrate usually take more 'active' (i.e. purposively constructed) forms, though some authors were eager to credit nature with its own inherent powers of resilience. Consider Charles Reade's description of a fictional Victorian gaol in *It is Never too Late to Mend*:

> Two round towers flank the principal entrance. On one side of the right-hand tower is a small house constructed in the same [Gothic] style as the grand pile. The castle is massive and grand: this, its satellite, is massive and tiny, like the frog doing his little bit of bull. . . . There is only one dimple to all this gloomy grandeur: a rich little flower-garden, whose frame of emerald turf goes smiling up to the very ankle of the frowning fortress . . . (p. 97)

The little flower garden at the base of the overshadowing prison is typical of the local, small-scale form of environmental manipulation described and celebrated in mid-Victorian literature of the city. Another, more imaginative adjustment to the pressure for space is the roof-top garden. The best known fictional example is probably the roof-top garden of Riah's house in *Our Mutual Friend* (1865). Dickens refuses to romanticize what is little more than 'a few boxes of humble flowers and evergreens' amid an 'encompassing wilderness of dowager old chimneys' (p. 279). But its 'humble creeper', trained about 'a blackened chimney stack', is a perfect if grotesque accommodation of nature to the city's artifacts. And it is here that the crippled Fanny Cleaver, now transformed into the strangely beautiful Jenny Wren, professes to find air and rest, and to experience by proxy the blessed release of peaceful death.

Dickens may have derived his idea of a roof-top garden from William Bridges-Adam, a contributor to *Once a Week*, who proposed a scheme to 'convert London into a garden'[30] by means of an intensive development of roof-gardens. A story more in keeping with the sanguine spirit of Bridges-Adam's plan was printed in *All The Year Round* in 1874. Its setting is Tony Spence's second-hand book shop in a backstreet of a town called Smokeford. Above the bookshop, we are told, 'flowers flourished wonderfully between sloping roofs'.[31]

The roof-garden was the most ingenious example of a range of garden developments that compensated for the shortage of ground space by taking advantage of the vertical dimension of urban buildings. From mid-century onwards, fictional accounts of 'portable gardens' were 'supplemented' by garden books and magazine articles advocating that gloomy city streets should be beautified and ruralized by the addition of balcony-gardens, window-boxes, and Wardian cases displayed for public viewing. A contributor to *Chambers's Journal* in the mid-1870s commented:

> No one who is observant of his surroundings in a walk through any great town or city in the United Kingdom can fail to recognise the great increase in the cultivation of flowers, and the adornments of the exterior of houses with devices and arrangements in which shrubs and plants of every description are prominent features. Those who can recall the condition of things twenty or thirty years ago, tell us of the dull, cheerless aspect of our streets, and the impossibility of seeing a growing leaf in our great cities, save in the conservatories of the wealthy, or the few trees that escaped the axe of the destroyer when some of the squares and streets were formed by builders.[32]

The assertion that mid-Victorian streets presented a 'cheerless aspect' is not, in fact, confirmed by many novels of the period. Victorian fiction also leaves little doubt that balcony gardens are a monopoly of the privileged rich. In *The History of Pendennis* (1850), Thackeray informs his readers that the Claverings' mansion in Grosvenor Square sported a

> balcony before the drawing-room [which] bloomed with a portable garden of the most beautiful plants, and with flowers, white and pink, and scarlet; the windows of the upper room . . . and even a pretty little casement of the third storey . . . were similarly adorned with floral ornaments. (p. 306)

Trollope more than once points out that the wealthy have the means to make city life a serviceable substitute for life in the country, either by using their money, as does Melmotte in *The Way We Live Now* (1874–5), to 'turn a London street into a bower of roses' (p. 188), or by acquiring desirable residences adjacent to beautiful parks and open spaces, as does Madame Goesler in *Phineas Finn* (1869). Her Park Lane 'cottage' has a particularly lovely view:

> It was May now . . . and the park opposite was beautiful with green things, and the air was soft and balmy . . . and the flowers in the balcony were full of perfume, and the charm of London—what London can be to the rich—was at its height. (p. 547)

Scores of now largely forgotten novels of upper-class London life attest to the contribution that portable gardens can make to 'the charm of London'. A typical example is Disraeli's description in *Henrietta Temple* of Bellair House, situated in fashionable Mayfair:

> It was a long building, in the Italian style, situate in the midst of gardens, which, though not very extensive, were laid out with so much art and taste, that it was very difficult to believe that you were in a great city. (p. 313)

In G. J. Whyte-Melville's *Kate Coventry* (1856), a novel of the metropolitan *beau monde*, London seems to begin and end at Belgravia. The heroine's 'sweet little house', 'a perfect jewel of its kind', has '*such* a lovely drawing-room, opening into a conservatory, with a fountain and gold fish, to say nothing of flowers. . . . There are always flowers in the balcony; and there's no great singularity about that' (p. 15). The great advantage of having a residence in Belgravia, says Kate, is that it 'is most conveniently situated for a morning ride or walk in the Park', which is one of the 'pleasantest things one does in London' (p. 6).

Kate Coventry's view is echoed throughout mid- and late Victorian literature of the city. With few exceptions, imaginative authors joined social commentators and environmentalists in lauding the provision of public parks and open garden spaces close to the most densely built-up areas of the metropolis.[33]

Public parks are extolled for a variety of apparently contradictory virtues. Two images dominate, though they characteristically take some composite form. The first is that of an oasis of quietude and beauty within a noisy desert of brick and mortar. In the 1860s, Hippolyte Taine found James's Park 'a real piece of country' and Regent's Park a 'backwater' in which 'the noise of traffic is no longer to be heard, London is forgotten, the place is solitude'.[34] To the speaker in Arnold's 'Lines Written in Kensington Gardens', the 'mountain sod' is 'scarce fresher' than his 'lone, open glade', and in Whyte-Melville's *Digby Grand* (1853) the titular hero comes close to experiencing a similar illusion of remoteness from the grimy city:

> People may sneer at the cockney-beauties of Kensington Gardens, but for my part I love those trim alleys and long deep glades as well as anything I have met with further afield; and were it not that the stems of the fine old trees become so engrained and blackened with soot, you might fancy, in the heart of that sylvan scenery, that you were a hundred miles from London. (p. 124)

As well as being conducive to the production of pleasing pastoral fictions, the green space of the Gardens offers the solitary figure breathing and thinking space and the experiential equivalent of the hurricane's eye. The most revealing phrase in the above passage is '*in the heart* of that sylvan scenery'. What it implies is that the solitude-affording trees compose a heart within a heart. Arnold's speaker also claims to occupy a bowery shelter in which he can experience 'peace for ever new' and from which he can observe the 'endless, active life' upon the open expanse before him. One of Hardy's short stories, 'A Son's Veto' (1891) in *Life's Little Ironies* (1894), opens with a scene in 'one of the minor parks . . . that are to be found in the suburbs of London' (p. 35). 'There are', says Hardy, 'worlds within worlds in the great city', and this garden is one such place, a place that 'nobody outside the immediate district had ever heard of' (p. 35). Partly because the city has become vast and complex, the kind of comprehensive vision which enabled Wordsworth, from his vantage point on Westminster Bridge in 1802, to apprehend London as one 'mighty heart',[35] is no longer possible. The lone observer now experiences the city as a nested hierarchy of zones or spaces, each one more private, more heart- or womb-like, than the one outside it.

More than just a soothing refuge, the innermost space of the public garden is an external correlative of inner space: a metaphor for the soul, the heart, or the centre of being. The 'embattled garden at the centre of Charlotte Brontë's *Villette*' (i.e. the garden behind the girls' school in the Rue Fossette) can be viewed in this way:

> What is it that such a garden contains, conserves, withholds from the hot grasp of the city? Not, certainly, merely a quantity of trees, flowers, and grass, but rather those feelings or potentialities for feeling that had long been linked with such objects or environments. . . .[36]

As a symbol of experiential enclosure, the garden in the city may have a temporal as well as a spatial dimension. Digby Grand looks back to the 'peaceful time' when he took 'very pleasant walks' in Kensington Gardens 'as a sort of smiling oasis in the waste of [his] reckless and tempestuous life' (p. 124). Alaric Tudor in Trollope's *The Three Clerks* also associates his walks through the parks of London with happier days:

> His office and house were so circumstanced that, though they were some two miles distant, he could walk from one to the other almost without taking his feet off the grass. This had been the cause of great enjoyment to him. . . . The time was gone when he could watch the gambols of children, smile at courtships of nursery-maids, watch the changes in the dark foliage of the trees, and bend from his direct path hither and thither to catch the effects of distant buildings, and make for his eyes half-rural landscapes in the middle of the metropolis. (pp. 437–8)

Here, the image of the park as a sweet breathing-space offering pleasing echoes of the countryside, is fused with the other image of the park as a community playground affording animated scenes and 'endless, active life'. Fiction writers who emphasize the latter image come close to the view of Tim Linkinwater in *Nicholas*

Nickleby, for whom the green spaces of the city have all the merits and none of the demerits of the country. In *Lucretia* (1847), Bulwer Lytton remarks that 'the parks and green Kensington Gardens . . . seem rural and country like, but yet with more life than the country' (p. 75). And Julian Gray in Wilkie Collins's *The New Magdalen* (1873) dilates enthusiastically upon his invigorating experience in Kensington Gardens:

> For some time past I have been living in a flat, ugly, barren agricultural district. You can't think how pleasant I found the picture presented by the Gardens, as a contrast. The ladies in their rich winter dresses, the smart nursery maids, the lovely children, the ever-moving crowd skating on the ice of the Round Pond, it was all so exhilirating after what I have been used to that I actually caught myself whistling as I walked through the brilliant scene. (p. 92)

Like a less riotous version of a crowd painting by Frith, this passage is a celebratory account of 'picturesque tumult'[37] in a pastoralized urban setting. An early Victorian reader might well have found it strange, for in pre-mid-century fiction public gardens are usually presented as the exclusive social arenas of the fashionable rich. But this depiction has much in common with other contemporary images of public gardens as egalitarian playgrounds, fantasy worlds, and social microcosms in which rich and poor sport in harmonious propinquity. Late in the century, Henry James described the public parks of the capital as 'the drawing rooms and clubs of the poor',[38] as well as the resorts of the better-off. Moreover, 'Sir James Barrie, devoted garden-lover, chose [Kensington] Gardens as a principal playground of his most famous creation, Peter Pan.'[39] During the present century, countless plays, musicals and films of the *Mary Poppins* ilk have persistently endorsed these images.

It is not difficult to understand why public gardens were generally presented so positively and romantically in the second half of the nineteenth century. For many middle-class observers of the time, the provision of open spaces for the masses afforded a tangible sign of social progress and a solution to some pressing city problems. Most obviously, it partially alleviated the distress of urban overcrowding. 'There are evidences', wrote one contributor to the *Quiver*, 'that the days of old were not better than these. The good new times have given us parks. In the old days towns had few of these beautiful healthy open recreation grounds.'[40]

Some contemporary novelists gave textual space to fictional advocates of public parks. In William Black's *The Strange Adventures of a Phaeton* (1878) a young Prussian officer in England is indignant that the 'various . . . open spaces around London' are wasted 'playgrounds' (p. 18) for the people. The government or the municipalities, he contends, should 'buy up the land, and provide amusements, and draw the people in to open air' (p. 19).

The enthusiasm for public parks, reflected in the passages I have quoted from *The Three Clerks* and *The New Magdalen*, suggests that they were seen also as a partial solution to what some middle-class Victorians considered a far more worrying problem than the lack of breathing space: the problem of too little physical and social contact between the social classes in great cities and, as a possible consequence of this, social disintegration and mob rule. The gardens of the Crystal Palace were repeatedly lauded for having facilitated social intercourse between the classes: 'As a garden alone', wrote one contributor to *All The Year Round*, the Crystal Palace 'serves to bring all classes of our pleasure-seekers together'.[41] The functions that Blanchard Jerrold ascribed to the Derby—'it gives all London an airing' and 'effects a beneficial commingling of classes'—he ascribed also to London's public gardens. Having averred that even 'the most obstinate and prejudiced traducer of London must admit that the Cockney is well provided with greenery', he proclaimed that 'in the St James's Park, betimes in Spring and Summer, are to be found men, women and children of all degrees, bowered in abundant greenery.'[42]

Other late Victorian writers tended to pastoralize the city,[43] and strained to see in its public parks and gardens the urban equivalents of the small country parish. What they appear to have sensed is that the public garden could effect, if only temporarily, a softening of antagonisms between the social classes—the principal virtue ascribed by detractors of cities to the small rural community. As one writer put it: 'The kindly intercourse that is promoted between the various classes is the best of all possible emollients in every season of political unrest.'[44] Perhaps they also took comfort from the perception that in the public garden the 'mob' is generally scattered into couples and knots, deprived of any collective perception of its identity, and encouraged to dissipate its energies in 'harmless' play.[45]

Amidst the generally positive descriptions of public gardens, the one conspicuously dissonant voice was that of George Gissing. In his *Private Papers*, Henry Ryecroft looks back from the comfort of his cottage near Exeter to his years as a struggling city writer. He recalls: 'For more than six years I trod the pavement, never once stepping upon mother earth—for the parks are but pavements disguised with a growth of grass' (p. 34). In contrast to, say, Alaric Tudor or Julian Gray, the lonely figures in Gissing's fiction who wander through the parks of London find nothing to exhilarate or cheer them. Their walks, like those of Mr Temperley in *A Poor Gentleman*, are desolate, and their encounters with fellow 'brethren in seclusion'[46] are mute and furtive. Similarly, the public garden gatherings in Gissing's novels are not disposed into innocently playful groups and couples like figures in a pastoral landscape. Rather, they rollick in drunken and quarrelsome disorder—as in Chapter 12 of *The Nether World*, where Gissing brilliantly describes the wedding excursion of Bob Hewett, his wife, and their nether-world companions to the grounds of the Crystal Palace.

Gissing's novels of the London poor consistently refuse both to collude with the practice of pastoralizing the urban environment, and to subscribe to the idea that gardens can improve the lot of working people: 'he was never tempted to see the city through the eyes of a Walt Whitman' for he 'knew too well the depressing effects of poverty on the urban proletariat to gloss light-heartedly over the plagues of unemployment, deplorable housing, lack of hygiene and ignorance.'[47]

Gissing's principal strategy for denying the pastoral aspects of the city is to focus upon 'the ironic disjunction between the idyllic name and the dingy actuality'[48] of a place. The filthy, dilapidated block of tenements at Clerkenwell in *The Nether World* where Mrs Candy lives bears the ironic name of Shooters Gardens. Of Paradise Street in *Thyrza*, the narrator points out that 'the name is less descriptive than it might be' (p. 25). In the same novel, Walnut Tree Walk is distinguished by its lack of walnut trees, whilst in *The Town Traveller* (1898) we are told that beneath the back window of Mr Gammon's room at Mrs Bubb's lodging house 'lay parallel strips of ground, divided from each other by low walls. These were called the "gardens" of the houses in Kennington Road, but no blade of grass ever showed upon the black, hard-trodden soil' (p. 277).

Gissing's message is clear: since slum dwellers have no access to gardens proper, gardens can do nothing to alleviate the ugliness of their living conditions. Nor, as Gissing makes plain in 'Transplanted' (1895), one of the sketches gathered together in *Human Odds and Ends*, can working people expect to find their lives transformed for the better if by some stroke of fortune they are transported to a real country garden. In 'Transplanted', a well-to-do 'young matron' takes pity on a physically wretched luggage carrier known by the name of Long Bill, and transplants him from London to her beautiful country house, where she puts him to work in the kitchen garden. Far from experiencing the regeneration of Oliver Twist under similar circumstances, Long Bill feels unutterably 'hopeless' and 'purposeless' (p. 247). He blames his benefactress for having uprooted him from his 'natural' home, and takes revenge by running riot in the grape-house and rose-garden. His mischief is discovered, and he runs away, only to die of a severe haemorrhage by the roadside.

In the companion piece to 'Transplanted', a sketch entitled 'A Son of the Soil' (1895), Gissing considers the consequences of transplantation in the opposite direction. Its subject, the farm labourer Jonas Clay, feels 'discordant with everything about him' (p. 297); when he becomes bewitched by a 'blurred, gaslight vision of a remote world' (p. 297), he abandons the mother who depends upon him, and leaves for London, where he finds every opportunity to lead a dissolute life. But he has no regrets: 'Nothing would have induced him to return to rural life; the smell of the pavement was very sweet in his nostrils, and he loathed the memory of the fields' (p. 301).

As these two pieces suggest, Gissing's sense of the urban/rural dichotomy was unusually complex. In contrast to Dickens, Gissing was not haunted by the pastoral frame of reference, though his novels and letters indicate that he preferred the countryside to the town, and that he regarded the country garden as a prerequisite or, at least, a concomitant of 'civilized' living—that is, an environment of leisure in which the gamut of human faculties could be fulfilled. In the novels of the 1880s and early 1890s, the model of the urbane lifestyle is the spacious country house and garden: The Firs in *A Life's Morning*, Knightswell in *Isabel Clarendon* (1886) and the Warricombes' home in *Born in Exile* (1892). In his final years, Gissing employed a simpler, 'cottage' model in *Our Friend the Charlatan* (1901), *The Private Papers of Henry Ryecroft* and *Will Warburton*, consonant, perhaps, with the back-to-the-land impulse in late-Victorian England.

However, Gissing's novels do on occasions accede that

comparatively well-to-do town dwellers could live in and among pleasant, country-like gardens. The educated and intellectual Thomas Meres lives with his daughter in the Cheyne Walk area of Chelsea, a place very favourably described in the first volume of *Isabel Clarendon*:

> Literally the air is pleasant; the flowing breadth of stream and the green extent of the opposite Park, the spacious Embankment with its patches of tree-planted garden, make a perceptible freshness. . . . There is peace to be found here in the morning hours, with pleasant haunting thoughts of great names and days gone by. (I, 121)

In *The Whirlpool*, Harvey Rolfe finds 'tranquility as he knew not how to find it elsewhere' in the house of his friend, the corn business proprietor Basil Morton. Morton's house is situated in an elm-bordered road in Greystone. 'It was in the town, yet nothing town-like. No sooty smother hung above the house-tops and smirched the garden leafage' (p. 332). Behind the house is a large, old-fashioned garden, in a 'bowered corner' of which Harvey luxuriates in dreams of his childhood.

And then, of course, there are the suburbs. Gissing's contributions to the imaginative literature of suburbia are of singular importance, though best understood within the context of that literature.

Depending on one's viewpoint, the Victorian suburb represents either a third configuration of garden/city relationships, or a stage between the *rus in urbe* idea and the topographical model in which distinctions between city and garden are collapsed or transformed virtually to the point of confusion. Some Victorians saw it as 'neither one thing nor the other' —[49] that is, as neither town nor country. Other commentators insist that it became an independent entity in its own right: 'neither the town spread thin nor the country built close, but a quite different type of development with its own inimitable characteristics.'[50]

What cannot be contested is the centrality of the garden in suburban life: conceptually, as the topographical image in which the concept of the suburb is perhaps most frequently embodied; physically, as an essential component of the individual suburban residence and of the ambience of the suburb in general; and ideologically, as the spatial expression or synecdoche of a culture of seclusion and privatism centred on the nuclear family. In addition, of course, the features of some suburban gardens are emblematic of the wealth and social status of their owners, though the ambivalent combination of display and concealment is one of the characteristic paradoxes of the suburban garden.

It was the desire to possess a house with a garden in an area of peaceful seclusion and floral beauty that prompted many middle-class Victorians to gravitate towards the suburbs. In *Cecil; or the Adventures of a Coxcomb* (1841) the narrator announces that 'Thriving merchants—popular actors—popular dentists—popular lawyers—popular all sorts of things, are sure to have their Tusculum, their *rus in urbe*, their Eden, their 'appiness 'ouse' (p. 129). Less popular 'sorts' were similarly motivated. In the Grossmiths' masterpiece of late-Victorian social comedy, *The Diary of a Nobody* (1892), the tell-tale name of the Pooters' house in suburban Holloway is 'The Laurels', and Mr Pooter's diary entries frequently betray his gardening interests.

According to one commentator, it was in the suburban garden that the 'owner might actually demonstrate his mastery over Nature, however minuscule, and relate directly to the soil and the environment as he could no longer to his fellow humans.'[51] Whatever the validity of this final clause, it is significant that the first substantial Victorian book on the garden, *The Suburban Gardener and Villa Companion*, was also the first of many to be directed, not at the owners of country estates, but at the swelling band of affluent suburban gardeners.

Though Victorian imaginative writers acknowledge the perceived attractiveness of the suburban garden, their images of it, and their responses to the suburb in general, are varied and complex. Three factors in particular help to account for this: the historical phase and character of suburban developments to which they refer; their historical perspectives; and their topographical perspectives, that is, whether they view the suburbs from within the city or from a point outside them.

Since Victorian suburbs differed enormously in kind, to speak of *the* suburb is extremely misleading. In the early nineteenth century, 'the norm was the detached "villa" standing in its own (and often substantial) grounds, very much a country seat in miniature and shorn of its tenant farms.'[52] It was this kind of exclusive development that Loudon had in mind when he declared his intention to prove 'that a suburban residence, with a very small portion of the land attached, will contain all that is essential to happiness, in the garden, park, and demesne of the most extensive country residence.'[53] Bulwer Lytton in *Kenelm Chillingly* presents a positive image of one such suburban garden: 'a broad gravel-drive, bordered with rare evergreens . . . a handsome house with a portico in front, and a long conservatory at the garden side'. It was, says the narrator, 'one of those houses which belong to "city gentlemen", and often contain more comfort and exhibit more luxury than many a stately manorial mansion' (p. 273).

A close cousin of the affluent city suburb is the dormitory settlement of the provincial town. In M. E. Braddon's *Just As I Am*, the narrator writes favourably of such a place. Avonmore, the residential settlement for the 'great iron town' of Blackford, is 'an elegant modern settlement, where the wealthy Blackfordians retired from the smoke of foundries and the labour of money-making, to clean air and conifer-shaded gardens, and the relaxation of money-spending' (p. 47). Elsewhere we are told that its 'gentle slopes . . . are dotted with white-walled villas, girdled with exquisitely kept gardens, rich in monkey-trees, deodoras, Wellingtonias, and all the aristocracy of foreign timber, (p. 167).

Waves of suburban expansion from the 1840s to the 1890s and, in particular, the development of lower middle-class suburbs characterized by repetitive and standardized layout, almost inevitably led to more varied literary images of the suburban garden. In the novels of Dickens there are at least three images, suggesting different responses to the idea of the suburb as a solution to inner-city problems. The first is exemplified by the attractive image of a garden in suburban Norwood in *David Copperfield*, written at a time when guide books were praising Norwood for its semi-rural charms:

> There was a lovely garden to Mr Spenlow's house; and though it was not the best time of year for seeing a garden, it was so beautifully kept, that I was quite enchanted. There was a charming lawn, there were clusters of trees; and there were perspective walks that I could just distinguish in the dark, arched over with trellis-work, on which shrubs and flowers grew in the growing season. (p. 368)

David's enchantment with Mr Spenlow's garden is heightened, no doubt, by his enchantment with Mr Spenlow's daughter; yet the garden described is charming in its own right.

A second, more idiosyncratic image is typified by Wemmick's 'castle' cottage and garden at Walworth in *Great Expectations*. This kind of suburban idyll, the locus of familial sentiments and emotional expressiveness, more clearly indicates Dickens's critical attitude towards the materialistic and de-personalizing conditions of the city itself. However, since Walworth for Wemmick is a purely residential suburb, it serves only to enforce a split between work and home life. Wemmick's lack of personal integration suggests that here the suburban idyll is no more than a partial and inadequate solution to the problems of urban existence.

Dickens's third image of the suburb is that of the blighted garden or wasteland. It occurs most conspicuously in his last completed novel, *Our Mutual Friend*, in the form of 'a tract of suburban Sahara' (p. 33) south of Holloway, and seems to be a comment on the mass movement of the lower middle classes to the suburbs in the 1860s.[54]

The second variable that helps to account for the variety of literary images of the suburban garden is temporal perspective. As a rule, writers who look back to suburbs of the past tend to present them more affectionately and positively than those who treat of contemporary developments. Dickens opens Chapter 4 of *Barnaby Rudge* (1841) with a description of the 'venerable suburb' of Clerkenwell in the mid-1770s. It recalls a nostalgic image of a green, pre-industrial London:

> There were gardens to many of the houses, and trees by the pavement side; with an air of freshness breathing up and down, which in these days would be sought in vain. . . . Nature was not so far removed or hard to get at, as in these days. . . . (p. 30)

In *The Doctor's Wife* (1864), *The Story of Barbara* (1880), and *A Lost Eden* (1904), M. E. Braddon looks back with affection to the Camberwell she knew in the early 1850s. Suburban gardens suggestive of the countryside are prominent in all three novels, and are presented in such a way as to imply that they offer their owners a more than adequate compensation for their lack of material wealth. The Trevernock family in *The Story of Barbara*, though 'absolutely poor', live in a 'little semi-detached house' with 'a dainty prettiness not always attainable by people of large means' (I, 3). They are 'always trying to surprise each other with some improvement in house or garden', if 'only a shilling rose-bush planted in the border, or a penny bunch of violets on the mantel-piece' (I, 4–5). In *The Doctor's Wife*, however, mid-Victorian Camberwell is not romanticized. Though there are 'pretty little villas and comfortable cottages nestling among trees' (I, 3), there is also a 'wild and sterile' canal and 'straggling rows of cottages dwindling away into pigsties' (I, 4). The garden of the Sleafords, once beautiful, is now unkempt: 'rare orchids' sprout 'out of beds that were full of chickweed, and liles-of-the-valley' flourish 'among the groundsel in a shady corner under the water-butt. . . . The odour of distant pigsties' mingles 'faintly with the perfume of the roses' (I, 31–2). Though the farmyard odours may detract from the beauty of the gardens, they also ratify its urban character.

A Lost Eden, the novel in which the perspective on mid-century Camberwell is most temporally distanced, is also the novel in which Braddon most insistently details the differences between what was and what is. The family the novel concerns, the Sandfords, have suffered a severe social decline, and yet their home of Chestnut Lodge is a detached house with a garden over two acres in size 'such . . . as no one could hope for nowadays [i.e. 1904] within five miles of London' (p. 74), and the novel contains a number of rhapsodic descriptions of it.

In contrast to writers who present nostalgic images of suburbs that no longer exist, those who view contemporary developments tend to withhold approval. Implicit in the following passage from Rhoda Broughton's *Belinda* (1883) is the conservative assumption that old and traditional topographies are superior to new and fashionable suburbs:

> It would be the opinion of outsiders, who have not visited Oxbridge . . . that the inhabitants of that university town dwell in grey and ancient houses, time-coloured and with flavours of old learning still hanging about their massy roof-trees. In point of fact, their lives are passed for the most part in flippant spick and span villas and villakins, each with its half acre of tennis-ground and double-daisies, all so neat that scarcely anyone has had the time to die there, though numerous people have taken leave to be born there, and forming, in their ensemble, an ugly, irrelevant, healthy suburb, that would not disgrace a cotton city of today. (pp. 251–2)

In a letter written in May 1873, Ruskin spoke of the 'pestilence' that 'has fallen on the suburbs of loathsome London', and left no doubt of his attitude towards standardization of design: 'Attached to every double block are exactly similar double parallelograms of garden, laid out in a new gravel and scanty turf, on the model of the pleasure grounds in the Crystal Palace, and enclosed by high, thin, and pale brick walls.' In the same letter, Ruskin recalled Herne Hill in the 1820s: 'a quiet secluded district of field and wood', in which cottages have 'their porches embroidered with honeysuckle, and their gardens with daisies' and in which a 'gentleman's house, with its lawn, gardens, offices, and attached fields' indicated 'a country life of long continuance and quiet respectability' (*RW*, IV, 528–9).

Gissing's images of suburban London are invariably in the present tense and, if not always disdainful, are characteristically intoned by a reporter who can find little to excite his interest or approval. However, Gissing's images resist easy generalization, partly because they map the subtle geographical and social variations of the suburban terrain, and partly because Gissing appreciated, as few other novelists of his time did, that for many of its inhabitants suburbia had become a whole world, not just a place in which to reside. For many of his men, it is the market from which they derive their money; for many of his women, it is the place in which their lives are spent (or wasted).

Suburbs, like individuals, are known in the first place by their names and faces—by what the eye can register. To respond to these aspects in isolation is analytically hazardous; and yet, as Gissing recognized, the visual appearance of the affluent suburb was all-important to those who aspired to live there. Gissing draws attention to this superficial response in the opening chapter of *In the Year of Jubilee* (1894):

> De Crespigny Park, a thoroughfare connecting Grove Lane, Camberwell, with Denmark Hill, presents a double row of similar dwellings; its clean breadth, with foliage of trees and shrubs in front gardens, makes it pleasant to the eye that finds pleasure in suburban London. In point of respectability, it has claims only to be appreciated by the ambitious middle-class of Camberwell. (p. 1)

'De Crespigny Park', the name, discloses the pretentions of its residents and the parodic character of a district that likes to think itself a country estate. *Front* gardens, the suburb's public faces, are the principal sites of affective displays. But front gardens can conceal as well as disclose; in Gissing's novels they conceal precisely and paradoxically those marital and generational tensions which the suburban home is intended to exorcise. Back gardens, too, may comment ironically on the confinement and enclosure of the family's individual members. The rear garden of the Lord family in *In the Year of Jubilee* is described in these terms:

> The garden was but a strip of ground, bounded by walls of four feet high; in the midst stood a laburnum, now heavy with golden bloom, and at the end grew a hollybush, flanked with laurels; a border flower-bed displayed Stephen Lord's taste and industry. (p. 30)

It is significant that the garden displays the 'taste and industry' of the father, for it is Stephen's patriarchal authority and indifference to 'culture' which brings him into conflict with his children. Nancy, his daughter, is frustrated by his refusal to move to a grander house as well as by what she takes to be her pointless existence. She realizes that her father can afford a garden expressive of greater affluence than his laurels and laburnums suggest. It is a tell-tale sign that Nancy and her weak-willed brother, Horace, use the garden not to be with their father but to escape him and to talk in private. On one occasion she 'carelessly' assents to seat herself on a rustic bench in the shadow of the laburnum while Horace stands languidly before her with one of the branches in his hand. Since both are bound in by the walls of the garden and the confinement they symbolize, their pastoral attitudes are strikingly ironic.

Considered solely in environmental terms, Gissing's suburbs are presented a good deal more positively than are the working class districts of the city. By dint of its foliage and variety, for example, Grove Lane where the Lords live—a 'bit of London which does not keep pace with the times' (p. 13)—is not unattractive. Gissing describes more favourably still the far more affluent district of Champion Hill which 'enjoys aristocratic seclusion' and from which 'is obtainable a glimpse of open fields' (p. 13).

The main point about topographical perspective is that the suburb is more likely to be presented approvingly if it is viewed from within the city than if it is viewed from a rural perspective. In a number of Wilkie Collins's novels, houses and gardens on the outskirts of London compare favourably with those nearer to its centre. The home of Amelius Goldenheart in *The Fallen Leaves* is situated in a by-road outside Regent's Park. This 'perfect little retreat' is simple, pretty and 'completely surrounded by its own tiny plot of garden-ground'. Toff, Goldenheart's old French servant, calls it a 'suburban Paradise' (p. 242). In the opening pages of *The Woman in White* (1860) Walter Hartwright is relieved to exchange the oppressive atmosphere and noise of 'the great heart of the city' for 'the cool night air in the suburbs' (p. 2) and his mother's Hampstead cottage. A different but no less favourably presented residence is Mablethorpe House, in suburban Kensington, the principal setting in *The New Magdalen*. Its conservatory, which 'varied and brightened the scene . . . forming an entrance to the rooms, through a winter garden of rare plants and flowers' bespoke 'the march of modern improvement' (p. 57).

By contrast, Trollope's narrators glance at the suburb from the implicit frame of reference of the country house. 'It is', he declares in *The Three Clerks*, 'very difficult nowadays to say where the suburbs of London come to an end, and where the country begins' (p. 22). That he does not approve of this blurring of the city/country distinction is evident in the description of Surbiton Cottage, home of the Woodwards, situated in one of those 'few nooks within reach of London which have not been be-villaed and be-terraced out of all look of rural charm' (p. 22). Surbiton cottage is appraised warmly only because it is atypical. It is not a villa 'but a small old-fashioned brick house abutting on to the road, but looking from its windows on to a lawn and gardens, which stretched down to the river'. The sentiments implied here are similar to those expressed by Mrs C. S. Peel in her manual of middle-class domesticity, *The New Home* (1898), 'that the suburbs of any large town appear to me detestable'. Such advantages as they could boast, she believed, were merely consolation prizes for 'those people who yearn for the pleasures of the country and who find their diversions in golf, tennis, bicycling, boating, or gardening, and whom cruel fate prevents from living in the real country.'[55]

Worth consideration, finally, are the contributions of imaginative writers to the fourth and most radical of city/garden models. As it is constructed upon the desire to eliminate blatant topographical dichotomies, this model is almost impossible to label by juggling the familiar categories of 'town', 'country' and 'garden'. Its most famous formulation is Garden City, though Ebenezer Howard's coinage upholds even as it qualifies the primacy of the city as the physical and conceptual core of the scheme. Though William Morris might well have thought the formulation inadequate, his

News from Nowhere is often cited as an important influence upon and even (though wrongly) as a blueprint for the Garden City project.[56] Because *News* is by far the most significant fictional exploration of the integrative topographical model at issue here, I shall make use of the expression at which Morris himself strongly hints: 'the city in the garden'. It retains the original nouns, but in Morris's utopian romance, the applications of both are transformed almost beyond recognition.

Whether expounded in fiction or in books on town planning, schemes designed to effect a comprehensive transformation of the humanized landscape are almost inevitably visionary and forward-looking rather than nostalgic genuflections to the myth of a past Golden Age—a fact which helps to explain their virtual absence in Victorian realist fiction. In addition to emphasizing the supreme importance of beautiful and healthy living conditions, they tend also to stress the concept of community. In 'socialist' versions, everyone lives in harmony in the same garden-like environment. In its most radical forms, the 'city in the garden' model entails the rejection of the two 'philosophies' implicit in the city/garden models examined previously: the philosophy of gradualism (that is, the idea that environmental change should be a gradual and probably piecemeal process rather than the result of cataclysmic political change), and the philosophy of accommodation, the principle that people better their living conditions by improving and adjusting to prevailing environmental conditions.

Few if any mid-Victorian writers were willing to advocate political revolution as a path to radical environmental change, though one or two foreshadow some aspects of Morris's utopian vision. In his lecture on 'Great Cities and their influence for Good and Evil', delivered in Bristol in 1857, Charles Kingsley declared that he looked forward to a time when it would be possible to 'build better things than cities', and when there would be 'a complete interpenetration of city and country, a complete fusion of their different modes of life, and a combination of the advantages of both, such as no country in the world had ever seen.'[57] Like Morris, Kingsley came to eschew the Romantic view of nature. The Great Exhibition taught him

> that man was now in a position to conquer and civilise Nature, to master his environment, and to lay the foundations of a new society, in which cities would no longer appear as

> diseased patches soiling the purity of the landscape, but as nuclei of organisations shining with the brightness of their regenerated state.[58]

But Kingsley was no revolutionary. He accepted that landed and commercial interests would retain their power to veto any programme for the comprehensive remodelling of the urban landscape. He believed also that model cities could only be imposed by despotic rulers or authoritarian states; he was thankful that the 'democratic' political institutions of Britain inhibited such shortcuts. Kingsley had faith in the evolution of capitalism to a stage when the social order would be more harmonious, and when enlightened industrialists would do for their employees what they had already done for themselves: import the city into the countryside so that 'the city would become what it ought to be; the workshop, and not the dwelling-house, of a mighty and healthy people.'[59]

One work of utopian fiction that at least nods in the direction of the 'city in the garden' ideal is Bulwer Lytton's *The Coming Race* (1871). The hero, an American, discovers a subterranean race, the Vril-ya, who owe their utopian existence to a fluid called 'vril', a force that has much in common with electricity. By means of this remarkable fluid, the Vril-ya have extinguished war, poverty and crime, and the state has dwindled to a benevolent patriarchy.

Their civilization appears to be a working model of social Darwinism, for in their rational pursuit of knowledge and the ideal society, the Vril-ya have weeded out institutions that have proved unfit—in other words, those likely to engender conflict and violent passions. They distrust the arts for precisely this reason. Their landscapes are not an expression of beauty for beauty's sake, but rather a reflection of the rational principles which govern every area of their lives. The city about which the hero is conducted is 'large in proportion to the territory round it' (p. 113), but still no bigger than a country estate. It would seem to approximate to the Garden City ideal, for 'the largeness of space, in proportion to the rural territory, occupied by the city, was occasioned by the custom of surrounding each house with a separate garden' (p. 117). Moreover, many of the houses display hanging gardens and their apartments are richly decorated with flowers.

Nonetheless, Bulwer Lytton appears not to have been able to conceive of a truly radically restructured landscape. The Vril-ya have no community gardens; all the gardens seem to be privately owned. In addition, town and country are not completely integrated, and the hero's guide finds it necessary to retire to his country estate whenever the opportunity arises.

In fairness to Bulwer Lytton, it ought to be said that *The Coming Race* is a vision of a society distinguished by its institutions and practices rather than by its environmental qualities—to which only limited attention is paid. To William Morris, on the other hand, the quality of the physical environment was all-important, not only because of the value he gave to beauty in everyday life, but also because he could not imagine a radically restructured landscape except as the product or concomitant of a radically restructured society—a socialist utopia.

Long before he wrote *News from Nowhere*, Morris repeatedly made it clear that he associated abundant gardens with a better society. His lectures and letters of the 1870s and 1880s are replete with declarations of what ought to be, and expressions of hope for what might be:

> In great towns, gardens both private and public are positive necessities, if the citizens are to live reasonable and healthy lives in body and mind. (*MW*, XXIV, 91)
>
> Every child should be able to play in a garden close to the place where his parents live. (*MW*, XXIII, 22)
>
> . . . suppose people lived in little communities among gardens and greenfields . . . then I think that one might say that civilization had really begun.[60]

When Morris addresses himself to the subject of a utopian future, the burden of 'garden' is significantly displaced from individual plots of land to the whole of the English landscape:

> I want the town to be impregnated with the country . . . I want every homestead to be . . . a lovely house surrounded by acres and acres of garden . . . I want the town to be . . . in short, a garden with beautiful houses in it.[61]

Morris came to realize that the garden, both as a concept and as a topography, had to expand so as to incorporate those features of the landscape to which it had previously been both physically and symbolically opposed. Only then would it be possible to transform 'this grimy back-yard of a workshop into a garden' (*MW*, XXII, 173) and so avoid the apocalyptic change, prophesied by Ruskin in the conclusion to *Sesame and Lilies*, in which the garden of England had become a coal mine.

The 'education' of Guest, the nineteenth-century narrator of *News from Nowhere* who awakens one day to find himself in post-revolutionary London, in part involves having to re-learn the concept of garden. At its simplest, this entails a renewed attentiveness to the importance of gardens as beautifying elements of the humanized landscape. He finds gardens everywhere and in the most unexpected places. Trafalgar Square is now the site of an apricot orchard. There are rose gardens where Endell Street once stood, gardens surround the mills dotted along the banks of the Thames, and from the end of Piccadilly to the British Museum 'each house stood in a garden carefully cultivated, and running over with flowers' (*MSW*, p. 38).

Guest's concept of garden is challenged more radically by the forms of some of the gardens he encounters in transformed London. Accustomed to thinking of gardens as units of private property and as symbols of social exclusiveness, he is confronted in Hammersmith with the sight of a row of houses with a '*continuous* garden in front of them' (my emphasis; *MSW*, p. 9). Guest makes little of this manifestation of community values, but the attentive reader will necessarily be struck by Guest's adjective, which 'indicates a *very* radical shift in property values'.[62]

Guest does at first find strange the larger applications that 'garden' has come to acquire in the socialist utopia. Hammond, his guide, informs him that England 'is now a garden, where nothing is wasted and nothing spoilt, with the necessary dwellings, sheds, and workshops scattered up and down the country, all trim and neat and pretty.' Guest seeks clarification:

> 'One thing, it seems to me, does not go with your word of "garden" for the country. You have spoken of wastes and forests, and I myself have seen the beginning of your Middlesex and Essex forest. Why do you keep such things in a garden? and isn't it very wasteful to do so?'
>
> 'My friend', he said, 'we like these pieces of wild nature, and can afford them, so we have them; let alone that as to the forests, we need a great deal of timber, and suppose that our sons and sons' sons will do the like. As to the land being a garden, I have heard that they used to have shrubberies and rockeries in gardens once; and though I might not like the artificial ones, I assure you that some of the natural

rockeries of our garden are worth seeing.' (*MSW*, p. 69)

Morris's vision of England transformed into a garden where the constituent elements also partake of garden-like qualities has nothing in common with the 'conservative' myth of the Garden of England. The latter is a product of selective perception, an illegitimate extrapolation from selected bits of the landscape to the country as a whole. But Morris's image of the comprehensive reconstruction of the physical environment justifies the application of 'garden' in its widest topographical sense. Remnants of pre-revolutionary England—Kensington Gardens, for instance—have been absorbed into a new cultural context, so that they now have totally different meanings and functions. (Significantly, Hammond cannot understand why Kensington *Gardens* is so called.)

Since the members of the socialist utopia make no distinctions between work and leisure, or between utility and beauty, 'garden' is no longer used exclusively to mark off those spaces reserved for refuge and recreation. 'Garden' now legitimately designates almost any feature of the humanized landscape expressive of the 'generosity and abundance of life' that brings Guest 'to a pitch that [he] had never yet reached' (*MSW*, p. 23). Thus, 'the fields were everywhere treated as a garden made for the pleasure as well as the livelihood of all . . .' (*MSW*, p. 179). This dramatically new application of 'garden' reflects at one and the same time a desire to live close to nature *and* a desire to control and shape it to human requirements.

It is no coincidence that *News from Nowhere* is both the most challenging exposition of city/garden relationships in Victorian imaginative literature and one of the least representative works of fiction produced in the nineteenth century. The originality of *News* lies partly in its invitation to the reader to rethink the nature of city/garden relationships within the context of a work that itself makes strange the literature in which those relationships are otherwise defined.[63]

CHAPTER NINE

Gardens, Homes and Women

Of the roughly 40,000 novels that the Victorians produced, the bulk are domestic novels. They deal with families and personal relationships within relatively small communities, as well as with the lives of particular individuals. Most fictional families are middle-class or (less frequently) upper-class. They may experience traumatic shifts of fortune, but for the most part they lead privileged lives in comfortable surroundings. They are more often seen at home and at play than at work; romance, marriage and quotidian domestic and social pursuits are their main preoccupations. Even the sensation novelists of the 1860s anchored their melodramatic stories in prosaic, domestic environments.

Little wonder, then, that the garden, the dominant bourgeois version of the *locus amoenus* and the aristocratic spatial model of gracious living, should have played such an important part in Victorian fiction. It was in their gardens more than anywhere else that privileged Victorians sported, courted and conversed. As an extension of the country house or suburban villa, the garden was an integral part of the domestic living space and the lifestyle it facilitated and expressed. At the same time, its circumscription made it conducive to the making and maintaining of fictions. Because it *looked* like a little world of its own, it could be conceived as one, and made to gratify the needs of one. This ambivalent ontological status—the garden as both everyday place and other world—lies at the heart of its functional significance in many literary texts.

Gardens play an especially important part in the works of many minor though often prolific Victorian novelists for whom bourgeois domesticity and romance appear to have been the only subjects of conceivable interest.Rhoda Broughton's *Doctor Cupid* (1887), for example, is a novel pervaded by garden scenes, thoughts and activities. It is chiefly concerned with the romantic interests of a group of sisters, who seem to spend the greater part of their time in gardens: lazing in hammmocks, playing tennis, wishing, crying, receiving nosegays, watering and admiring plants, working out their affairs of the heart, and evaluating residences in terms of the gardens of which they can or cannot boast. Their lives take their pattern from the seasonal rhythms of the gardener's calendar.

The spring inspection of the garden is a major event, as is Whitsuntide when 'devout souls . . . strip their hothouses and conservatories' (p. 241) to decorate country churches. The narrator, who embraces a mild form of environmental determinism, repeatedly relates their spirits to the state of their garden world. When one of the girls is made despondent in the autumn, the narrator comments:

> It seems such a folly and a shame to be miserable in the face of these yellow October days that by and by steal in, pranked out in the cheerful glory of their short-lived wealth . . . and with such an army of dahlias, ragged chrysanthemums, and 'Good-bye—summers', with their delicate broad disks, to greet you morning after morning as you pass in your pleasant ownership along their gossamered ranks. (p. 242)

In addition, *Doctor Cupid* is liberally laced with quotations from garden poets and authorities, some of which are fully integrated within the text and elicit a direct response from the narrator or the characters. Chapter 9, for example, opens with an extract from Bacon's essay on gardens, after which the narrator comments: 'I do not know whether Peggy had ever read Bacon, but she certainly endorsed his opinion' that gardening 'is the Purest of Humane pleasures' and 'the Greatest Refreshment to the Spirit of Man' (p. 68). Peggy herself declares that '"The garden is the only satisfactory thing" . . . as she stands besides her carnation-bed, and notes how many fat buds have, during the night, broken into pale sulphur and striped the blood-red flowers'. Though itself a part of the domestic sphere, the garden, as a dependable source of solace and pleasure, affords a buffer against the disappointments this sphere occasions. Here the garden's complex relations with the domestic world are again apparent, though the fact that the pain/pleasure balance sheet of garden experiences can stand comparison with the balance sheet of life itself gives some idea of its perceived importance.

Like Rhoda Broughton, many other Victorian novelists highlighted the socially privileged—at least in terms of textual space—which helps to explain both the amount and the kind of attention they devote to gardens. Many middle- and upper-class characters have so much leisure time that they can virtually live in their gardens—as Alfred Austin claimed to live in his; others (and here one thinks of many of Trollope's and some of Disraeli's characters) spend much of their time enjoying and more occasionally superintending their country estates. Moreover, their gardens are usually sufficiently spacious to serve as theatres for informal social dramas. By contrast, the poor person's garden is often small enough to be apprehended as a whole, thus furnishing a suitable subject for description, but inadequate to the needs of animated scenes. The affluent have lawns; the poor do not.[1] Hence most fictional cottage gardens are presented as entities rather than as settings, as static pictures for public inspection as opposed to communal spaces in private places.

This is one of the reasons that gardens are woven less into the fabric of fictional lives in novels of rural society—those of George Eliot and Hardy, for example—than in novels which concentrate on cossetted middle-class characters in cossetted middle-class settings. Another reason is that in novels concerned with rural communities, cottage and farmhouse gardens are typically components of the provincial 'pastoral' milieu rather than discrete domains. For instance, the garden of Hope Farm in Gaskell's *Cousin Phillis* is both physically and symbolically an element within what amounts to an edenic ecosystem, and no more or less distinct than any of the other elements. It is accommodated 'between the house and the shady, grassy lane' (p. 8), but there is no attempt to bracket it off; its flowers, we are told, 'crept out upon the low-covered wall and house-mount, and were even to be found self-sown upon the turf that bordered the path to the back of the house' (p. 12).

On those occasions when the rural worker's garden assumes greater than average proportions, its size is commensurate with the functions it is called upon to perform. Apart from its almost ungovernable fecundity, the chief distinguishing characteristic of Hall Farm Garden in *Adam Bede* is its size:

> In that leafy, flowery, bushy time, to look for any one in this garden was like playing at 'hide-and-seek'. . . . The garden was so large. There was always a superfluity of broad beans—it took nine or ten of Adam's strides to get to the end of the uncut grass walk that ran by the side of them. (p. 188)

The historical explanation is that it was formerly the kitchen garden of a manor house. This is significant fact, but also a convenient one, since it provides the pretext for a comprehensive and particularistic description of the garden's immense variety of vegetable life, as the narrator relates Adam's necessarily slow progress through it, and finally his meeting with Hetty in it. It also enables George Eliot to hint that Adam is of the 'organic' type, integrated in the 'natural' world, while its substantial proportions and the attention it can therefore sustain, mean that it can be interpreted, like the farm itself, as 'a major symbol of the vitality and stability' of the 'stable farming community'.[2]

In spite of the attention it receives in Chapter 20 of *Adam Bede*—where Eliot pulls out all the stops of pictorial realism—Hall Farm garden is essentially unique. This may seem a trivial point, but the fact that similar gardens are treated in like manner—described in depth and then despatched—appears to give credence to the idea that gardens are of continuous significance as settings and spaces only to those for whom they mean leisure and status rather than toil, food, and infrequent respite. After all, the brooding presences in rural novels are farms and fields, heaths and woodlands—places where work has to be done and wages earned. Gardens are the sites of occasional but sometimes intense and joyous expenditure of effort, a fact suggested by the concentrated bursts of description they are allocated in the rural novels of Eliot and Hardy.

The association of gardens with the privileged classes in their domestic spheres is further reinforced by the general absence of garden scenes and settings in novels which focus upon working-class life in urban environments. With few exceptions, the garden scenes in George Gissing's novels, for example, take place either in the English countryside or in the affluent, semi-rural suburbs of London. One thinks of the opening chapters of *A Life's Morning*, and of the Athel family gathered together in proximity to, and relaxing in, the garden of their 'delightful house in the midst of Surrey's fairest scenery' (p. 3); or, in *In the Year of Jubilee*, of Nancy Lord's first meeting with Lionel Tarrant in the 'aristocratic seclusion' of Mrs Vawdrey's substantial villa garden in Champion Hill, where 'the mellow sunlight, the garden odours, and the warm still air favoured a growth of intimacy' (p. 53). These kinds of felicitous garden scenes are few and far between in Gissing's novels, particularly his social novels, for Gissing's main concern is with the urban poor.[3]

Another reason for the absence of garden scenes in Gissing's fiction is his 'neglect' of conventional, middle-class domestic situations and marital relationships. Very few of his female characters are homemakers who competently perform a conventional domestic role. *Denzil Quarrier* (1892), *The Odd Women, In the Year of Jubilee*, and *The Whirlpool* all condemn 'women who neglect their households to pursue careers, affairs, or whatever'.[4]

It is virtually impossible to say anything about the garden in Victorian fiction without reference to the concept of home and the place of women within it.

Of the concept itself, little needs to be said here, since it is well known that most middle-class Victorians idealized family life, subscribing to Ruskin's celebratory notion of the ideal home as 'the place of peace; the shelter, not only from all injury, but from all terror, doubt, and division',[5] and concurring with the conviction that 'it is for the benefit of a family that a married woman should devote her time and affection almost exclusively to the ways of her household'.[6] Two other facts are equally familiar: that the conventionally-minded viewed the ideal home not only as a refuge from every kind of abrasive, confusing and corrupting influence, but also as a model for the whole social order; that 'ladies', though deprived of personal freedoms and legal rights, and exhorted to confine themselves to the domestic sphere, were idolized as the supreme moral guardians whose vocation it was to minister to the physical and spiritual needs of 'gentlemen' plunged daily into the brutalizing worlds of city and commerce.

The majority of Victorian writers, Dickens and Tennyson among them, seldom challenged the middle-class ideology of separate spheres and the domestic virtues upon which its cogency depended. It was partly through their presentation of the garden and their promulgation of garden codes that literary works affirmed the sovereignty of family life.

The identification of home and garden is established in various ways. They are synonymous concepts in the metaphorical Ruskinian sense of 'garden', in that the home is imaged as a walled garden ruled over by a domestic Queen. This metaphor had wide currency both in and out of fiction. The qualities of the ideal garden—beauty, oasis-like fertility, and enclosure—are those of the ideal home:

> And is it not a high vocation to make homes, like gardens, bloom in the wilderness of life; to be the centre around which hearts gather, and the fondest affections cling; to strengthen, brighten and beautify existence; to be the light of others' souls, and the good angels of others' paths. . . .

> And what to be mother? To give birth to young immortals! To guide and train the opening minds of those who shall influence the coming generation.[7]

Fictional gardens are frequently commended for their 'homely' appearance. (One reason that novelists lauded the old-fashioned cottage garden is that the constancy they impute to its plant life is suggestive of domestic stability; that is, its trusty perennials look like permanent residents and not, as is the case with bedding plants, mere tenants). Some gardens are described as 'bowers'; some (Helstone vicarage garden, for instance) as 'nests'.

As well as being apt, 'feminine' metaphors like 'nest' or 'bower', which characterize the ideal home as 'an all-encompassing desexualized womb into which [the man of the house] could retreat',[8] also have an unmistakably pastoral ring.[9] However, it was the walled garden, not the bucolic landscape, that the Victorian middle-classes took as their image of the ideal home. There were several important reasons for this.

Firstly, the enclosed garden is imagistically more appropriate than the open field to the conception of home as a sheltered enclosure, and to the family as 'a self-contained, autotelic unit, shut away from public view'.[10] Secondly, 'pastoral conventions were difficult to use in a fresh way in the nineteenth century, and bore the stigma of artificiality. They were no longer as immediate and appealing as they once had been.'[11] Hence, the major Victorian authors tend either to parody the pastoral vision, to expose it, as does Dickens in *Martin Chuzzlewit*, as 'an illusion, an absurd identification of the self with nature',[12] or to adopt the myth of the recent pastoral past 'in full awareness of its implications',[13] as does George Eliot in *Adam Bede*. Alternatively, they replace the pastoral convention with the less problematic image of the garden—less problematic because the garden can signify the positive qualities of the countryside without necessarily violating the mimetic conventions of realist fiction. Thirdly, and most obviously, the garden is an integral part of the physical structure of the ideal home and not simply an image of it.

The assumption that homes and gardens are related metonymically as well as metaphorically is almost ubiquitous in Victorian fiction. What it means in practice is that aesthetic and horticultural codes are often inseparable from domestic ones, that fictional gardens are evaluatively pre-stressed in terms of domestic as well as garden-specific frames of reference. Thus, for example, a positively evaluated garden not only conforms to commonly held notions of beauty and taste, but also implies a commitment to the values and virtues of home, and assists (rather than resists) the making and maintaining of happy family life. Moreover, fictional gardens frequently function as the barometers of family life: positively presented gardens are usually indicative of happy or efficient homes, negatively presented gardens of unhappy ones. A contributor to *The Cornhill* made this code explicit when he wrote that "though we may not always be right in the supposition that where there is a well-cultivated garden there is a well-ordered home, I doubt whether we should be often wrong in this surmise.'[14]

Dickens's works adhere almost unflinchingly to this code.[15] Since virtually all of his gardens reflect the assumption that only family-centred households have gardens worthy of the name, Dickens must be held responsible for helping to promote an unfalsifiable correspondence theory of homes and gardens.

In the model Dickensian home, home and garden are part of the same morphological entity. The Meagles's home in *Little Dorrit*, for example, is a homologue of the internal role structure of the family itself. The Meagles's cottage at Twickenham

> stood in a garden, no doubt as fresh and beautiful in the May of the Year, as Pet now was in the May of her life; and it was defended by a goodly show of handsome trees and spreading evergreens, as Pet was by Mr. and Mrs. Meagles. It was made out of an old brick house, of which a part had been altogether pulled down, and another part had been changed into the present cottage; so there was a hale elderly portion, to represent Mr. and Mrs. Meagles, and a young picturesque, very pretty portion to represent Pet. There was even the later addition of a conservatory sheltering itself against it, uncertain of hue in its deep-stained glass, and in its more transparent flashing to the sun's rays, now like fire and now like harmless water drops; which might have stood for Tattycoram. (p. 186)

Of the many homes in Dickens's novels which fall short of the ideal, some have gardens which reproduce the internal structure of the household, while others have gardens which reflect in a more general sense the perversion or absence of family relations. An example of the former is the secluded schoolroom garden of Dr Strong in *David Copperfield*. It comprises two contrasting features. First, 'two great aloes, in tubs, on the turf outside the windows', which symbolise the 'stiff' and rather sterile old schoolmaster. Second, peaches 'ripening on the sunny south wall' (p. 216)—representing, no doubt, the youthful Mrs Strong. The absence of plants symbolical of little Strongs hints at the incompleteness of the household. The 'gardens' of Dombey in *Dombey and Son* (1848) and of Gradgrind in *Hard Times*, the former 'a gravelled yard, where two gaunt trees, with blackened trunks and branches, rattled rather than rustled, their leaves were so smoke-dried' (p. 21), the latter 'a lawn and garden and an infant avenue, all ruled straight like a botanical account book' (p. 10), reflect in their different ways the domestic ethos of crushingly patriarchal households.

Some of Dickens's glowing families, too poor to possess a house with a garden, compensate by bringing the garden indoors. By means of a wall painting, the Plornishes in *Little Dorrit* convert their shop-parlour in Bleeding Heart Yard into a 'counterfeit cottage' and 'blooming garden' (p. 574). The Traddles in *David Copperfield* can do without even this little fiction for (Dickens implies) they enhance the interior with natural mirth. Dickens 'depicts Traddles' chambers in the law-engendered desert of Gray's Inn as an enchanted garden of richness, beauty, and warmth, a garden that blooms brightly and unexpectedly in a barren wilderness.'[16]

The point seems to be that good homes can thrive without actual gardens, but they cannot exist without the anti-materialistic values that impart to them a garden-like atmosphere. This metaphoric interchange of home and garden is supported by the assumption that blooming gardens are expressive of the traditional middle-class values that Dickens so much admired: among them, cheerful generosity, emotional spontaneity and imaginative freedom. When these values are adulterated and the assumption invalidated, the garden is just one more status symbol of the materialistic capitalist class.

It might indeed be argued, persuasively I believe, that if Dickens succeeds in his advocacy of the glowing home, then he does so more by counter example than by direct appeal, since the cutting edge of the former is blunted in the latter by a sentimentality that the emphasis on garden-like qualities serves only to compound.[17]

What is rather surprising about Dickens's use of the garden to highlight the domestic ideal, is that it is not much developed beyond the symbolic function. There are garden scenes in Dickens's novels, but comparatively few involve the exhibition of happy family groups. In the novels of many of Dickens's contemporaries, by contrast, garden scenes are commonplace. A typical group garden picture—one of a number recalled by the first-person narrator of *John Halifax, Gentleman*—features the hero's family in the garden of their smart country house:

> I could see him now, standing among the flower-beds, out in the sunny morning, the father's tall head in the centre of the group—for he was always the important person during the brief hour or two that he was able to be at home. The mother close beside him, and both knotted round with an interlaced mass of little arms and little eager faces, each waiting to hear everything and to look at everything—everybody to be first and nobody last. (p. 219)

Not all garden scenes are this mawkish, nor such obvious bourgeois propaganda for the nuclear family. But even when they do not overtly idealize domestic life, the ideal of the home tends to impinge in some form or other. When, for example, Margaret Hale returns to Helstone vicarage after an absence of several years, she finds its garden much altered, and bristling with the signs of active family life:

> The garden, the grass-plot, formerly so daintily trim that even a stray rose-leaf seemed like a fleck on its exquisite arrangement and propriety, was strewed with children's things: a bag of marbles here, a hoop there; a straw hat forced down upon a rose-tree as on a peg, to the destruction of a long, beautiful, tender branch laden with flowers, which in former days would have been trained up tenderly, as if beloved. (p. 469)

The garden is now truly lived in, and all the better for it.

Family group portraiture is often only one of a cluster of almost inseparable interests made manifest in garden scenes. View-painting, conversation-pieces, country-house portraits, and the novelistic equivalent of genre painting—some or all of these interests provide the motivation for, say, some of the garden scenes in *Lothair*, and the Cheverel Manor garden portrait that opens Eliot's 'Mr Gilfil's Love-Story'. In poetry, too, descriptions of family gatherings often have garden settings, notably in the poems of Tennyson, and particularly in *The Princess* and *In Memoriam*.

Gardens that resist the picturing of a family group within them—uncared-for gardens on the one hand, show-place gardens on the other—signify a want of homeliness. The Martindale gardens in *Heartsease*, a remarkably grand 'self-sacrifice to parade', reflect their owners, the highly respectable but emotionally inhibited Lord and Lady Martindale. Though the Martindales inspect their gardens, they never gather there as a convivial and cohesive group; or not, at least, until the close of the story, by which time the heads of the household have learned how to bestow upon their grandchildren the affection they have always withheld from their own children. One result of this belated discovery of familial feeling is the domestication (in this case, the simplification) of the gardens, which are stripped of much of their 'finery'. Now, realizing that her 'botanical pursuits' have diverted her from the joys of grandparenthood, Lady Martindale transfers her devotions to her grandchildren, and shows herself 'much too busy with the four black-eyed living blossoms to set her heart on any griffin-headed or monkey-faced orchids' (p. 466).

In part, of course, the original Martindale gardens are simply too bright and ornamental to provide a suitable backdrop to a family picture. More frequently, the garden uncongenial to domestic amusements and family gatherings is ugly and neglected. The gardens of Clavering Park in Trollope's *The Claverings* militate against use, and express the absence of the virtues of hearth and home in at least two ways. Firstly, because they 'were away from the house, and the cold desolate flat park came up close around the window' (p. 370). ('Cold' suggests the selfish Sir Hugh Clavering; 'desolate' the condition of his abused and lonely wife.) Secondly, they 'had but little of beauty to recommend them' (p. 1). It is in these gardens that the highly memorable first scene of the novel is set:

> It was now the end of August, and the parterres, beds, and bits of lawn were dry, disfigured, and almost ugly, from the efforts of a long drought. In gardens to which care and labour are given abundantly, flower-beds will be pretty, and grass will be green, let the weather be what it may; but care and labour were but scantily bestowed on the Clavering Gardens, and everything was yellow, adust, harsh, and dry. (p. 1)

Trollope leaves his readers to draw their own conclusions about the quality of family life at Clavering Park, though there seems precious little room for interpretive play; as one critic has observed, 'this paragraph should be equally understandable by someone unacquainted with English gardens, or a dry English August'.[18]

The final sentence of the paragraph quoted above brings in the actors: 'Over the burnt turf, towards a gate that led to the houses, a lady was walking, and by her side there walked a gentleman' (p. 1). The lady is not Lady Clavering but Julia Ongar; the gentleman is not Sir Hugh, but the poor relation, Harry Clavering. By placing comparative outsiders in a desiccated domestic garden, Trollope cleverly evokes the two conventions from which he departs: that only well-kept gardens provide backdrops for painterly family scenes; and that the central members of the family take pride of place within them.

In Victorian imaginative literature, the association of home and garden is cemented and naturalized in at least two other ways. First, and almost paradoxically, the event of leaving home is typically defined as an experience of enormous sadness, dislocation and loss. More often than not, it is the thought of leaving the garden, rather than of leaving the house, that most distresses the characters involved. Various reasons are given or implied for this. In contrast to the inanimate objects of the house, flowers are often seen as living familiars. Marianne Dashwood's apostrophe to her 'well known trees'[19] and Anne Elliott's lament on leaving the gardens of Kellynch Hall[20] set the pattern for later garden-centred farewells to a family home. Moreover, it is almost a convention in Victorian literature that garden-related experiences are happy ones. The assumption is implicit in the many verses written on the occasion of a garden leavetaking. The Dorset poet and parson, William Barnes, who declared that 'gardening is one of the sweetest amusements that an unambitious man, who lives far from the din of cities, can find', composed a farewell sonnet to his Chantry garden at Mere:

> No more, at breezy eve, or dewy morn,
> My gliding scythe shall shear the mossy green:
> No busy hands shall never more adorn.
> My eyes no more may see, this peaceful scene.
> But still, sweet spot, wherever I may be,
> My love-led soul will wander back to thee.[21]

What seems to make the garden a peculiarly poignant store of happy memories is its perceived perishability. Houses are relatively enduring structures; but gardens are precarious—and prickingly so to those about to leave a garden still in bloom. It is this perception that informs most farewell scenes, such as this one in *Doctor Cupid*:

> There is still lingering mignonette; plenty of Japanese anemones, their pure white faces pearled with the happy autumn dew; single dahlias, also, variously bright. It would have been easier to walk among them with that farewell feeling had the mignonette been sodden and dead, and the dahlias been frost-shrivelled up into black sticks. But no! they still light their gay cheeks to kiss the crisp air. (p. 178)

By the time that Margaret Hale is ready to depart her quiet New Forest parsonage, its garden, so bright but a few days before, is already dreary, as though resigned like the family to irrevocable change.

The Hales leave Helstone because Mr Hale's doctrinal doubts compel him to relinquish his living as a Church of England minister. Other farewells to gardens are similarly linked to personal traumas and domestic calamities. In Wilkie Collins's *No Name* (1862), Margaret Vanstone's goodbye to the garden of Coombe-Raven follows the sudden death of her father, and her shocked discovery that she and her sister are illegitimate and so without legal claim to the family property. Another of Collins's characters, Walter Hartwright in *The Woman in White*, also makes a shattering discovery that necessitates a wrench from the place that has become for him a second home. Having learned of Laura Fairlie's engagement to Sir Percival Glyde, Hartwright feels bound to take his leave of Limmeridge House and, in particular, of Laura's rose-garden to which he 'instinctively' turned to take, he says, 'my farewell of the scene which was associated with the brief dream-time of my happiness and my love' (p. 86).

The prodigious number of such valedictory garden experiences in Victorian literature hints strongly at the anxieties and insecurities that must have smouldered beneath the comfortable surface of middle-class domestic life. Bar bereavement, the prospect of being uprooted from a happy home was probably the greatest personal disaster of which the comfortably placed Victorian could conceive. Tennyson experienced this kind of dislocation; so also, still more acutely, did Dickens and Trollope. The Chatham home from which Dickens was torn (or so he came to feel) at the age of nine, is rendered pastoral and mythically recast as the Oedipal garden of David Copperfield's pre-Murdstone boyhood home at rural Blunderstone. Trollope's Chatham was Julians Hill at Harrow, 'the first house in which, as an adolescent, he had ceased to feel an outcast',[22] though he spent little more than a year there before the Trollope family fled to Belgium in 1834. Some thirty years later, Julians Hill was fictionally recreated as Orley Farm in the novel of the same name. Trollope's approbatory account of its straggling gardens—visualized in John Millais's drawing of Julians Hill that served as frontispiece to the novel—to say nothing of the lengths to which the protagonists are prepared to go to secure it for themselves, suggests the value that Trollope attached to the place in which he had felt secure and at home.

As a metonym of everything involved in the experience of departing a much loved place, the farewell to the garden scene naturalizes the association of home and garden, and emphasizes the importance of having roots in a stable, domestic environment. So also, but in a much more positive way, does the making or re-making of a garden. In Victorian fiction, the act of creating a garden is normally a gesture of commitment to a person, place and domestic futurity, particularly when it is undertaken with or for a loved partner. It is no coincidence that many Victorian novels end not only with a marriage (or the prospect of one) but also with the making of a domestic garden.

Silas Marner ends with both, and they dovetail perfectly, since Eppie's desire for a garden to complete her home is aroused by her desire for Aaron, the young man with whom she wishes to share it. Silas is willing to undertake, but physically incapable of, the spadework necessary to turn the stone-pits plot into a flower-garden, just as he is incapable of meeting the sexual and emotional needs of his teenage 'daughter'. His acceptance of the need to delegate this task symbolizes his recognition of the need to make way for the younger man who alone can ensure the happiness of Eppie's future.

Aaron is a gardener by occupation, and he promises to bring Eppie the slips of lavender of which she is so fond. That Eppie should have specified lavender is significant, for 'it was traditional for the countryman to plant a lavender-bed or -hedge for his bride. The lavender, being needed to scent the bed-linen, was thus a proper loving attention expected by custom.'[23] Since the lavender is to be brought from the Red House, its re-rooting in Marner's cottage garden betokens the eventual reconciliation of Godfrey Cass and his natural daughter. The wedding with which the novel ends takes place at the time of the year 'when the great lilacs and laburnums in the old-fashioned gardens showed their golden and purple wealth above the lichen-tinted walls' (p. 156)—a background symbolic both of stable community and fertile futurity. The final paragraph of the novel returns the reader to Eppie's garden, now a realized project, and the nucleus upon which the central figures in her small domestic community converge:

> Eppie had a larger garden than she had ever expected there now; and in other ways there had been alterations at the expense of Mr. Cass, the landlord, to suit Silas's larger family. For he and Eppie had declared that they would rather stay at the Stone-pits than go to any new home. The garden was fenced with stones on two sides, but in front there was an open fence, through which the flowers shone with answering gladness, as the four united people came within sight of them.
> 'O father', said Eppie, 'what a pretty home ours is! I think nobody could be happier than we are'. (p. 158)

The conclusion to *Silas Marner* would not have disappointed the expectations of Victorian readers accustomed to and conversant with the plot conventions of the unexceptional contemporary novel of social manners or domestic life. And yet, of course, Eliot's novel (or romance? or parabolic pastoral? or sociological fairy-tale?) is anything but unexceptional. That it closes with a marriage and the making of a garden has little to do with the author's deferential subscription to the home and hearth values of the urban bourgeoisie. Rather, the culminating discourse on gardens and flowers, within the context of an imminent marriage, is consistent with a fictional project that is more Bunyaneseque than Dickensian, and more folk-cultural than Bunyanesque. If Eppie's garden-making has a cognate cultural script, then it is a compound of the traditional harvest festival and pagan fertility rites enriched and Christianized by the religious symbolism of fruit and flowers.

There is another nineteenth-century novel, still more difficult to accommodate within the institution of bourgeois realist fiction, that also closes with the marriage of a young couple, and an account of their garden-making activities. The novel is *Wuthering Heights*, and even its general trajectory—from situations of interpersonal conflict and social dislocation to integration and the restitution of domestic harmony—bears a more than passing resemblance to that of *Silas Marner*.

Wuthering Heights concludes with Nelly Dean's account of the death of Heathcliff, and of the felicitous alliance of Hareton Earnshaw and the second Cathy. For some modern readers, the final note of peaceful domesticity is disappointingly tame, and even a capitulation to conventional morality.[24] But there is nothing tame about the determination of the second-generation children to transform the Heights into a flowery domicile. It is significant that they construct their flower garden while Heathcliff is still alive and, if only spasmodically violent, by no means a spent force. Nelly realizes just how daring they are, and later admits to having been 'terrified at the devastation which had been accomplished in a brief half hour' (p. 347). What is more, to clear the way for their stocks and wall-flowers, the young people uproot the currant and gooseberry bushes which are 'the apple of Joseph's eye'. Joseph is furious, and even Heathcliff is 'much surprised' by his daughter-in-law's temerity. When Heathcliff confronts her with it Cathy, far from quailing, braves an assertion of proprietary rights.

Brontë's Eve can confidently parry the curses of her dispossessing god because she has a clear and certain conception of the Eden she intends for herself and her Adam. This Eden is not a place to be entered but a space to be made. The garden she beguiles her Adam to make, though it represents faith in and commitment to the future, does not entail the suppression of the past, for it is clearly an echo of Cathy's edenic if cloistral childhood home. And though its flowers are 'emblems not so much of domestication as of the fertility of the future',[25] it nonetheless implies the desire for a more tender form of domesticity than Joseph's austere, crabbed, currant-bush kind. To be fit for this kind of domesticity, Hareton has to be educated and nurtured; the garden is part of Cathy's programme to socialize her husband. Finally, the garden is a declaration of intent: Cathy intends to claw back what is rightfully hers, join it to what is rightfully Hareton's and, in so doing, to heal the breach between the two households. Her garden is built at the Heights, but Thrushcross Grange is represented by the plants that have been imported from it.

It might fairly be said that Victorian fiction in general develops from, or stays within, the parameters of the situation with which *Wuthering Heights* closes. Indeed, the whole of this remarkable novel can be taken as a recapitulation of the processes by which the Romantic exaltation of topographical and experiential extremes becomes transformed in Victorian fiction into a metaphysics of 'lowland' realism, where nature is recuperated for human consumption, and where heroism dwells chiefly in community and home. The anticipatory mirroring of this transformation is an 'unconscious' effect of the novel's design.

Even a cursory analysis of *Wuthering Heights* would reveal that the oscillations between 'competing' landscapes and the modes of existence they symbolize become progressively less extreme as the novel unfolds. The violent antitheses which prevail in the environment of the first generation children—exposure v. enclosure, 'external rocks' v. seasonal foliage, abandonment to passion v. emotional constraint—are replaced in the environment of the second generation children by more moderate alternatives: Linton's ideal of the languid heath set against Cathy's ideal of the animated wood (see Ch. 24). Finally, even these mild alternatives converge upon the non-dialectic, unitary symbol of the garden. A concomitant trend involves the mollification of the domestic sphere itself: from the blazing inhospitality of the Heights in the early chapters to the softened, 'civilized' domesticity of the Heights at the end. Even the Victorian interrogation and transmutation of the picturesque is rehearsed in the harrowing experiences of Lockwood, the conventional city gentleman who is forced to confront the perceptual implications of his romantic expectations of nature, and whose touristic detachment seems finally to separate him from the only sources of real fulfilment and growth: home, place, and family life.

It has been said of *Wuthering Heights* that it 'speaks what realism knows but has been trained not to tell.'[26] This may be a valid point to make about large, seemingly characteristic stretches of the novel; but at its close, the novel seems to speak what Victorian realism knew and never tired of telling: that the domestic ideal is second to none. In calling its subjects into the garden, the dominant voice of Victorian realism inevitably beckons them away from competing arenas of action and commitment—arenas to which the experiences of fictional characters might theoretically have inclined them.

In making this important if obvious point, one might mention also the (revised) ending of *Great Expectations*, where Dickens contrives to have his world-weary protagonists, Pip and Estella, meet at the site of the ruins of Satis House. Significantly, though the buildings have disappeared, the wall of the old garden remains. Indeed, the scene flickers with the hope of future fecundity: 'The cleared space had been enclosed with a rough fence, and looking over it, I saw that some of the old ivy had struck root anew, and was growing green on low quiet mounds of ruin' (p. 458).[27] Though one can regard this ending as 'completely integrated into the fable-like quality of the tale', it is also true that Dickens's success in 'reducing his complex material to its simplest terms, to Pip's sustained quest for personal fulfilment', costs in terms of the options it closes. 'For the story eventually by-passes the world of public events and social themes, although these considerations have occupied large areas in the narrative. To our surprise the end of the third stage leads through the Forsaken Garden towards a far from Earthly Paradise.' It is crucially important here that 'Pip's exploration into things past which once seemed to threaten and expose the very foundations of law and order have not shaped him into a revolutionary, but given him these modified, subdued, yet acceptable grounds for hope in a future of domestic happiness'.[28]

Like many other Victorian novels, *Great Expectations* ends with the intimation of an unwritten sequel: unwritten because unnecessary, and unnecessary because 'known' in advance. Even the 'Reader, I married him' postscript is superfluous except where local conditions leave particular questions unresolved. (In *Jane Eyre*: Will Mr Rochester recover his sight? Will he and Jane have children?) The ending of *Great Expectations* is usually regarded as indeterminate, since we cannot be certain that Pip and Estella will eventually marry; but it may not have appeared so open-ended to the Victorian reader familiar with the conventional garden script finale to which Dickens's novel refers even as it departs from the convention.

As the primary site of happy domestic histories which unwritten sequels can afford to leave unchronicled, the garden is implicated in the classic empiricist project of wisdom through experience and the unscrambling of scrambled values through the transfiguring power of human (in the Victorian context, heterosexual) love. The wisdom the protagonists discover is that happiness and fulfilment lie in love within the context of marriage and family life. The reader has been privy to this knowledge throughout, since it is inscribed within the authorial discourse of the text and, what is more, assumed to be part of the fund of 'common-sense' knowledge.

To conclude this chapter, I wish to say something about the association of home and garden within a specifically aristocratic milieu. Though it occupies a space on the exotic and fabulous fringes of Victorian fiction, no novel illustrates this association better than Disraeli's *Lothair.*

The novel begins with an indoor scene—a 'happy picture' of Lady Corisande's family in the morning room at Brentham—and then immediately moves outdoors to the spectacular garden. The other major aristocratic family in *Lothair*, the St Jeromes, have an equally impressive garden at Vauxe, but it too is a family garden; a number of scenes in the novel show the St Jeromes actively engaged in the arrangement and care of it. To both Lothair and Disraeli's narrator, Brentham and Vauxe seem ideal because 'they combine the nuclear family with social intercourse in an elegant setting'.[29] Lothair's own garden at Muriel Towers is the most magnificent of them all, but it does not become an expression of domestic bliss until Lothair marries—an event deferred to the space beyond the text.

The stupendously wealthy young hero has three ambitions: to 'extinguish pauperism'; to lead a life that is 'entirely religious'; and to marry. The first goal is only touched upon. The second and third ambitions are paramount and interrelated.

Lothair's desire for domesticity ripens at the surprisingly early age of twenty. On the basis of one grand party, almost his only experience of Society Life, he declares himself to be disenchanted with the affectation of high society, and fully aware of the importance of having 'a happy home to fall back upon' (p. 16). (Lothair himself is an orphan.) As he wanders with the Duchess in the gardens of Brentham, he reveals that his 'ideal of a perfect society is being married, as I propose, and paying visits to Brentham' (p. 16). He wishes to propose to Corisande, but her mother persuades him to wait until he has more experience of the world.

These events take place in the first chapter. The major part of the rest of the novel is taken up with Lothair's involvement with the two other women who struggle for his allegiance. He falls initially under the spell of the 'divine Theodora', a passionate sympathizer with Garibaldi. Under her influence, Lothair leaves England to fight on the anti-papal side in the Italian revolution. When he is wounded, he becomes the victim of an elaborate and incredible plot to convince him that he has been fighting on the papal side, that the Virgin herself has intervened on his behalf, and that he is destined for the Roman Catholic Church. Clare Arundel, a staunch catholic and the other woman with whom Lothair becomes involved, is implicated in this scheme. When

Lothair finally extricates himself from it, he returns by way of Syria to England to pursue his conjugal ambitions. His proposal to Corisande, two years after the aborted attempt, occurs in the gardens of Brentham, against a background of talk on garden theory. The proposal itself takes the form of an invitation to join him in a collaborative horticultural venture: 'I wanted to speak to you about the garden at Muriel. I wanted to induce you to go there and help me to make it' (p. 466).

It is significant that the proposal scene takes place not in the modern pleasure-grounds, but in the 'remains of an ancient garden', preserved at the insistence of Corisande's grandfather, and now in the charge of Corisande herself. The physical context makes it clear that Lothair's commitment to domestic life is also a commitment to the traditions and values represented by Corisande and her garden. (Though she has 'the least striking personality of the three women . . . She is in the disciplined English tradition, Anglican and moderate—three very good things to be, according to [Disraeli's] mature opinion, in a dangerous world'.[30]) Old, thoroughly English, and unpretentiously aristocratic, Corisande's garden is perfectly emblematic of the kind of domestic future Disraeli decrees for his youthful hero.

Though much has been written about the presentation of women in Victorian literature, surprisingly little attention has been given specifically to the part played by the association of women and gardens in the construction of female stereotypes, and in the legitimizing of women's domestic and decorative functions. This is surprising, because imaginative writers place as much emphasis upon the Queen of the Garden role as upon the cognate role of Angel in the House. Indeed, because of the peculiarly appropriate associations of the garden—with love, beauty, nature, and leisure—no other part of the domestic sphere is more obviously consonant with the ideological project that seeks to beautify, sanctify and naturalize the confinement of women to it.

There is evidence to indicate that genteel Victorian girls received conflicting messages about the roles they were expected to play in life.[31] On the one hand, they were told that nature intended them to be gentle, submissive, dependent and decorative. On the other, they were expected to prepare for the business of procuring and subsequently of retaining a husband—a task which required them to execute their domestic duties with sufficient proficiency to please their husbands and thus to justify their parasitic dependence upon them. Translated into garden terms: young ladies were expected to embody the natural qualities of the gardens for which at the same time they were to be managerially responsible. In fiction, the conflict between the two roles is occasionally dramatized and exposed, apparently without the conscious intent of the author; more frequently it is dissolved by the supposition that women who turn to gardens are simply doing what comes naturally.

Victorian garden writers (of both sexes) never tire of asserting that women have an 'instinctive' love of gardens and a 'native' affinity with the plants they nurture. Novelists and poets more often endorse than question these attributions, and in general support the corollary belief that when women garden they do so as a willing expression both of their natural proclivities and domestic responsibilities. Exceptions turn out to be more apparent than real. For example, when in *North and South* Mr Lennox asks Margaret Hale whether she intends to engage in 'the proper employment for young ladies in the country' (p. 10) she replies, somewhat equivocally, that gardening is hard work. But at this stage in her life, Margaret has no domestic commitments to speak of, and indeed the rest of the novel shows that she is as fond of gardens and as certain of the eloquence of flowers as the next girl.

In fictional gardens, women engage in three main kinds of activity. Each is congruent with and serves to accentuate particular aspects of her femininity. Collectively, they have the effect of naturalizing the garden as the woman's domain.

Firstly, they are shown performing light gardening tasks such as cutting flowers, tying back roses, and nursing tender exotics—tasks appropriate to their assumed physical feebleness. They are rarely permitted to perform the physically demanding tasks of cutting flower beds or mowing lawns (which makes Margaret Hale's reference to 'hard work' rather puzzling). The few who are—Miss Wendover in M. E. Braddon's *The Golden Calf* (1883), for example—are middle-aged spinsters or honorary males (i.e. women who behave like men). Women leave the spade work to gardeners, or they charm their favourite men into doing it for them. Brontë's Catherine Heathcliff 'persuaded' and 'beguiled' Hareton to dig her flower garden, and when Eppie coaxes Aaron into digging hers, she declares with 'roguish triumph' that she knew he would. If Victorian women resented the restrictions imposed upon their physical gardening activities—and there is evidence that some did[32]—then their cries of protest are effectively smothered in fiction.

The second role that women play in the garden is a supervisory one. It illustrates their usefulness at a higher level, and exercises their intellect for what Ruskin famously defined as 'sweet ordering, arrangement, and decision' (*RW*, XVIII, 122). While her husband is doing the 'real' work, the selflessly devoted wife, Ursula Halifax in *John Halifax*, for instance, spends 'morning after morning superintending her domain' (p. 175).

It is noteworthy that women in Victorian fiction often prove more competent than their men-folk at handling stubborn and truculent gardeners. This competence is usually made to seem a matter of native wisdom. Molly Gibson proves adept at supervising the work of her muddle-headed old gardener, though she has had a sheltered upbringing and only a fraction of the education she would have received had she been a boy. The same can be said of Sylvia Blythe, the heroine of William Black's novel *Green Pastures and Piccadilly* (1878). The first two chapters portray her as a 'natural' product of her physical environment—the landscape park of her aristocratic father's estate. She is pictured by the lake, in the farthest reaches of the park, and on the high terrace. The narrator asks: 'What could be a fitter surrounding for this young English girl than this English-looking landscape? They were both of them in the freshness and beauty of their springtime, that comes but once in a year and once in a life' (p. 11). But before the story is much advanced, Sylvia is on the verge of marriage to an ambitious, London-based politician, Hugh Balfour. As if to provide some evidence that this vastly inexperienced girl has magically acquired the wherewithal to cope with complex domestic responsibilities, the narrator manoeuvres her into a situation where she has to confront the head gardener, 'a soured and disappointed man', 'curt of speech' and resentful of interference.

> On this occasion, moreover, he was in an ill-humour. But to his intense surprise his young mistress was not to be beaten off by short answers. Was her ladyship in an ill-humour too? Anyhow, she very quickly brought him to his senses; and one good issue of that day's worry was that old Blake was a great deal more civil to Lady Sylvia ever after. (pp. 65–6)

It is pertinent to mention here an issue much discussed by

Victorian garden writers and by no means neglected by authors of literary works: the question of whether the owner or the head gardener should have overall control of the garden. As a rule, both kinds of writers expressed or implied a preference for owners' gardens over gardeners' gardens. Most of the reasons for this need not concern us here. For novelists in particular, however, a major influencing factor was the need to find for their favoured female characters appropriate ways of expressing their domestic inclinations and competences. In practice this meant demoting professional gardeners so that the Queen of the Garden might be seen to act as sovereign in her own domain. One such queen is Lady Scamperley in J. G. Whyte-Melville's *Kate Coventry*. Her garden is described as

> a little *bijou* of a place, that bore ample witness to the good taste of its mistress. Every shrub had been transplanted under her own eyes, every border filled according to her own personal directions. She tied her own carnations, and budded her own roses, like the most exemplary clergyman's wife in England. (pp. 256–7)

Some domestic queens are responsible for transformations of a more remarkable kind. When Ferdinand Armine in *Henrietta Temple* first sets eyes on Ducie Bowers he declares it to be 'the most exquisite spot [he] ever beheld'. Mr Temple informs him that two years before the garden had been 'a perfect wilderness . . . one vast, desolate, and neglected lawn, used as a sheep-walk'. His daughter, the garden-loving Henrietta, had 'made everything' (p. 94). Similarly, when Nancy Cass in *Silas Marner* replaces the old Squire as the 'presiding spirit' of the Red House, she brings 'purity and order' in the form of flower-filled vases to its once dreary rooms. The results of Nancy's feminizing mission are evident also in the previously neglected garden. Fifteen years after her marriage to Godfrey, the garden boasts 'neatly-swept garden-walks, between . . . bright turf that contrasted pleasantly with the dark cones and arches and wall-like hedges of yew (p. 129).

For female characters with ambitions beyond as well as within their own domestic spheres, schemes for the improvement of other people's gardens offer one of the few socially acceptable opportunities for useful work. Hence, in *Middlemarch*, Dorothea Brooke's mortification at finding that the cottages on Casaubon's estate are in such good order—each has its strip of well-tended garden—that there is 'nothing for her to do in Lowick' (p. 54). M. O. Oliphant's Lucilla Marjoribanks in *Miss Marjoribanks*, a diluted Dorothea with Emma Woodhouse's penchant for matchmaking, has a keen eye for the philanthropic possibilities of which Dorothea is deprived. She is responsible for the creation of the garden of Miss Mortimer's 'little closed-up hermitage' (p. 208), an act not unconnected with her desire to engineer a marriage between Miss Mortimer and another minor character, the Archdeacon Mr Beverley.

The third major role that women play in the garden, that of the ornamental icon or spectacle, does most to naturalize their position within it. Victorian imaginative literature is punctuated by a quite remarkable number of descriptive passages in which the cynosure is a young woman in a private garden. These passages are distinguished less by their peculiar characteristics than by their high degree of conventionality and cross-echoing. The majority are doubly framed: firstly, by being bracketed off from the narrative flow, or by occupying a discrete area of textual space; secondly, by being highly pictorial. Intrusions in the form of other people or superfluous (non-garden) objects are blotted out. The woman at the centre of the picture, invariably a virgin heroine, a princess rather than a matronly queen, is silent, static, submissive, decorous and, above all, painterly. She tends to be striking an attitude that mimics the lines and sinuosities of the natural vegetation; the result of this is a kind of natural *pose plastique*. Either she stands out against a backdrop of trees and flowers, or she is so enveloped by them as to appear a natural component of the garden itself. In the latter case, the woman is not only removed from her usual context, transplanted from the social networks in which she is constituted as a social being, but seemingly arrested at a pre-Oedipal stage of development. Like the pre-linguistic 'self' of Lacan's *l'hommelette*, she merges with the surrounding natural forms in a closed circuit of visual exchange. As an innocent (because 'natural') *objet d'art*, the woman is an appropriate spectacle for public consumption. But within the text, she is almost always the ocular conquest of a privileged male observer, though every precaution is taken to de-eroticize the voyeuristic experience. The woman, unconscious of being the object of scrutiny, and thus never exhibitionistic, is usually self-absorbed. In contrast to the nudes in countless European paintings, her gaze is not directed towards the (absent) male consumer. The observer himself is placed at a reverential distance from the object of his adoration. The intervention of an aesthetic frame—a discrete passage of description resembling a painting and presented from the viewpoint of an artist—serves also to diminish his physical engagement.

Word pictures of women in gardens are particularly associated with first encounters with a wife or lover-to-be. They attest to what Tennyson's Arthur calls the 'authority of the eye'—according to one critic, the 'fundamental concept in Victorian aesthetics'[33] and to the validity of an authorial aside in *A Pair of Blue Eyes*. Hardy writes:

> Every woman who makes a permanent impression on a man is usually recalled to his mind's eye as she appeared in one particular scene, which seems ordained to be her special form of manifestation throughout the pages of his memory. (p. 18)

One such scene occurs in *The Woman in White*, when Walter Hartwright first sets eyes on Laura Fairlie. Laura is standing in a motionless 'attitude' in the doorway of 'a pretty summer-house' built 'in the form of a miniature Swiss chalet' (p. 34). The door affords a natural frame for the water-colour drawing that Walter subsequently produces; the 'dark greenish-brown background' of the summer-house serves as a tolerable substitute for the greenery of the garden, as well as an effective tonal contrast with the 'light youthful figure, clothed in a simple muslin dress, the pattern of it formed by broad alternate stripes of delicate blue and white' (p. 34). The detailed description which follows aspires to the apparent transparency of the iconic image upon which it is based. The setting of the ornamental summer-house—the child-woman's equivalent of the doll's house—fixes Laura in the role in which she is to remain. The best known of all asexual child-women in Victorian fiction, Dora Spenlow in *David Copperfield*, is pictured by David in a similar fairyland setting: among the geraniums clustered about the greenhouse in Mr Spenlow's Norwood garden.

Some virginal heroines emerge as apparitions in charmed garden settings which make them seem like native garden spirits. Lily Mordaunt in *Kenelm Chillingly* materializes before the titular hero as he reclines in a trellis-bound recess. As he looks up he sees 'the face of a girl in her first youth, framed round with the blossoms that festooned the trellis. How the face became the flowers! It seemed the fairy spirit of them' (p. 277). Lily's connections with gardens and nature are subsequently reinforced.

For example, Kenelm learns of her garden room in which she keeps a multitude of butterflies, some of which had learned to know her, and all of which she had 'tamed'. Much the same can be said of Henrietta Temple, who enters the story when she appears magically before Ferdinand Armine in the gardens of Armine Park. From that moment, she is hardly ever out of gardens, and forever declaring her interest in them.

The fixing of a female subject, from the moment of her entry into the text, as a static, visually delightful element of a garden scene, is a principal effect of the garden picture. In extreme cases, the woman is denied both a social dimension (since she seems to exist exclusively in the realms of nature and art) and independent existence as a social being (in that she is constituted entirely by the picture-making gaze of the male spectator). Tennyson's description of the gardener's daughter is, arguably, one such case, and probably the model for many others.

The Gardener's Daughter is subtitled 'the Picture'. The narrator, an artist, travels with his 'Brother in Art' to look upon the local beauty. The description of her is also a description of the painting that the narrator unveils at the end of the poem. It is, as Tennyson intended, 'full and rich . . . to a fault' (*TP*, p. 508). The girl is pictured first and most memorably in the Eve-like role of pinning back the flowers in the garden of a country house:

> For up the porch there grew an Eastern rose,
> That, flowering high, the last night's gale had caught,
> And blown across the walk. One arm aloft —
> Gown'd in pure white, to fix it back, she stood,
> A single stream of all her soft brown hair
> Pour'd on one side: the shadow of the flowers
> Stole all the golden gloss, and, wavering
> Lovingly lower, trembled on her waist —
> Ah, happy shade—and still went wavering down,
> But, ere it touch'd a foot, that might have danced
> The greensward into greener circles, dipt,
> And mix'd with shadows of the common ground!
> But the full day dwelt on her brows, and sunn'd
> Her violet eyes, and all her Hebe bloom,
> And doubled his own warmth against her lips,
> And on the bounteous wave of such a breast
> As never pencil drew. Half light, half shade,
> She stood, a sight to make an old man young. (*TP*, pp. 514–5)

The garden and the girl are difficult to separate, for the description functions to bring out the identification of the gardener's daughter with the natural world. She is flexuous as a flower, 'fitted to the shape of the plant she tends'; and her hair pours with the liquidity of a 'stream'. And as though 'violet eyes' and 'Hebe bloom' were not enough, Tennyson, with a forgivable heavy-handedness, leaves us in no doubt about the equivalence: 'she, a Rose / In roses, mingled with her fragrant toil' (p. 515). Though she is initially presented with (as Turner notes) a physical suggestiveness unusual in Tennyson, her sympathy with the spirit world of nature in 'that Eden where she dwelt' is elsewhere affirmed (p. 518, lines 195–202).

The chiaroscuro lighting effects of the passage above serve the treble function of interweaving the gardener's daughter with the natural setting, objectifying a felicitous mood, and casting the female figure in a light which is more than simply physical. The Marvellian parenthesis—'Ah, happy shade'—acts in this context to resist the improbable inclination to assign to the 'shadow of the flowers' any of those negative connotations of shadows and reflections so manifest in *Mariana* and *The Lady of Shalott*. More positively, it is one of many cues to the pictorial status of the passage; 'the immobility not only of that final "statue-like" but also of the "pause" with which Rose greets the narrator's extravagent courtesy has the poise and momentarily apprehended structure of a narrative picture'.[34]

Of course, the scene is not completely frozen; moreover, the pictorial treatment is justified by the narrator's occupation, and by his transmutation of Rose into a form that ratifies the past and enshrines her as his 'blessed memory'. But what ought not to be overlooked is that the qualities which render the gardener's daughter a painterly subject are precisely those aspects of her femininity which the garden setting serves to naturalize and enhance: rose-like bloom, fluidity of form, the absence of narcissistic self-possession, and the muteness that betokens modesty and innocence.

Equally salient is the fact that Rose is defined almost exclusively in terms of her relations with her environment and the male narrator. She is the product not so much of a garden estate as of a perfect world conceived as a garden state. Its location, 'Not wholly in the busy world nor quite / Beyond it' (p. 510), has the geographical imprecision of Milton's Hell; both are objective worlds that defy cartographical determination. Since Rose has almost nothing to say, and no dealings with anyone but the narrator, she is virtually a construct of his visual experiences. Save for the fleeting reference to her 'fragrant toil', there is no mention of her role within the social structure of the estate, nor of her position within a larger nexus of social relations. Tennyson's refusal to countenance any intrusion into the happy garden, even of those figures with a right to be there (the gardener, the owner, etc.) suggests the other-worldliness of the garden, its all too uncluttered simplicity. As one critic remarks, 'no parents exist for either the narrator or the girl to worry about a job, or about social class, or about money'.[35]

The Gardener's Daughter has a close parallel in J. G. Whyte-Melville's novel *The White Rose* (1868). In the early chapters, the nineteen-year-old hero, Gerard Ainslie, journeys from the town to the country parsonage of Mr Welby and his daughter, Norah. Like Tennyson's artist-narrator, he passes through transitional landscapes, and finally through a wicket gate, anticipating beyond it 'a smooth-shaven lawn, a spreading cypress, a wealth of roses, and the prettiest parsonage within four counties' (p. 13). The dream image is realized, and the scene which follows it, like the central picture of the gardener's daughter, a *memento mori*. Norah, like Rose, is made to seem an integral part of the garden scene:

> She was sitting in a white dress beneath the drooping lime-tree that gleamed and quivered in the sunbeams, alive with its hum of insects, heavy in its wealth of summer fragrance, and raining its shower of blossoms with every breath that whispered through its leaves. For many a year after, perhaps his whole life long, he never forgot her as she sat before him then; never forgot the gold on her rich chestnut hair, the light in her deep fond eyes, nor the tremble of happiness in her voice. (p. 13)

Another word portrait of a woman in a garden also suggests the influence of *The Gardener's Daughter*—even in its title: 'A Picture'. It is by the hymn writer and poet, Dora Greenwell:

> It was in autumn that I met
>   Her whom I love; the sunflowers bold
> Stood up like guards around her set,
> And all the air with mignonette
>   Was warm within the garden old;

Beside her feet the marigold
Glowed star-like, and the sweet-pea sent
A sigh to follow as she went
Slowly adown the terrace;—there
I saw thee, oh my love! and thou wert fair.

She stood in the full noonday, unafraid,
As one beloved of sunlight, for awhile
She leant upon the timeworn balustrade;
The white clematis wooed her, and the clove
Hung all its burning heart upon her smile;
And on her cheek and in her eyes was love;
And on her lips that, like an opening rose,
Seemed parting some sweet secret to disclose,
The soul of all the summer lingered;—there
I saw thee, oh my love! and thou wert fair.[36]

There is little point in quoting more texts of this kind. Suffice it to say that there are masses of them, that they have a range of visual counterparts in the form of photographs, paintings, and book and magazine illustrations, and that they bring together a variety of Victorian interests, including gardens, scene paintings, narrative pictures, tableaux, static mimes and peep shows to produce one of the most persuasive and seductive of gender stereotypes in Victorian literature.[37] Whatever the motivations behind them (and one must surely have been the sublimation and aesthetic transformation of sexual impulses), their chief potential effect is to make 'feminine' qualities seem natural, essential and desirable. But since women can achieve the status of 'natural' objects only by conforming to the dominant, male-constructed concepts of their place and form, garden pictures carry within them the seeds of their own ideological deconstruction.

Garden scenes in which men are the objects of attention, and women the spectators, are, not surprisingly, extremely rare. The few that do exist are qualitatively different from those which feature women. Consider the following passage from Chapter 36 of Charlotte Brontë's *Villette*. The speaker/observer is Lucy Snowe:

> M. Emanuel had a taste for gardening; he liked to tend and foster plants. I used to think that working amongst shrubs with a spade or watering-pot soothed his nerves; it was a recreation to which he often had recourse; and now he looked to the orange trees, the geraniums, the gorgeous

> cactuses, and revived them all with the refreshment their drought needed. His lips meantime sustained his precious cigar, that (for him) first necessary and prime luxury of life; its blue wreaths curled prettily enough amongst the flowers, and in the evening light. (p. 398)

There are three things to notice here. First, that Paul Emanuel is *working* in the garden; he is neither passive nor ornamentally idle. Second, that his gardening is a form of 'recreation'—a welcome break from (by implication) the pressures of the job to which, as a man, he has necessarily to devote the greater part of his time. And third, that he neither craves nor requires an appreciative audience; he needs only his 'precious cigar' to feel independent and fulfilled. It is with this symbol of masculine luxury that the female onlooker must compete for his attention on manifestly unequal terms.

A few other points should be made about the association of women and gardens in Victorian literature. One is that young, conventionally attractive women tend to retain their ornamental and painterly qualities after they are married. Significantly, however, they are usually pictured *with* their husbands. There would seem to be two explanations for this. First, the husband-and-wife scene offered a novelist the opportunity of beautifying the institution of marriage by presenting the happy couple in poses indicative of conjugal bliss and perfect complementarity. Mrs Craik, being one such novelist, has Phineas Fletcher recall a garden scene enacted by John and Ursula Halifax in which the attitudes of the young couple, 'he kneeling, planting box-edging, she standing by him with her hand on his shoulder' (p. 168), are clearly intended to be metonymical of their domestic roles and metaphorical of their love and unity. Second, to have a husband dwell admiringly on the ornamental qualities of his wife would expose him to the charge of gloating over a prized possession, for the obvious reason that husbands cannot be expected to maintain a reverential distance from the women they have the privilege of observing. Thus, when Charlotte M. Yonge concocts an overtly pictorial garden scene in *Heartsease*, she contrives for Arthur to join his young wife, thereby dissociating him from the picture-making operations of those who witness the scene from a window.

With few exceptions—one of which is Meredith's presentation of the Sir Willoughby Patterne/Clara Middleton relationship in

The Egoist—Victorian novelists appear deliberately to suppress the connection between the decorative qualities of women and the status-symbolic aspirations of men. The idle, beautiful wife is valued for enhancing the beauty of her surroundings, rather than for enhancing the status of her husband. And yet

> The perfect lady of the mid-Victorian years, removed not only from worldly concerns, but also from household ones, was a symbol of her husband's wealth and status. She was part of the leisure class, but in somewhat the same way as an unemployed man was—by compulsion. . . . Conspicuous leisure and conspicuous consumption were a mark of status, their utility for purposes of respectability lying in the element of waste common to both—waste of time and effort, or waste of goods.[38]

The myth that women install themselves in gardens (and thus, by implication, in the domestic sphere) instinctively and of their own volition, does not pass completely unchallenged in Victorian literature. The so-called 'New Women' of late-Victorian fiction assault the myth directly; but it is exposed unconsciously by the considerable number of episodes in which women are compelled to use gardens for clandestine trysts to escape the prying eyes of parents and other authority figures. Secret garden meetings reveal splits and strains within the domestic sphere. They also highlight a contradiction: that gardens afford women in constrained circumstances a significant degree of privacy and freedom only when prised from the houses to which they are joined and to which they owe their existence. Since domestic gardens have no real autonomy, their female sovereigns can be queens in name only.

Tennyson's *Maud* is a case in point. In the early part of the poem, the speaker correctly identifies Maud as an integral part of the physical and social world of the manorial Hall. He sees her 'pass like a light' 'up in the high Hall-garden' (*TP* p. 1048). Maud is not simply Maud, but her brother's 'lady-sister'. Though filtered through a jaundiced perception, the speaker's description of Maud's physical characteristics—her 'passionless', 'icily regular', 'cold and clear-cut face' (p. 1047)—implies an attentiveness to the visible marks of social etching. Maud is the product of her social environment; it shows in her face. The speaker realises also that, as the daughter of a wealthy man, Maud is subject to the usual controls imposed upon unmarried daughters by male guardians concerned with land, money, and class alliances. He knows that he has little chance with Maud because 'there is fatter game on the moor' (p. 1045): in particular, the suitor favoured by Maud's father and brother—the 'new-made lord' whose wealth is derived from the mines in which 'grimy nakedness drags his truck' (p. 1057).

All this changes when the speaker becomes intoxicated with Maud's beauty, and when he succumbs to the fiction that Maud can make the bitter world sweet, for this fiction can be maintained only by a perception devoid of social and historical awareness. He dislocates Maud from her defining social context by convincing himself that she is the product of a genetic miracle working in his favour: she is 'only the child of her mother'. By this magic, she has escaped the fate of her brother who alone has 'inherited' from the father 'the huge scape goat of the race' (p. 1063). Maud is all purity, her brother all corruption. This genetic bifurcation is reinforced by a separating consciousness which keeps Maud and her brother apart.[39]

In addition, the narrator dissociates Maud from the network of social relationships in which she is constituted by transferring her from the Hall to the Hall-garden. He now construes her as a product of the innocent, natural world of the garden. She has 'but fed on the roses and lain in the lilies of life' (p. 1052). She is not the lady of the Hall but a rose or a 'Bright English Lily' (p. 1072). In the 'Go not, happy day' song of XVII, he separates her still further from the immediate social context by situating her within a symbolic geography of global proportions:

> Rosy is the West,
>   Rosy is the South,
> Rosy are her cheeks,
>   And a rose her mouth. (p. 1066)

Almost immediately he proceeds to rob Maud of historical specificity by transforming her Victorian rose-garden into the *hortus conclusus* of the Virgin Mary and the 'thornless garden' of 'snow-limbed Eve' (p. 1068).

'Eden, finally, is the only world in which he [the narrator] can live'.[40] But Eden had a male-dominated authority structure—a male overlord and a superintending God. The narrator rids Maud's garden of the men he loathes—Maud's brother and her 'dandy-despot' suitor—by defining them in eastern and baroque imagery which makes them into preposterously and opulently un-

English tyrants of another age. The suitor becomes a 'jewelled mass of millinery'; the brother, a 'Sultan' and an 'oiled and curled Assyrian Bull' (p. 1054). Maud remains the undisputed sovereign of the garden world. She is Queen Maud, 'Queen rose of the rosebud garden girls', 'Queen lily and rose in one' (p. 1077). Her Kingdom comprises 'a garden of roses / And lilies fair on the lawn; / There she walks in her state / And tends upon bed and bower' (p. 1064). This independent state is separated from the fallen world by a wall with its 'own garden-gate' upon which ramps a lion 'claspt by a passion-flower' (p. 1064)—emblematic of the values of the garden state: love and sacrifice.

Yet the garden is not an autonomous realm, but private property. It belongs not to Maud but to her capitalist brother. He permits her the 'freedom' of it, doubtless because it suits his interests to do so; it locks her away from the 'nameless and poor' and presents her in a showcase setting calculated to enhance her market value. The hyphenated 'Hall-garden' underscores the physical and economic unity of house and garden. The narrator's rapturous nocturnal experience in the garden (XXII) takes place in what is virtually an outdoor room, in which flowers dance to the rhythms of the polka wafting from the ballroom within. The brother's final and fatal entry into the garden shatters for good the speaker's illusion that the garden is Maud's and Maud's alone.

Very occasionally, the confinement of women to the domestic garden is presented as just that: literal imprisonment. Edith, the tragic heroine of Tennyson's *Aylmer's Field*, is incarcerated in the garden of her father's manor house: 'Kept to the garden . . . and groves of pine, / Watched even there' (p. 1175). Like the speaker of *Maud*, Edith's orphan sweetheart, Leolin, is a self-acknowledged victim of the 'filthy marriage-hindering Mammon' (p. 1170). It is the money-conscious, status-minded Sir Aylmer who prevents his re-entering the garden in which he played with Edith as a child.

A variant of the garden prison of the romantic heroine is the ruined garden of the blighted bride. Dickens's Miss Havisham, falsely installed in the domestic sphere by a perfidious lover, is fated never to be called into the garden to assume the role of queen. Her hopes and expectations shattered by a capricious exercise of male power, she withers in self-imposed immurement. At the same time, she contrives to make her rotting garden the stage for an ironic enactment of the love scenes she has never played out. Estella and Pip, the icily beautiful princess and the dutiful page, orbit the neglected garden of Satis House, the human instruments of a desolated spinster's retribution. The performance, however, serves only to confirm the normality of the reverse situation, and the unspoken assumptions upon which it rests: that women belong in gardens, are congruent with them, and flourish like gardens when, and only when, they realize the role of dutiful wife.

In spite of her peculiarities (her economic independence, for example), Miss Havisham is as weak a vessel as any romantic heroine for whom the needs of the heart are paramount. For Miss Havisham, the cost of this total dependence upon emotional gratification is wasted fecundity—of which the rotting garden is a major symbol.

Dickens's deployment of this symbol may owe something to his reading of Tennyson's *Mariana*, a poem which has as its 'unconscious' message the ideologically weighted idea that women depend upon men to make their domestic gardens bloom—literally as well as figuratively. Thus, in spite of its medieval setting, *Mariana* has a relevance to the social formation in which it was received, particularly when read against the arguments of Auguste Comte and others that 'women have unconsciously preserved medieval traditions and saved moral culture', so enabling them to 'assume their rightful position as objects of veneration'.[41] For many Victorians, as I have shown, one of the principal sites of veneration was the enclosed domestic garden, itself a kind of contemporary version of the medieval *hortus conclusus*, retaining its connections with the religious associations of the *hortus conclusus* in its literary forms through the ideological practice which sanctified women as the privileged bearers of moral and spiritual values. This makes it possible to read *Mariana* as a kind of negatively transformed version of the figure in the enclosed garden and of the emblematic associations which attend it. Such a reading both endorses the idea that women rely upon men for healthy development, and betrays the ills to which the casualties of male irresponsibility are heir.

CHAPTER 10

Garden Settings and Scenes

> A garden on a warm summer night offers opportunities no schemer should neglect.[1]
>
> To turn the pages of the Victorian novelists would be to find garden picture after garden picture, each one a setting for a Victorian conversation piece.[2]

Many of the scenes and events in Victorian fiction have garden settings. The obvious reason for this is that middle- and upper-class characters tend to use their gardens as outdoor rooms. A less obvious but exceedingly important reason is that novelists exploited the theatrical and regulatory potentialities of country house and suburban villa gardens. In countless narrative texts, garden design exerts a controlling influence upon the actions of the characters, and gardens provide stages for behaviour with consequences at the level of plot, and sometimes at other, higher levels as well. Action-advancing activities such as hiding, spying, discovering, eavesdropping, and conniving are made possible by the disposition of distinctively Victorian garden features, so much so that it is often hard to imagine alternative arenas to which they might successfully have been transferred.

The point has been made that nature in the form of the suburban villa garden 'ameliorated the staginess of the interior'.[3] For the 'plotting' novelists, however, staginess was at a premium outside the house as well as inside it. The ideal garden for their purposes included features of exposure, prospect, refuge and concealment. One of the basic models of Victorian garden design afforded the perfect arrangement: highly 'artificial' elements in the form of terraces, parterres and gravel paths in the immediate vicinity of the house, more 'naturalistic' features such as shrubberies and winding walks farthest from it, with a broad stretch of lawn in between.

This design, advocated by theorists such as Shirley Hibberd and Joseph Paxton, was in part intended to maximise the range of uses to which the garden could be put. The features closest to the house were formal and functional extensions of the interior living space. Consequently, the activities to which they were deemed appropriate—public or frontstage[4] activities such as conversing and spectating—were those most rigidly regulated by the codes of behaviour which operated indoors. The most distant features were those thought to bear the greatest resemblance to natural elements of the landscape. Since they were the features least visible from the house, they offered the imaginative and behavioural freedom appropriate to private or backstage activities such as plotting, spying and meeting in secret. A third, more ambivalent, set of features included conservatories and summer-houses. Though their architectural forms and, usually, their locations set them in the public domain, they lent themselves to private and secret encounters.

Imaginative writers exploited the opportunities offered by these features, and almost certainly helped to script them by defining the kinds of uses to which they could be put.

THE GRAVEL PATH

The giveaway gravel path has its own little part to play in Victorian fiction. Lewis Carroll draws attention to the presence-betraying function of the gravel path in his parody of the talking flowers section of *Maud*:

> 'She's coming!' cried the larkspur.
> 'I hear her footsteps, thump, thump, thump, along the gravel walk!'[5]

Before the proposal scene in the garden of Thornfield on Midsummer Eve, Jane Eyre attempts to conceal her presence from Mr Rochester. 'I trod on an edging of turf,' she says, 'that the crackle of pebbly gravel might not betray me' (p. 277). In detective novels, gravel paths betray the presence of intruders. Since gravel walks were expensive to lay and maintain, they also indicate wealth and status.

THE TERRACE

Like the billowing lawn, the stately terrace is an integral element of the *mise en scene* of the country house. As such, it helps to give environmental expression to a lifestyle that its admirers characterized as graceful, elegant and leisurely. But as regards its more pragmatic functions in fiction, it is probably the least utilized of the architectural garden features. Its contiguity with the house occasionally makes it useful as an additional room. In *The Woman in White*, Wilkie Collins manoeuvres Laura Fairlie onto the terrace of Limmeridge House, leaving Walter Hartwright and Marion Halcombe free to rummage through the letters in which they hope to find a clue to the identity of the woman in white. As a rule, the terrace is scripted as a public place appropriate to country house tea parties, as in *The Way We Live Now* and Henry James's *The Awkward Age* (1899), and to semi-formal encounters. In *A Country Gentleman and his Family*, the young widow, Lady Markland, considers the terrace a fitting place to entertain the young man who woos her. Only when they become more intimate does she invite him indoors (see II, 15).

The only other significant use of the terrace is as a vantage point for spectators. In this respect, the terrace serves much the same function as an upstairs window. From both viewpoints, the more interesting vistal experiences are those which suggest psychological motives or effects. There is a good example in Hardy's *Desperate Remedies* (1871): to convey Cytherea Graye's state of mind on her arrival as lady's-maid at Knapwater House, Hardy has her look out from a bedroom window upon the scene before her:

> Here she sat down by the open window, leant out the sill like another Blessed Damozel, and listlessly looked down upon the brilliant pattern of colours formed by the flower-beds on the lawn—now richly crowded with late summer blossom. But the vivacity of spirit which had hitherto enlivened her was fast ebbing under the pressures of prosaic realities, and the warm scarlet of the geraniums, glowing most conspicuously, and mingling with the vivid cold red and green of the verbenas, the rich depth of the dahlia, and the ripe mellowness of the calceolarias, backed by the pale hue of a flock of sheep feeding in the open park, close to the other side of the fence, were, to a great extent, lost upon her eyes. (p. 92)

Views from a window or terrace can also have a temporal dimension. A magazine poem called 'On the Terrace' opens with a scene-setting stanza:

> The stately lady, the grave calm man,
> Stood on the terrace together;
> 'Mid the bright rose thicket the revellers strayed,
> And hidden music sweet melodies made,
> At the fete in the July weather.[6]

Then, after snatches of conversation in a manner of 'careless languid courtesy', the old couple are prompted by the scene before them to recollect their happier youth together.

Finally, mention should be made of Henry James—the only late nineteenth-century novelist fully to exploit the prospective symbolism and hermeneutic implications of the terrace view. This is not the place to discuss in detail this aspect of James's fiction; in any case, his use of terrace views, his concept of vista, and his appreciation of the psychological implications of physical space have received a good deal of critical attention.[7] But at least passing reference should be made to the two works in which the terrace view is supremely important: *Daisy Miller* (1878) and the early novella, *Madame de Mauvres* (1874).[8]

THE LAWN

The well-shaven lawn proved invaluable to Victorian novelists, if only because it had no exact equivalent within the house. To be sure, as regards its visible physical and decorative properties, it seemed to many Victorians to resemble an indoor room, and is often depicted as such. The lawn of Hamley House garden in *Wives and Daughters* is converted into an 'open-air summer parlour' by the presence of 'chairs, tables, books and tangled work' and 'a sofa placed under the shadow of the great cedar-tree on the lawn' (p. 109). The justly famous description of Grandcourt in the opening chapter of *The Portrait of a Lady* (1881) strives for a still more homologous correspondence:

> The wide carpet of turf that covered the level hilltop seemed but the extension of a luxurious interior. The great still oaks and beeches flung down a shade as dense as that of velvet curtains; and the place was furnished, like a room, with cushioned seats, with rich-coloured rugs, with the books and papers that lay on the grass. (p. 33)

But the spatial poetics of the lawn, those atmospheric qualities of airiness, lightness, and scented warmth to which imaginative writers were keenly sensitive, are quite different from those of any indoor room. The lawn is also a peculiar kind of social space. Though Victorian photographs suggest that it could be as formal and stuffy as the drawing-room,[9] novelists tend to script it as a comparatively public space conducive to informal and relaxed encounters. Consider the lawn as a setting in W. H. Mallock's *The New Republic* (1877). The weekend party assembled at Otho Laurence's country house spends most of its time indoors, discussing the topics selected by the host. The conversation is witty, heated, and sometimes acrid. When the party is ushered into the garden, there is a change of mood. Upon the open, more imaginative stage of the lawn, relations seem less prickly, exchanges less caustic, and the emphasis is upon conviviality and enjoyment of the scene:

> . . . the party had already assembled, disposed in an easy group upon the grass. The place was an amphitheatre of turf, set round with laurels and all kinds of shrubs; in the arena of which—if one may so speak—a little fountain splashed cool and restless in a porphyry basin. . . . The whole scene was curiously picturesque. . . . And here, as the lights and shades flickered over them, they seemed altogether like a party from which an imaginative onlooker might have expected a new Decameron. (p. 150)

As the hub of a larger topographical structure, the lawn provided a suitable subject for view-painting, and a suitable setting for portraiture, conversation-pieces, more animated social activities, or for any combination of these. The mode of presentation could be scenic in the graphic or pictorial sense, or scenic in the theatrical sense, or the one could modulate into the other. Characters could be brought 'on location' or depicted in their 'native' habitats, selected for individual close-up portraits, considered as a collectivity, or disposed so as to bring out the relationships between them. In the passage quoted above, the lawn is simultaneously a stage for interpersonal encounters (an 'amphitheatre' 'screened' by the surrounding trees), an 'arena' for verbal duelling, and a picture.

An additional advantage of the lawn setting is that it does not necessarily require an on-the-spot or behind-closed-doors observer of the scene. If they are conducted on the lawn, most private exchanges may be exposed to view. Victorian novelists often exploited the possibilities of the concealed observer. For example, in Chapter 27 of Hardy's *Two on a Tower*, Swithin St Cleeve stations himself in a belfry from which he commands a view of Viviette Constantine, her brother Luis, and her admirer, Bishop Helmsdale, promenading and conversing on the lawn of Welland House. Swithin is angered by Viviette's attentions to the bishop, and unplacated by the conspiratorial kisses she blows him from the garden.

A much more professional spy is Charlotte Brontë's Paul Emmanuel in *Villette*, who shocks Lucy Snowe with a brazen-faced account of his voyeuristic activities at the window of the school house:

> That is a room I have hired, nominally for a study—virtually for a post of observation. There I sit and read for hours together: it is my way—my taste. My book is this garden, its contents are human nature—female human nature. I know you all by heart. (p. 353)

Whatever the implication of this (perhaps that the 'real' nature of women can be discovered only by observing them in their 'natural' habitat) the plot significance is that M. Emmanuel's spying has saved him from marrying Zelie St Pierre.

It is by means of an unseen and unidentified observer that George Eliot presents the description of Cheverel Manor in 'Mr Gilfil's Love-Story' in *Scenes of Clerical Life*. Its lawn serves initially as a backdrop for close-up portraits of Caterina Sarti and Lady Cheverel, then becomes an element in a pictorially composed landscape, and finally turns into the setting for a conversation-piece. The women

> sat down, making two bright patches of red and white and blue on the green background of the laurels and the lawn, which looked none the less pretty because one of the women's hearts was rather cold and the other rather sad.
>
> And a charming picture Cheverel Manor would have made that evening, if some English Watteau had been there to paint it . . . the broad gravel-walk winding on the right, by a row of tall pines, alongside the pool—on the left branching out among swelling grassy mounds, surmounted by clumps of trees, where the red trunk of the Scotch fir glows in the descending sunlight against the bright green of limes and acacias; the great pool, where a pair of swans are swimming lazily with one leg tucked under a wing, and where the open water-lilies lie calmly accepting the kisses of the flittering

> light-sparkles; the lawn, with its smooth emerald greenness, sloping down to the rougher and browner herbage of the park, from which it is invisibly fenced by a little stream that winds away from the pool, and disappears under the wooden bridge in the distant pleasure-ground; and on this lawn our two ladies, whose part in this landscape the painter, standing at a favourable point of view in the park, would represent with a few little dabs of red and white and blue. (p. 84)

The final (duplicative) image of the women splashed on the lawn prepares for the transition into a description of the interior of Cheverel, and thence to a conversation-piece. It may also represent a bid to rescue the key elements from a sea of details.[10] Painterly interests are clearly paramount, but so too are they in more focused descriptions of lawn-centred scenes. Though there are usually text-specific reasons for this, a more general reason may be that novelists wrote with an eye to the illustrative potentialities of their material. It has been argued that 'group scenes were the preferred matter for the illustrations of many Victorian serials, since they offered variety and a chance for a "full" engraving, thus giving the audience as much visual material as possible.'[11] The lawn provided both pretext and context for a visually appealing group scene with illustrative possibilities.

Moreover, aspects of character not revealed in the drawing room can be displayed on the lawn. A scene of this sort can also define relationships, not only between the participants themselves, but also between those participants and anyone who may observe them from within the house.

I have said that the lawn is generally scripted as a public place. It would be truer to say that it is a public place in a private world. This is not the trivial qualification it may seem to be. One of Austin Dobson's *Vers de Société*, 'A Sonnet in Dialogue', is a playful exchange between a man and a woman—presumably husband and wife—he on the lawn, she in the house. In a series of dovetailed one-liners, he tempts her to the terrace, while she teases him with good-humoured excuses. Their dialogue has the reciprocity of polite public speech appropriate to the lawn; but it is not intended for public consumption, and could only have taken place in a space sealed off from outsiders (see *DP*, pp. 291–2).

The nested arrangement of public lawn within private world is put to more poignant effect in *Modern Love* (1862). Meredith's sonnet sequence dramatizes the torments of a husband and wife whose relationship is in the process of inexorable decay. For the most part, they suffer their emotional estrangement together in the backstage privacy of the house they still share. But in Sonnet XXI the scene shifts to the 'cedar-shadowed lawn' made frontstage by the presence of a third party. When the friend enthuses about his forthcoming marriage, they struggle to respond appropriately, until the strain of keeping up appearances finally tells on the wife. She faints, and the ignorant friend infers from this that she is pregnant:

> When she wakes,
> She looks the star that thro' the cedar shakes:
> Her lost moist hand clings mortally to mine. (*MP*, p. 142)

This ending to the sonnet is a 'compassionate assent to their shared meaning'. 'The irony that the estrangement increases their sensitivity to each other'[12] is an effect of having the couple endure their private agony on the public lawn.

In novels, the lawn provides an ideal site for gathering together a group of characters, exploring their frontstage relationships, and isolating them from the world beyond. These are precisely the uses to which Henry James puts the lawn in the opening scene of *The Portrait of a Lady*. Having described the characters, the setting, its tea-party props and its atmospheric isolation ('privacy here reigned supreme' (p. 33)), the narrator withdraws. Save for the occasional stage direction, he permits the characters to present themselves through dialogue alone.

In Trollope's *The Small House at Allington*, the dramaturgical function of the lawns of the Allington houses is one of a hierarchy of interrelated functions. At the symbolic level they offer a topographical image of what in many ways aspires to be a socially self-sufficient and morally autonomous country community. Within this circumscribed world, the lawns serve both to divide and to connect the two houses, by means of a foot-bridge over a ditch, and to give their members a shared space for communal activities. On the lawn of the Small House, croquet is 'quite an institution'. And so, for the younger members, is dancing. For this activity, the lawn has the advantages over the drawing-room which Lily spells out: 'we've only got four young gentlemen . . . and they will look stupid standing up properly in a room, as though we had a regular party. . . . But out on the lawn it won't look stupid at all' (p. 73). It is on the lawn that the Dales of both houses meet on Sunday mornings before Church. On these occasions, the Squire finds an additional use for the lawn, and one which reinforces the idea of the garden as a domain:

> [He] would stand in the middle of the grass-plot, surveying his grounds, and taking stock of the shrubs and flowers, and fruit-trees around him; for he never forgot that it was all his own . . . . (p. 109)

Since the Allington community is not entirely cohesive and secure, the gardens are also sites significant for the social politics of the group, behaviour sites of 'manoevring for territorial advantage'.[13] Partly to maintain his position as head of the household, Christopher Dale remains on home ground whenever possible. Lily Dale employs the same tactic in her dealings with Hopkins, the irascible gardener:

> I always like to get him into the house, because he feels himself a little abashed by the chairs and tables; or, perhaps, it is the carpet that is too much for him. Out on the gravel-walks he is such a terrible tyrant, and in the greenhouse he almost tramples upon one. (p. 536)

Like Hopkins, Johnny Eames senses that the garden regulates encounters in ways that favour the 'politically' disadvantaged. When he comes to the Small House to propose to Lily, she attempts to manoeuvre him into the drawing-room, 'feeling that she would be in some degree safer there than out among the shrubs and paths in the garden.' 'John Eames also had some feeling of this kind, for he determined to remain out in the garden, if he could manage it' (p. 205). He does manage it, and gets the opportunity to make his declaration.

There are parallel scenes to these in Meredith's *The Egoist*, another novel much concerned with power plays and manoeuvring for territorial advantage. The lawns of Patterne Hall, more even than those of the houses at Allington, derive their dramaturgical and plot significance from their contiguity with other, less frontstage garden features. Early in the novel, Sir Willoughby is content with a public show of his power over Clara Middleton: 'He led her about the flower-beds; too much as if he were giving a convalescent an airing. She chafed at it, and pricked herself with remorse' (I, 70). But later, when his animal passions are stirred, he attempts to nudge her into a backstage quarter of the garden: 'his design was to conduct her through the covert of a group of laurels, there to revel in her soft confusion. She resisted, nay, resolutely returned to the lawn-sward' (I, 132).

Nowhere does the novel look more to Restoration comedy than in the closing pages of *The Egoist*, where garden and drawing-room settings interconnect to form a network of stages that contribute to the impressions of staginess and manic pace. At this point (Chapter 46) pairings are still uncertain, and so still the subject of elaborate plots and negotiations. Vernon Whitford is 'pushed forth on the lawn' by Sir Willoughby, then whisked away into the privacy of the shrubbery by Mrs Mountstuart—presumably to sound him out on the idea of marrying Clara—and finally returned to 'the open turf-spaces' (II, 572). The principal manipulators

> perceived Dr. Middleton wandering over the lawn, and Willoughby went to put him on the wrong track: Mrs. Mountstuart swept into the drawing-room. Willoughby quitted the Rev. Doctor, and hung about the bower where he supposed the pair of doves [Clara and Vernon] had by this time ceased to stutter mutually:—or what if they had found the world of harmony? He could bear that, just bear it. He rounded the shrubs, and behold, both had vanished. The trellis decorated the emptiness. (II, 573)

As the site of public and group activities, the country-house lawn has a vital but curiously passive part to play in some of Wilkie Collins's novels. In *Man and Wife* (1870) its importance lies precisely in the fact that it is *not* where the real action takes place. In the early chapters of the First Scene, this role falls to the summer-house at Windygates. It is here that the principal characters are introduced, first as a group, and then, when the setting turns into a stage, in a string of dyadic, private and increasingly dramatic exchanges: first between Arnold Brinkworth and Sir Patrick Lundie; then between Arnold and Blanche Lundie; finally between Anne Sylvester and Geoffrey Delamayn. Throughout this sequence, the lawn remains 'out there', the offstage area to or from which the actors make their exits. As the realm of the ordinary, the social and the leisurely, it serves to heighten by contrast the melodramatic intensity of the extraordinary private dramas enacted in the summer-house that stands in its midst.

In the later Windygate scenes, the lawn retains importance as the place to which unimplicated characters are shunted, leaving those directly involved in the action to scheme and confabulate in the privacy of the library (from which the lawn is viewed). On the lawn, characters are undifferentiated. When they leave it to enter the library, they are immediately individuated. And when the plotting characters seek solitude to think things out, they head for a secluded part of the garden well away from the lawn. In Chapter 22, Geoffrey Delamayn ignores the 'idling' friends who beckon him from the lawn, makes for the remote kitchen garden, and there soliloquizes on his predicament, hitting finally upon a plan to rid himself of the woman who stands between him and a glorious career on the running track.

SHRUBBERIES, SUMMER-HOUSES AND CONSERVATORIES

Lawns provided Victorian novelists with ideal settings for social rituals and interpersonal exchanges of the more leisurely and 'overt' kinds. For the staging of private or secret encounters, writers turned to other popular features of the larger garden: in particular, to shrubberies, summer-houses and conservatories.

If the Victorians had known nothing of shrubberies, contemporary novelists would probably have had to invent them. In some respects they did. Actual Victorian shrubberies tended to be irregular plantings. Fictional examples are also irregular, though perhaps less for reasons of mimetic fidelity than for purposes of concealment. But whereas actual shrubs were usually well-spaced (in accordance with the principles of the gardenesque), fictional shrubberies are characteristically dense—again, an adjustment to functional requirements. One simple example can be found in Chapter 8 of Gissing's *Isabel Clarendon*, in which Vincent Lacour pays a visit to Ada Warren. To enter the house unseen, he makes his way through the shrubbery of Knightswell garden, and then climbs in through the library window. He leaves the way he came, but is startled when discovered by Isabel emerging from 'the impenetrable gloom of the shrubbery' (I, 161).

Like the lawn, the shrubbery is important as a setting because it is not easily interchangeable with any interior room. Its functions are attributable to its distinctive characteristics, to which those of no room exactly correspond. One of these characteristics is visibility. Though scripted as a place for private negotiations and secret trysts, the shrubbery can usually be seen by an observer on the lawn or in the house. Its location is also distinctive.

Because it is removed from the house, approaching it, entering it, and emerging from it are actions requiring time and effort, which novelists can chart and pronounce for dramatic effect. There is an excellent example of this use of the shrubbery in Chapter 14 of *The Eustace Diamonds* (1873), in which Lord Fawn attempts to persuade Lizzie Eustace to give up the diamond necklace to which, he believes, she has no legal claim. The exchange is conducted with the interlocutors on the move, and the details of this motion are carefully noted. The couple meet in the hall of Fawn Court, then move away from the house, across the lawn, and into the shrubbery. Here the scene reaches a peak of tension, as Frederic hints for the first time that Lizzie's restoration of the diamonds is a precondition of his marrying her. The interview ends in deadlock, with the couple emerging from the privacy of the shrubbery to the communality of the lawn, where the 'elders' are leaving for church.

Because it is dense and distanced from the house, the shrubbery is the preeminent setting for amatory and often clandestine meetings of youthful lovers. Many such scenes are presented with dramatic effect from the point of view of an outside observer. In the latter part of *Wives and Daughters*, there is a scene in which Roger Hamley calls on Cynthia Kirkpatrick, resolved to make 'one strong manly attempt to overcome the obstacles . . . that she had conjured up against the continuance of the relations to each other' (p. 697). He is received by Molly Gibson, who is seated in 'the bow-window which commanded the garden' (p. 698). Molly is flustered, partly because of her own feelings for Roger, but chiefly because she knows that her coquettish stepsister is at that moment in the shrubbery with another of her admirers. The episode reaches a climax when

> Suddenly . . . the merry murmur of distant happy voices in the garden came nearer and nearer; Molly looked more and more uneasy and flushed, and in spite of herself kept watching Roger's face. He could see over her into the garden. A sudden deep colour overspread him, as if his heart had sent his blood out coursing at full gallop. Cynthia and Mr. Henderson had come in sight; he eagerly talked to her as he bent forward to look into her face; she, her looks half averted in pretty shyness, was evidently coquetting about some flowers, which she either would not give, or would not take . . . the lovers had emerged from the shrubbery into

> comparatively public life. (pp. 698–9)

When the alarmed spectator is a parent, a shrubbery scene may not only ginger the action and complicate relations between the characters involved, but also disclose something about the politics of family life. Young women, precluded by restrictive social conventions or parental disapproval from conducting their romantic affairs in the open, are compelled to conduct them in secret. This is the latent, if not always the manifest, message of shrubbery scenes. In Charles Reade's *Hard Cash* (1863), for example, Mrs Dodd, a respectable middle-class mother, warns her nineteen-year-old daughter Julia to stay clear of Alfred Hardie, of whom she strongly disapproves. Her advice apparently goes unheeded, for she sees Julia and Alfred walking in the garden of her suburban villa. Mrs Dodd's initial impulse is 'to dart from her ambush and protect her young'. She then has second thoughts:

> besides, the young people were now almost at the shrubbery; so the mischief, if any, was done.
>
> They entered the shrubbery.
>
> To Mrs. Dodd's suprise and dismay, they did not come out this side so quickly. She darted her eye into the plantation; and lo! Alfred had seized the fatal opportunity foliage offers, even when thinnish: he held Julia's hand, and was pleading eagerly for something she seemed not disposed to grant; for she turned away and made an effort to leave him. (p. 80)

In so far as it is a place for private, dyadic exchanges, the summer-house is similar in function to the shrubbery. In other respects, however, the summer-house script is peculiar. It lends itself to a nocturnal setting, with the moon supplying the illumination for a romantic picture of the woman. The man, who in most scenes encounters her by chance, is struck for the first time by her beauty and desirability. In what is contextually defined as an emotionally heightened atmosphere, he makes a sudden, unpremeditated display of affection—with momentous consequences.

In two strikingly similar scenes of this kind, one in Gissing's *A Life's Morning*, the other in Collins's *The Evil Genius*, the relationship of the couple is best described as exogamous. In both, the woman is a governess, the man her social superior. This fact is not without significance, for it seems to suggest that under the extraordinary phenomenal and psychological conditions in which summer-house scenes take place, normal social codes are nullified. Asymmetrical relationships are balanced, as it were, so that governesses are no longer seen as employees but as women. There is a further suggestion: since place affects moods and actions, the man in particular is a victim of circumstances rather than the calculating perpetrator of domestic crimes—marital infidelity from one point of view, seduction and the excitation of false hopes from another. Actions which would have seemed reprehensible in the drawing-room seem less so in the summer-house.

Take the scene expansively and meticulously developed in Chapter 9 of *The Evil Genius*. It begins with the hero, Herbert Linley, strolling late at night in the grounds of Mount Morven, his Scottish mansion. He is surprised to encounter Sydney Westerfield, the poor but pretty governess he has altruistically rescued from a life of misery. They soon discover that all the doors of the house are locked. Concerned for his 'innocent' companion and the 'evil construction which might be placed on their appearance together', Herbert suggests that they make for the summer-house rather than attempt to rouse the servants. He hesitates before entering, but Sydney's 'fearless ignorance' compels him to join her inside. In a spontaneous gesture of gratitude, Sydney kisses his hand. When Herbert recoils, Sydney is distraught with the guilt of having behaved improperly. The sight of her 'tortured face' impels him to return her kiss, and then to declare his love for her. Passion soon gives way to guilt on both sides. Sydney resolves to leave Mount Morven, but Herbert persuades her to stay for a while to spare the feelings of his devoted wife. When Mrs Presty (the evil genius of the title) discovers and makes public their secret, Sydney is disgraced and Herbert loses his wife. The repercussions of the summer-house scene are felt throughout the rest of the novel. What should be stressed here is that the setting itself provides the mitigating circumstances for Herbert's actions, which in turn make it possible for the reader to sympathize with his subsequent plight.

The scene in *A Life's Morning* between Emily Hood and her employer's son, Wilfrid Athel, is also 'a turning-point of fate' (p. 45), though a less catastrophic one. When Wilfrid encounters Emily in the summer-house doorway, he sees her as he has never seen her before. 'Without reflection' he declares his love for her. Again, the presentation of the scene is such as to leave no doubt that the actions of the man are precipitated by the setting and the beauty of the garden at night.

Though an important, plot-significant setting in a handful of novels, the summer-house figures far less prominently in Victorian fiction than that other, preeminently Victorian garden room, the conservatory. Some of the reasons for this are relatively obvious. 'The conservatory played an essential part in upper-class Victorian social life'[14]—Disraeli's Ferdinand Armine avows that it is impossible to live without one[15]—and it provided affluent Victorians and fictional characters with a symbol of status and wealth more egregious than that of any other item of garden furniture. Moreover, as I have suggested elsewhere,[16] the conservatory captured the Victorian imagination in much the same way and for much the same reasons as did two other Victorian institutions, one indigenous, the other appropriated, and both applauded for their marvellous and miraculous effects: the greatest of all glass palaces, the Crystal Palace, and translations of the *Arabian Nights*, to which the Great Exhibition was often compared.

Not surprisingly, then, the conservatory in fiction is typically presented as an image of a delightful, trouble-free world beyond the imperfect present[17] and, within the here-and-now world of the privileged classes, as an enchanted bubble appropriate to encounters of the more intimate kinds.

Most conservatory scenes have their motivational origins in a public place—usually a ball-room—from which the couple in question leave to be alone or to escape the unwanted attentions of others. Whereas actual Victorian conservatories were used mainly 'for reading, lounging, or taking light refreshments',[18] fictional conservatories are reserved almost exclusively for the private meetings of lovers. Narrators explicitly script it as such. In Wilkie Collins's *The Black Robe* (1881) we are told that 'lovers (in earnest or not in earnest) discovered, in a dimly-lit conservatory with many recesses, that ideal of discreet retirement which combines solitude and society under one roof' (p. 116).

Once in the conservatory, lovers find privacy, and experience a sense of being in an other-world environment. Exotic plants, dizzying scents, chinese lanterns, and magical oxymoronic compounds of coolness and heat, airiness and profusion, and darkness and luminosity, conspire with the conservatory's ambiguous threshold locations[19] to raise the emotional temperature and suspend the operation of public codes of behaviour.

This is a composite picture. Though the fairy tale effects are constant, the particular ingredients naturally vary in accordance with the atmospheric requirements of specific scenes. One can observe such variations in the stage-setting descriptions below. The first is from Rhoda Broughton's *Not Wisely, but Too Well.* The emphasis here is upon the heady and the sensuous, an atmosphere fitting the steamy scene between Kate Chester and Dale Stamer into which the description dissolves. The second, from J. G. Whyte-Melville's *The White Rose*, opens the exchange between the young and innocent heroine, Norah Welby, and the scheming Squire Vandeleur. The latter has 'rescued' Norah from some over-enthusiastic admirers in order that he might seduce her in the absence of her sweetheart. In the interests of Vandeleur and dramatic suspense it is important that Norah does not immediately suspect the motives of her host. A sensuous atmosphere might have put her on her guard.

> And how marvellously pleasant it was when they were fairly inside that 'box where sweets compacted lie'; how almost oppressive, overpowering, the fragrance of the warm, damp atmosphere, where a thousand sweet smells strove perpetually for the mastery. There, side by side, gathered from the far east and the far west, blossomed and reigned Nature's most regal flower-daughters. Gorgeous stately flowers, that had hitherto revealed their passionate hearts, fold after fold, to the fainting air of some cloudless, rainless, brazen tropic sky, now poured forth all their sweets, put on all their brilliant apparel, under our watery, sickly sunbeams. . . . What of man's devising can be more intoxicating than one of these temples dedicated to rich odours and brave tints? And when there stands in this temple, among these gorgeous flowers, a lovely woman . . . the subjugation of the senses may be supposed to be complete. Kate was in ecstasies. (p. 107)

> 'This is delightful!' exclaimed Norah, drawing a full breath of the pure, cool night air, that played through the roomy conservatory, and looking round in admiration on the quaintly-twisted pillars, the inlaid pavement, the glittering plants and gorgeous flowers. It seemed a different world from the ballroom and would have been Paradise, if only Gerard had been there. (p. 70)

The rise in emotional temperature in the conservatory, sufficient to melt the constraints imposed upon courting couples under less stimulating circumstances, may occur by mutual consent, but more frequently the woman under threat strives to continue the small-talk of the ballroom while the man attempts to divert the exchange into a more erotic direction. The tension that results is nicely captured in the principal conservatory scene in *Henrietta Temple*. Among the 'orange groves' of the Ducie Bower conservatory, Ferdinand is eager to play out a mildly sexual fantasy in which he is cast as an enchanted prince and Henrietta as a Sicilian princess. Henrietta endeavours to focus the conversation on plants, until she terminates it with what appears to be a playful threat of symbolic castration: 'Cut off your tendrils and drown you with a watering-pot', she says (see pp. 96–7).

Perhaps the best-known conservatory scene in Victorian fiction provides as good an example as any of the dramatic usefulness of the conservatory setting. In Chapter 10 of the sixth book of *The Mill on the Floss*, Maggie Tulliver attends a dance at Stephen Guest's home of Park House. Stephen, overcome with passion for Maggie, leads her from the 'stifling' ballroom to the 'cool retreat' of the conservatory. The scene proceeds, conventionally, with an observation upon the environmental peculiarities of the setting:

> 'How strange and unreal the trees and flowers look with the lights among them!' said Maggie, in a low voice. 'They look as if they belonged to an enchanted land, and would never fade away—I could fancy they all were made of jewels.' (p. 408)

At first the exchange is silent but emotionally intense. Maggie gazes at the flowers; Stephen gazes at Maggie. Then, when they reach the end of the conservatory, Maggie feels the pressure of 'a new consciousness' (p. 409). Attempting to 'dissipate the burning sense of irretrievable confusion', she remarks on a half-opened rose, and stretches her arm towards it. Seized by a 'mad impulse', Stephen 'darted towards the arm, and showered kisses on it, clasping the wrist (p. 409). Maggie declares that he has insulted her, and commands him to avoid her in the future. Stephen returns to the ballroom; Maggie follows shortly afterwards, now feeling exultantly free from any temptation to take Stephen away from Lucy.

The Cornhill Magazine of January 1893 carried a story entitled 'The Arbour in the Garden'. The story concerns a young woman by the name of Adelaide Lilburne who is engaged to be married to the 'heavy and stupid' Augustus Chessall. Both live in the remote Devonshire village of Knagford. Adelaide has doubts about her forthcoming marriage, and foresees only tedium in store for herself. Six weeks before the wedding is to take place, an old flame returns to Knagford. He is Dr Ernest Wilson, formerly the village GP, but now, having spent five years in Borneo, a distinguished traveller and explorer. He makes it clear to Adelaide that he wishes to resume their intimacy. Though still in love with Ernest, Adelaide asks him to leave, since she feels conscience-bound to honour her commitment to Augustus.

In the Lilburnes's garden there is a 'sort of rustic arbour formed of trellis-work and overhanging creepers'.[20] It was in this arbour that Adelaide first became intimate with Ernest, and it is the place she most associates with the lover she has lost. It has a similar significance for Ernest. The moment he gives up hope of persuading Adelaide to change her mind, he returns to the arbour for a final gaze:

> He wanted to look once more at the place where he had taken his final farewell of Adelaide, five years before. It had been her favourite haunt, and he sighed profoundly as he thought of it. As he reached the entrance, he saw the place was not untenanted. A tall girl was sitting with a book before her intently reading. It was Maud Lilburne, and Dr. Wilson saw that she was not aware of his presence. He stood quite still for a few seconds watching her. Maud, with clear-cut features, seen in profile, her long lashes drooping a little, and her youthfully rounded figure bending a little forward, made a very pretty picture in the green foliage. One ray of sunlight, struggling through the leaves, lighted up the gold of her hair. Dr. Wilson gazed for a few seconds, and then a sigh betrayed him.[21]

The predictable happens. Ernest and Maud, Adelaide's younger sister, fall in love, but keep their romance a secret. One month later, Adelaide returns to the arbour to consider her situation; it is there that she resolves to break her engagement, and admit 'what her heart really prompted'. No sooner has she made her decision than she recognizes the voices of Maud and Ernest in the garden. She hears them kiss and talk of their plans to marry. She knows that she must resign herself to a dreary future with Augustus.

As the principal *mise en scène*, the arbour plays a crucial role, as the title indicates, in the romantic career charted by the story. It provides the meeting-place for intimate encounters, the subject for a garden picture that ratifies the femininity of the heroine's rival, and the setting for experiences of discovery which advance the action. It would be difficult to conceive of another device of equally various uses—except, perhaps, some similar item of garden architecture. The arbour has a cluster of apposite connotations—romance, rusticity, privacy, and quasi-naturalness —which no interior room, for example, can exactly match.

'The Arbour in the Garden' is notable only because it is not unusual. In countless Victorian narrative texts, gardens are places where things are discovered, connived at, and covertly observed. One reason that gardens are favoured settings for these activities should by now be clear: by virtue of their features and the spatial relations between them, distinctively Victorian gardens afforded fitting and credible settings for certain experiences significant to the narrative plot. But this alone does not suggest the significance of garden experiences at levels 'higher' than the plot; nor, indeed, does it explain why some are recurrent.

The most recurrent of all such experiences is that of the unwitting eavesdropper. Many a fictional character is the unintended beneficiary of information which affects, sometimes profoundly, his or her subsequent actions, self-image, and relationships with others.

At the level of expediency, the unwitting eavesdropper seems to be a device for obviating the necessity of resolving or confronting problems of interpersonal relationships by means of direct, face-to-face exchanges. The most generous explanation of its deployment is that it frequently represents a saving of textual space. Both of these functions are fulfilled in the scene in Collins's *No Name* in which Mr Pendril, the Vanstones's family solicitor, divulges to Miss Garth, the governess and family friend, that Norah and Magdalen Vanstone are illegitimate and thus effectively penniless and homeless. Throughout the interview, attention is periodically directed to the 'humming of flies among the evergreen shrubs under the window [which] penetrated drowsily into the room' (p. 83). In the next chapter but one, the significance of this is made apparent. From under the open window, Magdalen has heard the entire interview, so that Miss Garth has no longer to agonize over how she is to tell the girls of their misfortune.

But the device of the unwitting eavesdropper may also seem to reveal a want of inventiveness, and even, perhaps, an abnegation of authorial responsibility to work out or through the situation that he or she has contrived. In the Brussels section of *The Professor*, Brontë traces the growth of William Crimsworth's sexual attraction to the enigmatic Mlle. Reuter. It is clear, however, that Brontë's decent hero must sooner or later be brought to realize that Zoraïde Reuter is not the woman for him. This could have been achieved by bringing the two into direct confrontation. Instead, Crimsworth is allowed to overhear a conversation in the school-house garden between Zoraïde and her lover, Pelet, as they take a midnight stroll. Almost instantaneously, Crimsworth recovers from his infatuation, and the very next morning meets Francis Henri for the first time. The rest of the novel is devoted to the development of the love between them.

The device of the garden eavesdropper has particularly serious thematic implications in texts which treat of the possibilites of exogamous marriages. A prime example is Gissing's *Thyrza*, one of the narrative threads of which concerns the mutual attraction which develops between Walter Egremont, a wealthy Oxford graduate with a social conscience, and Thyrza Trent, a beautiful working-class girl. Unable to resist his love for Thyrza, but determined not to stand between her and the scholarly workman, Gilbert Grail, Egremont leaves England. To avoid marrying Grail, Thyrza leaves Lambeth for Eastbourne, where she is given refuge by an altruistic matron, Mrs Ormonde. Screened by a trellis in Mrs Ormonde's garden, Thyrza overhears a conversation between her benefactress and Egremont. The latter declares his wish to marry Thyrza, but is persuaded to wait for two years until Thyrza has been educated to make her a suitable partner for Egremont. Heartened by what she has overheard, Thyrza sets about 'improving' herself, and so successfully that Mrs Ormonde is convinced that she is happy. When Egremont returns, she tells him that Thyrza has become too fine for him, that she is happy as she is, and that marriage would only be to her disadvantage. Egremont leaves and finally turns to a girl of his own class. Thyrza dies without recovering from her disappointment.

In *Thyrza*, then, the expedient of the eavesdropper in the garden not only has extensive consequences for the action; it also vitiates the anti-romantic premise that underlies the action. Since Egremont and Thyrza are not allowed to confront their predicament, the hypothesis that inter-class marriages are impossible or unwise is never put to the test, and so never confirmed or rejected.

The recurrence of the unwitting eavesdropper scene hints at a significance beyond and disproportionate to its specific function as a plot mechanism. Since it suggests something about the hermeneutics of daily experience, and something about the quality of personal relationships in the social worlds of the novels in which it occurs, it may be appropriate to call it an ideological significance.[22] At any rate, the garden setting implies that duplicity and subterfuge have infiltrated the domestic sphere itself. And though it reaffirms the conventional moral judgement that the truth will always come out, it betrays—perhaps as unintentionally as the overheard speaker in the garden—the realist's nightmare that the truth can only be stumbled upon by accident or glimpsed through the crack in the garden wall.[23]

Many reluctant eavesdroppers discover not just unwanted information, but also the unpalatable truth that the only messages with any real credence are those unintentionally overheard. This is the experience of Ada Warren in Gissing's *Isabel Clarendon*, a novel in which the principal characters knew much less about each other than they suppose. There is a crucial scene in Chapter 11 in which Ada, seated on the garden side of the conservatory of Knightswell, overhears Isabel and a friend, Mrs Stratton, discussing within the rotunda Ada's relations with Vincent Lacour and Bernard Kingcote. Their highly unflattering remarks are capped by Mrs Stratton's observation that Ada 'isn't as ugly as she was'. Ada, shocked and hardened by what she has heard, decides to accept Lacour's proposal of marriage, in part, presumably, to escape from a house in which she feels ill at ease.

As we might expect, eavesdropping experiences figure significantly in novels which attach particular importance to the part played by chance and accident in human affairs. Many of Hardy's works provide obvious examples. In Chapter 3 of *The Woodlanders*, Marty South overhears Mr and Mrs Melbury conversing in their garden. Melbury speaks of his regret of having to atone for his own sins by sacrificing his daughter, Grace, to Giles Winterbourne. Marty, now realizing that Giles cannot be hers, 'mercilessly' cuts off her beautiful hair for the two sovereigns promised by Mr Percomb.

For reasons that have more to do with their revolt against the conventions of the domestic novel than with more general philosophic convictions, the plotting novelists of the sensation school assert what one may call 'the primacy of accident'.[24] Unintentionally overheard conversations are common in the novels of Wilkie Collins. For example, the titular protagonist of *Basil* is privy to a conspiratorial conversation between the woman he has recently married, rashly and to the ignorance of his family, and her mother, Mrs Sherwin, as he gathers flowers in the garden of their 'gaudy' suburban house. For the first time, Basil begins to feel 'a little uneasiness' at 'certain peculiarities in Margaret's character and conduct' (p. 131).

In the sensation novels of the 1860s and after, eavesdropping is not always unintentional; neither is it the only symptom of disorder and deception in the domestic sphere. Spying and the plotting and perpetration of crimes and intrigues commonly take place in domestic gardens. One explanation for this is the apparent familiarity and ordinariness of the garden. As a respectable bourgeois environment, it provides a credible physical setting for extraordinary and often melodramatic goings-on. Indeed 'it is the mixture of different "realities", the startling contrast between the event and its mundane surroundings, that gives the sensation novel its special pungency and its undeniable effect.'[25]

Many contemporary commentators were alarmed by this contrast; almost all of them drew attention to it. In a major review of 'The Sensation School', a contributor to the *Temple Bar* wrote: 'It is on our domestic hearths that we are taught to look for the incredible . . . our innocent-looking garden walks hold the secret of treacherous murders . . .'[26]

The allusion here is almost certainly to *Lady Audley's Secret* (1862), the novel that cannoned M. E. Braddon to fame, and virtually exploded the script of the 'innocent' country garden. The contrast between honorific setting and horrific event is hinted at in the opening pages of the novel. A eulogistic description of the 'glorious old place' of Audley Court culminates in an account of its two most enigmatic garden features: an old well 'half buried among the tangled branches and the neglected weeds' of the shrubbery, and a lime-tree walk,

> an avenue so shaded from the sun and sky, so screened from observation by the thick shelter of the over-arching trees that it seemed a chosen place for secret meetings or for stolen interviews; a place in which a conspiracy might have been planned or a lover's vow registered with equal safety; and yet it was scarcely twenty paces from the house. (p. 3)

A reader might well conclude that this passage exceeds the minimal scene-setting requirements; and calculatedly so, for the expectations it arouses, and the questions it poses (to what uses *are* these mysterious features to be put?) are important elements in the novel's hermeneutic code. After many twists of narrative suspense, Robert and the reader finally discover the full significance of the shrubbery: it is the site of 'murder' and of Lady Audley's secret.

It is worth reiterating that the attempted murder does not take place, as one recent writer has inaccurately stated, 'in a remote corner of the garden',[27] but in unnervingly close proximity to the house. The implication of this—and one in keeping with the general philosophy of the sensationalist project—is not that chaos and illicit passions are nibbling at the edges of the comfortable bourgeois world, but rather that they have eaten into its very heart. Like the physical gap between Audley Court and its shrubbery, the dividing lines between order and disorder, the familiar and the unknown, domestic stability and romantic energy are terrifyingly but titillatingly thin, intensifying the vicarious excitement of readers for whom the sensation novel affords a 'harmless refuge from the established tyranny of the principle that all human happiness begins and ends at home'.[28]

To assault this principle and, inevitably, to 'violate some of the conventionalities of sentimental fiction',[29] Braddon and Collins present the middle-class domestic paradise as anything but humdrum and, often, as anything but paradise. The garden frequently turns out to be a place of danger and drama; its sentimental codifications are subverted and its theatrical possibilities exploited. It is no coincidence that those of Collins's fictional gardens and garden rooms in which most incidents occur can be found in works conceived or adapted for the stage: *The Frozen Deep* (written 1856), *The Woman in White*, *Man and Wife*, and *The New Magdalen*—all exhibiting his preference for 'the strikingly dramatic incident, and for a series of well-staged episodes rather than the slow accumulation of detail.'[30] Two examples will suffice. In Chapter 47 of *Man and Wife*, there is an eavesdropping scene so theatrical that it must surely have been conceived with the stage in mind. Blanche Lundie, concealed at Lady Lundie's behest on the garden side of a projecting window, hears her husband from inside the house 'confess' to Lady Lundie in the garden that he has secretly 'married' Blanche's friend and governess, Anne Sylvester. Blanche believes that her domestic happiness has been shattered, and immediately prepares to take leave of her husband.

The second example is from *The New Magdalen*. When Grace Roseberry discovers that both her identity and her place as companion to Lady Janet of Mablethorpe House have been taken by Mercy Merrick, a reformed prostitute but a winning person, she resolves to gain entry into Mablethorpe by way of its conservatory. There are some dramatic scenes in which Grace, secreted behind the glass-house shrubs, surveys the proceedings in the reception room. Since the real Grace is presented as a much more objectionable individual than the counterfeit one, her presence in the conservatory represents a threat to the domestic order of Mablethorpe. One could scarcely find a more blatant example of drama seasoning and passion imperilling the equanimity of the respectable Victorian home.

For numerous and diverse reasons, then, gardens provide the settings for a variety of fictional events, many of which would have been difficult or impossible to present in other kinds of settings, and some of which are significant at a variety of textual levels.

CHAPTER ELEVEN

The Garden Within

Thus far I have considered the garden as an external landscape related to other external landscapes by contrast or similarity. But in Victorian literature the garden also occurs as an internal or internalised landscape—a spatial or aesthetic analogue of consciousness, for example—that serves to articulate a range of subjective and intrapersonal experiences and concerns. This chapter will examine the internal and internalized gardens in the work of the poet whose interests can be plotted in terms of their varying uses: Tennyson.

A crude synopsis of Tennyson's career as a 'landscape' poet might note that after an early flirtation with romantic mountain scenery, Tennyson turned to the garden: initially, for topographical images of embowerment; subsequently, to explore the social implications of landscape. There are other ways of expressing this trajectory. Perspectivally, for instance, one can speak of a shift from 'vertical' to 'horizontal' landscapes and viewpoints, with a parallel shift of interest from the figure in the garden to the figure excluded from it. Or one can remark a movement away from pastoral and mythological 'lawns' to the 'lawns' of contemporary English gardens: from the lawns of Lotos-land, and the 'vale of Ida' in *Oenone*, to those of Somersby and Swainston, and the garden estates of the *English Idylls*, *The Princess*, and *Aylmer's Field*. Or one can trace a shedding of Romantic attachments, and a concomitant desire to invest the domesticated garden landscape with the heroism and idealism formerly associated with mountains.

Something of the latter can be seen in the very early poem, *On Sublimity*. Having spurned the 'vales of tenderest green', the speaker calls for the 'wild cascade' and 'rugged scene' (*TP*, p. 116). He knows that these 'sad views' can only 'charm the awe-struck sole which doats on solitude' (p. 116), and yet he sees them as more challenging than 'Fancy's vales' (p. 119). In later poems, mountains tend to be seen either as pastoralized (as in *Oenone*) or as places of splendid but pleasureless isolation to which the idealist like Sir Galahad sets out or from which she (it is always a she) is beckoned to 'Come Down'—as in the famous lyric from the *The Princess*. From the 1830 volume onwards, gardens and bowers displaced mountains as Tennyson's principal landscapes of refuge and withdrawal from active social life. For the kinds of experiences with which he wished to deal, gardens had the more appropriate connotations: enclosure rather than exposure; stasis rather than action; escape rather than heroic endeavour; sensuousness rather than strenuousness. Moreover, since mountains suggested to Tennyson both solitude *and* heroic action, they resolved or, more precisely, dissolved the very opposition that he was seeking to map through the topographical symbolism of his early poems: 'the old conflict between the claims of the active and the contemplative life'.[1] Eden-like gardens encompassed by landscapes associated with the social world had the virtue of maintaining this dualism.

One commentator has identified in 'virtually all the more significant early poems . . . the opposition of still point and turning world . . . so characteristic of Tennyson's symbolic projection of the quarrel with himself and the world.' He continues: 'The still point is generally associated with the isolated and alienated self, aestheticism, sensuousness—with private poetry; the turning world with involvement with humanity and its essential concerns—with public poetry'.[2]

Though the still point is usually imaged as 'the secreted island or garden (or both together)',[3] and the turning world as wildscape or community, their relations are variable. In some poems, *The Lady of Shalott*, for example, the still point/turning world antithesis is strongly marked; in others it is intentionally weakened, and more by implication than by overt description—as is the case with *Mariana*. The comparative dangers and attractions of still point and turning world also vary from poem to poem. In *The Poet's Mind* Tennyson considers the garden's appeal as a refuge and sacred bower with fewer reservations than in the decidedly more enigmatic *The Hesperides*.

Another way in which Tennyson explores the comparative attractions of still point and turning world is through the concomitant distinction of being and world. Although this relation is similarly variable, it veers not so much between collapse and maintenance as between different degrees of dissolution. This dissolution is most extreme in *Mariana*, where the decaying house and garden seem either the 'embodiment of Mariana's consciousness'[4] or the effect of her 'imposing upon the landscape her own frustrated and tortured soul'.[5] Either way, landscape and mindscape are largely indistinguishable. A similar identification of self and setting obtains in *Youth*, between the insentient speaker and the 'scentless flowers' among which he paralytically sits. But here the speaker is conscious of the boundary between self and world, and accepts that its dissolution can be, must be, merely temporary. By contrast, the speaker in *The Poet* would gladly annul the distinction between garden mindscape and garden world—provided the latter could project and transcribe the vision of the former—a distinction which the speaker in *The Poet's Mind* insists upon as a prerequisite of uncontaminated poetic activity.

Tennyson achieves the opposition between garden and turning world in three other ways: first, in terms of the constituent features and atmospheric qualities of his landscapes (the quality of weightiness distinguishes many of his gardens); second, through the framework of a symbolic geography conceived in terms of the East-West polarity; finally, by textual reinforcement through the use of verse techniques and the shape of the text on the page.

All three means are at work in *Youth*. Here the garden is presented as a 'middle way' for the undecided, an arena of conflict rather than a place of repose. The speaker languishes in a field of opposing forces: between the East and the West; between the voice which calls him to 'come back' to the exotic and 'far away', and the voice which urges him to come along. The voice which calls him from 'distant fields' is 'low' and 'sweet' (p. 578) but less joyful than it once had sounded. The seemingly stronger voice which urges him forward is associated with 'agony', 'labour' and the 'groans of men' (p. 580).

Significantly, the lines in which the speaker describes his present condition occupy the dead centre of the poem—the textual equivalent of the hurricane's eye:

Confused, and ceasing from my quest,
  I loitered in the middle way,
So pausing 'twixt the East and West,

I found the present where I stay:

Now idly in my natal bowers,
Unvext by doubts I cannot solve,
I sit among the scentless flowers
And see and hear the world revolve:

Yet well I know that nothing stays
And I must traverse yonder plain:
Sooner or later from the haze
The second voice will peal again. (*TP*, p. 579)

The speaker's mental state is an uneasy mixture of certain knowledge and unconvincing self-deception. (His claim to be 'Unvext by doubt' is patently disingenuous.) It is clear that the garden can afford nothing more than a temporary refuge for the torn and uncommitted.

Youth, together with a number of Tennyson's other early poems, and a few of the later ones as well, can be regarded as a 'garden of the mind' poem. The phrase 'garden of the mind'—it comes from *Ode to Memory* (*TP*, p. 211)—has three main applications: to poems in which the speaker travels to gardens in his imagination; to poems in which the speaker's memories of a garden play an important part in the experiences he articulates; and to poems in which the garden objectifies a mood or provides an analogue of the poet's mind.

The Hesperides is an example of the latter category. At least, the poem can be and has been read as Tennyson's most complicated and equivocal statement on the nature of art, the situation of the artist and, more specifically, the poet's need to protect his creative imagination from disturbing forces.

The garden isle of *The Hesperides* is the most isolated symbolic environment presented by any of the poems concerned with the poet's inner life. It is remote in time as well as space, as the allusions to Eden, and the mythological echoes—to Hercules, to sacred pagan bowers—remind us. Moreover, the cosmology of the poem is on a grand scale. For the speaker of *Youth*, the duality of East and West was little more than a spatial projection of conflicting impulses. In *The Hesperides*, the East-West dichotomy emerges naturally from the location of the Hesperidian gardens, from Hesperus, the evening star, and from its daughters who guard the golden apple—'the treasure / Of the wisdom of the West' (*TP*, p. 425).

Robert G. Stange has no doubts about the importance of the contrast: 'the varied associations of East and West establish a kind of symbolic geography which enforces the central duality of the poem and underlies its pattern of emotional contrasts'.[6] The West stands for rest, warmth, mystery, and death; the East for activity, for the dawning of a new bold age. The West 'incorporates the notion of a retreat to the past and an envisioning of the lost paradise',[7] while it is from the everyday world of the East that someone may voyage to steal the magic fruit.

In some respects, *The Hesperides* is Tennyson's most compelling argument for granting to the poet and his art a privileged status. In no other garden-as-refuge poem does he more precisely elucidate the levels and interactions of what might be termed the garden-poetic ecosystem. There is first the 'awful mystery' of the protective chain of 'Five and three':

> Five links—a golden chain are we —
> Hesper, the Dragon, and sisters three
> Bound about the golden tree. (*TP*, p. 427)

Taken as a unit, the 'Five links' suggest the five senses which nourish the poet, and over which—if he is to master his craft—he must lord. The smaller chain of three suggests, in addition to the obvious referent, the 'threefold music' by which the sap is induced to rise and the blossom to 'bloweth'. It suggests also the three interdependent parts of the tree: the 'charmed root', the 'gnarled bole', and the 'hallowed fruit' (pp. 428–9).

The protective chain is symbiotically 'bound' to the object it guards. The maidens' unceasing incantation is both cause and effect of the sacred fruit. They must sing if the fruit is to grow, and from the active life of the tree they receive the inspiration for their song. Symbolically, this is 'a figure of the connections among the artist, his art, and his inspiration'.[8]

Finally, there is a further, more subliminal source of strength for the tree: the sea

> Every flower and every fruit the redolent breath
> Of the warm seawind ripeneth,
> Arching the billow in his sleep. (*TP*, p. 428)

The poet, Tennyson implies, requires nourishment from more primal or less conscious sources than the garden itself can supply.

As a plea for a sacred bower of poetic inspiration, the strength of this poem lies not only in its identification of the web of relations between the components of the garden (and, by analogy, between the poet, his work, and his environment), but also in its emphasis upon the essentially mysterious nature of the processes involved. Through his distancing and mythologizing of the garden-poetic ecosystem, Tennyson achieves a 'dream-like air of mystery combined with intense concreteness'.[9]

Nonetheless, *The Hesperides* is problematic. Like Milton's paradisaical home of the Attendant spirit, Tennyson's Hesperidian gardens are conceived as 'a restful abode for the privileged spirit and as a source of creativity'.[10] The speaker insists that the garden and its sacred fruit must be protected from mankind in general since the apple would make them 'overwise' and 'cure the old wound of the world' (p. 427). It is hard not to feel that the protection of a fruit with such miraculous powers amounts to indefensible sacerdotalism. Given the astonishing precariousness of the fruit (should not the stuff of poetry be more robust?), the effort expended on its protection (is the 'external pleasure' it affords worth 'external want of rest'?), and the arcane code of the maidens' song (the details of which are 'meant to baffle the outsider who dares to invade the holy precincts of poetry'[11]), we may well feel that the poem rings with 'a sense of disengagement from life and human sympathies'.[12]

The speaker's insistence upon the absolute purity and sanctity of the garden and its fruit, his refusal to countenance the merest trace of human occupation, suggests, perhaps, a failure of vision, an inability to see what many poets have seen: that the garden can function as a poignant symbol only if there is the possibility of its being subverted, violated, destroyed.

This is a problem for any poet who uses the garden as an image of ordered harmony and secure happiness. 'The most tactful poetic solution' is 'to treat it as an unrealized possibility, a place which we are just on the point of occupying or which we might have occupied'.[13] Hence, Coleridge's Kubla Khan decrees the laying-out of his pleasure garden, but does not enter it. Similarly, Milton emphasizes the transcience of the cloistral delight of the happy human pair, and has the 'first grand Thief' break into the fold to destroy it; the Eden garden, 'epitome of the sure dispensation, would have been totally uncompelling without the satanic assault'.[14]

Tennyson permits no such possibility. He emphasizes the fragility of the garden, but without a corresponding emphasis upon the potentially insinuating forces of the East. Encircled by a sleepy yet mountainous terrain, an equally somnolent wildlife which, in an emergency, might yet be roused to serve as a first line of defence, and an expanse of ocean formidable enough to deter all but the most determined intruders, the maidens of the Hesperides seem as safe as on a distant planet. Against this background, the incantations of the three maidens seem the otiose strains of a paranoiac aesthete. Since the only real signs of life are there in the garden, the antithesis of still point and turning world is all but inverted.

It is difficult to know whether Tennyson himself was aware of these 'difficulties'. The fact that he never republished the poem has often been cited as evidence of his subsequent dissatisfaction with its garden-of-privileged-refuge aesthetic. Internal evidence may suggest that we are expected to interpret the poem critically, perhaps even ironically. While some critics have focused upon the patterns of unity linking the elements of the garden, other writers have emphasized patterns of disjunction.[15] It seems likely that Tennyson eventually rejected the Hesperidian model of the poetic world because he came to see that the poet must situate his garden of art in the social world, address social themes, and engage in human affairs, rather than strive to maintain his own brand of aesthetic occultism.

It is this perception that informs *The Lotos-Eaters*, a poem which, like *The Hesperides*, deals with the theme of escape from the brazen world and with the importance of fulfilling the escapist's dreams. For this reason, the poems invite comparison and very often receive it. But to focus upon the differences in the biogeographical details of the poems is to become aware that *The Lotos-Eaters* subverts the escapist's dream of a garden paradise, not by foregrounding its precariousness and the unceasing effort required to protect it, but by robbing it of edenic attractions. Indeed, the most important thing about Lotosland is that it is not a garden.

For one thing, Lotosland does not conform to the aesthete's ideal of the garden—a sacred bower for the privileged few—since it entertains the very representatives of ordinary humanity which the guardians of the Hesperidian garden seek actively to exclude. Lotosland can comfortably admit the mariners of Ulysses because it has nothing to fear from them. In contrast to the Gardens of the Hesperides, Lotosland proffers its fruits, for their consumption will ensure compliance with its natural rhythms. The mariners are powerless to change what is fundamentally unchanging. Only gardens, which almost by definition are time-bound and capable of being transformed (into wildscape), are endangered by the predatorily self-indulgent. To the travel-weary sailors, Lotosland is a place where 'all things seemed the same' (*TP*, p. 431). Here as elsewhere in the poem, 'seemed' is used to draw attention to the illusory nature of the mariners' perceptions rather than to imply the mutability of Lotosland itself. And, of course, it is the apparent permanence of its forms, the essentially *un*-gardenlike nature of the place, that most attracts the mariners to it.

Lotosland differs from gardens proper—and from the Hesperidian gardens in particular—in terms of its contents and form. Gone is the exotic island garden with its complex syntagm of precisely delineated forms. In its place, paradigmatic profusion, where any internal differences are of a formal rather than of a functional kind. Everything tends to sameness. Absolutes like 'all' and 'every' abound, and there is a pervasive atmosphere of heaviness and decay—a kind of sterile fecundity. The 'long-leaved flowers weep', 'the poppy hangs in sleep' (p. 433) and 'the full-juiced apple, waxing over-mellow, / Droops in a silent autumn night' (p. 432).

In Lotosland, then, Tennyson has created not a garden of forms but a nebulous symbolic landscape with no internal structure to speak of. Apparently he was attempting to fashion an environment and a vegetable life both seemingly consonant with the immediate mood of the mariners, and finally inimical to their ultimate needs and interests. The landscape of undifferentiated natural forms appears to gratify their present desires: sybaritic fusion with nature, and the urge towards undifferentiated being and union with the gods. But Lotosland is not paradise; 'its satisfactions are enervating and narcotic'.[16] The mariners, Tennyson implies, must struggle towards this realization, must use what resources they have to combat its monopolizing and homogenizing effects on their perception. The task will not be easy, for Tennyson has deliberately placed them in a landscape which resists the kinds of categorizing operations they must perform if they are to recognize their separateness and nature as outsiders.

The struggle takes the form of sensory submission versus rhetorical assertiveness, and is mimetically patterned in the structure of the Choric song, where verse paragraphs of description alternate with those in which the mariners reluctantly express a nagging sense of responsibility to the world beyond.

There is a third and related reason why Lotosland is not a garden. In the garden man must labour. Only unfallen man has the privilege of living without need of a spade. Even the magical Hesperidian garden is a place of toil. *The Hesperides* is full of injunctions to action, like 'watch' and 'guard', and the sap must work relentlessly to nourish the garden fruit. Lotosland is the antithesis of the well-kept, ordered garden; this is its appeal to the labour-exhausted mariners.

One of the problems of knowing exactly what to make of the revolt against toil in *The Lotos-Eaters* is Tennyson's decision (albeit a decision constrained by literary sources) to populate his illusionary paradise with sailors rather than poets. This has led some critics to suggest that Tennyson was entirely sympathetic to the mariners' quest. Both this interpretation and the slightly more sophisticated thesis that '*Officially* he is writing a denunciation; *creatively* he is making a defence',[17] rest upon the assumption that Tennyson is concerned exclusively with the plight of working people in general, and thus very little with the particular plight of the poet. If this assumption is invalid (as I believe it is) then there is no justification for thinking that Tennyson is expressing unqualified approval of the mariners' idleness. Sloth, after all, is peculiarly unpoetic. To live forever in a subjective world, 'Falling asleep in a half-dream', is to remain forever an unrealized poet. Tennyson could not approve of this (though he could understand it) which may help to explain the rhetorical energy the mariners expend in arguing themselves into torpor. Should it succeed—and we are surely meant to believe it will not—the mariners would be submitting to a land which 'offers not abundant life but spiritual death', for Lotosland is 'no garden of the Hesperides but a magnificently ironic variation upon a wasteland'.[18]

In neither *The Hesperides* nor *The Lotos-Eaters* is the poet's mind explicitly linked with emblematic garden landscapes. Two poems in the 1830 volume do make this explicit linkage.

The Poet, heavily influenced by Shelley, is a rhapsodic vision of the poet as universal gardener. If the poem is stripped of its decorative trimmings and some of its more obvious emphases, we can discern three main stages in its development. The first deals with what the poet is; the second with what he does; the third with the consequences of what he does.

The poet is credited with enormous power, knowledge, and percipience: 'He saw thro' life and death, thro' good and ill, / . . . thro' his own soul'. Thus gifted, he is able to perform his seminal mission. 'Like Indian seeds blown from his silver tongue' he shoots 'The viewless arrows; his thoughts' (*TP*, p. 222) into the fields of the world. His seeds of truth take root, and blossom into golden flowers, which furnish further 'winged shafts of truth', until 'the world / Like one great garden show'd'. In the garden's sunrise, Freedom is reared; embroidered on her 'raiment's hem' is the flaming tag, 'Wisdom' (p. 223). Fed by the poet's texts, she 'gather[ed] thunder', until with 'one poor poet's scroll . . . she shook the world' (p. 224).

The poet of *The Poet's Mind* is no less special or privileged, but wholly concerned with pursuing his hieratic craft in necessary isolation from the threatening world. The poem itself is a plainer, less ambiguous version of *The Hesperides*. Like its more exotic successor, *The Poet's Mind* adumbrates a poetic-garden ecosystem, though its formal characteristics are different. The poet's mind is imaged as a garden enclosed, a space of 'holy ground' hedged round by 'laurel-shrub'. In the middle leaps a fountain, springing from 'a level of bowery lawn'. The song it sings—a 'song of undying love'—is the source of the poet's imagination, though its ultimate source is 'the brain of the purple mountain / Which stands in the distance yonder'. In turn, the mountain 'draws from the Heavens above' (*TP*, p. 225). Hence, the poet's mind is connected, through a chain of natural forms, to God himself. The flow of energy along this chain is apparently uni-directional, thus this poetic-garden ecosystem is less involved, and less complete than that in *The Hesperides*.

Like the Hesperidian gardens, the poet's garden mind is threatened from without; not, this time, by humanity in general, but by a more particular foe: the 'Dark-brow'd sophist' (p. 224). He is portrayed as a withering anti-gardener, an insentient and insensitive outsider. There is death in his eye and frost in his breath. Were he to penetrate the sacred garden he would 'blight the plants' and unperch the 'merry bird' that 'chants' (p. 225) at its heart.

To repel his foe, the poet has only vexed injunctions—which accounts for the tone of paranoia as well as of antipathy in his voice. The poet's garden possesses none of the defenses afforded by the song of the Hesperidian maidens, and so its survival depends entirely upon the sophist's compliance with the poet's commands. Should he dispute the poet's claims to mystery and sacerdotal privilege, the garden is his to trammel at will.

The Poet's Mind has received only scant critical attention. It tends to be passed over as thematically straightforward, and interesting for only two reasons—firstly, because it presents a clear statement of Tennyson's resentment 'at attempts of those of an intellectual bent to enter into any sort of examination or analysis of the poet's mind';[19] secondly, because it forms a puzzling contrast to *The Poet*.

However, *The Poet's Mind* becomes an altogether more interesting poem when one considers why the poet's mind is imaged as an enclosed garden rather than as some more expansive and 'naturalistic' topographical figure. The reasons, I suggest, are historical as well as personal; Tennyson's deployment of the enclosed garden resulted not simply from his perception of its representational possibilities, but also from his having written the poem within earshot of the Romantic poets he nonetheless felt his otherness from. Placed in this historical context, *The Poet's Mind* can be taken as an implied statement of the need to reclaim for the poet the privileged and identifying environment of the *hortus conclusus*, which the Romantics had shunned.[20] Similarly, Tennyson's obsessive concern with the vulnerability of the poet's world, and his decision to image this world as a walled garden, can be illuminated by the history of poet/landscape identifications, in which Tennyson's place is significantly different from that of the poets he immediately succeeded.

It has long been recognized that certain kinds of gardens are peculiarly appropriate settings in which to pursue certain kinds of aesthetic activity.[21] It is also significant that poets of various ages have found in garden landscapes analogues of and correspondences to other kinds of 'landscape'—social, political, and aesthetic. The last of these analogues—the codification of aesthetic *Gestalten* in the imagery and syntax of the appropriate garden type—is especially pertinent to the present discussion. The dialectic between different levels of identification is particularly significant when the poet's predilections for a garden type superbly conducive to his thoughts and feelings emerges as an objective correlative of the geography of his inner landscape.

The relevance of these relationships to *The Poet's Mind* may not be immediately apparent, since Tennyson deploys the enclosed garden as an aesthetic analogue, but offers no explicit argument for its restoration as a physical setting for poetic production. The point to stress here is that Tennyson's sense of the need to reassert the identity and status of the poet is not unconnected with the fact that the Romantics had found their symbols of greatest power and beauty among more natural landscapes.

If Tennyson's poem could not have been written by any one of the major Romantic poets, neither could it have been written without them; for *The Poet's Mind* is simultaneously a modification, extension and repudiation of the Romantic conception of the poet's place in the process of poetic production. On the one hand, some of the Romantic poets were imaginatively attracted to the *topos* of the enclosed garden, in part because they foreshadowed Tennyson's interest in aesthetic self-clarification, and his desire to distinguish the poet's domain from that of the philosopher. The Romantic poet's transactions with the physical world necessarily involved a conceptualization of the poetic self. To some degree all the major Romantic poets addressed themselves to the task of formulating an image of their inner terrain: How are mental images related to the configuration of objects in the phenomenal world? Does the human imagination construct or reconstruct the world in its 'ennobling interchange' with it?

On the other hand, the imaginative appeal of the enclosed garden never quite crystallized into a Romantic image of the poet's mind comparable with Tennyson's, in part because of the celebrated environmental predilections of the Romantics. For while their intense engagement with nature in its magnificent, sublime, and less cultivated forms facilitated perceptions of the most complex kinds, it also worked actively to resist the conditions under which the poet could picture his mind in terms of an image of appropriate equivalences. This is partly a matter of the excesses of nature uncontained, and the problem of extracting from the abundance of the natural world a coherent and precisely delineated analogue of the poet's mind and art. The task is compounded when the distinction between perceiving subject and perceived object is all but blurred, as it is in those moments of profound interpenetration of self and world that readers have tended to value most in Romantic poetry.[22]

The Romantic 'solution' was to set or find enclosed 'gardens' in the *midst* of natural scenery. One such naturally sequestered 'garden' is the 'green and silent spot, amid the hills' in which the speaker in Coleridge's *Fears in Solitude* finds himself.[23] There are similar spots in the poetic landscapes of Keats: the 'tasteful nook' in *Endymion*, for example, and the natural 'garden' which Keats presents as an image of the poet's mind in the final stanza of *Ode to Psyche*.[24]

In exchanging the naturally sequestered 'garden' for a cultivated fully enclosed garden, Tennyson signalled a set of attitudes towards the natural world that differed significantly from those of his immediate predecessors. Tennyson's poetry lacks 'anything like the complete ecstatic self-abandonment to the world-process shown by Goethe in his *Fragment über die Natur*'.[25] Nor did he share Wordsworth's effusiveness over nature and the wholehearted belief in its beneficence. Moreover, Tennyson was predominantly a dualist by temperament, was unsympathetic to the monistic 'craving to reduce all the phenomena of the universe to a single term and therefore obliterate the distinction between objective and subjective.'[26] By picturing the poet's mind as a cultivated garden, linked to but distinguishable from the natural world, Tennyson was able to maintain this distinction.

Tennyson apparently sensed that he could best assert his identity as a poet by providing an exactly defined and recognisable image of his mind and art. The enclosed garden had precisely the appropriate properties and associations. It approximated more closely to Tennyson's ideas of art than nature untransformed ever could, and the enclosed garden had those qualities that Tennyson favoured most in his own art. It was compact, coherent and clearly delineated; it had a framed and picture-like quality; and because of its historical associations—with the medieval world, in particular—it suggested distance in time and space. As external evidence, there is Tennyson's oft-quoted remark to Knowles: 'it is the distance that charms me in the landscape, the picture and the past'.[27] The observation that Tennyson 'needed an art that isolated, distanced, and preserved even the immediate and contemporary within its own world of precision and ideal form',[28] is clearly to the point. It is characteristic of Tennyson that he should pluck from history and mythology a garden type with countless apposite connotations (privilege, refuge, holiness, order, delight, and so forth) and appropriate it to very specific aesthetic demands.

Though the garden in *The Poet's Mind* is a felicitous, functional enclosure, Tennyson more commonly deploys the enclosed garden as an image of isolation and imprisonment. The garden of the poet's mind may be antisocial, but it is full of life, and precious because of its vulnerability. This is not the case with the enclosed gardens of the island tower of *The Lady of Shalott* and of the 'sinful soul' in *The Palace of Art*. In both, the garden elements are firmly contained by and very literally overshadowed by incarcerating structures:

> Four gray walls, and four gray towers
> Overlook a space of flowers, (*TP*, p. 355)
>
> Four courts I made, East, West, South and North,
> In each a squared lawn . . . (*TP*, p. 402)

The 'space of flowers' and the 'squared lawn[s]' suggest neatness, and deliberate exclusion of the creative energies of the wilderness admitted into the poet's garden via the spring which has its source in the distant purple mountains. Squeezed between 'four gray towers', the garden of the Lady of Shalott is dislocated not only from the turning social world but also from the Lady herself. When Tennyson revised the poem in 1842, he emphasized the austerity of the garden, and made it a still more telling image of alienated poetic consciousness, by expunging the references to the roses which 'overtrailed' the 'little isle' (*TP*, p. 355).

In *The Palace of Art*, the soul's palatial monstrosity has as its prototypical model Kubla Khan's pleasaunce, against which, Tennyson's 'Lordly pleasure-house' seems 'merely gimcrack'.[29] The palace, and the self-indulgent aestheticism which inspires it, is expressed in the dedicatory verse to the poem in quasi-allegorical terms as 'A spacious garden full of flowering weeds' (*TP*, p. 399). Nature enters the palace garden in elements of grotesquerie, and many of its features suggest an attempt to upstage the garden of Timon's Villa in Pope's *Epistle to Burlington*, a garden built for self-aggrandisement and show. Statues feature prominently in both poems, as do fountains of a sort. 'Two cupids squirt before' Timon's Villa; in the palace gardens 'The golden gorge of dragons spouted forth / A flood of fountain foam'. And the final impression of the palace (the soul's as well as the reader's) is also of 'a labour'd Quarry above ground'.[30]

The soul's palace is more complex than Timon's Villa, and less symmetrically structured. It is also more attractive since, superficially at least, it has an 'artful wildness' which Timon's tasteless villa garden lacks. But neither is raised with the happy cooperation of nature. To emphasize the point, both Pope and Tennyson supply landscapes to contrast with those they condemn—with one important difference. Pope's alternative vision of the good estate is a full contrast; Tennyson's cottage in the vale is a feeble half-contrast. It can be nothing more than this because it is itself 'an artistic image'.[31] The issues of the cottage garden aesthetic lie dormant and unquestioned. Moreover, the palace is not so much abandoned in utter disillusionment as vacated until such time as the soul can be 'purged' of its 'guilt' (p. 418).

In *The Poet's Mind*, the poet's garden is threatened from without; in *The Lady of Shalott* and *The Palace of Art* it is sapped from within. The garden is no longer co-extensive with the poetic consciousness, but a feature of it, much reduced in size, significance, and vitality, and displaced both spatially and symbolically from the centre of the aesthete's world. In these poems, Tennyson traces one stage of the process by which the beautiful garden retreat of the poet's mind is perceptually redefined as a place of debilitating isolation. The ultimate stage is presented in *Mariana*. The imaginatively (but ironically) fertile 'heroine' of the poem cannot or will not escape from the withering immurement of her moated grange. The opening lines of the poem refer us to the wasteland into which the delightfully ordered garden of the mind has degenerated:

> With blackest moss the flower-pots
> Were thickly crusted, one and all:
> The rusted nails fell from the knots
> That held the pear to the gable-wall.
> The broken sheds looked sad and strange:
> Uplifted was the clinking latch;
> Weeded and worn the ancient thatch
> Upon the lonely moated grange. (*TP*, pp. 187–8)

These features are the secretions of a debilitated, morbidly introspective Romantic consciouness. They are also absence-in-presence reminders of what was or might have been: a flourishing country-house world, a vital garden of the mind.

In a number of the early poems, then, Tennyson uses the image of the enclosed garden to explore the problem of the poet who wishes to defend himself from a hostile world but who frets about the devitalizing effects of embowerment. In the poems I have discussed, the problem seems insoluble. To remain in the enclosed garden, like Mariana, is to experience a disastrous wilting of the poetic libido. To leave the protective enclosure inadequately equipped to reconcile the creative spirit with life in the busy world is to die like the Lady of Shalott. To depart like the sinful soul with every intention of returning is to do no more than gesture towards the social world.

That Tennyson found other uses for the garden suggests that he found ways of circumventing or dissolving this dilemma. The first possibility that seems to have occurred to him was to focus upon gardens *in* rather than *of* the mind: the poet was better off *inventing* gardens—that is, exercising his creative powers—than confining himself within them.

A product of this perception is *Recollections of the Arabian Nights*, one of the few early poems in which enclosed gardens are not associated with stasis and imprisonment. The speaker finds refuge from the 'forward-flowing tide of time' by embarking on a dreamlike voyage through exotic gardens inaccessible to prisoners of reality:

> Black the garden-bowers and grots
> Slumbered: the solemn palms were ranged
> Above, unwoo'd of summer wind:
> A sudden splendour from behind
> Flushed all the leaves with rich gold-green. (*TP*, p. 208)

If the first lines bring to mind Mariana's wasteland garden, the impressions of gloom and rotting stillness are dispelled by the final lines. Again, like Mariana's garden and Lotosland, these 'High-walled' oriental gardens are heavy (with scents and blooms) but the connotations of weightiness are quite different. In *Mariana*, weightiness suggests stagnancy and spiritual oppression; in *The Lotos-Eaters*, somnolence and rankness. In *Recollections*, the heaviness of 'eastern flowers large' has the positive connotations of the luxuriant, the sensuous, and the entrancing.

It has been said that *Recollections* 'is one of the few poems of Tennyson's in which a personal mythology prevailed.'[32] In this respect, the poem is less derivative than, say, the 'holy garden' poems which owe more than a little to Tennyson's reading of George Stanley Faber, the nineteenth-century mythologist. Even so, the idea of a dreamlike voyage through sensuous gardens was probably suggested by Shelley's *Alastor*, and though the poet's grandson may be right in supposing that "it is the song of a Lincolnshire nightingale, not of the Arabian bulbul, which makes the poem spring to life',[33] the gardens Tennyson describes bear little resemblance to the gardens with which he was personally familiar.

As Tennyson became less introspectively concerned with the garden of the poet's mind, he drew increasingly upon his experiences of actual gardens. There are two main reasons for this. Firstly, as gardens were experientially linked with his moods and memories they permitted him to focus and convey feelings of personal significance but of more general interest than those of the isolated Romantic aesthete. Secondly, as Tennyson developed an interest in social themes—the family, education for women, class relations—his attention switched from internal gardens to external gardens and their social implications.

There is a third, more general reason. Landscapes, humanized landscapes, gradually acquired for Tennyson a degree of significance proportional to his sense of their otherness from nature. This sense was relatively weak in the youthful Tennyson. In *On Sublimity*, the speaker feels that mountains are not only more exhilarating than gentle valleys, but also more real, ontologically more compelling. In other words, he comes close to confusing mountain scenery with nature itself. Tennyson came to view this correspondence theory of nature and scenery with grave suspicion, a position resulting from theological uncertainties, scientific theories of evolution, and doubts about the healthiness of the Romantic predilections he exorcised through his 'garden of the mind' poems. For Tennyson, external nature came to mean both a world of material things and an 'abstract and amoral process',[34] fundamentally indifferent to human needs, sometimes hostile, and neither therapeutic nor spiritually illuminating. Only at fleeting, mystical moments, he believed, did it interpenetrate with human experience. By contrast, landscape scenery is always of human significance. Because it is always cultivated and particularized, it cannot be mistaken for the general principle of nature. It appeals to the conscious pictorial artist, it has direct links with human experience, and for Tennyson it 'is almost invariably stamped with the associations of immemorial social use'.[35] Tennyson himself declared: 'A known landskip is to me an old friend, that continually talks to me of my own youth, and half-forgotten things, and indeed does more for me than many an old friend that I know.'[36]

Even in the 1830 poems, a 'known landskip'—the gardens and purlieus of Somersby—give what Charles Tennyson called 'life and passion' to the 'most striking lyrics of the collection'.[37] The flat topography of Lincolnshire inspired the description of Mariana's desolate grange garden. Close in feeling to *Mariana* is the beautiful lyric *Song*, 'A Spirit haunts the year's last hours'. The setting is an autumnal garden, and its contents establish the poem's mood. Again, the principal feature of the garden is its weightiness, here connoting grief and melancholy, though tempered by suggestions of richness synaesthetically rendered as the 'moist rich smell of rotting leaves' (*TP*, p. 215). As in *The Lotos-Eaters*, the various significations of heaviness are closely bound up with thematic concerns. The mariners' state of mind must ultimately be construed as false consciousness, because they mistake the connection between their own feelings of weariness, and the heavy forms of Lotosland; they identify with the sensuousness, but not with the oppressive rankness, of its flowers. By contrast, and as an effect of Tennyson's concentration upon the mood of a familiar landscape, the spirit who stalks it is near to unison with its flowers and rhythms. The only question mark hangs over the usefulness of the job he performs; since the flowers are drooping beneath their own weight ('Heavily hangs the broad sunflower', / Heavily hangs the hollyhocks'), his own contribution ('Earthward he boweth the heavy stalks / Of the mouldering flowers') seems redundant. Apparently he wishes to accelerate the natural processes of decay—to hasten the realization of his death wish. But unlike Blake's sunflower, which also yearns for release from the world, Tennyson's spirit seems not to long for a golden clime beyond and above the world of wearying experience. What is more, his actions seem wantonly destructive. In this, he seems to represent the masculine counterpart of Keats's female spirit of autumn—the animus as opposed to the anima—'who instead of tying up the drooping flowers, like Eve in *Paradise Lost* (IX), relentlessly forces them down'. He is 'an anti-gardener, depressive in temperament, and presenting one of the traditional symptoms of mental derangement ("To himself he talks")'.[38]

In this respect, *Song* may be regarded as the forerunner of many Victorian verses which similarly associate heavy or dying gardens with sick and dying humans.[39] This connection has something to do with the problems many Victorians appear to have experienced in confronting the fact of death directly and, consequently, their attempts to soften its harsher edges through the dying blooms of scented gardens. It is what might be called the alchemical use of the garden, through which base experiences are transmuted into golden memories. I have noted already how the melancholy evocations of drooping flowers in the *Song* garden are qualified by a suggestion of pleasurable luxuriance. The equivocal mood of the garden setting seems to be an expression of the equivocal atmosphere of his Somersby home and/or a poetic act of mental management: a means of rendering the wintry memories of an overbearing father less stark.

Another of the early poems laced with garden imagery is *Ode to Memory*. Here, as in many later poems, the emphasis is upon the restorative powers of garden memories as opposed to the contemplative and protective uses of garden enclosures. The speaker, 'faint in obscurity', draws eagerly upon revivifying memory pictures of the garden and purlieus of Somersby rectory:

> The seven elms, the poplars four
> That stand beside my father's door,
> And chiefly for the brook that loves
> To purl o'er matted cress and ribbed sand.
>
> . . . .
>
> Or a garden bower'd close
> With plaited alleys of the trailing rose,
> Long alleys falling down to the twilight grots,
> Or opening upon level plots
> Of crowned lilies, standing near
> Purple-spiked lavender. (*TP*, pp. 212; 213–4)

Before invoking these memories that 'Never grow sere', the poet 'rejects the picturesque and exotic landscapes that he had often used in his earlier poems presumably because they are not personal memories.'[40] 'Tennyson is quite consciously making a statement about the sources of his poetic inspiration, rejecting outside influences, and rooting his poetry in his own experience.'[41]

Tennyson's own experiences were typically constituted by the experiential associations of particular places at particular times. More thoroughly even than Wordsworth, Tennyson internalized familiar landscapes, evaluating their subjective significance in terms of their power to move him.

Many of these familiar landscapes are gardens, most obviously because some of Tennyson's most poignant experiences occurred in gardens or were connected with them, less obviously because gardens register change, loss, and the passing of time—the processes which animate the associations of place—more swiftly, sensitively, and conspicuously than, for example, the buildings to which they are attached. Thus, in the famous 'farewell to Somersby' section of *In Memoriam* (Section CI), Tennyson focuses upon the transient garden and the surrounding landscape, rather than upon the rectory itself (*TP*, p. 954).

Tennyson's apparent ability to recall the details of the 'well-beloved' garden accentuates the feeling of regret. But in a curious way, the poet's grasp of the experience is only made possible by his withdrawal from the familiar landscape. It would seem that in order to organize, comprehend, and ultimately to come to terms with experience, Tennyson needed to contain it within a discrete but temporally distanced spatial structure. Similarly, he seems to have required the intensely visual elements of a living landscape to 'observe' the processes of time. The combination of temporal distance and topographical acuity complicates the poet's response to the passing of time, which is experienced neither as atrophyingly linear (since separation from the garden does not diminish its visual or affective intensity), nor as joyfully circular (since the seasonal rhythms continue 'Unwatch'd' and 'Unloved'), but as reflexive or helical (since we can recall but never repeat even a repetitive experience). Hence, the tonal quality of the section: sadness for what was, tempered by acceptance of what is and hope for what will be.

Elsewhere in *In Memoriam*, Tennyson's memory pictures are framed more literally and iconically in garden terms, embodying the associations of place in a sharply-focused visual image. More than once he recalls the tree-encompassed lawn of Somersby, with its checkered pattern of shade and light: 'Witch-elms that counterchange the floor / Of this flat lawn with dusk and bright' (*TP*, p. 940). We might see in this chiaroscuro landscape a symbolization of the two spirits who, in the garden-walks on the eve of his depature, 'Contend for loving masterdom': the 'light' spirit of boyhood and family love, and the spirit of Hallam, the 'lost friend among the bowers' (p. 955), whose death has cast a shadow upon the garden of felicitous memories. The tree-framed garden is the topographical equivalent of the 'one pure image of regret' into which the contending spirits finally 'mix' (p. 955). At any rate, Tennyson's communion with the past is facilitated by his 'Artist-like' memory which, 'Ever retiring' to 'gaze / On the prime labour of its early days' (p. 213), fixes upon a vivid garden structure from the aperture of the present and along 'the vista of long grief and pain'.[42] Because of its familiarity, discreteness, and iconicity, the garden served Tennyson well as a means of making intelligible the kinds of mystical experience he relates in Sections XCV and CIII of *In Memoriam*. In the latter, for example, 'the visionary excitement is carefully placed in a context of Victorian circumstances, a country house with distinct landscapes of blossom, maple and stream'.[43]

Tennyson knew also that gardens have the additional virtue of keeping alive the associations which made them memorable. In *The Gardener's Daughter*, the painterly description of Rose in her garden appears also to be a description of the painting of Rose—a permanent pictorial record to comfort the husband (or lover?) she has left behind. But Tennyson did not even need to go back to once-loved gardens to fix them in his mind, or revive the sensations of which they were originally productive.

When he did revisit such gardens, they functioned anamnesically, but more importantly, they brought to mind past experiences *within* the context of a physical landscape more or less unaltered by the loss of the loves or lives which gave them their emotional resonance. A good example of this process can be found in the little autobiographical poem, 'The Roses on the Terrace':

> Rose, on this terrace fifty years ago,
> When I was in my June, you in your May,
> Two words, '*My* Rose' set all your face aglow,
> And now that I am white, and you are gray,
> That blush of fifty years ago, my dear,
> Blooms in the Past, but close to me to-day
> As this red rose, which on our terrace here
> Glows in the blue of fifty miles away. (*TP*, p. 1423)

Like the gardener's daughter, Rose is equated with the blooms of the garden, only more so, for she lives on in the red rose itself. Here, too, Tennyson combines the Wordsworthian belief in the restorative powers of the memory, the more Proustian coupling of memory with desire, and the process of an unresolved dialectic, which nevertheless yields moments of harmony.

An earlier 'garden' poem of recollection is *In the Garden at Swainston*, composed on the occasion of the funeral of Tennyson's friend and neighbour, Sir John Simeon, in 1870, though first published four years later. Again, tender memories are evoked within a familiar garden, the plenitude of which persists in the absence of the people with whom it is connected:

> Nightingales warbled without,
> Within was warbling for thee:
> Shadows of three dead men
> Walked in the walks with me,
> Shadows of three dead men and thou wast one of the three.
>
> Nightingales sang in his woods:
> The Master was far away:
> Nightingales warbled and sang
> Of a passion that lasts but a day;
> Still in the house in his coffin the Prince of courtesy lay.
>
> Two dead men have I known
> In courtesy like to thee:
> Two dead men have I loved
> With a love that ever will be:
> Three dead men have I loved and thou art last of the three. (*TP*, pp. 1219–20)

Why the *garden* (as opposed to the *house*) of Swainston? Again, it would seem to be a combination of biographical significance and environmental appropriateness. It was in the garden of Swainston in the early-mid 1850s that Tennyson composed those sections of *Maud* that may have been inspired by its Cedars of Lebanon. Tennyson would have known that his fondness for Swainston was not peculiar, that its scenery had been lauded in a long series of guides and tours to the Isle of Wight, itself a favourite haunt of hunters of the picturesque. By the time of the poem's composition, 'Swainston and its surroundings had long been celebrated as a showplace. In the poem its very name for scenic history and beauty adds poignancy to its role as a scene of death'.[45] Moreover, the speaker's experience is here constructed out of oppositions which emerge naturally from the garden setting: absence/presence; within/without; transience/permanence; recurrence/finality; silence/noise; action/stasis. As the (ironically) seasonal agents and reminders of a continuing or permanent state of affairs, the nightingales play a role akin in function and importance to that of the roses in *Roses on the Terrace.*

If space permitted, one might both extend this discussion so as to trace Tennyson's more 'social' uses of the garden, and expand it to consider the metaphorical applications of 'garden' in Victorian literature of various kinds. Tennyson's own deployment of the garden to articulate a range of personal experiences and concerns itself offers a paradigm of the Victorian predilection for mapping the inner life in garden imagery.

Conclusion

When I embarked on this study, my intention was not to unpack a neatly parcelled thesis, but rather to explore the relations between gardens and literature within the Victorian cultural context in which both are embedded. What in the first place attracted me to it was the challenge of grappling with a genuinely interdisciplinary and potentially integrative concept: the concept of the garden. I expected to have to accommodate and synthesize inputs from a number of seemingly disparate fields of enquiry. I expected also that the word 'garden' would afford me access to many Victorian ideas, institutions and social practices and, in particular, to their mediation in works of imaginative literature.

My expectations have not been disappointed. I believe I can claim also that my decision not to be bound in by a formal definition of 'garden' has been fully vindicated. Indeed, so various are the forms and functions of 'garden', that a merely informal and abbreviated inventory turns out to be strikingly catholic: cultivated plot, aesthetic composition, aesthetic analogue, social image, humanized landscape, symbolic landscape, representational text, therapeutic environment, domestic sanctuary, domestic prison, recreational space, community playground, social setting, civilizing agency, socializing institution, and locus of cultural values.

It is to the last of these 'functions' that I wish to devote the final pages of this study, for it seems to me that the significance of the garden elements in Victorian imaginative literature may lie ultimately in their hidden curriculum—that is, in the implicit and probably unintended messages of cultural or ideological significance that they convey. I have in mind the assumptions upon which garden descriptions rest, and the ideas, beliefs and values they tend to emphasize. I want, if I can, to identify a few of the more common of these, and to present them as simple postulates. If they seem banal then it is probably because they have the character of all potentially ideological myths that masquerade as common-sense truths.

Perhaps the principal postulate is that gardens reflect their owners. In *The Garden that I Love*, Alfred Austin gave explicit formulation to a belief almost ubiquitous in Victorian imaginative literature: the belief that gardens express the values, attitudes and personalities of their owners:

> A garden that one makes oneself becomes associated with one's personal history and that of one's friends, interwoven with one's tastes, preferences, and character, and constitutes a sort of unwritten, but withal, manifest autobiography. Show me your garden, provided it be your own, and I will tell you what you are like. (p. 112)

In the novels of Dickens, Trollope and most other Victorian novelists the semiotic consonance between gardens and their owners is so consistent that it amounts to a kind of tautology. Gardens mirror their owners; owners mirror their gardens. Favourably presented characters have favourably presented gardens; unfavourably presented characters have unfavourably presented gardens—or no gardens at all.[1]

The signifying practice of what might be called topographical phrenology implies a set of widely-shared assumptions: in particular, that gardens are autonomous 'texts', the meanings of which are determined largely by individual 'authors' rather than by, say, culture-specific codes and conventions over which individual owners have little or no control. 'Authors' are also assumed, to some extent, to have unique, stable and unitary characters which their gardens diagrammatically represent.[2]

These assumptions are reflected in a novel by Charlotte Yonge entitled *Nuttie's Father* (1885). In the opening chapter there is a description of a row of houses, each one of which has a garden which reflects its owner in some significant respect. The garden of Mr Dutton ('the old bachelor of the Road') reflects his passion for tidiness and order:

> . . . was not his house, with lovely sill boxes full of flowers in the windows, the neatest of the neat; and did not the tiny conservatory over his dining-room window always produce the flowers much needed for the altar roses, and likewise bouquets for the tables of favoured ladies. Why, the very daisies never durst lift their heads on his little lawn, which even bore a French-looking glass globe in the centre. (p. 6)

When Mr Dutton moves to London, he constructs another garden, expressive again of his peculiar and unchanging personality:

> . . . there was a perfect order and trimness about the shaven lawn, the little fountain in the midst, the flower-beds gay with pansies, forget-me-nots, and other early beauties, and

> the freshly-rolled gravel paths, that made Nuttie exclaim: 'Ah! I should have known this for yours anywhere.' (p. 306)

Gardens do not necessarily have to be made by the characters of whom they are meant to be expressive. In Trollope's novels, maintaining an inherited garden is as indexical of character and squirarchical responsibility as is making a garden from scratch. The landed gentleman expresses his sense of self with reference to his relations with past and future stewards of the same estate. He must either acknowledge or deny his partnerships with them. Though impoverished, the Greshams of *Dr Thorne* are true gentlemen because they decline to meddle with the 'multitude of trim gardens' on the Greshamsbury estate—'one of the well-known landmarks of the family' (p. 10). Similarly, Roger Carbury shows himself to be a thoroughly dependable and, in the best sense, a disinterested, landed gentleman by maintaining the gardens of Carbury Manor House. By contrast, Sir Hugh Clavering is an irresponsible and neglectful steward as well as a cold and selfish man. His gardens have the characteristic demerits of those of Trollope's imperfect estate owners: a bleak and naked lawn that comes right up to the house front; and a neglected flower-garden inhospitably remote from the house.

To most Victorian readers, the expressive assumptions underpinning garden descriptions would probably have seemed too obvious to question. The ideological significance of these assumptions lies precisely in the apparent self-evidence of the values they endorse: the importance of private property, the naturalness of individual ownership, and the ideology of individualism itself. Gardens can be defined as expressive of the values, attitudes and characters of particular individuals only if they are assumed to be owned and controlled by individuals. The creative contribution of an employed labour force must be played down—as it generally is in Victorian fiction—and attention must focus on garden texts rather than contexts. Hence, fictional gardens tend to be bracketed off from the economic structures which support them (the garden is one thing, the factory another), and from the agencies—nursery firms, garden magazines, horticultural societies, and the like—which supply them with materials and ideas. Moreover, the illusion of expressive individuality can be sustained only by suppressing the conventional significations of garden design, and by subordinating imitativeness to originality. Gardens of purely conventional or imitative design are rarely evaluated positively, and rarely associated with particular individuals.

Finally, the emphasis on expressive individualism silences or perhaps makes unthinkable other conceptualizations of the garden and the social conditions under which they might be realized. The idea of a garden as something owned and maintained by communities, of gardening as joyful collaborative labour—what Morris called 'skilled cooperative gardening for beauty's sake'[3]—is almost totally absent in Victorian literature of all kinds.

A related postulate is that gardening is an 'innocent' and virtuous activity that enhances the quality of life for those who engage in it. The belief that gardens bring moral and personal benefits to those who care deeply for their gardens is a bedrock assumption of Victorian literature—both imaginative and technical. In novels, only sympathetically presented characters are allowed to cherish gardens for their own sakes. Such characters tend also to display the qualities of industry, patience, kindness and compassion which, according to countless garden writers, gardening serves to inculcate.

Characters who cherish their gardens are presented not only as 'better' people than those who do not; they are also presented as better off—a seemingly crude but, nonetheless, remarkably valid generalization. Underpinning this belief is the supposition that the possession of a much-loved garden implies the possession of other prerequisites for a contented existence—in particular, a stable and happy home. Regardless of their economic status, characters who value their gardens are seldom dissatisfied with their general lot. If they are comparatively poor, the possession of natural wealth (that is, wealth in the form of flowers and other living things) implies a more than adequate compensation for the lack of material wealth (this is surely the implicit message of most cottage garden descriptions). If they are comparatively well off, their gardens testify to their moral incorruptibility. Only characters seduced by wealth turn their gardens into ostentatious but joyless displays of riches. In short, gardens are a reward for virtue. They reward the poor man for his contentment with wealth in the form of flowers rather than bank notes. They reward the rich man for having the decency (or efficiency?) to convert (or disguise?) his material privileges into a currency which seems more 'natural' and acceptable. And they reward everyone who subscribes to the theory that the best kinds of commitments to make are those involving a home and a family.

In identifying these implicit messages I am making no

suppositions about conscious intent. In general, these messages seem to have been spoken through rather than by their 'authors'. Yet they serve to produce as well as to reflect consensual definitions of the situation for the very reason that they are so rarely subverted or challenged. For example, I know of only one moment in Victorian fiction (and it is only a moment) when gardening is defined in terms of its political as opposed to its moral and personal functions. Field, a Chartist leader and one of the least savoury characters in Disraeli's *Sybil*, denounces Trafford, the model factory owner, as 'a most inveterate Capitalist' who 'would divert the minds of the people from the Five Points by allotting them gardens and giving them baths' (p. 479).

From Field's perspective, gardening is anything but a virtuous and innocent activity, since its effect is to atomize the working class, and to divert the minds and energies of working people from the collective political action necessary to improve the conditions of their existence. That Field's view is given virtually no space in Victorian fiction does not mean that Victorian fiction is apolitical or ideologically neutral. The implicit messages of garden elements tend to privilege the definition of the situation to which Field is radically opposed. This is the view that gardening is socially integrative, an interest capable of uniting people from every section of society and of promoting a common culture that cuts across or transcends the divisions of class. Among the middle classes, the concept of a supra-class community based on the virtues of the garden had many exponents, presumably because this kind of demotic culture in no way threatened the existing social order. A contributor to *The Quarterly Review* of 1842 wrote:

> . . . as long . . . as this common interest pervades every class of society, so long shall we cling to the hope that our country is destined to outlive all her difficulties and dangers. Not because, like the Peris, we fight with flowers, and build amaranth bowers, and bind our enemies with links of roses—but because all this implies mutual interest and intercourse of every rank, and dependence of one class upon another—because it promotes an interchange of kindness and favours—because it speaks of proprietors dwelling on their hereditary acres, and the poorest labourer having an interest in the soil—because it gives local attachment, and healthy exercise and innocent recreation, and excites a love of the country and love of our own country, and a spirit of

> emulation devoid of bitterness—because it tells of wealth wisely spent, and competence widely diffused, of taste cultivated, and science practically applied—because . . . it *does* bring 'peace to the cottage', while it blesses the palace, and every virtuous home between these wide extremes—because it bespeaks the appreciation of what is natural and simple, and pure—teaches men to set the divine law of excellence above the low human standard of utility. . . .[4]

Much in Victorian imaginative literature appears to give the lie to the notion that garden lovers constitute a homogeneous community. For example, while the love of gardens is not presented as specific to any given class, certain horticultural practices and codes most certainly are. When Molly Gibson in *Wives and Daughters* and Violet Martindale in *Heartsease* enter upper-class gardens for the first time (those of Cumnor Towers and Martindale respectively), they are struck not just by the novelty but also by the unintelligibility of what they see before them—clear evidence that garden experiences have a social dimension. Occasionally, more specific question marks are suspended above the concept of a common floral culture in passages which draw attention to the unequal distribution of goods and wealth. Aaron, gardener to the Raveloe gentry, comments in *Silas Marner*:

> There's never a garden in all the parish but what there's endless waste in it for want o' somebody as could use everything up. It's what I think to myself sometimes, as there need nobody run short o' victuals if the land was made the most on, and there was never a morsel but what could find its way to a mouth. It sets one thinking o' that—gardening does. (p. 121)

On the other hand, the most pervasive assumptions and implicit messages in imaginative literature are consonant with the myth of a common (horti)culture. An avowed antipathy to flowers and gardens is repeatedly defined as a mark of moral perversity and cultural deviance. Trollope's Felix Carbury in *The Way We Live Now* says that he doesn't care for flowers or gardens; Carbury is a thoroughly nasty young cad. Collins's Dr Benjulia in *Heart and Science*, says, 'I don't care about trees and gardens' (p. 101) and he refuses to have a flower garden; Benjulia is a cruel and heartless 'scientist'. In the dining-room of the French sisters in *In the Year of Jubilee* 'not a flower appeared among the pretentious ornaments' (p. 2); the French sisters are idle, slovenly philistines. The exceptions prove the rule—that only 'good' people really care for flowers and gardens, and that 'good' people are to be found in all social classes. Again, the propositions seem crude, but on the broadest level they are surprisingly sound.

From the implicit messages I have identified here, there can be little doubt that the hidden curriculum of garden elements is (for want of a better term) conservative in its bias. This is nowhere more evident than in the model of time and change that garden elements tend to prefer. The positive emphasis upon old-fashioned and long-established plants and gardens and upon picturesqueness by default, the association of gardens with rootedness in a stable and familiar domestic world, with happy experiences and pleasing memories—these things are consonant with the conservative and culturally dominant model of gradualism, itself a conceptual outgrowth of Lyell's uniformitarian theory of gradual geological change. It has been argued that the ideology of gradualism infiltrated every major sphere of Victorian culture,[5] and that Victorian scientists and imaginative writers alike shared a 'preference for gradualism as opposed to catastrophism, evolution as opposed to revolution'.[6] Gradualist principles necessarily legitimized a cautious, not to say grindingly slow, approach to social and political change.

Perhaps the most powerful effect of many garden scenes and descriptions is that of endorsing the appeal of gradualist modes of thought and feeling. For one thing, gardens seem often to translate the inscrutable pace of geological change to graspable human time scales—to, for example, the seasonal rhythms of the gardener's calendar. For another, the leisurely garden scenes beloved of so many Victorian novelists seem to fix or suspend the flux of time, so that Victorian readers could indulge, like Henry James, 'in the happy belief that the world is all an English garden and time a fine old English afternoon'.[7] Gatherings on the lawn of the country house—itself so often a symbol of temporal and cultural continuity—imply the gradualist supposition that life at its best moves at an easy pace. Indeed, the very expansiveness of the villa or country house garden suggests an analogue of temporal stability—as though space has dilated to compensate for the exigencies of time, the experiential convulsions, and the 'sick hurry' and 'divided aims'[8] of the world at large.

Significantly, gardens are rarely the sites or victims of catastrophic upheaval and, where they do occur, such changes in a garden are invariably construed as deleterious. Mrs Henry Wood's *Oswald Cray* (1864), for example, opens with an account of the 'bitter feud' between the older inhabitants of Hallingham who fought to retain their cherished Abbey Gardens—'not so long ago the evening recreation of the townspeople, who would promenade there at sunset'—and the railway company who sought to appropriate it for their own uses. The railway company triumphed, and so 'trains for London . . . would go shrieking and whistling through the town at any hour of the day or night . . . peace for Hallingham was over' (p. 1). The narrator's sympathies are transparently obvious. A better-known example is the episode in Trollope's *The Prime Minister* (1876) in which Lady Glencora completely reconstructs the gardens at Gatherum in preparation for the grand reception proposed to promote her husband's government. Her husband, the Duke, is horrified at what he considers to be the brutal disfigurement of a garden that had taken many generations to compose. He denounces the look of 'raw newness' (I, 211) brought about by the cataclysmic change.

A more positive expression of gradualist predilections is the honorific status accorded by many writers to garden features of inherently slow maturation. One such feature is the time-worn wall. In *Impressions of Theophrastus Such* (1879), George Eliot confesses a 'tender attachment' to those features of Midland scenery which 'have never lost their familiar expression and conservative spirit for me'. One of the 'signs of permanence' she singles out is 'a crumbling bit of wall where the delicate ivy-leaved toad-flax hangs its light branches . . .'[9]. Old garden walls also stimulate pleasing reflections on times past. The garden of Mr Longdon in Henry James's *The Awkward Age* 'had for its greatest wonder the extent and colour of its old brick wall, of which the pink and purple surface was the fruit of the mild ages, and the protective function, for a visitor strolling, sitting, talking, reading, that of a sort of nurse of reverie' (p. 275).

More revered even than old garden walls are trees of venerable age. In novels of country house life, like those by Disraeli and Trollope, old trees, particularly oaks, are symbols of temporal continuity, synecdoches of the estates they occupy, and certificates of pedigree. Since their growth is very gradual, they cannot be bought with money. As Lady Ongar tells Florence Burton in *The Claverings*, 'fine trees . . . are the only things which one cannot by any possibility command' (p. 503). The Treasury Secretary in *Phineas Finn* (1869) makes a similar point. As he views Mr Kennedy's estate at Loughlinter, he remarks: 'Very grand;—but the young trees show the new man. A new man may buy a forest; but he can't get park trees' (p. 157).

One could give further examples of the more subtle means by which imaginative writers imply a preference for gradualism over any theory or programme of rapid change. Enough, however, has been said about this and some of the other implicit messages of garden scenes and descriptions to indicate that the garden elements in Victorian literature are not just 'about' flowers, lawns and trees, nor even solely about what people do in and with them. That I have been able to suggest these things is not unconnected with the implicit message of my own study, which is: the wider the net, the bigger the catch. Eschewing a 'major authors' approach has allowed the identification of commonalities and relationships between seemingly disparate authors, some of whom have long been forgotten. I should like to think that the present study may have done something to suggest the merits of placing evaluative criteria to one side, and of restructuring the institution of Victorian imaginative literature on the basis of the ideas, values, and predilections of all the writers of that period.

Notes and References

NOTES TO THE INTRODUCTION

1. Perhaps the main reason that garden historians have paid only scant attention to the garden in Victorian imaginative literature is that the abundance of technical garden literature of the period renders 'evidence' derived from novels and poems of little importance. By contrast, the comparative lack of surviving practical manuals of horticulture and garden designs from earlier periods has meant that garden historians of those periods have been forced to rely heavily on literary texts for 'evidence'.
2. 'Victorian garden design', in *The Garden: A Celebration of One Thousand Years of British Gardening*, pp. 56–63 (p. 57).
3. As far as I know, the only nominal reference to Loudon in Victorian fiction occurs in *Middlemarch*, Chapter 3, where Dorothea Brooke informs Sir James Cheetham that she has been studying 'all the plans for cottages in Loudon's book'. The book in question is probably *A Manual of Cottage Gardening, Husbandry, and Architecture* (London, 1830).
4. J. C. Loudon, *The Suburban Gardener and Villa Companion*, p. 161.
5. 'The gardenesque garden', *The Garden: A Celebration*, pp. 47–55 (p. 55).
6. *The Landscape Gardening and Landscape Architecture of the Late H. Repton Esq.*, pp. viii–ix.
7. 'Landscape Gardening', *Quarterly Review* 98 (1855), pp. 189–220 (p. 206).
8. 'Tennyson's Garden of Art: A Study of the *Hesperides*', *PMLA* 67 (1952), pp. 732–43; reprinted in *Critical Essays on the Poetry of Tennyson*, ed. John Killham, pp. 99–125 (p. 105).

CHAPTER ONE: THE TRIM GARDEN

1. 'Landscape Gardening', *Quarterly Review* 37 (1828), pp. 303–44 (p. 307).
2. *Rustic Adornments for Homes of Taste*, p. 279.
3. *Essays on the Nature and Principles of Taste* (Edinburgh, 1790), p. 5. Alison's influence on Loudon's aesthetics has long been recognized. Recently, attention has also been drawn to the influence upon Loudon

of the French theorist Antoine C. Quatremere de Quincy. See Melanie L. Simo, 'John Claudius Loudon: On Planning and Design For the Garden Metropolis', *Garden History* 9, No. 2 (1981), pp. 184–201.
4. J. C. Loudon, *An Encyclopaedia of Gardening* (1835), quoted by Elizabeth Burton in *The Early Victorians at Home*, p. 280.
5. Anon., 'The Flower Garden', *Quarterly Review* 70 (1842), pp. 196–243 (p. 207).
6. H. Repton, *An Enquiry into the Changes of Taste in Landscape Gardening* (1806), quoted by Miles Hadfield in *A History of British Gardening*, p. 245.
7. See note 5 above, p. 221.
8. Trim gardens in general, and well kept lawns in particular, were felt by many Victorians to be peculiarly English and especially attractive to foreign visitors. An enormous number of American visitors, for example, confessed to being charmed by the neat, finished appearance of English gardens. See Allison Lockwood, *Passionate Pilgrims: The American Traveler in Great Britain 1800–1914*, p. 444 et passim, and Christopher Mulvey, *Anglo-American Landscapes: A Study of nineteenth-century Anglo-American travel literature*, pp. 126–8.
9. *English Hours*, p. 127.
10. *The Wild Garden*, p. 13.
11. Reginald Blomfield launched his attack on Robinson in *The Formal Garden in England* (1892). J. D. Sedding's most famous book was the justly applauded *Garden-Craft Old and New* (1891).
12. Such gardens are portrayed in the illuminated manuscript *Roman de la Rose*, 1485 (British Library, Harley Ms. 4425). For other examples, see John Harvey, *Medieval Gardens* (London, 1981).
13. 'Hopes and Fears For Art' (1882), *MW*, XXII, p. 90.
14. In a letter to Mrs Burne-Jones (17 Jan. 1882) he wrote: 'We are hard at work gardening here: making dry paths and a sublimely tidy box edging. How I do love tidiness!' Quoted by Paul Meier in *William Morris: The Marxist Dreamer*, II, p. xiii.
15. Roland Barthes, *S/Z*, translated by Richard Miller (Paris, 1970; transl. London, 1974), p. 55.
16. *Quarterly Review* 70 (1842), p. 206.
17. Introduction to *Gardener's Magazine* 1 (1826), pp. 1–7 (p. 6).
18. 'Remarks on Laying out Public Gardens and Promenades', *Gardener's Magazine* 2 (1835), pp. 648–64 (p. 649).
19. Ibid., p. 650.
20. Ibid., p. 650.
21. 'At present, the most general mode of laying out pleasure-grounds . . . is to adopt the architectural, or the Italian style, immediately on the

lawn front of the house; and, where this style terminates, to commence either with the picturesque or the gardenesque style'. 'On Laying out and Planting the Lawn, Shrubbery, and Flower-Garden', *Gardener's Magazine* 19 (1843), pp. 166–77 (p. 168).
22. Elizabeth Barrett Browning, 'Aurora Leigh' (1856) in *Aurora Leigh And Other Poems*, introd. by Cora Kaplan (London, 1978), p. 56.
23. Ibid., p. 57.
24. For Aurora Leigh, the 'tamed' and 'domestic' English landscape is an image of England itself. See Kenneth Churchill, *Italy and English Literature 1764–1930* (London and Basingstoke, 1980), pp. 102–3.
25. Introduction to *Lothair* (London, 1975), p. xvi.
26. Anne Scott-James and Osbert Lancaster describe Disraeli as 'intoxicated with the gay parterres' of bedded-out gardens (*The Pleasure Garden: An Illustrated History of British Gardening*, p. 72). See also Muriel Masefield, *Peacocks and Primroses: A Survey of Disraeli's Novels*, passim.
27. Disraeli's comments on the gardens he himself visited seem to confirm this. See *Disraeli's Reminiscences*, pp. 113, 140.
28. *Rustic Adornments for Homes of Taste*, p. 5.
29. *The Amateur's Flower Garden*, p. 5.
30. *Floral World* (1869), quoted by Richard Gorer in *The Flower Garden in England*, p. 115.
31. *The History of Gardens*, p. 242.
32. In 'Victorian garden design', Brent Elliott quotes a contributor to the *Athenaeum*: 'in these magnificent arcades we have something new to our country and our century—something exquisitely Italian . . . in these successions of terraces, in these artificial canals, in these highly ornamental flower-works we have something of the taste and splendour of Louis Quatorze' (*The Garden: A Celebration*, p. 59).
33. 'Notes and Reflections made during a Tour through Parts of France and Germany in the Autumn of the Year 1828', *Gardener's Magazine* 7 (1830), p. 7.
34. *Parks, Promenades and Gardens of Paris* (1869), quoted by Christopher Thacker in *The History of Gardens*, p. 248.
35. *Irish Gardens and Demesnes from 1830*, p.106.
36. H. E., 'Some Famous English Gardens', *Leisure Hour* (1886), pp. 405–9 (p. 408).
37. Robert Kerr, for instance. Of Italian gardens, he wrote: 'Ostentation has to be avoided; the succession of Terraces, the lines of statues, the Fountain-groups, and the stately flights of steps, must be kept within limits of effect, as if matters of necessity rather than effort, and of subdued vigour rather than overelaboration. It is on these conditions alone, this as in other questions too easily transgressed, that grandeur

is allowable in the home of an English family' (*The Gentleman's House*, p. 335).

38. I mean by this that the champions of Italian gardens tended to regard them as in the authentic English style which pre-dated the eighteenth-century landscape garden.

39. Robert Pattison, *Tennyson and Tradition*, p. 96.

40. The negative significations of excessive stonework are also exploited in Dickens's description of the chateau of Monsieur the Marquis which opens Chapter 9 of *A Tale of Two Cities*.

41. There were, perhaps, a few novelists of little fame who drew attention to the bedding-out craze. For example, Thomas Miller's novel, *My Father's Garden* (1867), concerns a young man by the name of George Abel who achieves success as a florist by supplying people's parks with geraniums and other bedders. I am indebted to Beverly Seaton, whose article 'The Garden Writings of Henry Arthur Bright' (*Garden History* 10, No. 1 [1982], pp. 74–9), drew my attention to Miller's book.

42. Bogdanor, Introduction to *Lothair*, p. xvi.

43. Tom Braun, *Disraeli the Novelist*, p. 144. For this and other indications of Disraeli's fondness for show and affluence, see Eric Forbes-Boyd, 'Disraeli the Novelist' in *Essays and Studies* (London, 1950), pp. 100–117.

44. Robert Lee Wollf, *Gains and Losses: Novels of Faith and Doubt in Victorian England*, p. 162.

45. *The Garden* 8 (11 December 1875).

46. In an editorial entitled "The Next Fashion in Floriculture" (*Floral World* 8, No. 3 [1865], pp. 43–4), Shirley Hibberd predicted "the revival of a fashion of the past time—viz., the cultivation of hardy herbaceous plants of kinds suitable for exhibition' (pp. 43–4), and cheerfully announced that 'there is taking place on every hand a reaction against the meretricious attractions of the bedding system' (p. 44).

47. Jay Appleton, *The Experience of Landscape*.

48. Margaret Mave and Alicia C. Percival, *Victorian Best-Seller: The World of Charlotte M. Yonge*, p. 156.

49. Alfred Austin, *The Garden that I Love*, p. 13.

50. Quoted by Geoffrey Taylor in *The Victorian Flower Garden*, p. 114.

51. An Optimist, 'On Gardening', *Cornhill Magazine* 26 (1872), pp. 424–39 (p. 429).

52. [Mary Dickens], 'Charles Dickens at Home', *Cornhill Magazine* NS 4 (1885), pp. 32–51 (p. 43).

CHAPTER TWO: THE SCENTED GARDEN

1. Gover takes 1895 as a 'convenient pivot'; see *The Flower Garden in England*, p. 112.
2. *The Wild Garden*, p. 6.
3. William Beach Thomas, *Gardens*, p. 95.
4. Note the specification of mignonette. Anne Scott-James, who quotes this passage, says that 'scarcely any other flower is so often mentioned in Victorian literature'. If we exclude the rose, she is probably correct (*The Cottage Garden*, p. 67).
5. For example, in *Musings over the 'Christian Year'* Charlotte Yonge recalled happy moments in the 1840s spent at John Keble's annual feast at Hursley: "How exquisite it used to be to stand on the terrace in the fresh evening scents of early summer. . . .' Quoted by Mare and Percival in *Victorian Best-Seller*, p. 126.
6. *Tennyson's Major Poems: the Comic and Ironic Patterns*, p. 164.
7. *Tennyson's Style*, p. 138.
8. 'Vision and Revision: *In Memoriam* XCV', *Victorian Poetry* 18 (1980), pp. 135–46 (p. 142).
9. Yi-Fu Tuan, *Topophilia: A Study of Environmental Perception, Attitudes, and Values*, p. 10.
10. William A. Madden, *Matthew Arnold: A Study of the Aesthetic Temperament in Victorian England*, p. 70.
11. *The Disappearance of God: Five Nineteenth-Century Writers*, p. 216.
12. *Elizabeth Gaskell and the English Provincial Novel*, p. 258.
13. *A Nineteenth-Century Garden*, p. 36.
14. Quoted by Scott-James in *The Cottage Garden*, p. 97.
15. 'Hopes and Fears for Art' (1882), *MW*, XXII, p. 90.

CHAPTER THREE: OLD-FASHIONED GARDENS

1. Forbes Watson, *Flowers and Gardens: Notes on Plant Beauty*, p. 103.
2. Both poems are reprinted in *The Modern Elocutionist* (Dublin, 1882), respectively pp. 141, 509.
3. Michael Irwin, *Picturing: Description and Illusion in the Nineteenth-Century Novel*, p. 115.
4. Henry Arthur Bright, 'The English Flower-Garden', *Quarterly Review* 149 (1880), pp. 331–60 (p. 340). See also, Richard Jefferies, 'Flowers and Fruit', *Globe*, 19 July 1877; reprinted in *Richard Jefferies, Landscape and Labour: A New Collection of Essays*, ed. John Pearson (Wiltshire, 1979), pp. 59–62 (p. 59).

5. 'The Victorian Self-Image and the Emergent City Sensibility', *University of Toronto Quarterly* 33, No. 1 (1963), pp. 61–77 (p. 66). Forsyth's citation is of *Blackwood's Magazine* 129 (1881), pp. 256–7.
6. 'Felicitous Space: The Cottage Controversy', *Nature and the Victorian Imagination*, pp. 29–48 (p. 37).
7. Anne Scott-James, *The Cottage Garden*, p. 100.
8. *The Mayor of Casterbridge*, pp. 63–4. From a distant, bird's-eye view, Casterbridge itself resembles an old-fashioned garden of modest formality. '"What an old-fashioned place it seems to be!" said Elizabeth-Jane . . ., "It is huddled all together, like a plot of garden ground by a box edging"' (p. 31).
9. Walter F. Wright observes: 'Mrs Fleming is not practical; her unimaginative husband is especially unappreciative of flowers and all the tangibles which they suggest.' Wright construes these 'cardinal defects' as the 'weaknesses in a civilization' which makes 'a separation between duty and toil, on the one hand, and beauty and enjoyment, on the other.' *Art and Substance in George Meredith: A Study of Narrative*, p. 135. Brian Taylor sums up Iden as 'sensitized, educated, but hopelessly impractical'. *Richard Jefferies*, p. 91.
10. Basil Willey, *Ideas and Beliefs of the Victorians*, ed. Harman Grisewood (London, 1949), pp. 43–4.
11. Quoted by C. H. Salter in *Good Little Thomas Hardy*, p. 34.
12. F. S. Schwarzbach, *Dickens and the City*, p. 61.
13. In fact, there is some doubt about the extent of Blackmore's business acumen. The general view is that he was unbusinesslike. See, for example, Quincy Guy Burris, *Richard Doddridge Blackmore: His Life and Novels* (Westport, Connecticut, 1973), p. 331, and Miles Hadfield, *Gardening in Britain*, p. 347. Waldo Hilary Dunn contests this view: 'Some have maintained that he played at the task [of fruit-growing], followed it simply as a hobby, and did not practice business-like methods. It would appear, however, that he applied himself to the work as few would have done, and in doing so was as business-like and economical as possible'. *R. D. Blackmore* (London, 1956), p. 108. Although I have not found space to discuss in detail the garden writings of Blackmore, they deserve consideration, if only because he was probably the only Victorian to combine fiction-writing and commercial gardening. Useful material can be found in the works cited above, and in the novels. See, in particular, *Alice Lorraine: A tale of the South Downs*, 3 vols. (London, 1875); *Christowell: A Dartmore Tale*, 3 vols. (London, 1882); and *Kit and Kitty: a story of West Middlesex*, 3 vols. (London, 1890).
14. *Blackwood's Magazine* 116 (1874), p. 686.
15. The term 'gothic Eden' is John D. Rosenberg's in *The Darkening*

Glass: A Portrait of Ruskin's Genius (New York, 1961), p. 52.
16. *The Garden* 15 (15 April 1879), pp. 298–300.
17. 'William Morris', *Ecologist* 4, No. 6 (July 1974), pp. 210–12 (p. 211).
18. K. B. Valentine, 'Motifs from Nature in the Design Work and Prose Romances of William Morris, 1876–1896', *Victorian Poetry*, 13 (1975), pp. 83–9 (p. 83).
19. Georgiana Burne-Jones, *Memorials of Edward B.-J.*, p. 212.
20. Ibid., p. 420.
21. Philip Henderson, *William Morris: His Life, Work and Friends*, p. 34.
22. W. B. Yeats, 'The Happiest of Poets' (1902) in *Essays and Introductions* (London and Basingstoke, 1961), pp. 53–64 (p. 60).
23. Peter Faulkner, *Against the Age: An Introduction to William Morris*, p. 20.
24. R. C. Ellison, '"The Undying Glory of Dreams": William Morris and the "Northland of Old"', in *Victorian Poetry*, Stratford-Upon-Avon Studies 15, ed. Malcolm Bradbury and David Palmer (London, 1972), pp. 139–75 (p. 142). For a similar view, see Eric S. Rabkin, *The Fantastic in Literature*, (Princeton, 1979), pp. 88–90.
25. Jeffrey L. Spear, 'Political Questing: Ruskin, Morris and Romance', in *New Approaches to Ruskin: Thirteen Essays*, ed. Robert Hewison, pp. 174–93 (p. 182).
26. Ibid., p. 189.
27. *Sweetness and Light: The 'Queen Anne' Movement 1860–1900*, p. 152. Girouard quotes Bell Scott's sonnet on page 154.
28. Rodney Engen, *Kate Greenaway: A Biography*, p. 91.
29. 'Garden Design on Old-Fashioned Lines', *Black's Gardening Dictionary*; reprinted in *A Gardener's Testament: A Selection of Articles and Notes By Gertrude Jekyll*, ed. Francis Jekyll and G. C. Taylor (Antique Collectors' Club, 1982), pp. 57–8 (p. 57).
30. *Mary's Meadow* first appeared in *Aunt Judy's Magazine* between November 1883 and March 1884. According to Horatia Gatting, its author 'received many letters of enquiry about the various plants mentioned in the tale', to which she responded in the Correspondence sections of the magazine. As a consequence, the idea of forming a Parkinson Society was mooted in July 1884. *Mary's Meadow*, Preface.
31. See Girouard, *Sweetness and Light*, p. 156.
32. Peter Davey, *Arts and Crafts Architecture: The Search for Earthly Paradise*, p. 74. For a fuller discussion of the 'William Morris cult' in relation to garden design, see Mavis Batey, *Oxford Gardens: The university's influence on garden history* (Amersham, 1982), pp. 174–80.
33. See Robert Schmutzler, 'Blake and Art Nouveau', *Architectural Review* 118 (1955), pp. 90–7.

34. Isobel Spencer, *Walter Crane*, p. 138.
35. *The Aesthetic Movement in England*, p. 35.
36. Quoted by Hamilton, p. 102.
37. *The Poems of Algernon Charles Swinburne*, 6 vols. VI, pp. 4–23 (p. 11).

CHAPTER FOUR: THE PICTURESQUE GARDEN

1. *The Picturesque: Studies in a Point of View*, p. 2.
2. As Ruskin observed in 1849, 'probably no word in the language, (exclusive of theological expressions), has been the subject of so frequent or so prolonged dispute; yet none more vague in their acceptance.' "The Seven Lamps of Architecture", *RW*, VIII, p. 235.
3. One of the few recent discussions which does not stop short at the 1830s is Alexander M. Ross's illuminating essay, 'The Picturesque in Nineteenth Century Fiction', in *English Studies Today*, ed. Spencer Tonguc (Istanbul, 1973), pp. 327–58, though Ross has virtually nothing to say specifically on the picturesque garden. Most other relevant studies treat of the picturesque in relation to particular authors. For George Eliot and the picturesque see Hugh Witemeyer, *George Eliot and the Visual Arts* (New Haven and London, 1979). For Dickens and the picturesque see Nancy K. Hill, *A Reformer's Art: Dickens's Picturesque and Grotesque Imagery* (Athens, 1981). For useful considerations of the picturesque and Jane Austen see Alistair Duckworth, *The Improvement of the Estate: A Study of Jane Austen's Novels* (Baltimore and London, 1971); Ann Banfield, 'The Moral Landscape of Jane Austen', in *Nineteenth-Century Fiction* 26 (June 1971), pp. 1–24; and Rosemarie Bodenheimer, 'Looking at the Landscape in Jane Austen', in *Studies in English Literature 1500–1900* 21 (1981), pp. 605–23.
4. *The Picturesque*, p. 242.
5. David Watkin, *The English Vision: The Picturesque in Architecture, Landscape and Garden Design*, p. 88. It would be truer to say that the picturesque maintained its appeal through its transmutations into the gardenesque, and through its accommodation by other garden styles.
6. Introduction to Robert Kerr, *The Gentleman's House*, p. x.
7. *The Gothic Revival: An Essay on the History of Taste*, p. 67.
8. *A Dream of Order: The Medieval Ideal in Nineteenth-Century Literature.*
9. *English Landscaping and Literature 1660–1840*, pp. 142–6.
10. *Essays on the Nature and Principles of Taste*, p. 29.
11. Witemeyer, *George Eliot and the Visual Arts*, p. 128.
12. Chandler, *A Dream of Order*, p. 185.
13. David Lowenthal and Hugh C. Prince, 'English Landscape Tastes',

Geographical Review 55 (1965), pp. 186–222 (p. 203).
14. An important element of picturesque theory was, as Gerald Finley points out, 'that landscape was considered to be more than mere topography: it was the silent witness to the events of human history.' *Landscapes of Memory*, p. 21.
15. George L. Hersey, *High Victorian Gothic: A Study in Associationism*, p. 13.
16. *Victorian Homes*, p. 38.
17. Nicholas Taylor, 'The Awful Sublimity of the Victorian City', in *The Victorian City: Images and Realities*, ed. H. J. Dyos and Michael Wolff, 2 vols. (London and Boston, 1973), II, pp. 431–47 (p. 433).
18. William Gilpin, *Three Essays: On Picturesque Beauty; On Picturesque Travel; and On Sketching Landscape*, pp. 7–8.
19. Hersey, *High Victorian Gothic*, p. 53.
20. A. Dwight Culler, *The Poetry of Tennyson*, p. 79.
21. See Raymond Williams, *The Country and the City*.
22. *Sketches of English Life and Character*, p. 54.
23. Gillian Darley, *Villages of Vision*, p. 115.
24. Samuel H. Monk, *The Sublime: A Study of Critical Theories in XVIII-Century England*, (Michigan 1960), p. 204.
25. Sheila M. Smith, *The Other Nation: The Poor in English Novels of the 1840s and 1850s*, p. 102. References to Howitt's *The Rural Life of England* are to the new edition (London, 1844).
26. Robert Bernard Martin suggests that Shirley's house is made to resemble a Girtin watercolour (*The Accents of Persuasion: Charlotte Brontë's Novels*, p. 109).
27. The stress on growth by gradual accretion is particularly strong in pre- and early-Victorian fiction. In the opening chapter of *Hillingdon Hall*, R. S. Surtees lavishes description on the 'rich and picturesque domain' (p. 4) of Hillingdon Hall, and says of the 'old-fashioned manor-house' itself: 'there was no attempt at architectural symmetry. . . . Each room had been added separately and stuck in, as it were, so as not to interfere with its neighbours' (p. 2).
28. See Witemeyer, *George Eliot and the Visual Arts*, p. 129.
29. 'Southey's *Colloquies*' (January 1830), in *The Works of Lord Macaulay*, 12 vols. (London 1898), V, p. 342.
30. 'The Natural History of German Life', *Westminster Review* (July 1856), quoted in *Essays of George Eliot*, ed. Thomas Pinney (London, 1963), p. 268.
31. As George H. Ford points out; see 'Felicitous Space: The Cottage Controversy', p. 37.
32. Witemeyer, *George Eliot and the Visual Arts*, p. 130.

33. *The Westminster Review* (April 1851), pp. 343–4.
34. *George Eliot and the Visual Arts*, p. 130.
35. Peter Conrad, *The Victorian Treasure House*, p. 39.
36. *Christmas Books*, pp. 131–2.
37. Quoted by Margaret Reynolds, review of *A Reformer's Art: Dickens's Picturesque and Grotesque Imagery*, by Nancy K. Hill, in *The Dickensian* 78, No. 398 (1982), pp. 170–2 (p. 170).
38. According to George H. Ford in 'Felicitous Space: The Cottage Controversy', the cottage controversy centres on the question of whether or not 'the poet's picture of the cottage is fatuously unrealistic, untrue or unrepresentative' (p. 33).
39. *Our Old Home, and English Note-Books*, 2 vols., I, p. 483.
40. Quoted by Geoffrey Taylor in *Some Nineteenth Century Gardeners* (London, 1951), p. 45.
41. *Quarterly Review* 70 (1842), pp. 207, 202.
42. 'Observations on the Improvement of Flower-Gardens', *Gardener's Magazine* 5 (1829), pp. 48–9 (p. 49).
43. Review of *Practical Hints on Landscape Gardening*, by W. Sawrey Gilpin, *Gardener's Magazine* 8 (1832), pp. 700–702 (p. 701).
44. 'On Laying Out and Planting the Lawn, Shrubbery and Flower-Garden', *Gardener's Magazine* 19 (1843), pp. 166–77 (p. 167).
45. An Amateur, 'Remarks on the present style of Ornamental Gardening in this country, and Suggestions for Improvement', *Gardener's Magazine* 4 (1828), pp. 86–90 (p. 88).
46. 'Landscape Gardening', *Quarterly Review*, 98 (1855), pp. 212, 206.
47. 'The After-Season in Rome' (1873), quoted by Charles R. Anderson in *Person, Place and Thing in Henry James's Novels*, p. 16. For a consideration of James's notion of the picturesque see Viola Hopkins Winner, *Henry James and the Visual Arts* (Charlottesville, 1970).
48. *Stories and Sketches*, p. 218.
49. *Gardens and Grim Ravines: The Language of Landscape in Victorian Poetry*, p. 247.
50. Rosemarie Bodenheimer, 'Looking at the Landscape in Jane Austen', *Studies in English Literature 1500–1900* 21 (1981), pp. 605–23 (p. 606).
51. In *The Victorian Treasure House*, Peter Conrad considers the ways in which 'the Victorians transferred the picturesque from the country to the city' (p. 89). I deal more fully with the application of 'picturesque' to city gardens in Chapter 8.

CHAPTER FIVE: IMAGINATIVE LITERATURE AND GARDEN CONSCIOUSNESS

1. Quoted as a press notice in *The Garden that I Love*, n.p.
2. 'The Garden', *Blackwood's Magazine* 73 (1854), pp. 129–44 (p. 142).
3. 'The *Graphic* on Flower Gardening', *The Garden* 4 (6 December 1873), p. 460.
4. [Henry Arthur Bright], 'The English Flower Garden', *Quarterly Review* 149 (1880), pp. 331–60 (p. 357).
5. Quoted by Tom Braun, *Disraeli the Novelist*, p. 132.
6. 'Herbaceous Gardens', in *Victorian Cottage Residences*, p. 246.
7. There is copious evidence of this in Hallam Tennyson, *Alfred Lord Tennyson: A Memoir*, 2 vols. Hallam records that his father 'delighted . . . to recall the rare richness of the bowery lanes . . . the flowers, the mosses, and the ferns' around Somersby (*Memoir*, I, p. 3). The *Memoir* is punctuated also with recollections of Tennyson's gardening activities. Tennyson's interests can be gauged, as well, from the books in his library, which included Baxter's *Flowering Plants* (see *Memoir*, I, p. 369), and Rev. Henry Burgess's *The Amateur gardener's year-book* (Edinburgh, 1854). See *Tennyson in Lincoln*, ed. Nancie Campbell (Lincoln: Tennyson Research Society), I, p. 37.
8. Lecky declared that some of his happiest memories of Tennyson went back 'to many different scenes, to the gardens and downs of Farringford, to the lovely terrace at Aldworth' (*Memoir*, II, pp. 206–7). Bishop Brooks recorded his impressions of Farringford in 1883 (*Memoir*, II, pp. 295–6) and in his *Hundred Days in Europe*, Oliver Wendell Holmes gave an account of his visit to Farringford in June 1886 (*Memoir*, II, p. 324).
9. A 'careless ordered garden' was Mrs Bradley's assessment of Farringford in or about 1860 (*Memoir*, I, p. 467).
10. *Country Pleasures: The Chronicles of a Year, chiefly in a Garden*, quoted by Alfred Forbes Sieveking, in *The Praise of Gardens: An Epitome of the Literature of The Garden-Art*, p. 299.
11. The influence of Tennyson's surroundings upon his poetry has for long been a subject of interest. Early studies include John Cumming Walters, *In Tennyson Land* (London, 1890), and E. L. Cary, *Tennyson: His Homes, His Friends, His Work* (New York, 1898). Much of Tennyson's poetry issued from his own garden-related experiences (see Chapter 11), and Tennyson's gardening activities occasionally impinged directly upon his poetry. Mrs Richard Ward reported, for example, that 'the lines on "The Flower" were the result of an investigation of the "love-

in-idleness" growing at Farringford—he made them nearly all on the spot' (*Memoir*, II, p. 11).

12. The poet-gardener analogy figures in a quatrain written in 1892 in response 'to one of the many American editions which reprinted poems that Tennyson had suppressed' (*TP*, p. 1448). On the other hand, Tennyson vehemently denied that *The Flower* referred to his poetry (see *TP*, p. 1185). See Chapter 11.

13. Geoffrey Taylor, *The Victorian Flower Garden*, p. 199.

14. *Quarterly Review*, 149 (1880), p. 349.

15. 'Roses', *Sunday Magazine* (1889), p. 455.

16. Donald S. Hair, *Domestic and Heroic in Tennyson's Poetry*, p. 40.

17. A. J. Downing, *Rural Essays*, pp. lvii–lviii.

18. John Dixon Hunt and David Palmer, 'Tennyson', in *English Poetry*, pp. 131–47 (p. 133).

19. Review of *Poems, Chiefly Lyrical*, in *London Review* (July 1835), I, pp. 402–24, reprinted in *Tennyson: The Critical Heritage*, ed. John D. Jump (London, 1967), pp. 84–97 (p. 86).

20. The ways in which *Mariana* 'exercised a considerable hold over Dickens's imagination' are discussed by Robin Gilmour in 'Dickens, Tennyson, and the Past', *The Dickensian* 75, No. 389 (1979), pp. 130–42.

21. *Dickens and the Invisible World: Fairy-Tales, Fantasy and Novel-Making*, p. 292.

22. 'The Middle Years, from the *Carol* to *Copperfield*', *Dickens Memorial Lectures* (1970), pp. 12–13.

23. Geoffrey Tillotson remarks that it was from his reading of Tennyson's *Poems* of 1842 that Dickens 'learned how to build up a great description of external nature'. Afterward to *Bleak House* (The New American Library of World Literature, 1964), p. 886.

24. Kincaid, *Tennyson's Major Poems*, p. 22.

25. 'The Colours of Trees in Autumn', *Floral World*, 11, No. 10 (1867), pp. 299–301 (p. 299).

26. Basil Willey, Quoted by K. W. Gransden, *Tennyson: In Memoriam*, p. 28.

27. 'Some Types and Emblems in Victorian Poetry', *The Listener* (25 May 1967), p. 679.

28. 'Lord Byron', *Quarterly Review* 131 (1871), pp. 354–92 (p. 371).

29. Andrea Rose, *The Pre-Raphaelites*, p. 18.

30. Frances Spalding, *Magnificent Dreams: Burne-Jones and the Late Victorians*, p. 47.

31. Cited by Allen Staley in *The Pre-Raphaelite Landscape*, p. 115.

32. *The Amateur's Flower Garden*, p. 4.

33. *The Wild Garden*, p. 11.

CHAPTER SIX: FLORAL CODES

1. 'Letters From a Little Garden', Letter 1, *Aunt Judy's Magazine* (November 1884), p. 79.
2. Quoted by Robert L. Herbert in *The Art Criticism of John Ruskin* (New York, 1964), p. 32.
3. Quoted by Geoffrey Taylor in *The Victorian Flower Garden*, pp. 101–2.
4. In *Gardening of Britain*, Miles Hadfield quotes one anonymous writer of the period who observed that the auricula 'is to be found in the highest perfection in the gardens of the manufacturing class, who devote much time and attention on this and a few other flowers, as the tulip and the pink' (p. 72).
5. *The Garden that I Love*, pp. 1–2.
6. 'Flowers and Fruit', *The Quiver* 20 (1885), pp. 763–4.
7. Flora, 'What becomes of the flowers?', *Floral World*, 3, No. 2 (1868), pp. 42–3 (p. 43).
8. Anon., *The Language of Flowers* (London, n.d.), p. 5.
9. *The Language of Flowers; or, Floral Emblems of Thoughts, Feelings, and Sentiments*, p. x.
10. *The Secret Lore of Plants and Flowers*, p. 53.
11. Jean Marsh, *Language of Flowers*, Illustrated by Kate Greenaway, p. 14.
12. Quoted by Josephine Miles in *Pathetic Fallacy in the Nineteenth Century: A Study of Changing Relations Between Object and Emotion* (New York, 1965), p. 30.
13. Fletcher, *The Listener* (25 May 1967), p. 680.
14. Gisela Hönnighausen, 'Emblematic Tendencies in the Works of Christina Rossetti', *Victorian Poetry* 10 (1972), pp. 1–15 (p. 6).
15. Dinah Birch, 'Ruskin and the Science of *Proserpina*', in *New Approaches to Ruskin*, pp. 142–56 (p. 148).
16. Quoted by Geoffrey Eley in *The Ruined Maid: Modes and Manners of Victorian Women* (Royston, 1970), p. 41.
17. *The Complete Poetical Works of Thomas Hood*, p. 424.
18. *The Poetical Works of Leigh Hunt*, II, pp. 169–70. According to Claire Powell, it was Hunt who 'established the Victorian convention that it was chiefly of love that flowers spoke' (*The Meaning of Flowers: A Garland of Plant Lore and Symbolism from Popular Custom and Literature*, p. 18).
19. In, for example, W. M. Thackeray, *Vanity Fair* (1848), p. 46, Samuel Butler, *The Way of All Flesh* (1903), p. 408, and Charlotte M. Yonge, *The Daisy Chain* (1856), in which the children of the family are referred to as 'daisies'.
20. William R. Campbell, 'A Note on the Flowers in *Pippa Passes*',

Victorian Poetry 14 (1976), pp. 59–62; Ramona Merchant 'Pippa's Garden', *Studies in Browning and His Circle* 2, No. 2 (1974), pp. 9–20, and others.
21. Gisela Hönnighausen, 'Emblematic Tendencies in the Works of Christina Rossetti', (see note 14 above).
22. *A Lost Eden* (1904), p. 76.
23. This fact is recorded by H. G. Witham Fogg in *History of Popular Garden Plants From A to Z* (London, 1976), p. 115.
24. *The Garden that I Love*, p. 17.
25. 'The Garden', *Blackwood's Magazine* 73 (1853), p. 133.
26. For an account of the cultivation and media celebration of the Victoria Regia, see 'The Chatsworth Lily: Paxton's Great Exhibition', *The Listener* (29 August 1974), pp. 269–71. See also Anne Grosthwait, 'Discovering the Giant Water-Lily', *Country Life* 144 (1968), pp. 550–1.
27. See note 25 above.
28. *Flowers and Gardens: Notes on Plant Beauty*, p. 99.
29. *Quarterly Review* 149 (1880), p. 360.
30. W. W., *The Garden* I (4 May 1872), pp. 517–18 (p. 517).
31. *The Amateur's Flower Garden*, pp. 33–4.
32. *Essays and Studies* (London, 1888), p. 97.
33. Paul Meire, *William Morris: The Marxist Dreamer*, II, pp. 420–1.
34. Jack Harness, 'Old Garden Roses', in *The Love of Gardening*, ed. Kenneth A. Beckett (London, 1980), pp. 86–92 (p. 86).
35. [Shirley Hibberd], *Floral World* 5, No. 3. (1862), pp. 41–5 (p. 41).
36. 'Crimson and Purple Leaved Bedders', *Floral World* 8, No. 4 (1865), pp. 69–72.
37. The assault on modernity and the reaction against the aesthetic impoverishment of the bourgeoisie were not unrelated. In an essay entitled 'The Ugliness of Modern Life', Ouida lumped 'glaring geometrical flower-beds' together with subways, trams, and the lath and plaster of jerry builders as 'dreary suburban features'. She added: 'Amongst even the most cultured classes few have any sensibility to beauty'. *Critical Studies: A Set of Essays by OUIDA* (London, 1900), pp. 222, 215.
38. 'Flower Factories', *All The Year Round*, NS 8 (1872), p. 116.
39. An Optimist, 'On Gardening', *Cornhill Magazine* 26 (1872), pp. 424–39 (p. 429).
40. See William Robinson's letter to Ruskin (4 July 1885) in *RW*, XXV, p. 533.
41. *Sketches of English Life and Character*, pp. 15–16.
42. In 'Mrs Gardiner' (1843), Thomas Hood concludes his attack upon the 'scientific Godfathers and Godmothers' who baptise plants with

'bombastical and pedantical titles' with the following comment: 'It looks selfish, in the learned, to invent such difficult nomenclatures, as if they wished to keep the character, habits, origin, and properties of new plants to themselves.' *The Works of Thomas Hood*, 7 vols. vi, pp. 167–92 (p. 178).
43. *Barchester Towers*, p. 90.
44. *Sweetness and Light*, p. 29.
45. According to Edward Thomas, Jefferies 'saw foreign shrubs and trees, the emblems of sudden riches, rhododendron and plane especially, taking possession of gardens where he longed to see oaks and filbert walks'. *Richard Jefferies* (1909; rpt. London, 1979), p. 105. See also 'Trees about Town', in *Richard Jefferies' London*, ed. with an introduction by Samuel J. Looker (London, 1944), pp. 78–9.
46. For these details of the 'social overtones' of suburban vegetation, I am indebted to H. J. Dyos, *Victorian Suburb: A Study of the Growth of Clerkenwell* (Leicester, 1961), p. 188. In some of Gissing's novels, the 'social overtones' of plants, trees and shrubs help to render the status gradations within Gissing's version of suburban London. See Chapter 8 for a consideration of the differences in vegetation between Grove Lane, de Crespigney Park, and Champion Hill in *In the Year of Jubilee.*
47. 'The Influence of Flowers', *The Gardeners' Chronicle and Agricultural Gazette*, August 1861.
48. *Saturday Magazine*, 12 September 1840, pp. 103–4 (p. 103).
49. *Home: a Victorian Vignette* (London, 1938), p. 49.
50. *The Amateur Gardener's year-book*, p. 13.
51. Ibid., p. 14.
52. *Floral World*, 1, No. 2 (1866), pp. 18–23 (p. 18).
53. Quoted by Rachel Anderson in *The Purple Heart Throbs: the sub-literature of love* (London, 1974), p. 53.
54. Donald S. Hair, *Domestic and Heroic in Tennyson's Poetry*, p. 121.
55. *Tennysonian Love*, p. 97.
56. The flower image seems to imply that the development of women as individuals is biologically pre-determined by immutable natural laws. In the light of this, consider the following comment by Nina Auerbach in 'Alice in Wonderland: A curious child:': 'Cast as they are in the role of emotional and spiritual catalysts, it is not surprising that girls who function as protagonists in Victorian literature are rarely allowed to develop: in its refusal to subject females to the evolutionary process, the Victorian novel takes a significant step backward from one of its principle [sic] sources, the novels of Jane Austen.' *Victorian Studies* 17 (1973), pp. 31–47 (p. 45).
57. See Park Honan, *Browning's Characters: A Study in Poetic Technique*, pp. 75–6.

58. *Quiver*, 12 (1877), p. 670.
59. J. T. B. Steene, *Tennyson*, p. 119.
60. Roland Prothero, *Edinburgh Review* 158 (1886), p. 495. For discussions of the floral symbols in *Maud*, see J. D. Yohannon, 'Tennyson and Persian Poetry', *MLN* 57 (1942), pp. 83–92; E. D. H. Johnson, 'The Lily and the Rose: Symbolic Meaning in Tennyson's *Maud*', *PMLA* 64 (1949), pp. 1222–7; and John W. Crawford, 'A Unifying Element in Tennyson's *Maud*', *Victorian Poetry* 7 (1969), pp. 64–6. For flower symbols in *The Princess*, see Gerard Joseph, *Tennysonian Love*, pp. 95–6; and Wendell Stacy Johnson, *Sex and Marriage in Victorian Poetry* (Ithaca, 1975), pp. 131–2. For flower and colour symbolism in *Idylls of the King*, see Jerome H. Buckley, *Tennyson: the Growth of a Poet*, pp. 182–4; and R. Altick, 'The Lily Maid and Scarlet Sleeve: White and Red in Tennyson's *Idylls*', *University Review* 34 (1967), pp. 65–71. There are also helpful footnotes on the significance of flowers in Tennyson's poetry in J. M. Gray, *Tennyson's Doppelganger: 'Balin and Balan'* (Lincoln, The Tennyson Society, 1971).
61. Rosalind Miles, 'The Woman of Wessex', in *The Novels of Thomas Hardy*, pp. 23–44 (pp. 30, 31).
62. R. C. Terry, *Victorian Popular Fiction 1860–80*, p. 112.
63. *The Works of Thomas Hood*, VI, pp. 167–92.
64. See Peter K. Garrett, *Scene and Symbol from George Eliot to James Joyce* (New Haven, 1969), pp. 83–91.
65. Patricia Stubbs, *Women and Fiction: Feminism and the Novel 1880–1920*, p. 159.
66. Fraser Harrison, *The Dark Angel: Aspects of Victorian Sexuality*, p. 29.
67. For a consideration of this myth from a feminist perspective see Penelope Brown and L. J. Jordanova, 'Oppressive Dichotomies: The nature/culture debate', *Women in Society: Interdisciplinary Essays*, The Cambridge Women's Studies Group (London, 1981), pp. 224–41.
68. Robert Ashley, *Wilkie Collins*, p. 117.
69. *The Subjection of Women*, p. 21.
70. Hazel Mews, *Frail Vessels: Women's Role in Women's Novels from Fanny Burney to George Eliot*, p. 121.
71. Rosalind Miles, 'The Women of Wessex', p. 30.
72. Patricia Stubbs, *Women and Fiction*, p. 49.
73. *RW*, XVIII, pp. 109–44. Ruskin refers to what he calls 'feeble florets'. Kate Millett points out that this is 'full period euphemism for whore'. *Sexual Politics* (London, 1971), p. 107.

CHAPTER SEVEN: GARDENS, LANDSCAPES, AND NATURE

1. Robert L. Patten, '"A Surprising Transformation": Dickens and the Hearth', in *Nature and the Victorian Imagination*, pp. 153–70 (p. 154).
2. Walter E. Houghton, *The Victorian Frame of Mind, 1830–1870*, p. 79.
3. Fraser Neiman, *Matthew Arnold*, p. 67.
4. J. Hillis Miller, *The Disappearance of God*, p. 234.
5. *Charles Kingsley: His Letters and Memories of His Life*, edited by his wife [Fanny E. Kingsley], 2 vols., I, p. 70.
6. Alan Roper, *Arnold's Poetic Landscapes*, p. 49.
7. Significantly, the speaker in Dobson's poem sees, in the arrangement of flowers in his garden, not a reflection of the contemporary class-structured society but an older hierarchical social structure. As Harold Perkins points out, 'the very concept of class, in the modern sense of broad, mutually hostile bands based on conflicting economic interests, is a product of the British Industrial Revolution. Until then . . . its place [was] supplied by the "ranks", "orders" and "degrees" of a more finely graded hierarchy of great subtlety and discrimination' (*The Structured Crowd: Essays in English Social History* [Sussex, 1981], p. 11). By using the older terms, Dobson's speaker emphasises the vertical bonds of patronage and dependency which cut across horizontal antagonisms, making both nature and society seem integrated and neighbourly.
8. George Levine, 'High and Low: Ruskin and the Victorian novelists', in *Nature and the Victorian Imagination*, pp. 137–52.
9. Pauline Fletcher, *Gardens and Grim Ravines*, pp. 3, 8, 9.
10. *A Year at Hartlebury: or The Election* was published in 2 vols. by Saunders and Otley in March 1834 under the authorship of 'Cherry and Fair Star'. That these were the pseudonyms of Benjamin and Sarah Disraeli was revealed in the Fall 1979 issue of the *Disraeli Newsletter*.
11. Pauline Fletcher, *Gardens and Grim Ravines*, p. 7.
12. See, for example, Edith G. Hoare, *A Faulty Courtship: A Tyrolese Romance* (London, 1899).
13. Leo Marx, *The Machine in the Garden*.
14. Jean-Paul Hulin, '"Rus in Urbe": A Key to Victorian Anti-Urbanism?' in *Victorian Writers and the City*, ed. Jean-Paul Hulin and Pierre Coustillas, pp. 11–40 (p. 15).
15. *My Lady Ludlow And Other Tales*, p. 464.
16. 'A Study of Hopkins' Use of Nature', *Victorian Poetry*, 5 (1967), pp. 79–92 (p. 79).
17. R. A. Forsyth, 'The Victorian Self-Image and the Emergent City Sensibility', *Univ. of Toronto Quarterly* 33, No. 1 (1963), pp. 61–77 (p. 66).

18. *Saturday Magazine*, 21 August 1841, p. 72.
19. Jerome Buckley, *Tennyson: The Growth of a Poet*, p. 177.
20. James R. Kincaid, *Tennyson's Major Poems*, p. 155.
21. *Gardens and Grim Ravines*, p. 37.
22. *Tennyson's Major Poems*, p. 183. Henry Kozicki also takes Vivien to represent the 'interests of savage nature and the sexual fires that animate it'. *Tennyson and Clio: History in the Major Poems* (Baltimore, 1979), p. 131.
23. S. Baring Gould, *Old Country Life*, p. 102.
24. 'Country Life', *Quarterly Review* 158 (1884), pp. 400–30 (p. 420).
25. Unsigned Review, *Athenaeum* (25 December 1847), pp. 1324–5, reprinted in *The Brontës: The Critical Heritage*, ed. Miriam Allott, pp. 218–9 (p. 218).
26. Unsigned Review of *Wuthering Heights, Britannia* (15 January 1848), pp. 42–3, reprinted in *The Brontës: The Critical Heritage*, pp. 223–6 (p. 224).
27. Houghton, *The Victorian Frame of Mind*, p. 267.
28. Quoted by Malcolm Andrews in *Dickens on England and the English* (Sussex, 1979), p. 44.
29. *The Letters of Charles Dickens*, IV, ed. Kathleen Tillotson, pp. 629–30.
30. *American Notes and Pictures from Italy*, p. 200.
31. Samuel M. Sipe, 'The Intentional World of Dickens', *Nineteenth Century Fiction* 30, No. 1. (1975), pp. 1–19 (p. 13).
32. *American Notes and Pictures from Italy*, pp. 419, 182.
33. F. S. Schwarzbach, *Dickens and the City*, p. 90.
34. George Levine, 'High and Low: Ruskin and the Novelists', p. 148.
35. 'No Thoroughfare' (1867) is reprinted in *Christmas Stories* (London, 1956), pp. 539–859.
36. 'High and Low: Ruskin and the Novelists', p. 152.
37. As Louis Cazamian has asserted; see *The Social Novel in England 1830–1850*, p. 164.
38. J. Hillis Miller, *Charles Dicken: The World of His Novels*, p. 71.
39. James F. Marlow, 'Memory, Romance, and the Expressive Symbol in Dickens', *Nineteenth-Century Fiction* 30, No. 1 (1975), pp. 20–32 (p. 22).
40. Curtis Dahl, 'The Victorian Wasteland', *College English* 16 (1955), pp. 341–7, rpt. in *Victorian Literature: Modern Essays in Criticism*, ed. Austin Wright, pp. 32–40 (p. 32).
41. *Chambers's Journal*, No. 718 (29 September 1877), p. 624.
42. Coral Lansbury, *Elizabeth Gaskell: The Novel of Social Crisis*, p. 190.
43. Yi-Fu Tuan, *Topophilia*, p. 109.
44. Mrs Gaskell, *The Life of Charlotte Brontë*, 2 vols., II, p. 54.

45. *The Poems of Anne Brontë: A New Text and Commentary*, ed. Edward Chittham, pp. 101–103 (p. 101).
46. *The Poems of Anne Brontë*, pp. 99–100, (p. 100).
47. 'A Faith on Trial', *MP*, p. 356.
48. Unsigned review, *Westminster Review* 128 (September 1887), rpt. in *Norman Meredith: The Critical Heritage*, ed. Ioan Williams, pp. 297–392 (p. 299).
49. Kelvin, *A Troubled Eden: Nature and Society in the Works of George Meredith*, p. 3.
50. *Back to the Land: The Pastoral Impulse in England, from 1880 to 1914*, p. 34.
51. Tess Cosslett, *The 'Scientific Movement' and Victorian Literature*, p. 101.
52. Ebbatson, *Lawrence and the Nature Tradition*, p. 74.
53. *The Letters of George Meredith*, 2 vols. (New York, 1912), I, p. 33, quoted by J. W. Beach in *The Concept of Nature in Nineteenth Century England*, p. 480.
54. Quoted by Ebbatson in *Lawrence and the Nature Tradition*, p. 75.
55. Michael Wheeler, *The Art of Allusion in Victorian Fiction*, p. 114.
56. Mohammed Shaheen, *George Meredith: A Reappraisal of the Novels*, p. 176.
57. Bernard A. Richards, '*One of Our Conquerors* and the Country of the Blue', in *Meredith Now: Some Critical Essays*, ed. Ian Fletcher, pp. 281–94 (p. 283).
58. Andrew Enstice, *Thomas Hardy: Landscapes of the Mind*, p. 42.
59. Margaret Drabble, 'Hardy and the natural world', in *The Genius of Thomas Hardy*, ed. Margaret Drabble, pp. 162–9, (p. 166).
60. *The Collected Poems of Thomas Hardy*, p. 405.
61. J. R. Osgerby, 'Tess of the D'Urbervilles', *The Use of English* 14, No. 2 (1962), pp. 109–15 (p. 112).
62. Bruce Johnson, '"The Perfection of Species" and Hardy's Tess', in *Nature and the Victorian Imagination*, pp. 259–77 (p. 266).
63. David Lodge, *Language of Fiction*, pp. 182, 184.
64. Marsh, *Back to the Land*, p. 39.
65. Havelock Ellis, 'Thomas Hardy's Novels', *Westminster Review* 119 (April 1983), pp. 334–64, rpt. in *Thomas Hardy: The Critical Heritage*, ed. R. G. Cox, pp. 103–32 (p. 120).
66. *Spectator*, 26 March 1887, pp. 419–20, reprinted in *Thomas Hardy: The Critical Heritage*, pp. 142–5 (p. 145).
67. Lance St. John Butler, *Thomas Hardy*, p. 81.
68. Graham Hough, Introduction to *Selected Poems of George Meredith*, p. 5.

69. Consider, in particular, *A Forsaken Garden*. See also Pauline Fletcher's discussion of Swinburne in *Gardens and Grim Ravines*, Chapter 7.
70. George Bornstein, 'Miscultivated Field and Corrupted Garden: Imagery in *Hard Times*', *Nineteenth-Century Fiction*, 26, No. 2 (September 1971), pp. 158–70 (p. 159).

CHAPTER EIGHT: GARDENS AND CITIES

1. Christopher Mulvey, *Anglo-American Landscapes*. Mulvey quotes E. S. Nadal, *Impressions of London Social Life with Other Papers Suggested by an English Residence* (New York, 1875), p. 172.
2. See note 70 above.
3. *The Woman in White*, p. 322.
4. Little Dorrit in the novel of the same name sees London as a place 'so large, so barren, and so wild' (p. 165). The popular Victorian preacher, Charles Spurgeon, said that 'a great city is a great wilderness'. Quoted by David Skilton in *The English Novel*, p. 102.
5. Bruce B. Redford, 'Ruskin Unparadised: Emblems of Eden in *Praeterita*', *Studies in English Literature 1500–1900*, 22 No. 4 (1982), pp. 675–87 (p. 677).
6. The novels are *The Doctor's Wife* (1864), *The Story of Barbara* (1880), and *A Lost Eden* (1904).
7. *A Lost Eden*, p. 74.
8. For elaboration of this point, see Gillian Tindall, *The Born Exile*, p. 41.
9. 'The Garden', *Blackwood's Magazine*, 73 (1853), p. 131.
10. Ivanka Kovačević and S. Barbara Kanner, 'Blue Book Into Novel: The Forgotten Industrial Fiction of Charlotte Elizabeth Tonna', *Nineteenth-Century Fiction*, 25, No. 2 (September 1970), 152–73 (p. 160).
11. Quoted by Ivanka Kovačević in *Fact into Fiction*, p. 55.
12. For a perceptive analysis of the ambiguities and contradictions of *Sybil* relevant to my argument, see Patrick Brantlinger, *The Spirit of Reform*, pp. 96–104.
13. Trafford's model factory and village, and its 'real' world equivalents like Colonel Edward Akroyd's model suburban community at Halifax, look back to aristocratic models of country landowners.
14. *Mary Barton*, Preface to First Edition.
15. *Elizabeth Gaskell: Four Short Stories*, introduced by Anna Walters, p. 10.
16. *The Country and the City*, p. 281.

17. David Skilton, *The English Novel*, p. 131.
18. I am thinking in particular of novelists who deal almost exclusively with the socially privileged classes, and with novelists of provincial and rural societies. Perhaps even George Eliot can be regarded as one such novelist. Of her novels, only *Felix Holt* has a contemporary historical context, and her fiction is skewed in favour of her own topographical (i.e. rural) predilections.
19. Jean-Paul Hulin, Quoted in '"Rus in Urbe": A Key to Victorian Anti-Urbanism?' p. 16.
20. *The Poetical Works of Eliza Cook*, p. 276.
21. *Lays and Lyrics*, pp. 89–93.
22. Dobson, *Poetical Works*, pp. 269–70, 409–10.
23. John Lucas, *The Melancholy Man: A Study of Dickens's Novels*, p. 36.
24. '"Rus in Urbe": A Key to Victorian Anti-Urbanism?' p. 30.
25. Samuel M. Sipe, 'The Intentional World of Dickens', *Nineteenth-Century Fiction*, 30, No. 1 (June 1975), pp. 1–19 (p. 18).
26. Ibid., p. 19.
27. '"Rus in Urbe": A Key to Victorian Anti-Urbanism?' p. 25.
28. *Household Words*, 9, No. 225 (July 1854), pp. 543–6 (p. 543).
29. Ibid., p. 544.
30. 'How to Convert London into a Garden', *Once a Week*, I (1859), pp. 519–22.
31. 'The Country Cousin', *All The Year Round*, NS, 12, No. 285 (May 1874), Chapter 1, pp. 115–20 (p. 115).
32. 'Home Flowers', *Chambers's Journal*, No. 642 (15 April 1876), pp. 241–4 (p. 241).
33. Social observers were equally enthusiastic about the public parks opened up from the late 1840s onward in the major industrial towns of central and northern England, many of which were funded by wealthy individuals and private enterprise schemes. It is a mark of the metropolitan bias of later nineteenth-century fiction that novelists confine their comments and descriptions almost exclusively to the public parks of London.
34. Hippolyte Taine, *Notes on England* (1860–70), tr. Edward Hyams.
35. 'Composed Upon Westminster Bridge, September 3, 1802' (Published 1807), *The Poetical Works of Wordsworth* (London, 1951), p. 214.
36. Andrew Griffin, 'The Interior Garden and John Stuart Mill', in *Nature and the Victorian Imagination*, pp. 171–86 (p. 172).
37. 'Picturesque tumult' is Jerrold's phrase for Billingsgate in *London: A Pilgrimage*, p.80.
38. *English Hours*, p. xxxi.
39. Guy Williams, *The Royal Parks of London* (London, 1975), p. 78.

See also J. M. Barrie, 'The Grand Tour of the Gardens', in *The Little White Bird* (London, 1902), Chapter 13.
40. 'Public Parks', *Quiver* 13 (1878), p. 687.
41. 'Out of Doors', *All The Year Round*, NS, 4, No. 99 (October 1870), pp. 487–90 (p. 489).
42. *London: A Pilgrimage*, pp. 80, 101, 104.
43. Consider Henry James's comment on London's parks: 'They spread themselves with such a luxury of space in the centre of the town that they form . . . a pastoral landscape under the smoky sky.' *English Hours*, p. 11.
44. Th.[omas] Chalmers, 'Causes and Cure of Pauperism', *Edinburgh Review* 28, No. 55 (1817), pp. 16–17.
45. In the 1860s, a rich businessman in Manchester told Hippolyte Taine that Peel Park 'keeps our working men occupied and gives them something to think about. They must have something to amuse them; and besides, every hour spent here is one hour less in the public houses'. *Notes on England*, p. 234.
46. Quoted by Pierre Coustillas in 'Gissing's Variations on Urban and Rural Life', in *Victorian Writers And The City*, pp. 115–45 (p. 138).
47. Ibid., p. 131.
48. John Goode, *George Gissing: Ideology and Fiction*, p. 73.
49. Donald J. Olsen, *The Growth of Victorian London*, p. 204.
50. J. M. Richards, *Castles on the Ground* p. 2.
51. Walter L. Creese, 'Imagination in the Suburb', in *Nature and the Victorian Imagination*, pp. 49–67 (p. 49).
52. B. I. Coleman, 'The Idea of the Suburb: Suburbanization and Suburbanism in Victorian England', in *London in Literature*, A Symposium organised by the English Syndicate of the Roehampton Institute, May 1979 (Roehampton Institute, 1979), pp. 73–90 (p. 76).
53. *The Suburban Garden and Villa Companion*, p. 8.
54. It is a negative image, but 'it is suburbia unfinished that Dickens is portraying here'; consequently his 'conclusions are incomplete' (B. I. Coleman, *London in Literature*, p. 78).
55. Quoted by H. J. Dyos in *Victorian Suburb*, pp. 26–7.
56. For example, Ian Bradley asserts that Morris 'was one of the originators of the idea of the Garden City . . .'; see *William Morris and his World* (London, 1978), p. 114.
57. *Miscellanies*, second edition, 2 vols., II, pp. 318–45 (pp. 339–40).
58. Marc Reboul, 'Charles Kingsley: The Rector in the City', in *Victorian Writers and the City*, pp. 41–72 (p. 62).
59. *Miscellanies*, II, p. 340.
60. Letter to Mrs Alfred Baldwin (26 March 1874), in *The Letters of*

William Morris to his Family and Friends, ed. and introd. Philip Henderson, p. 62.
61. 'The Lesser Arts' (1882), quoted by Roderick Marshal in *William Morris and his Earthly Paradises* (Wiltshire, 1979), p. 242.
62. Bernard Sharratt, '*News from Nowhere*: Detail and Desire', in *Reading the Victorian Novel: Detail into Form*, pp. 288–305 (p. 295).
63. For considerations of *News from Nowhere* as a conscious anti-novel produced in opposition to bourgeois realist fiction, see Bernard Sharratt (above); Patrick Brantlinger, '"News from Nowhere": Morris's Socialist Anti-Novel', *Victorian Studies*, 19, No. 1 (September 1975), pp. 35–50; and Michael Wilding, *Political Fictions* (London, 1980), pp. 48–90.

CHAPTER NINE: GARDENS, HOMES AND WOMEN

1. Gillian Darley has made this point in regard to actual cottage gardens. See 'Cottage and suburban gardens', in *The Garden: A Celebration*, pp. 151–8 (p. 152).
2. Ian Adam, *George Eliot*, p. 10.
3. As he noted in *The Nether World*, 'The poor can seldom command privacy'. Adrian Poole writes: 'Rooms and streets—these are the dominant locations in Gissing. The single room is set against the streets as the locus for all the most intense emotion.' *Gissing in Context* (London, 1975), p. 45. John Halperin makes a similar point: 'We can see why so many stories Gissing wrote in the nineties are set in a lodging house: the place was for him a symbol of social anomalousness.' *Gissing: A Life in Books* (Oxford, 1982), p. 162.
4. *Gissing: A Life in Books*, p. 239.
5. 'Of Queen's Gardens', *RW*, XVIII, p. 122.
6. John Angell James, 'The Family Monitor', in *The Works of John Angell James*, edited by T. F. James (Birmingham, 1860), p. 56.
7. Joseph Shillito, *Womanhood: Its Duties, Temptations and Privileges* (1877), quoted by Jenni Calder in *Women and Marriage in Victorian Fiction* (London, 1976), p. 169.
8. Duncan Crow, *The Victorian Woman*, p. 52.
9. Of relevance here is the often quoted assertion that 'in the recoil from the City, the home was irradiated by the light of a pastoral imagination' (Walter E. Houghton, *The Victorian Frame of Mind*, p. 344).
10. Jan B. Gordon, 'The ALICE Books and the Metaphor of Victorian Childhood', in *Aspects of Alice: Lewis Carroll's Dreamchild as seen through the Critics' Looking-Glass 1865–1971*, ed. Robert Phillips (London, 1972), pp. 93–113 (p. 97).

11. Donald S. Hair, *Domestic and Heroic in Tennyson's Poetry*, p. 224.
12. Steven Marcus, *Dickens: From Pickwick to Dombey*, p. 253.
13. '*Adam Bede* and "the Story of the Past"', in *George Eliot: Centenary Essays And An Unpublished Fragment*, ed. Anne Smith, pp. 55–76 (p. 56).
14. An Optimist, *Cornhill Magazine* 26 (1872), pp. 424–39 (p. 427).
15. As John Carey says, his gardens 'frequently symbolize their owners as tellingly as the little chandelier symbolized Volumnia Dedlock'. *The Violent Effigy: a study of Dickens' Imagination*, p. 126.
16. Harry Stone, *Dickens and the Invisible World*, p. 254.
17. James M. Brown argues a similar view. He acknowledges that in Dickens's novels 'the ideal home operates as a microcosm of a social environment within which relations are healthy and qualitative, representing a radical criticism of the materialistic values and loss of community in the wider environment.' And yet, Brown contends, 'the fact that Dickens is utilising the middle-class myth of the Victorian hearth to clarify (by opposition) what is wrong with the system dilutes and emasculates his social criticism by cloaking it within a cosy, sentimental gloss so that the criticism becomes as comfortable as the tool used to convey it' (*Dickens: Novelist in the Market Place* (London, 1982), p. 44).
18. David Skilton, *Anthony Trollope and his Contemporaries*, p. 147.
19. *Sense and Sensibility*, Chapter 3.
20. *Persuasion*. Anne Elliott's attachment to the gardens of Kellynch is frequently remarked upon.
21. Quoted by Brenda Collombs in *Victorian Country Parsons* (London, 1977).
22. James Pope Hennessy, *Anthony Trollope*, p. 48.
23. Q. D. Leavis, Notes to *Silas Marner* (Harmondsworth, 1967), p. 263.
24. Consider Thomas Moser's essay, 'Conflicting Impulses in *Wuthering Heights*', *Nineteenth-Century Fiction* 17, No. 1 (June 1962). According to David Daiches, Moser's Freudian interpretation of the novel involves 'an admission that the latter part of the book . . . is inferior and indeed novelettish, the grafting on to the real novel of a conventional moral pattern involving the relation between the children of the storm and the children of the calm, as Lord David Cecil sees it' (Introduction to *Wuthering Heights* [Harmondsworth, 1965], p. 26). Barbary Hardy also entertains the possibility of a disappointed response, and asks her readers to consider whether 'the domestic peace of Hareton and Cathy represents a tamer and easier love than the endurance and affinity and painful rapture of Heathcliff and Catherine' (*Wuthering Heights* (Oxford, 1963), p. 54).
25. Stevie Davies, *Emily Brontë: The Artist As A Free Woman*, p. 169.

26. George Levine, *The Realist Imagination*, p. 215.
27. Consider Jane Eyre's words to Rochester in their reconciliation in the garden at Ferndean: 'You are no ruin, sir—no lightning-struck tree: you are green and vigorous. Plants will grow about your roots, whether you ask them or not . . .' (*Jane Eyre*, p. 469).
28. R. George Thomas, *Charles Dickens: Great Expectations*, p. 58.
29. Daniel R. Swarz, *Disraeli's Fiction*, p. 131.
30. Paul Bloomfield, *Disraeli*, p. 32.
31. For a discussion of the conflicting messages imparted to middle-class girls, see Deborah Gorham, *The Victorian Girl and the Feminine Ideal* (Bloomington, 1982).
32. Consider 'Elizabeth's [E. M. Russell's] outburst in *The Solitary Summer*: 'I sometimes literally ache with envy when I watch the men going about their pleasant work in the sunshine, turning up the luscious damp earth, raking, weeding, watering, planting, cutting the grass, pruning the trees' (p. 14).
33. William E. Buckler, *The Victorian Imagination*, p. 61.
34. John Dixon Hunt, *Story Painters and Picture Writers*, p. 192.
35. Christopher Ricks, *Tennyson*, p. 102.
36. *Everyman's Book of Victorian Verse*, ed. J. R. Watson (London, 1982), p. 200.
37. The embowered maiden was a favourite subject of Victorian photographers. One good example is Julia Margaret Cameron's photograph of Alice Liddell, aged 20, taken in 1872 (reproduced in Gus Macdonald, *Camera: Victorian Eyewitness* London, 1979, p. 28). Much the same can be said of D. G. Rossetti's painting, 'The Day-dream'. It depicts an idealised woman in a state of reverie, distanced from the adoring male spectator by 'The thronged boughs of the shadowy sycamore' which protect, enshrine and seem almost to grow out of her. Of the many paintings depicting women in garden settings, two watercolours by Frederick Walker, 'Lilies' (1868) and 'A Lady in a Garden, Perthshire' (1889), are among the better known examples.
38. Hugh Cunningham, 'Class and Leisure in Mid-Victorian England', reprinted from *Leisure in the Industrial Revolution* (1980) in *Popular Culture: Past and Present*, ed. Bernard Waites, et al. (London, 1982), pp. 66–91 (p. 82).
39. As Kincaid observes, the narrator 'almost never speaks of them together' (*Tennyson's Major Poems*, p. 123).
40. Ibid., p. 125.
41. Quoted by Marlene Springer in 'Angels and Other Women in Victorian Literature', in *What Manner of Women*, pp. 124–59 (p. 126).

CHAPTER TEN: GARDEN SETTINGS AND SCENES

1. Mrs Humphry Ward, *Robert Elsemere*, p. 35.
2. Geoffrey Taylor, *The Victorian Flower Garden*, p. 201.
3. Walter L. Creese, 'Imagination in the Suburb', p. 50.
4. In making use of terms such as 'frontstage', 'backstage' and (social) 'scripts', I am adopting the dramaturgical perspective of sociologists and social psychologists who view social life as a kind of improvised drama. From this perspective, social 'performances' are assumed to be 'scripted' in that they depend upon intersubjectively recognized rules of behaviour and sequences of behaviour appropriate to particular social situations. 'Frontstage' and 'backstage' are adopted from Erving Goffman, who posits the idea of a structural division of social establishments into 'front' regions (meeting places where guests are entertained) and 'back' regions (places to which the 'home team' retires between performances to relax and engage in more intimate activities). See Erving Goffman, *The Presentation of Self in Everyday Life* (Garden City, New York, 1959), pp. 144–5.
5. *Alice's Adventures in Wonderland and Through the Looking-Glass*, p. 141.
6. Anon., 'On the Terrace', *All The Year Round* 12, No. 303 (September 1874), p. 540.
7. See Richard Gill, *Happy Rural Seat: The English Country House and the Literary Imagination* (New Haven and London, 1972); Charles R. Anderson, *Person, Place and Thing in Henry James*, pp. 89–123; and Kenneth Graham, *Henry James: The Drama of Fulfilment. An Approach to the Novels*.
8. Perhaps the best discussion of these is by Kenneth Graham, who, having asserted that 'any approach to Henry James should open at once on a balcony or terrace', goes on to consider 'the way in which the grand terrace-view of Parisian and other possibilities becomes at once the view taken by a particular man of a particular enigmatic young woman' (*Henry James: The Drama of Fulfilment*, pp. 1, 2).
9. See William Sansom and Harold Chapman, *Victorian Life in Photographs* (London, 1977), p. 140.
10. For some readers, the description of Cheverel Manor is flat and overcrowded. Thomas A. Noble complains of being 'wearied with the seemingly endless process of adding phrase on phrase' (*George Eliot's 'Scenes of Clerical Life'*, p. 125).
11. Arlene M. Jackson, *Illustration and the Novels of Thomas Hardy*, p. 134.
12. Patricia M. Ball, *The Heart's Events*, p. 116.
13. Juliet McMaster, *Trollope's Palliser Novels*, p. 109.

14. Ronald King, *The Quest for Paradise*, p. 204.
15. *Henrietta Temple*, p. 95.
16. See my article, 'The Conservatory in Victorian Literature', *Journal of Garden History* 2, No. 3 (1982), pp. 273–84.
17. Consider Norman May's description of the conservatory at Abbotstoke Grange in Charlotte Yonge's *The Daisy Chain*: 'It's a real bower for a maiden of romance, with its rich green fragrance in the midst of winter. It is like a picture in a dream. One could imagine it as a fairyland, where no care, or grief or weariness could come.' Quoted by Mark Girouard in *The Victorian Country House*, p. 38.
18. Priscilla Boniface, *The Garden Room*, p. iii.
19. Significantly, the great majority of fictional conservatories are attached to, and accessible from within, the house. Hence, they tend to be ambiguous not only in form (built like the house, 'natural' like the garden), but also in location (part of the house? the garden?). Because they straddle the boundary between house and garden, they acquire those characteristics—'abnormal, timeless, ambiguous, at the edge, sacred'—which Edmund Leach ascribes to social boundary zones. See *Culture and Communication: the logic by which symbols are connected* (Cambridge, 1976), especially p. 35.
20. *The Cornhill Magazine*, NS, 20 (January 1893), pp. 509–24 (p. 510).
21. Ibid., p. 518.
22. Although I have chosen to concentrate upon fictional examples of the eavesdropping experience, there are similar scenes in Victorian narrative poetry, some of which are clearly symptomatic of the mistrust, deception and secrecy pervasive in the social worlds of the texts in which they occur. If we subscribe to the view that Tennyson's Arthurian characters are 'really' Victorians in drag—'men and women of the nineteenth century' as W. H. Mallock put it—then the abundant instances of spying and eavesdropping in the *Idylls of the King* offer oblique comments on the quality of communicative relationships in Victorian England. The experience of the luckless Balin in 'Balin and Balan' (*TP*, pp. 1583–4) is as shattering in its consequences as any other scene of its kind in Victorian literature. In one of the Camelot gardens, Balin bears witness to an apparently adulterous encounter between Lancelot and Guinevere, the latter hitherto his model of purity and grace. Once undeceived, Balin dashes away "mad for strange adventure" to the forest. Disillusionment leads to personal disintegration and finally to death.
23. It is through a crack in a garden wall that the (presumably) guiltless maiden portrayed in P. H. Calderon's well-known painting 'Broken

Vows' (1857) glimpses her perfidious lover in the act of flirting with another woman.
24. Winifred Hughes, *The Maniac in the Cellar*, p. 65.
25. Ibid., p. 17.
26. 'Our Novels: The Sensation School', *Temple Bar* 29 (July 1870), p. 422.
27. Robert Lee Wolff, *Sensational Victorian*, p. 4.
28. Wilkie Collins, *Armadale*, p. 622.
29. Wilkie Collins, Letter of Dedication to *Basil* (1862 ed.), p. iv.
30. Sue Lonoff, *Wilkie Collins and His Victorian Readers*, pp. 22–3.

CHAPTER ELEVEN: THE GARDEN WITHIN

1. David Palmer, 'Tennyson', in *English Poetry*, p. 145.
2. John Pettigrew, *Tennyson: The Early Poems*, pp. 12–13.
3. Ibid., p. 13.
4. David Palmer, 'Tennyson's Romantic Heritage', in *Tennyson*, ed. D. J. Palmer, pp. 23–51 (p. 25).
5. John Dixon Hunt, 'Tennyson', in *English Poetry*, p. 133.
6. 'Tennyson's Garden of Art: A Study of the Hesperides', in *Critical Essays*, p. 103.
7. Ibid., p. 104.
8. Ibid., p. 103.
9. Ibid., p. 101.
10. Ibid., p. 101.
11. Paul Turner, *Tennyson*, p. 66.
12. David Palmer, 'Tennyson's Romantic Heritage', p. 33.
13. John Armstrong, *The Paradise Myth* (London, 1969), p. 109.
14. Ibid., p. 110.
15. W. David Shaw, for example, draws attention to the syntactic isolation of the poem's opening lines, the detachment of the proem from the song that follows, and the way in which the song itself presents a series of discrete pictures. See *Tennyson's Style*, p. 62.
16. Ibid., p. 66.
17. J. B. Steane, *Tennyson*, p. 46.
18. Pettigrew, *Tennyson: the Early Poems*, p. 38.
19. William R. Brashear, *The Living Will*, p. 65.
20. I have chosen not to explain the Romantic thrust towards aesthetic self-determination from a specifically Marxian perspective. Had I done so, I should have interpreted the emergence of a garden-of-art aesthetic as a reaction to the dominant ideologies and social practices of early

industrial capitalism: to incipient Utilitarianism, empiricism, the forces of the market, and alienated labour. From such a perspective, the poetic-garden ecosystem is an image both of the organic, unitary and ahistorical work of solitary creative labour, and of the conditions under which such works have of necessity to be produced in an age in which creative writers are deprived of any significant or central social function. See Terry Eagleton, *Literary Theory: An Introduction* (Oxford, 1983), especially pp. 19–21.

21. Consider, for example, the predilection of Renaissance poet-philosophers, caught up in the prevailing cult of melancholy, for the comparatively naturalistic groves and bosky plantings which lay *outside* the confining walls of enclosed gardens. For a consideration of Renaissance illustrations of the poet-philosopher's environmental preferences, and their effects on garden design, see Roy Strong, *The Garden in England in the Renaissance* (London, 1977).

22. As evidence, consider the irony that the key 'structural' terms in Wordsworth's poetry, 'image', 'form', and 'shape', are precisely those which offer maximum resistance to structurization and determination. For Wordsworth, as C. C. Clarke has argued, 'image (i.e. sense-image) comes to mean neither "object of perception" simply nor "object" simply, neither "appearance" nor "thing" but a fusion or amalgam . . . of both' (*Romantic Paradox: An Essay on the Poetry of Wordsworth* (London, 1962), p. 95).

23. Quoted in Marshall Suther *Visions of Xanadu* (New York, 1965) p. 111.

24. *The Poetical Works of John Keats* (London, 1908), pp. 102–3, 236–7.

25. Beach, *The Concept of Nature in Nineteenth-Century English Poetry*, p. 406.

26. Ibid., p. 407.

27. Quoted by John Dixon Hunt in 'The Poetry of Distance: Tennyson's "Idylls of the King"', in *Victorian Poetry*, pp. 89–121 (p. 89).

28. Ibid., pp. 89–90.

29. Ricks, *Tennyson*, p. 93.

30. *Pope: Poetical Works*, edited by Herbert Davis (London, 1966), pp. 314–21.

31. John Dixon Hunt, 'Tennyson', in *English Poetry*, p. 135.

32. E. H. Waterston, 'Symbolism in Tennyson's Minor Poems', *Univ. of Toronto Quarterly* 20 (1951), pp. 369–80, reprinted in *Critical Essays*, pp. 113–25 (p. 120).

33. Charles Tennyson, *Alfred Tennyson*, p. 88.

34. K. W. Gransden, *Tennyson: In Memoriam*, p. 28.

35. Beach, *The Concept of Nature in Nineteenth-Century English Poetry*, p. 406.
36. Hallam, Tennyson, *Memoir*, I, p. 172.
37. Charles Tennyson, *Alfred Tennyson*, p. 88.
38. Paul Turner, *Tennyson*, p. 50.
39. The softening and sentimentalizing of death through association with gardens and flowers is particularly conspicuous in minor poems and magazine verses. See, for example, Austin Dobson's 'A Song of Angiola in Heaven' (*Poetical Works*, pp. 130–32); Samuel H. Gowan's 'Hally's Flower' (reprinted in *The Modern Elocutionist*, pp. 48–50); and M. G. Watkin's 'In Mother's Garden' (*Quiver* 1875, pp. 657--8).
40. Pauline Fletcher, *Gardens and Grim Ravines*, p. 49.
41. Ibid., p. 50.
42. I have borrowed this fine phrase from Christopher Ricks in 'Tennyson Inheriting the Earth', *Studies in Tennyson*, ed. Hallam Tennyson, (London, 1981), p. 77.
43. John Dixon Hunt, '"Story Painters and Picture Writers": Tennyson's Idylls and Victorian Painting', p. 184.
44. Of Tennyson's concept of the process of the non-finalist dialectic, Allan Danzig has this to say: 'the two terms of a contrary, in precarious balance, are equally valid and equally necessary to human life, which exists in the tension of their irresolvable polarity.' See 'The Contraries: A Central Concept in Tennyson's Poetry', *PMLA* 77, No. 5 (December 1962), pp. 577–85, reprinted in *British Victorian Literature: Recent Revaluations*, ed. Shiv Kumar (New York, 1969), pp. 112–30 (p. 117).
45. L. G. Whitbread, 'Tennyson's "In the Garden at Swainston"', *Victorian Poetry*, 13 (1975), pp. 61–9 (p. 66).

NOTES TO THE CONCLUSION

1. The point has not passed unobserved. See John Carey, *The Violent Effigy*, p. 127 and Juliet McMaster, 'Trollope's Country Estates', in *Trollope Centenary Essays*, ed. John Halperin (London, 1982), pp. 70–85 (p. 71).
2. Many garden writers expressed the view that gardens tended by their owners are superior to those entrusted entirely to paid employees. Novelists appear to have concurred with the view, for the great majority of favourably presented gardens are owners's gardens. There appear to be two main explanations for this bias. The first is the supposition that only owners indifferent to their gardens would relinquish responsibility for them. It follows from this that gardeners's gardens register the

indifference of their owners. The second explanation is that paid employees do not put their hearts into their work. Most professional gardeners in fiction are presented in unflattering terms; consider, for example, Hopkins in *The Small House at Allington*, Craig in *Adam Bede*, Hawkins in *Lothair*, and Blake in William Black's *Green Pastures and Piccadilly*. For critical remarks on gardeners in general see *The Belton Estate*, Chapter 7, *The Eustace Diamonds* II, pp. 192–3, and *Lothair*, p. 54 et passim.

3. 'A Factory as It Might Be', *MSW*, p. 647.
4. *Quarterly Review* 70 (1842), p. 240.
5. A. Dwight Culler, *The Poetry of Tennyson*. See, in particular, p. 15.
6. Tess Cosslett, *The 'Scientific Movement' and Victorian Literature*, p. 4.
7. Quoted in *English Hours*, p. 210.
8. Matthew Arnold, 'The Scholar Gipsy', *AP*, p. 366.
9. Quoted by John Holloway in *The Victorian Sage*, p. 136.

Bibliography

This bibliography is a list of works cited. For reasons of economy, it excludes (i) most works consulted but not cited, and (ii) many of the books, essays and articles to which only fleeting reference is made in the text and/or notes. Dates and titular forms are of editions used. Place of publication London, unless otherwise stated.

PRIMARY TEXTS I

The following list includes works of prose fiction, poems, and collected works.

Arnold, Matthew, *The Poems of Matthew Arnold*, ed. Kenneth Allott; 2nd ed. Miriam Allott (Longman, 1979).

Austin, Alfred, *The Garden that I love* (Macmillan, 1896).

——, *In Veronica's Garden* (Macmillan, 1897).

Barrie, J. M., *The Little White Bird* (Hodder and Stoughton, 1902).

Black, William, *Green Pastures and Piccadilly* (Macmillan, 1878).

——, *The Strange Adventures of a Phaeton* (Macmillan, 1878).

Blackmore, Richard Doddridge, *Alice Lorraine: A Tale of the South Downs*, 3 vols. (Sampson Low, 1875).

——, *Christowell: A Dartmore Tale*, 3 vols. (Sampson Low, 1882).

——, *Kit and Kitty: a story of West Middlesex* (Sampson Low, 1890).

Braddon, Mary Elizabeth, *Lady Audley's Secret* (New York: Dover Publications, Inc., 1974).

——, *The Doctor's Wife*, 3 vols. (John Maxwell and Co., 1864).

——, *The Golden Calf* (Simpkin, Marshall, Hamilton, Kent, and Co., n.d.).

——, *Just as I Am* (John and Robert Maxwell, n.d.).

——, The *Story of Barbara; her splendid marriage, and her gilded cage*, 3 vols. (John and Robert Maxwell, n.d.).

——, *A Lost Eden* (Hutchinson, 1904).

Brontë, Anne, *Agnes Grey* (Thomas Nelson, n.d.).

——, *The Poems of Anne Brontë: A New Text and Commentary*, ed. Edward Chittham (Macmillan, 1979).

Brontë, Charlotte, *Jane Eyre: An Autobiography* (Harmondsworth: Penguin, 1966).

——, *Shirley: A Tale* (Collins, 1953).

——, *Villette* (Collins, 1953).
——, *The Professor: A Tale*, in *The Professor: Tales From Angria; Emma: A Fragment* (Collins, 1954).
Brontë, Emily, *Wuthering Heights* (Harmondsworth: Penguin, 1965).
Broughton, Rhoda, *Not Wisely, but Too Well* (Richard Bentley, 1884).
——, *Belinda* (Richard Bentley, 1884).
——, *Doctor Cupid* (Richard Bentley, 1887).
Browning, Elizabeth Barrett, *Aurora Leigh And Other Poems*, intr. Cora Kaplan (The Women's Press, 1978).
Browning, Robert, *Browning: Poetical Works 1883–1864*, ed. Ian Jack (Oxford Univ. Press, 1970).
Butler, Samuel, *The Way of All Flesh* (Oxford Univ. Press, 1936).
'Carroll, Lewis' (Charles Lutwidge Dodgson), *Alice's Adventures in Wonderland AND Through the Looking-Glass*, ed. with an intro. Roger Lancelyn Green (Oxford Univ. Press, 1971).
Collins, Wilkie. *The Woman in White* (Chatto and Windus, 1886).
——, *Basil* (rev. ed., 1862; rpt. New York: Dover Publications, Inc., 1980).
——, *No Name* (Chatto and Windus, 1898).
——, *Armadale* (Chatto and Windus, 1897).
——, *The Moonstone: A Romance* (Chatto and Windus, 1871).
——, *Man and Wife* (Chatto and Windus, 1871).
——, *The Fallen Leaves* (Chatto and Windus, 1879).
——, *The Black Robe* (Chatto and Windus, 1897).
——, *Heart and Science* (Chatto and Windus, 1917).
——, *The Evil Genius; A Domestic Story* (Chatto and Windus, 1899).
——, *Blind Love* (Chatto and Windus, 1890).
——, *The New Magdalen* (Chatto and Windus, 1894).
Cook, Eliza, *The Poetical Works of Eliza Cook* (F. Warne, 1869).
'Craik, Mrs' (Dinah Maria Mullock), *John Halifax, Gentleman* (W. Nicholson, n.d.).
Deland, Margaret, *Old Garden and Other Verses* (Osgood and McIlvaine, 1893).
Dickens, Charles, *Sketches By Boz* (Oxford Univ. Press, 1957).
——, *The Posthumous Papers of The Pickwick Club* (Oxford Univ. Press, 1948).
——, *Oliver Twist* (Oxford Univ. Press, 1949).
——, *Nicholas Nickleby* (Oxford Univ. Press, 1950).
——, *The Old Curiosity Shop* (Oxford Univ. Press, 1951).
——, *Barnaby Rudge* (Oxford Univ. Press, 1954).
——, *American Notes AND Pictures from Italy* (Oxford Univ. Press, 1957).

——, *Martin Chuzzlewit* (Oxford Univ. Press, 1951).
——, *Dombey and Son* (Oxford Univ. Press, 1950).
——, *David Copperfield* (Oxford Univ. Press, 1948).
——, *Christmas Books* (Oxford Univ. Press, 1954).
——, *Bleak House* (Oxford Univ. Press, 1948).
——, *Hard Times* (Oxford Univ. Press, 1955).
——, *Little Dorrit* (Oxford Univ. Press, 1953).
——, *A Tale of Two Cities* (Oxford Univ. Press, 1956).
——, *Great Expectations* (Oxford Univ. Press, 1948).
——, *Our Mutual Friend* (Oxford Univ. Press, 1952).
——, *The Mystery of Edwin Drood* (Oxford Univ. Press, 1956).
——, *Christmas Stories* (Oxford Univ. Press, 1956).
Disraeli, Benjamin, *Henrietta Temple* (Peter Davies, 1927).
——, *Venetia* (Peter Davies, 1927).
——, *Coningsby* (Peter Davies, 1927).
——, *Sybil or The Two Nations* (Peter Davies, 1927).
——, *Lothair* (Peter Davies, 1927).
——, *Endymion* (Peter Davies, 1927).
——, and Sarah Disraeli ['Cherry and Fair Star'], *A Year at Hartlebury or The Election* (John Murray, 1983).
Dobson, Austin, *The Complete Poetical Works of Austin Dobson* (Oxford Univ. Press, 1923).
Dore, Gustave, and Blanchard Jerrold, *London: A Pilgrimage* (New York: Dover Publications, 1970).
Eden, Emily, *The Semi-attached Couple AND The Semi-attached House* (Virago, 1979).
'Eliot, George' (Mary Ann Cross, born Evans), *Scenes of Clerical Life* (Collins, n.d).
——, *Adam Bede* (Edinburgh and London: William Blackwood, n.d.).
——, *The Mill on the Floss* (Edinburgh and London: William Blackwood, n.d.).
——, *Silas Marner: The Weaver of Raveloe* (Edinburgh and London: William Blackwood, n.d.).
——, *Felix Holt the Radical* (Edinburgh and London: William Blackwood, n.d.).
——, *Middlemarch: A Study of Provincial Life* (Edinburgh and London: William Blackwood, 1875).
——, *Daniel Deronda* (Edinburgh and London: William Blackwood, 1889).
——, *Essays of George Eliot*, ed. Thomas Pinney (Routledge and Kegan Paul, 1963).

'Elizabeth' (Elizabeth Mary, Countess Russell), *Elizabeth and her German Garden* (Macmillan, 1928).
——, *The Solitary Summer* (Macmillan, 1901).
Ewing, Juliana, *Mary's Meadow* ed. H. K. F. Gatty (Society for Promoting Christian Knowledge, 1886).
Gaskell, Elizabeth, *Mary Barton* (Smith, Elder, and Co., 1906).
——, *Cranford* (Smith, Elder, and Co., 1906).
——, *North and South* (Smith, Elder, and Co., 1906).
——, *Ruth (Oxford Univ. Press, 1906).*
——, *My Lady Ludlow and Other Tales* (Smith, Elder, and Co., n.d.).
——, *Cousin Phillis and Other Tales* (Smith, Elder, and Co., 1906).
——, *Wives and Daughters* (Smith, Elder, and Co., 1906).
——, *Elizabeth Gaskell: Four Short Stories* intro. Anna Walters (Pandora Press, 1983).
——, *The Life of Charlotte Brontë*, 2 vols. (Smith, Elder and Co., 1857).
Gatty, Mrs [H. K. F.], *Parables from Nature* (Thomas Nelson, n.d.).
Gissing, George, *Demos: A Story of English Socialism* (Eveleigh Nash and Grayson, 1928).
——, *Isabel Clarendon*, 2 vols. (Sussex: Harvester Press, 1969).
——, *Thyrza: A Tale* (John Murray, 1907).
——, *A Life's Morning* (Eveleigh Nash and Grayson, 1928).
——, *The Nether World* (Dent, 1973).
——, *Born in Exile* (Thomas Nelson, n.d.).
——, *The Odd Women* (Thomas Nelson, n.d.).
——, *In the Year of Jubilee* (Sussex: Harvester Press, 1976).
——, *The Whirlpool* (Lawrence and Bullen, 1897).
——, *Human Odds and Ends: Stories and Sketches* (Sidgwick and Jackson, 1911).
——, *The Town Traveller* (Thomas Nelson, n.d.).
——, *The Private Papers of Henry Ryecroft* (New York: The New American Library of World Literature Inc., 1961).
——, *A Victim of Circumstances And Other Stories* (Constable, 1927).
——, *Will Warburton: A Romance of Real Life* (Constable, 1905).
——, *Stories and Sketches* (Michael Joseph, 1938).
Gore, Catherine, *Cecil; or, the Adventures of a Coxcomb* (n.p., 1841).
Grossmith, George, and Weedon, *The Diary of a Nobody* (Dent, 1940).
Hardy, Thomas, *The Collected Poems of Thomas Hardy* (Macmillan, 1952).
——, *Desperate Remedies* (Macmillan, 1952).
——, *Under the Greenwood Tree* (Macmillan, 1935).
——, *A Pair of Blue Eyes* (Macmillan, 1952).
——, *Far From the Madding Crowd* (Macmillan, 1974).
——, *The Return of the Native* (Macmillan, 1935).

——, *The Trumpet-Major* (Macmillan, 1962).
——, *Two on a Tower* (Macmillan, 1952).
——, *The Mayor of Casterbridge* (Macmillan, 1958).
——, *The Woodlanders* (Macmillan, 1934).
——, *Tess of the D'Urbervilles* (Collins, 1958).
——, *Life's Little Ironies* (Macmillan, 1952).
Hawthorne, Nathaniel, *Our Old Home, and English Note-Books*, 2 vols. (Kegan Paul and Trench, 1883).
——, *The Centenary Edition of the Works of Nathaniel Hawthorne* (Ohio: Ohio State Univ. Press, 1963–).
Hemans, Mrs [Felicia Dorothea], *Works of Mrs. Hemans With A Memoir By Her Sister* [Harriet Hughes] (Edinburgh: Blackwood, 1839).
Hood, Thomas, *The Works of Thomas Hood*, 7 vols. (Edward Moxon, 1862).
——, *The Complete Poetical Works of Thomas Hood*, ed. Walter Jerrold. (Henry Frowde, 1906).
Hunt, Leigh, *The Poetical Works of Leigh Hunt*, ed. S. Adams Lee (Boston: n.p., 1866).
James Henry, *Roderick Hudson* (Oxford: Oxford Univ. Press, 1980).
——, *The Portrait of a Lady* (Bodley Head, 1968).
——, *The Aspern Papers*, in *The Turn of the Screw, The Aspern Papers and Other Stories* (Collins, 1956).
——, *The Awkward Age* (Bodley Head, 1967).
——, *The Ambassadors* (Bodley Head, 1970).
——, *English Hours*, ed. with an intro. by Alma Louise Lowe (Heinemann, 1962).
Jefferies, Richard, *Amaryllis at the Fair*, in *After London, and Amaryllis at the Fair* (Dent, 1932).
——, *Richard Jefferies' London*, ed. with an intro. by Samuel J. Looker (Lutterworth Press, 1944).
——, *Richard Jefferies, Landscape and Labour: A New Collection of Essays*, ed. John Pearson (Wiltshire: Moonraker Press, 1979).
Kingsley, Charles, *Glaucus; or, The Wonders of the Shore* (Cambridge, Macmillan, 1855).
——, *Miscellanies*, 2 vols. (John W. Parker, 1860).
Lytton, Edward Bulwer, *Eugene Aram: A Tale* (George Routledge, 1851).
——, *Godolphin* (Routledge, Warne, and Routledge, 1865).
——, *Ernest Maltravers* (George Routledge, 1840).
——, *Alice; or the Mysteries* (George Routledge, 1851).
——, *Lucretia; or, The Children of Night* (George Routledge, 1953).
——, *Night and Morning* (George Routledge, 1851).
——, *The Coming Race* (Leipzig: Tauchnitz, 1873).

——, *Kenelm Chillingly: His Adventures and Opinions* (George Routledge, 1873).
Macaulay, Thomas Babington, *The Works of Lord Macaulay*, 12 vols. (Longmans, 1898).
Mallock, W. H., *The New Republic: Culture, Faith and Philosophy in an English Country House* (Leicester: Leicester Univ. Press, 1975).
Marshall, Emma, *In the City of Flowers* (Seeley, 1889).
Meredith, George, *The Poetical Works of George Meredith*, notes by G. M. Trevelyan (Constable, 1912).
——, *Sandra Belloni* (Constable, 1904).
——, *Rhoda Fleming* (Constable, 1910).
——, *The Egoist: A Comedy in Narrative*, 2 vols. (Constable, 1910).
——, *Diana of the Crossways* (Constable, 1906).
——, *One of Our Conquerors* (Constable, 1910).
Mill, John Stuart, *The Subjection of Women*, ed. Sue Mansfield (Illinois, Arlington Heights: AHM Publishing Corporation, 1980).
Miller, Thomas, *My Father's Garden* (n.p., 1867).
Mitford, Mary Russell, *Our Village* (Macmillan, 1926).
——, *Sketches of English Life and Character* (John Lane, 1928).
Morris, William, *The Collected Works of William Morris*, ed. May Morris, 24 vols. (Longmans, Green, and Co., 1910–15).
——, *William Morris: Selected Writings*, ed. G. D. H. Cole (Nonesuch Press, 1946).
Oliphant, Mrs [M. O.], *Chronicles of Carlingford: Salem Chapel* (Edinburgh and London: William Blackwood, 1863).
——, *Miss Marjoribanks* (Zodiac Press, 1969).
——, *A Country Gentleman and his Family*, 3 vols. (Macmillan, 1886).
'Ouida' (Marie Louise Ramé), *Moths* (Chatto and Windus, 1902).
——, *Critical Studies: A Set of Essays by OUIDA* (T. Fisher Unwin, 1900).
Reade, Charles, *It is Never Too Late to Mend* (Collins, n.d.).
——, *Hard Cash: A Matter-of-Fact Romance* (Chatto and Windus, 1922).
——, *A Woman-Hater* (Chatto and Windus, 1896).
Ruskin, John, *Library Edition of The Works of John Ruskin*, ed. E. T. Cook and Alexander Wedderburn, 39 vols. (George Allen, 1903–12).
'Rutherford, Mark' (William Hale White), *Catherine Furze* (T. F. Unwin, 1893).
Scott, Clement, *Lays and Lyrics* (Routledge, 1888).
Sieveking, Albert Forbes, ed., *The Praise of Gardens: An Epitome of the Literature of The Garden-Art* (Dent, 1899).
Surtees, R. S., *Hillingdon Hall or The Cockney Squire: A Tale of Country Life* (Methuen, 1844).

Swinburne, A. C., *The Poems of Algernon Charles Swinburne*, 6 vols. (Chatto and Windus, 1904).
——, *Essays and Studies* (Chatto and Windus, 1888).
Tennyson, Alfred, *The Poems of Tennyson*, ed. Christopher Ricks (Longmans, 1969).
Thackeray, William Makepeace, *Vanity Fair: or, a Novel without a Hero* (Thomas Nelson, n.d.).
——, *The History of Pendennis* (Macmillan, 1901).
——, *The Newcomes: Memoirs of a most respectable family* (Macmillan, 1907).
[Tonna], Charlotte Elizabeth, *Helen Fleetwood* (R. B. Seeley, 1841).
Trollope, Anthony, *Barchester Towers* (Dent, 1906).
——, *Dr. Thorne* (Oxford Univ. Press, 1926).
——, *The Three Clerks* (Oxford Univ. Press, 1907).
——, *Framley Parsonage* (Zodiac Press, 1972).
——, *Castle Richmond* (John Lane, 1906).
——, *Orley Farm*, 2 vols. (Oxford Univ. Press, 1935).
——, *Rachel Ray* (Oxford Univ. Press, 1924).
——, *Can You Forgive Her?* 2 vols. in one (Oxford Univ. Press, 1953).
——, *The Small House at Allington* (Zodiac Press, 1973).
——, *Phineas Finn, the Irish Member* (Harmondsworth: Penguin, 1972).
——, *The Claverings* (Oxford Univ. Press, 1924).
——, *The Eustace Diamonds* 2 vols. in one (Oxford Univ. Press, 1973).
——, *The Way We Live Now* (Oxford Univ. Press, 1951).
——, *The Prime Minister*, 2 vols. in one (Oxford Univ. Press, 1938).
——, *The American Senator* (Oxford Univ. Press, 1931).
——, *An Eye For An Eye* (Anthony Blond, 1966).
——, *Ayala's Angel* (Oxford Univ. Press, 1929).
Ward, Mrs Humphry [Mary Augusta], *Robert Elsemere* (Lincoln: Univ. of Nebraska Press, 1967).
Whyte-Melville, G. J., *Digby Grand: An Autobiography* (Longmans, Green, And Co., 1890).
——, *Tilbury Nogo; or, Passages in the Life of An Unsuccessful Man* (Ward, Lock, Bowden, And Co., 1858).
——, *Kate Coventry: An Autobiography* (Longmans, Green, And Co., 1882).
——, *Cerise: A Tale of the Last Century* (Chapman and Hall, 1866).
——, *The White Rose* (n.p., 1868).
Wood, Mrs Henry [Ellen], *The Channings* (Walter Scott Publishing Co., n.d.).
——, *Oswald Cray* (Macmillan, 1901).
Yonge, Charlotte M., *The Heir of Redclyffe* (Macmillan, 1901).

——, *Heartsease; or, The Brother's Wife* (Macmillan, 1906).
——, *The Daisy Chain* (Macmillan, 1879).
——, *The Pillars of the House; or, Under Wode, Under Rode*, 2 vols. (Macmillan, 1893).
——, *Nuttie's Father* (Macmillan, 1886).

PRIMARY TEXTS II

This list includes nineteenth-century works on garden theory and practice. It excludes all but a few of the most substantial and frequently cited articles from contemporary journals.

Alison, Archibald, *Essays on the Nature and Principles of Taste* (Edinburgh: Bell and Bradfute, 1790).
Anon., 'The Garden', *Blackwood's Magazine* 73 (1853), pp. 129–44.
Blomfield, Reginald, *The Formal Garden in England* (Macmillan, 1892).
Bridges-Adam, William, 'How to Convert London into a Garden', *Once a Week* 1 (1859), pp. 519–22.
[Bright, Henry Arthur], 'The English Flower Garden', *Quarterly Review* 149 (1880), pp. 331–60.
Burgess, Henry, *The Amateur Gardener's year-book* (Edinburgh: A. and C. Black, 1854).
An Optimist, 'On Gardening', *Cornhill Magazine* 26 (1872), pp. 424–39.
Downing, Andrew Jackson, *Victorian Cottage Residences* (rev. 5th ed., 1873; rpt. New York: Dover Publications, Inc., 1981).
——, *Rural Essays*, ed. with a memoir by George William Curtis (New York: Leavitt and Allen, 1856).
Gould, S. Baring, *Old Country Life* (Macmillan, 1895).
Hibberd, Shirley, *Rustic Adornments for Homes of Taste* (Groombridge, 1870).
——, *The Amateur's Flower Garden* (Groombridge, 1875).
Howitt, William, *The Rural Life of England* (Longman, Brown, Green, and Longmans, 1844).
Kerr, Robert, *The Gentleman's House* (New York: Johnson Reprint Corporation, 1972).
Loudon, John Claudius, *An Encyclopaedia of Gardening* (Longman, Rees, Orme, Brown, and Green, 1828).
——, *The Suburban Gardener and Villa Companion* (Longman, Orme, Brown, Green, and Longmans, 1838).
——, Introduction to *Gardener's Magazine* 1 (1825), pp. 1–7.
——, 'Remarks on Laying Out Public Gardens and Promenades',

Gardener's Magazine 2 (1835), pp. 648–64.
——, 'On Laying Out and Planting the Lawn, Shrubbery, and Flower-Garden', *Gardener's Magazine* 19 (1843), pp. 166–77.
Milner, George, *Country Pleasures: The Chronicle of a Year, chiefly in a garden* (Longmans, 1881).
Morris, William, 'Hopes and Fears for Art' (1882), in *The Collected Works of William Morris*, ed. May Morris, 24 vols. (Longmans, Green, and Co., 1910–15), XXII, pp. 87–90.
Paul, Margaret A., 'Old Fashioned Gardening', *Nineteenth Century* 7 (1880), pp. 128–35.
Repton, Humphry, *An Enquiry into the Changes of Taste in Landscape Gardening* (Taylor, 1806).
——, *The Landscape Gardening and Landscape Architecture of the Late H. Repton*, intro. J. C. L[oudon] (Longman, 1840).
Robinson, William, *The Wild Garden; or, Our Groves And Shrubberies Made Beautiful By The Naturalization Of Hardy Exotic Plants* (John Murray, 1870).
Anon., 'The Flower Garden', *Quarterly Review* 70 (1842), pp. 196–243.
Anon., 'Landscape Gardening', *Quarterly Review* 37 (1855), pp. 189–220.
[Scott, Sir Walter], 'Landscape Gardening', *Quarterly Review* 37 (1828), pp. 303–44.
Sedding, J. D., *Garden-craft, old and new* (Kegan Paul, 1891).
Tyas, Robert, *The Language of Flowers; or, Floral Emblems of Thoughts, Feelings, and Sentiments* (Routledge, 1869).

SECONDARY MATERIAL I

This list includes twentieth-century studies of Victorian gardens and gardening, and more general works treating of Victorian attitudes toward nature and landscapes.

Appleton, Jay, *The Experience of Landscape* (John Wiley, 1975).
Batey, Mavis, *Oxford Gardens: The university's influence on garden history* (Amersham: Avebury, 1982).
Beach, Joseph Warren, *The Concept of Nature in Nineteenth-Century English Poetry* (Macmillan, 1966).
Darley, Gillian, *Villages of Vision* (Architectural Press, 1975).
Davey, Peter, *Arts and Crafts Architecture: The Search for Earthly Paradise* (Architectural Press, 1980).
Girouard, Mark, *Sweetness and Light: The 'Queen Anne' Movement 1860–1900* (Oxford: Clarendon Press, 1977).

——, *The Victorian Country House* (New Haven: Yale Univ. Press, 1979).
Gorer, Richard, *The Flower Garden In England* (Batsford, 1975).
Hadfield, Miles, *A History of British Gardening* (Hutchinson, 1960).
——, *Topiary and Ornamental Hedges* (A. and C. Black, 1971).
Harling, Robert, *Home: a Victorian Vignette* (Constable, 1938).
Harris, John, ed., *The Garden: A Celebration of One Thousand Years of British Gardening: the Guide to the Exhibition Presented by the Victoria and Albert Museum* (New Perspectives, 1979).
Hussey, Christopher, *The Picturesque: Studies in a Point of View* (Cass, 1967).
King, Ronald, *The Quest for Paradise: A History of the World's Gardens* (Weybridge, Surrey: Whittet Books, 1979).
Knoepflmacher, U. C., and G. B. Tennyson, eds., *Nature and the Victorian Imagination* (Berkeley and Los Angeles: Univ. of California Press, 1977).
Malins, Edward, *English Landscaping and Literature 1660–1840* (Oxford Univ. Press, 1966).
——, and Patrick Bowe, *Irish Gardens and Demesnes from 1830* (Barrie and Jenkins, 1980).
Maple, Eric, *The Secret Lore of Plants and Flowers* (Robert Hale, 1980).
Marsh, Jan, *Back to the Land: The Pastoral Impulse in England, from 1880 to 1914* (Quartet Books, 1982).
Marsh, Jean, *Language of Flowers*, illus. Kate Greenaway (Macdonald and Jane's, 1978).
Powell, Claire, *The Meaning of Flowers: A Garland of Plant Lore and Symbolism from Popular Culture and Literature* (Jupiter Books, 1977).
Ravensway, Charles Van, *A Nineteenth-Century Garden* (New York: Universe Books, 1977).
Roberts, Harry, *English Gardens* (Collins, 1944).
Rubenstein, David, *Victorian Homes* (David Charles, 1974).
Scott-James, Anne, *The Cottage Garden* (Allen Lane, 1981).
——, and Osbert Lancaster, *The Pleasure Garden: An Illustrated History of British Gardening* (Harmondsworth: Penguin, 1977).
Seaton, Beverly, 'The Garden Writings of Henry Arthur Bright', *Garden History* 10, No. 1 (1982), pp. 74–9.
Taylor, Geoffrey, *Some Nineteenth Century Gardeners* (Skeffington, 1951).
——, *The Victorian Flower Garden* (Skeffington, 1952).
Thacker, Christopher, *The History of Gardens* (Croom Helm, 1979).
Thomas, William Beach, *Gardens* (Burke, 1952).
Tuan, Yi-Fu, *Topophilia: A Study of Environmental Perception, Attitudes, and Values* (New Jersey: Prentice-Hall, 1974).
Waters, Michael, 'The Conservatory in Victorian Literature', *Journal of*

Garden History 2, No. 3 (1982), pp. 273–84.
Watkin, David, *The English Vision: The Picturesque in Architecture, Landscape and Garden Design* (John Murray, 1982).

SECONDARY MATERIAL II

This list includes historical, biographical, and critical studies.

Adam, Ian, *George Eliot* (Routledge and Kegan Paul, 1969).
Allott, Miriam, ed., *The Brontës: The Critical Heritage* (Routledge and Kegan Paul, 1974).
Anderson, Charles R., *Person, Place and Thing in Henry James's Novels* (Durham, North Carolina: Duke Univ. Press, 1977).
Anderson, Rachel, *The Purple Heart Throbs: The sub-literature of love* (Hodder and Stoughton, 1974).
Andrews, Malcolm, *Dickens on England and the English* (Sussex: Harvester Press, 1979).
Ashley, Robert, *Wilkie Collins* (Arthur Barker, 1952).
Ball, Patricia M., *The Heart's Events: The Victorian Poetry of Relationships* (Athlone Press, 1976).
Bradbury, Malcolm, and David Palmer, eds., *Victorian Poetry* Stratford-Upon-Avon Studies 15 (Arnold, 1972).
Brantlinger, Patrick, '"News from Nowhere": Morris's Socialist Anti-Novel', *Victorian Studies* 19, No. 1 (September 1975), pp. 35–50.
——, *The Spirit of Reform: British Literature and Politics, 1832–1867* (Cambridge, Mass.: Harvard Univ. Press, 1977).
——, 'What is "sensational" about the "Sensation Novel"?' *Nineteenth-Century Fiction* 37, No. 1 (June 1982), pp. 1–28.
Brashear, William R., *The Living Will: A Study of Tennyson and Nineteenth-Century Subjectivism* (The Hague: Mouton, 1969).
Braun, Tom, *Disraeli the Novelist* (George Allen, 1981).
Brown, James M., *Dickens: Novelist in the Market Place* (Macmillan, 1982).
Buckler, William E., *The Victorian Imagination: Essays in Aesthetic Exploration* (Sussex: Harvester Press, 1980).
Buckley, Jerome H., *Tennyson: The Growth of a Poet* (Cambridge, Mass.: Harvard Univ. Press, 1960).
Burne-Jones, Georgiana, *Memorials of Edward B.-J.* (n.p., 1904).
Burris, Quincy Guy, *Richard Doddridge Blackmore: His Life and Novels* (Westport, Connecticut: Greenwood Press, 1973).
Burton, Elizabeth, *The Early Victorians at Home* (Longman, 1972).

Calhoun, Blue, *The Pastoral Vision of William Morris: 'The Earthly Paradise'* (Athens: Univ. of Georgia Press, 1975).

Carey, John, *The Violent Effigy: a study of Dickens' Imagination* (Faber and Faber, 1979).

Chandler, Alice, *A Dream of Order: The Medieval Ideal in Nineteenth-Century Literature* (Routledge and Kegan Paul, 1971).

Churchill, Kenneth, *Italy and English Literature 1764–1930* (Macmillan, 1980).

Collie, Michael, *The Alien Art: A Critical Study of George Gissing's Novels* (Dawson: Archon Books, 1979).

Collombs, Brenda, *Victorian Country Parsons* (Constable, 1977).

Conrad, Peter, *The Victorian Treasure House* (Collins, 1973).

Cosslett, Tess, *The 'Scientific Movement' and Victorian Literature* (Sussex: Harvester Press, 1982).

Craik, W. A., *Elizabeth Gaskell and the English Provincial Novel* (Methuen, 1975).

Crow, Duncan, *The Victorian Woman* (George Allen and Unwin, 1971).

Culler, A. Dwight, *The Poetry of Tennyson* (New Haven: Yale Univ. Press, 1977).

Cunningham, Hugh, *Leisure and the Industrial Revolution* (Croom Helm, 1980).

Davies, Stevie, *Emily Brontë: The Artist As A Free Woman* (Manchester: Carcanet, 1983).

Dickens, Charles, *The Letters of Charles Dickens*, various eds. and dates (Oxford: Clarendon Press).

Drabble, Margaret, ed., *The Genius of Thomas Hardy* (Weidenfeld and Nicolson, 1976).

Dunn, Waldo Hilary, *R. D. Blackmore* (Robert Hale, 1950).

Dyos, H. J., *Victorian Suburb: A Study of the Growth of Clerkenwell* (Leicester: Leicester Univ. Press, 1961).

——, and Michael Wolff, eds., *The Victorian City: Images and Reality*, 2 vols. (Routledge and Kegan Paul, 1973).

Easson, Angus, *Elizabeth Gaskell* (Routledge and Kegan Paul, 1979).

Ebbatson, Roger, *Lawrence and the Nature Tradition: A Theme in English Fiction 1859–1914* (Sussex: Harvester Press, 1980).

Eley, Geoffrey, *The Ruined Maid: Modes and Manners of Victorian Women* (Royston, Herts.: Priory Press, 1970).

Engen, Rodney, *Kate Greenaway: A Biography* (Macdonald Futura Publishers, 1981).

Enstice, Andrew, *Thomas Hardy: Landscapes of the Mind* (Macmillan, 1979).

Faulkner, Peter, *Against the Age: An Introduction to William Morris* (George Allen and Unwin, 1980).

Finley, Gerald, *Landscapes of Memory: Turner as Illustrator to Scott* (Scolar Press, 1980).

Fletcher, Ian, ed., *Meredith Now: Some Critical Essays* (Routledge and Kegan Paul, 1971).

Fletcher, Pauline, *Gardens and Grim Ravines: The Language of Landscape in Victorian Poetry* (New Jersey, Princeton: Princeton Univ. Press, 1983).

Forster, Margaret, *William Makepeace Thackeray: Memoirs of a Victorian Gentleman* (Secker and Warburg, 1978).

Forsyth, R. A., 'The Victorian Self-Image and the Emergent City Sensibility', *Univ. of Toronto Quarterly* 33, No. 1 (1963), pp. 61–77.

Garrett, Peter K., *Scene and Symbol from George Eliot to James Joyce* (New Haven: Yale Univ. Press, 1969).

Gill, Richard, *Happy Rural Seat: The English Country House and the Literary Imagination* (New Haven: Yale Univ. Press, 1972).

Goode, John, *George Gissing: Ideology and Fiction* (Vision Press, 1978).

Graham, Kenneth, *Henry James: The Drama of Fulfilment. An Approach to the Novels* (Oxford: Clarendon Press, 1975).

Gransden, K. W., *Tennyson: In Memoriam* (Arnold, 1964).

Gray, J. M., *Tennyson's Doppleganger: 'Balin and Balan'* (Lincoln: Tennyson Research Centre, 1971).

Gregor, Ian, ed., *Reading the Victorian Novel: Detail into Form* (Vision Press, 1980).

Hair, Donald S., *Domestic and Heroic in Tennyson's Poetry* (Toronto: Univ. of Toronto Press, 1981).

Halperin, John, *Gissing: A Life in Books* (Oxford Univ. Press, 1982).

Hamilton, Walter, *The Aesthetic Movement in England* (New York: Ams Press, 1971).

Harrison, Fraser, *The Dark Angel: Aspects of Victorian Sexuality* (Sheldon Press, 1977).

Henderson, Philip, ed., *The Letters of William Morris to his Family and Friends* (Longmans, Green, and Co., 1950).

——, *William Morris: His Life, Work, and Friends* (Thames and Hudson, 1967).

Hennessy, James Pope, *Anthony Trollope* (Jonathan Cape, 1971).

Hersey, George L., *High Victorian Gothic: A Study in Associationism* (Johns Hopkins Univ. Press, 1972).

Hewison, Robert, ed., *New Approaches to Ruskin: Thirteen Essays* (Routledge and Kegan Paul, 1981).

Hill, Nancy, *A Reformer's Art: Dickens's Picturesque and Grotesque Imagery*

(Athens: Ohio Univ. Press, 1981).
Holloway, John, *The Victorian Sage: Studies in Argument* (Archon Books, 1962).
Honan, Park, *Browning's Characters: A Study in Poetic Technique* (New Haven: Yale Univ. Press, 1969).
Hönnighausen, Gisela, 'Emblematic Tendencies in the Works of Christina Rossetti', *Victorian Poetry* 10 (1972), pp. 1–15.
Houghton, Walter, E., *The Victorian Frame of Mind, 1830–1870* (New Haven: Yale Univ. Press, 1957).
Hughes, Winifred, *The Maniac in the Cellar: Sensation Novels of the 1860s* (New Jersey, Princeton: Princeton Univ. Press, 1980).
Hulin, Jean-Paul, and Pierre Coustillas, eds., *Victorian Writers and the City* (Centre D'Etudes Victoriennes: publications de l'université de Lille III, n.d.).
Hunt, John Dixon, 'The Poetry of Distance: Tennyson's "Idylls of the King"', in *Victorian Poetry*, ed. Malcolm Bradbury and David Palmer (1972), pp. 89–121.
——, '"Story Painters and Picture Writers": Tennyson's Idylls and Victorian Painting', in *Tennyson*, ed. D. J. Palmer (Bell, 1973), pp. 181–202.
——, and David Palmer, 'Tennyson', in *English Poetry* (Sussex Books, 1976).
Irwin, Michael, *Picturing: Description and Illusion in the Nineteenth-Century Novel* (George Allen and Unwin, 1979).
Jackson, Arlene M., *Illustration and the Novels of Thomas Hardy* (Macmillan, 1982).
Johnson, Wendell Stacy, *Sex and Marriage in Victorian Poetry* (Ithaca: Cornwall Univ. Press, 1975).
Joseph, Gerard, *Tennysonian Love: The Strange Diagonal* (Minneapolis: Minnesota Univ. Press, 1969).
Kelvin, Norman, *A Troubled Eden: Nature and Society in the Works of George Meredith* (Oliver and Boyd, 1961).
Killham, John, ed., *Critical Essays on the Poetry of Tennyson* (Routledge and Kegan Paul, 1960).
Kincaid, James R., *Tennyson's Major Poems: The Comic and Ironic Patterns* (New Haven: Yale Univ. Press, 1975).
Kingsley, Charles, *Charles Kingsley: His Letters and Memories of His Life*, ed. by his wife [Fanny E. Kingsley], 2 vols. (H. S. King, 1877).
Kovačević, Ivanka, *Fact into Fiction: English Literature and the industrial scene 1750–1850* (Leicester Univ. Press, 1975).
——, and S. Barbara Kanner, 'Blue Book Into Novel: The Forgotten Industrial Fiction of Charlotte Elizabeth Tonna', *Nineteenth-Century*

Fiction 25, No. 2 (September 1970), pp. 152–73.

Kumar, Shiv, ed., *British Victorian Literature: Recent Revaluations* (New York: New York Univ. Press, 1962).

Lerner, Laurence, ed., *The Victorians* (Methuen, 1978).

Levine, George, *The Realist Imagination: English Fiction from Frankenstein to Lady Chatterley* (Chicago: Univ. of Chicago Press, 1981).

Lockwood, Allison, *Passionate Pilgrims: The American Traveler in Great Britain 1800–1914* (New York: Cornwall Books, 1981).

London in Literature. A symposium organised by the English Syndicate of the Roehampton Institute, May 1979 (Roehampton Institute, 1979).

Lonoff, Sue, *Wilkie Collins and His Victorian Readers: A Study in the Rhetoric of Authorship* (New York: Ams. Press, 1982).

Lucas, John, *The Melancholy Man: A Study of Dickens's Novels* (2nd ed., Sussex: Harvester Press, 1980).

Madden, William A., *Matthew Arnold: A Study of the Aesthetic Temperament in Victorian England* (Bloomington: Indiana Univ. Press, 1967).

Marcus, Steven, *Dickens: From Pickwick to Dombey* (Chatto and Windus, 1965).

Mare, Margaret, and Alicia C. Percival, *Victorian Best-Seller: The World of Charlotte M. Yonge* (Harrap, 1948).

Masefield, Muriel, *Peacocks and Primroses: A Survey of Disraeli's Novels* (Geoffrey Bles, 1953).

Marlow, James F., 'Memory, Romance, and the Expressive Symbol in Dickens', *Nineteenth-Century Fiction* 30, No. 1 (1975), pp. 20–32.

Martin, Robert Bernard, *The Accents of Persuasion: Charlotte Brontë's Novels* (Faber and Faber, 1966).

Marx, Leo, *The Machine in the Garden: Technology and the Pastoral Ideal in America* (New York: Oxford Univ. Press, 1964).

McMaster, Juliet, *Trollope's Palliser Novels: Theme and Pattern* (Macmillan, 1978).

——, 'Trollope's Country Estates', in *Trollope Centenary Essays*, ed. John Halperin (Macmillan, 1982, pp. 70–85).

Meier, Paul, *William Morris: The Marxist Dreamer*, trans. Frank Gubb, 2 vols. (Sussex: Harvester Press, 1978).

Mews, Hazel, *Frail Vessels: Women's Role in Women's Novels from Fanny Burney to George Eliot* (Athlone Press, 1969).

Miles, Josephine, *Pathetic Fallacy in the Nineteenth Century: A Study of Changing Relations Between Object and Emotion* (New York: Octagon Books, 1965).

Miller, J. Hillis, *The Disappearance of God: Five Nineteenth-Century Writers* (Cambridge, Mass: Harvard Univ. Press, 1963).

Mitford, Mary Russell, *The Life and Letters of Mary Russell Mitford*, ed.

A. G. l'Estrange, 2 vols. (New York: Harper, 1870).

Mulvey, Christopher, *Anglo-American Landscapes: A study of nineteenth-century Anglo-American travel literature* (Cambridge: Cambridge Univ. Press, 1983).

Noble, Thomas A., *George Eliot's 'Scenes of Clerical Life'* (New Haven: Yale Univ. Press, 1965).

Olsen, Donald J., *The Growth of Victorian London* (Batsford, 1976).

Palmer, D. J., ed., *Tennyson* (Bell, 1973).

Pattison, Robert, *Tennyson and Tradition* (Cambridge, Mass.: Harvard Univ. Press, 1979).

Pettigrew, John, *Tennyson: The Early Poems* (Arnold, 1970).

Poole, Adrian, *Gissing in Context* (Macmillan, 1975).

Relph, Edward, *Place and Placelessness* (Pion, 1975).

Richards, J. M., *Castles on the Ground: The Anatomy of Suburbia* (Murray, 1973).

Ricks, Christopher, *Tennyson* (Macmillan, 1977).

Roper, Alan, *Arnold's Poetic Landscapes* (Baltimore: Johns Hopkins Univ. Press, 1969).

Rose, Andrea, *The Pre-Raphaelites* (Oxford: Phaidon, 1981).

Ross, Alexander M., 'The Picturesque in Nineteenth-Century Fiction', in *English Studies Today*, ed. Spencer Tonguc (Istanbul, n.p., 1973), pp. 327–58.

Salter, C. H., *Good Little Thomas Hardy* (Macmillan, 1981).

Schwarzbach, F. S., *Dickens and the City* (Athlone Press, 1979).

Shaheen, Mohammad, *George Meredith: A Reappraisal of the Novels* (Macmillan, 1981).

Shaw, W. David, *Tennyson's Style* (Ithaca: Cornell Univ. Press, 1976).

Sinfield, Allan, *The Language of Tennyson's "In Memoriam"* (Oxford: Basil Blackwell, 1971).

Sipe, Samuel M., 'The Intentional World of Dickens', *Nineteenth-Century Fiction* 30, No. 1 (June 1975), pp. 1–19.

Skilton, David, *Anthony Trollope and his Contemporaries: A Study in the theory and conventions of mid-Victorian fiction* (Longmans, 1972).

——, *The English Novel: Defoe to the Victorians* (Newton Abbot: David and Charles, 1977).

Smith, Anne, ed., *The Novels of Thomas Hardy* (Vision Press, 1979).

——, ed., *George Eliot: Centenary Essays And An Unpublished Fragment* (Vision Press, 1980).

Smith, Sheila M., *The Other Nation: The Poor in English Novels of the 1840s and 1850s* (Oxford: Clarendon Press, 1980).

Spalding, Frances, *Magnificent Dreams: Burne-Jones and the Late Victorians* (Oxford: Phaidon, 1978).

Spencer, Isobel, *Walter Crane* (Studio Vista, 1975).
Springer, Marlene, ed., *What Manner of Women: Essays on English and American Life and Literature* (Oxford: Basil Blackwell, 1978).
Staley, Allen, *The Pre-Raphaelite Landscape* (Oxford: Clarendon Press, 1973).
Steane, J. B., *Tennyson* (Evans, 1966).
Stone, Donald D., *The Romantic Impulse in Victorian Fiction* (Cambridge, Mass.: Harvard Univ. Press, 1980).
Stone, Harvey, *Dickens and the Invisible World: Fairy-Tales, Fantasy and Novel-Making* (Macmillan, 1980).
Stubbs, Patricia, *Women and Fiction: Feminism and the Novel 1880–1920* (Sussex: Harvester Press, 1979).
Suther, Marshall, *Visions of Xanadu* (New York: Columbia Univ. Press, 1965).
Swartz, Helen M., and Marvin, eds., *Disraeli's Reminiscences* (Hamish Hamilton, 1975).
Swarz, Daniel R., *Disraeli's Fiction* (Macmillan, 1979).
Taine, Hippolyte, *Notes on England*, trans. Edward Hyams (Thames and Hudson, 1957).
Taylor, Brian, *Richard Jefferies* (Boston: Twayne, 1982).
Tennyson, Charles, *Alfred Tennyson* (Macmillan, 1949).
Tennyson, Hallam, *Alfred Lord Tennyson*: A Memoir, 2 vols. (Macmillan, 1892).
Terry, R. C., *Victorian Popular Fiction 1860–80* (Macmillan, 1983).
Thomas, Edward, *Richard Jefferies* (Faber and Faber, 1978).
Thomas, R. George, *Charles Dickens: Great Expectations* (Arnold, 1964).
Tindall, Gillian, *The Born Exile: George Gissing* (Temple Smith, 1974).
Turner, Paul, *Tennyson* (Routledge and Kegan Paul, 1976).
Wheeler, Michael, *The Art of Allusion in Victorian Fiction* (Macmillan, 1979).
Wilding, Michael, *Political Fictions* (Routledge and Kegan Paul, 1980).
Williams, Ioan, ed., *Meredith: The Critical Heritage* (Routledge and Kegan Paul, 1971).
Williams, Raymond, *The Country and the City* (Chatto and Windus, 1973).
Winner, Viola Hopkins, *Henry James and the Visual Arts* (Charlottesville: Univ. Press of Virginia, 1970).
Witemeyer, Hugh, *George Eliot and The Visual Arts* (New Haven: Yale Univ. Press, 1979).
Wolff, Robert Lee, *Gains and Losses: Novels of Faith and Doubt in Victorian England* (John Murray, 1977).
——, *Sensational Victorian: The Life and Fiction of Mary Elizabeth Braddon*

(New York: Garland Publishing, 1979).

Wright, Austin, ed., *Victorian Literature: Modern Essays in Criticism* (Oxford Univ. Press, 1968).

Wright, Walter F., *Art and Substance in George Meredith: A Study of Narrative* (Westport, Connecticut: Greenwood Press, 1980).

Index